Trade unions in Britain today

Second edition

Politics today

Series editor: Bill Jones

Trade unions in Britain today

Second edition

John McIlroy

Manchester University Press

Manchester and New York

Distributed exclusively in the USA and Canada by St. Martin's Press

Copyright © John McIlroy 1995

First edition 1988, reprinted 1990

Published by Manchester University Press
Oxford Road, Manchester M13 9NR, UK
and Room 400, 175 Fifth Avenue, New York, NY 10010, USA

Distributed exclusively in the USA and Canada
by St. Martin's Press, Inc., 175 Fifth Avenue, New York, NY 10010, USA

British Library Cataloguing-in-Publication Data
A catalogue record for this book is available from the British Library

Library of Congress Cataloging-in-Publication Data
McIlroy, John
    Trade unions in Britain today / John McIlroy. — 2nd ed.
        p.   cm. — (Politics today)
    Includes bibliographical references and index.
    ISBN 0–7190–3982–7. — ISBN 0–7190–3983–5 (pbk.)
    1. Trade-unions—Great Britain.   I. Title.   II. Series: Politics
    today (Manchester, England)
    HD6664.M37   1995
    331.88′0941—dc20

                                                                    94–31957

ISBN 0 7190 3982 7 *hardback*
        0 7190 3983 5 *paperback*

Phototypeset in Linotron Ehrhardt
by Northern Phototypesetting Co. Ltd, Bolton

Printed in Great Britain
by Bell & Bain Ltd, Glasgow

Contents

Figures

Tables

Preface and acknowledgements

For this edition of *Trade unions in Britain today*, I have completely rewritten and updated the text to take account of developments since 1988. The book has been expanded and reorganised. There is a new introductory chapter on the development of trade unions and their contemporary organisation and structure. The important subject of the unions' involvement in politics is now given more detailed analysis with the TUC and the Labour Party treated separately. There are new chapters on 'Bargaining and the workplace' and on trade unions and Europe. Considerations of balance and space have required the chapter on new technology to be laid aside although the union response is briefly dealt with in the chapter on workplace trade unionism. I hope this revised approach provides for a more rounded analysis of trade unionism at all levels, located in its essential economic and social context.

The purpose of the book remains to provide an accessible but rigorous account of the key issues currently confronting trade unions. *Trade unions in Britain today* looks in turn at the changing economic, social and industrial background; the diverse factors challenging unions at the workplace and their effect on workplace organisation; the contentious issues of union democracy; and the unions' contemporary involvement in politics in relation to the state and the Labour Party. The ever growing legal framework of industrial relations and its impact on union organisation and activity is examined, the labour movement's new commitment to Europe is analysed, and recent developments relating to the perennial and unresolved problems of worker participation and industrial democracy are discussed. In the concluding chapter, 'The state of the unions', I attempt to pull the strands together and assess the arguments about what has been happening to trade unions since the advent of Thatcherism, what their current response should be, and what the future holds for them.

The book attempts to provide a picture of trade unionism in the last decade of the twentieth century, place important issues in the context of political controversy, and relate them to recent research in industrial relations to help understanding and strengthen public debate. Both myself and colleagues have found it useful in a range of undergraduate and postgraduate courses in industrial relations, management, politics and economics, as well as in shorter courses for trade unionists and managers, and classes in adult education. I hope the book will also be of interest to the general reader.

It owes a particular debt to students on the distance learning courses organised for many years now at the universities of Liverpool and Manchester, in collaboration with students of the Transport and General Workers' Union, and more latterly, UNISON. I am also indebted to Tony Carew, John Kelly and Peter Nolan, who read drafts of the text and made many valuable comments, and to Stephanie Jackson and Barbara Littler for help in word processing the text.

Abbreviations

AA	Automobile Association
ACAS	Advisory, Conciliation, and Arbitration Service
AEEU	Amalgamated Engineering and Electrical Union
AES	Alternative Economic Strategy
AEU	Amalgamated Engineering Union (now AEEU)
AFL-CIO	American Federation of Labor – Congress of Industrial Organizations
APEX	Association of Professional, Executive, Clerical and Computer Staff (now GMB)
ASLEF	Associated Society of Locomotive Engineers and Firemen
ASTMS	Association of Scientific, Technical and Managerial Staffs (now MSF)
AUT	Association of University Teachers
BALPA	British Airline Pilots' Association
BIFU	Banking Insurance and Finance Union
BSC	British Steel Corporation (now British Steel)
BUPA	British United Provident Association
CAP	Common Agricultural Policy
CBI	Confederation of British Industries
CEEP	European Centre of Public Enterprises
CCT	Compulsory Competitive Tendering
CLP	Constituency Labour Party
COHSE	Confederation of Health Service Employees (now UNISON)

CP	Communist Party
CPSA	Civil and Public Services Association
CROTUM	Commissioner For the Rights of Trade Union Members
CSEU	Confederation of Shipbuilding and Engineering Unions
CTUC	Commonwealth Trade Union Council
DE	Department of Employment
DHV	Deutschnationaler Handlungsgehilfenverband – German National Commercial Employees Association
EEF	Engineering Employers' Federation
EETPU	Electrical Electronic Telecommunication and Plumbing Union (now AEEU)
EPIU	Electrical and Plumbing Industries' Union
ERM	(EU) Exchange Rate Mechanism
ESOPs	Employee Share Ownership Plans
ESRC	Economic and Social Research Council
ETU	Electrical Trades Union
ETUC	European Trade Union Confederation
ETUI	European Trade Union Institute
EU	European Union
FDA	First Division Association
GATT	General Agreement on Tariffs and Trade
GCHQ	Government Communications Headquarters
GDP	Gross Domestic Product
GLEB	Greater London Enterprise Board
GMB	General Municipal and Boilermakers' Union
GPMU	Graphical, Paper and Media Union
HRM	Human Resource Management
IBM	International Business Machines
ICFTU	International Confederation of Free Trade Unions
ILO	International Labour Organisation
IMF	International Monetary Fund
IPM	Institute of Personnel Management
IPMS	Institution of Professionals, Managers and

	Specialists
IRSF	Inland Revenue Staff Federation
ISTC	Iron and Steel Trades Confederation
KFAT	National Union of Knitwear, Footwear and Apparel Trades
LRD	Labour Research Department
MORI	Market and Opinion Research International
MSC	Manpower Services Commission
MSF	Manufacturing, Science and Finance Union
NACODS	National Association of Colliery Overmen, Deputies and Shotfirers
NALGO	National and Local Government Officers' Association (now UNISON)
NAPO	National Association of Probation Officers
NAS/UWT	National Association of School Masters and Union of Women Teachers
NATFHE	National Association of Teachers in Further and Higher Education
NATSOPA	National Society of Operative Printers, Graphical and Media Personnel (now GPMU)
NCU	National Communications Union
NEB	National Enterprise Board
NEC	National Executive Committee
NEDC	National Economic Development Council
NGA	National Graphical Association (now GPMU)
NHS	National Health Service
NIRC	National Industrial Relations Court
NTA	New Technology Agreement
NUCPS	National Union of Civil and Public Servants
NUJ	National Union of Journalists
NUM	National Union of Mineworkers
NUPE	National Union of Public Employees (now UNISON)
NUR	National Union of Railwaymen (now RMT)
NUS	National Union of Seamen (now RMT)
NUT	National Union of Teachers
NUTGW	National Union of Tailor and Garment Workers

	(now GMB)
OECD	Organisation for Economic Co-operation and Development
POEU	Post Office Engineering Union (now NCU)
RCN	Royal College of Nursing
RMT	National Union of Rail, Maritime and Transport Workers
SDP	Social Democratic Party (now Liberal Democrats)
SEM	Single European Market
SOGAT	Society of Graphical and Allied Trades (now GPMU)
TASS	Technical Administrative and Supervisory Union (now MSF)
TECs	Training and Enterprise Councils
TGWU	Transport and General Workers' Union
TQM	Total Quality Management
TUC	Trades Union Congress
TUFL	Trade Unions for Labour
TULV	Trade Unions for a Labour Victory
UCATT	Union of Construction, Allied Trades and Technicians
UCW	Union of Communication Workers
UDM	Union of Democratic Mineworkers
UNICE	Union of Industrial and Employers' Confederations of Europe
USDAW	Union of Shop, Distributive and Allied Workers
WFTU	World Federation of Trades Unions
WIRS	Workplace Industrial Relations Survey

1

Trade unions: organisation and structure

Britain's trade unions possess the longest history of workers' organisations anywhere in the world. In the 1990s they face deep-seated problems – yet they are more popular than at any time since the 1960s. Despite reverses around half the workforce is still covered by collective bargaining. Unions still negotiate with employers in 47 of *The Times* top 50 companies. The average wage premium for members over non-members is around 10%. In 1992 unions won £300 million for their members in legal awards alone. They have not outlived their time. Every day in workplaces up and down the country dedicated, unpaid union representatives sort out problems, prevent injustice and make workers' lives a little better. Rights to organise collectively, bargain with employers and withdraw labour remain essential protections and basic human rights. Unions are the custodians and guarantors of these rights, a hallmark and a bulwark of a free society. Of course, all is not well with the unions. The pages of this book are witness to their dilemmas. They remain essential institutions contributing to fairness and justice in the workplace and wider, to the democracy of Britain and to the well-being of its citizens. This chapter provides background on the organisation and structure of unions in Britain.

What are trade unions?

Trade unions are inseparable from the society in which they are created and recreated. Collective organisations of workers by hand and brain they came into being as a response to *capitalism*. Capitalism is a form of social and economic organisation where ownership of the means of production is concentrated in private hands, where the object of production is to produce commodities for profit through the market and where the majority, excluded from ownership of the means of production, are compelled to sell their labour power in order to live. For workers a well paid secure job is a major objective, an essential basis for a decent life. But their labour and wages are for employers an economic cost and productive resource, a cost to be minimised, a resource to be exploited to the maximum and dispensed with when markets so dictate. Antagonism therefore arises over terms and conditions of employment. Conflict is structured by the interest of employers in maximising profits which competes with the employees' interest in maximising wages and by the imbalance of power between individual workers and employers.

Whatever the impact of changes in labour and product markets or political regimes, pushing power a little this way or a little that way, whatever the potential for co-operation between employer and workers in day to day dealings, conflicts of interest and disparity of power define the employment relationship. The contract of employment arrived at through free negotiation between equal individuals is a legal fiction given the greater power of capital or the state. In reality the employer is already a collective entity with all the resources that involves. In the long run, as Adam Smith observed, the worker may be as necessary to the employer as the employer to the worker: the necessity is less immediate. As for the contract of employment 'it is an act of submission, in its operation it is a condition of subordination' (Kahn-Freund, 1977, 6).

Collective organisation is an expression of the realities of power and conflict at work and in society. Unions mobilise power to redress the bargaining imbalance between employer and employee, articulate the conflict between capital and labour and render it more equal. By combining together individuals aggregate power algebraically more than arithmetically: the power of collectivity is qualitatively different from the mere sum of strength of its members as isolated individuals (Hyman, 1975, 35). The creation of unions is a rational act no matter how much it may be branded irrational by those pursuing conflicting economic interests. Its logic is to oppose the rationality of capital and replace self-defeating competition over jobs and terms of employment by collective regulation which provides a superior basis for maximisation of wages and security of employment.

Unions are *class* organisations: they consist of 'workers by hand and brain'; but they organise *fragments* of the class on a *sectional* basis. They thus represent tendencies to both sectionalism, as demonstrated by the map of union structure and any study of strike action and unity, as demonstrated by the existence of different groups of workers in the same organisation, affiliation to the TUC and Labour Party and solidarity action. The form unions take will be determined by their members. That determination will also bear the mark of employers and the state as well as the forceps of the industrial structure that brought them to birth. Unions initially faced coercive hostility from employers and state. The small fragmented scale of capitalist enterprise until well into the twentieth century, the privileged position of Britain in the capitalist world and the relatively undeveloped nature of management produced, after initial bitter resistance, accommodation. A role for unions in the regulation of the enterprise developed as a response to the tenacious attachment of British workers to collective organisation. This as well as the stance of a weak and abstentionist state has permanently marked unions.

The best known definition of a trade union remains that of the Webbs: 'a continuous association of wage-earners for the purpose of maintaining or improving the conditions of their working lives' (Webb and Webb, 1920, 1). It is still echoed by official statements: 'trade unions are organisations of workers set up to improve the status, pay and conditions of employment of their members' (ACAS, 1980, 39). Legal definitions such as that in section 1 of The Trade Union and Labour Relations (Consolidation) Act, 1992 emphasise unions may be *temporary* or permanent and consist wholly or *mainly* of workers, stressing their 'principal purposes' as the regulation of relations between workers and employers.

These definitions are unspecific as to the methods unions use. The major instrument we associate with the regulation of employer–employee relations today is **collective bargaining**. The Webbs emphasised its centrality but also noted that unions attempted to achieve their purposes through **mutual insurance**, the provision of welfare services and benefits to members and **legal enactment**, the use of political pressure to achieve statutory support. Some unions pride themselves on rejecting political action. Many in the past and today in Africa, Asia and South America prioritise political action. They are no less trade unions because of that.

Different kinds of union

As a tool for analysing unions R. M. Blackburn put forward the concept of **unionateness**, a rough measure of how far different organisations reflected 'the general principles and ideology of trade unionism'. Unionateness embodied seven criteria:

1 It regards collective bargaining and protection of the interests of members, as employees, as its main function, rather than professional activities or welfare schemes.
2 It is independent of employers.
3 It is prepared to be militant using all forms of industrial action.
4 It declares itself a union.
5 It is registered as a union.
6 It is affiliated to the TUC.
7 It is affiliated to the Labour Party (Blackburn, 1967, 18–19).

Unions are complete, fully unionate, if they meet all seven criteria. Britain's biggest union UNISON would be less unionate than the second largest union – the TGWU – for one of its constituent parts, NALGO, is not affiliated to the Labour Party. Similarly, between 1988 and 1993 the long established EETPU was not affiliated to the TUC whilst the militant National Graphical Association was not a member from 1971 to 1974 because of differences over the Industrial Relations Act. Another of the ten biggest unions, the Royal College of Nursing, is affiliated to neither the TUC nor the Labour Party.

But how many – and which – of the criteria must be met to qualify as *a trade union*? Most people would probably accept that organisations which meet points 1–3 are inside the definition. The other criteria are less fundamental. Points 4 and 5 may be regarded as inessential: a union may be very much a union although it calls itself an 'association' or 'society'. Points 1–3 moreover are imprecise compared with points 4–7: the measurement of militancy or independence may be difficult. Some might argue possession of a political fund is as important as affiliation to the Labour Party. Others might claim that the National Union of Teachers or the National Union of Journalists are no less complete as unions because they have neither political fund nor party affiliation. If we see unions as industrial organisations the first three points in Blackburn's definition may seem most important. If we see trade unionism as industrial organisation *and* social movement we may require that all criteria except perhaps the fifth be met. However a militant union which disaffiliates from the Labour Party because of its lack of socialist principles may be demonstrating a lack of attachment to the wider movement. But it may be very much a union in the essential sense of defending and advancing its members' interests against the employers.

The criterion of independence is important. Organisations which are the creatures of employers or the state as in the former Soviet Union cannot be classified as unions. For they are controlled not by their members but by an external agency. A fundamental requirement is that the organisation has been created or recreated by its members. But unionateness can change over time. NALGO and the NUT only affiliated to the TUC in the 1960s after a long history. A number of prominent unions began life as Staff Associations. But membership creation is a hallmark of British unions. Unlike many organisations elsewhere they grew spontaneously from workplace needs, not the offices of political parties or religious groups. Made and re-made through the struggles of working people they remain a major cultural achievement of the working class.

Blackburn's criteria are historically and geographically specific. The early craft unions were very much unions even though they *opposed* collective bargaining in favour of unilateral regulation with unions laying down terms and conditions of employment to employers on a 'take it or leave it' basis. The Industrial Workers of the World, 'the Wobblies', were trade unionists though they prioritised the general strike. In the 1920s and 1930s the United Clothing Workers and the United Mineworkers of Scotland were unions although established and influenced by the Communist Party. In Germany before Hitler the DHV, the largest white collar workers' union propagated racialist ideology and excluded Jews; until recently in South Africa many unions excluded black workers. If, as the Webbs put it, 'The trade union is an organ of revolt against the capitalist system' it can take many different forms. Developing capitalism generates many different oppositionary responses.

The value of Blackburn's criteria in relation to contemporary British trade unionism lies in their breadth. Unions may be collective bargaining agents but are often more than that. They must be viewed as social and political as well as industrial actors. They are best conceptualised and studied, not in isolation, as **industrial bargainers**, but as part of a wider totality, **a labour movement** with industrial and political wings.

Union goals and objectives

Some writers distinguish between *substantive* goals such as the union's fundamental mission to protect workers' terms and conditions of employment and the *procedural* goal of control over the work process and the rules which regulate it, itself an instrument for attaining substantive goals. Goals may be *defensive*, aimed at protecting existing terms and conditions or *aggressive*, seeking in favourable economic conditions to increase wages, reduce hours and secure improved working conditions (Crouch, 1982, 121ff.).

The breadth of current goals may be seen from TUC statements which list: improved terms of employment; improved physical environment at work; full employment; security of employment and income; improved social security; fair shares in national income and wealth; industrial democracy; improved social services; planning of industry; and a voice in government. Goals may be industrial, social or political. Trade unionists may seek changes in the ownership of industry, the education system or foreign policy as a means of improving the quality of working lives. The revolt against capitalism often takes shape as an attempt to extract more from the system and achieve reform of its structure. Trade unionists may go further and seek to change the very basis of society. Union constitutions sometimes codify wide purposes such as the railway workers': 'the supercession of the capitalist system by a socialist order of society'. As the product of specific struggles goals change over time. Rulebook objectives may cease to represent – if they ever did – the aspirations of the majority of members or even activists. They continue to possess some mobilising power and reflect perhaps the aspirations of a minority.

'The goals of trade unionism' must, in the end, be referred to 'the goals set by trade unionists'. But the organisation may develop institutional goals (Hyman and Fryer, 1975). **Survival** and **security** will be fundamental goals influencing behaviour. Unions will seek to gain acceptance by employers and the state if they are to sustain themselves. But institutional needs for recognition or the introduction of favourable legislation may affect policy on wages or industrial action. Similarly desire for **financial stability** to enhance bargaining power may lead to the inhibition of strikes and thus diminish bargaining power. **Efficiency** may conflict with democracy and stimulate centralisation of authority. Another common goal is **growth** which can increase power and enhance survival and stability even at the cost of transforming the organisation by merger. **Unity**, often vital to the full mobilisation of power in organisations characterised by sectionalism, is an important goal: it may however conflict with democracy. Institutional goals, in their inception an essential means of articulating substantive and procedural goals, may conflict with them and displace them.

This process may be stimulated by employers and the state.

Union types

Unions have traditionally been classified in a number of categories. The first permanent organisations, the **craft unions**, were based on small scale handicraft production recruiting printers, engineers, carpenters and textile workers. Their object was to exploit the scarcity of members' skill by controlling its supply through apprenticeship, the closed shop and imposition of the rules and custom of the craft. Craft unions favoured unilateral regulation rather than collective bargaining.

Strikes were unusual: employers who refused society rates and rules were boycotted. This necessitated unemployment benefit, other welfare provision and 'tramping'. Craft unions grew with the emergence of national labour markets and larger employers from local societies to the 'new model unions' of Engineers, Carpenters and Joiners and Tailors. They were the first to introduce administrative structures and employ full-time officers in the 1850s and 1860s. They were exclusive and defensive, often politically conservative. Closed to the majority of workers who were viewed as unorganisable they benefited from Britain's position as the first capitalist nation and workshop of the world. As the 'aristocrats of labour' they were uninterested in size, antagonistic to technical innovation and organised horizontally across industry. There was always difficulty in demarcating the boundaries of the craft and craft unions were undermined by deskilling and technological change.

In industries such as mining and iron and steel the ability of employers to bring in substitute labour in the event of conflict and the drive of less skilled workers towards trade unionism produced an emphasis on **vertical** rather than **horizontal** organisation. The establishment of the Miners' Federation of Great Britain in 1889 as a national organisation for all miners heralded the growth of **industrial unionism**. This developed with the creation of the National Union of Railwaymen in 1913 and the Iron and Steel Trades Confederation four years later.

There were again difficulties in defining an industry: was vehicle production 'the car industry' or part of the engineering industry? Economic and industrial change moved boundaries: old industries declined, new ones emerged. Craft unions already occupied job territory limiting the realisation of all inclusive membership. Some unions such as the National Union of Public Employees simply declared themselves industrial unions in defiance of the facts.

If the aspiration of industrial unionism was to organise **vertically** and represent all workers in one industry, the impetus of the **general unionism** which developed in the last two decades of the nineteenth century was to organise **horizontally**, recruiting in all industries. The object was the unskilled general labourer. Excluded from craft protection or hierarchical promotion structures, often working seasonally across a range of industries, lacking in financial resources and education, the unskilled worker had been regarded as unorganisable. Given inability to control the labour supply in the face of easy substitutability of workers the aim of the general union was all embracing organisation, strength in numbers and collective bargaining.

Industrial weakness produced an emphasis on **independent political action**. 'The new unionism' coincided with the disintegration of economic supremacy and the growth of socialist ideas. It was initially influenced by socialist leaders such as Tom Mann, Will Thorne and Eleanor Marx and was contrasted with the stereotype of the 'top-hatted' craft unionists who looked to the Liberal Party. As with the earlier general unionism of the 1830s the dynamic towards one big union was arrested. Unlike its predecessor this organising wave left stable organisation outside the craft areas in the docks, road transport, gas and manufacturing industry generally.

General unionism continued to advance in the first two decades of the twentieth century whilst the idea of industrial unionism as a weapon of radical political change was taken up by advocates of syndicalist ideas who established bases in the Miners' Federation and the NUR. Its legacy was not 'one big union' but a number of powerful expansionist general unions such as the Transport and

General Workers Union and the General and Municipal Workers' Union. They competed with each other and increasingly with the craft organisations as unions such as the Amalgamated Engineering Union, confronted with loss of job territory through technological change, opened their gates to semi-skilled workers.

Matters were further complicated by the emergence of **white collar unions**. Some were formed in the last century but became established after World War I. Some were occupational like the teaching unions. Others like NALGO developed vertically, beginning by recruiting senior town hall staff and then all white collar employees in local government and beyond. Explosive growth took place after World War II, particularly between 1968 and 1979, in defiance of established wisdom that employers and employees were resistant to white collar unionisation. The overall picture became even more complex: in response to the growth of white collar unions the established organisations created white collar sections to recruit these workers. Despite overlapping and reverses these trends produced growth in union membership which compared with similar countries was healthy and resilient (see Table 1.1).

Finally, we should mention the importance since the 1960s of **public sector trade unionism**, manual and white collar. The National Union of Public Employees grew from 200,000 members in 1960 to 700,000 in 1979. NALGO had 274,000 members in 1960 and 753,000 in 1979. There were around 370,000 union members in the NHS in 1967 and 1.3 million in 1979. These developments did much to change the face of British trade unionism which had previously possessed the stamp of the private sector.

Contemporary classifications

Traditional classifications are useful for understanding the development of unions, less so in categorising them today. They help us understand the complexity of present structures, the product of more than two centuries of *laissez-faire* development unpunctuated by major social upheaval. History left its mark.

Table 1.1 *Union membership, selected years*

Year	Union membership (000s)	Union density % of labour force
1910	2,565	14.6
1913	4,135	22.1
1917	5,499	30.2
1920	8,348	45.2
1921	6,633	35.8
1923	5,429	30.2
1926	5,219	28.3
1933	4,392	22.6
1938	6,053	30.5
1945	7,875	38.6
1950	9,289	44.1
1955	9,741	44.5

Source: Bain, 1970.

From the early unions came the impulse towards self-government and control of work and the creation of working-class institutions to mark out independent space within an apparently immutable if reformable system. From the new unions and the industrial unions came a recognition of the breadth of the working class, the need for a more inclusive industrial movement and an *independent* political arm. The radical ideologies which initially influenced the new unionism and 'the great unrest', 1900–21, remained a minority strand. The establishment of the Labour Party represented its political limits, the Communist Party never occupied an important role. **Labourism**, the philosophy of gradual social change within capitalism, dominated horizons: practice was based on 'a fair day's work for a fair day's pay' rather than 'the abolition of the wages system'.

The craft unions rarely achieved their full agenda. In periods of boom they met success in imposing conditions on employers but were gradually driven into collective bargaining. There were until recently residues of craft control of labour in the hiring system operated by SLADE the lithographers' union and the NGA (now merged in the Graphical, Paper and Media Union). But the weakening of these unions by computerised print-setting in the 1980s demonstrated yet again the craft as victim of technological development. Sooner or later the choice for craft unions is to merge, to broaden their recruitment territory or head for Jurassic Park. By the 1990s a union like the Lancashire Box and Packing Case Society was reduced to 200 members and absorbed by the TGWU. The only pure craft unions were bodies such as the Society of Shuttlemakers or the Military and Orchestral Musical Instrument Makers' Trade Society – each of which had under 100 members. Unions such as the AEU and ETU preferred diversification to slow decline and lost their craft identity in the process.

Bodies such as ASLEF, the train drivers' union, or BALPA, the airline pilots' association, were based on the scarcity of skills but were perhaps viewed best as occupational unions. The arbitrary nature of categorisation is demonstrated by the fact that the former has generally been classified as a manual union and the latter as a white collar organisation.

Similarly the industrial unions never succeeded in recruiting all workers in an industry. The National Union of Mineworkers, for example, failed to achieve completeness, for supervisory workers were members of the National Association of Colliery Overmen, Deputies and Shotfirers and managers of the British Association of Colliery Managers. After 1985 there was also the breakaway Union of Democratic Mineworkers. Moreover, craft workers in the industry were members of the craft unions. On the railways the NUR recruited the majority of employees but the drivers were members of ASLEF and office staff of the Transport and Salaried Staffs' Association. Both these unions deserved the appellation 'single industry union' rather than industrial union. Just like the craft unions, they became victims of social change. As the traditional heavy industries contracted so the membership of the ISTC and the NUM tumbled.

General unions proved more resilient. Unlike the craft and industrial unions they spread their risks and recruited wherever they were not prohibited by powerful competitors or TUC regulation. However, there is again no pure example of a general union, recruiting all workers in all industries and it is the impulse to organisation across boundaries that has become dominant, partially through mergers, not the traditional general unions such as the TGWU or the GMB. What we are seeing is not the simple expansion of the general unions but the development of hybrid, conglomerate organisations.

This raises the question of the utility of the white collar category. It was the product of a period when trade unionism was conceived of as largely the accomplishment and preserve of manual workers. We have seen blurring of lines between blue collar and white collar driven by technological change and this has been reproduced in union structures with the development of hybrid organisation and the fulcrum of British trade unionism shifting towards white collar workers. With privatisation public sector trade unionism is another changing category.

The developing impulse to cross boundaries was recognised as long ago as the 1960s by H. A. Turner. Focusing on dynamics and strategy rather than historical forms he distinguished between **open** and **closed** unions. **Open organisations** are expansionist seeking to increase the range of their membership and recruit new types of worker in new industries. **Closed unions** are more restricted concentrating on demarcated groups of workers. Open unions seek to expand their power base through expanding the population from which they recruit. Closed unions attempt to expand their power base by expanding the material rewards, status, job control and demand for the skills of well defined groups of workers. Over time unions may revise their strategy just as the electricians and the engineers moved from closed to open unions (Turner, 1962).

This distinction provides a useful lens through which to look at the development of union structure. But whilst closed organisations such as BALPA continue to thrive, the current impulse is powerfully towards openness; the closed category is a declining one. ASLEF, for example, had 80,000 members after the war: today it has 19,000. Yet it has to continue to service its members efficiently on a national basis. The logic is towards merger.

Current structure

Many of these points are underlined if we examine the major
unions (see Table 1.2). UNISON is the result of a 1993 merger
between three public service unions. NALGO was an all grades
union for white collar staff in local government but also recruited
in the health service, gas, electricity, water, transport and higher
education. The National Union of Public Employees was
NALGO's manual opposite number while the Confederation of
Health Service Employees had aspired to be an industrial union
for the NHS but was limited by the presence of NALGO, NUPE
and former craft unions. Given recent privatisation UNISON
recruits in both public and private sectors.

The TGWU, long Britain's biggest union, is in contrast the
product of a 1920s amalgamation of general unions with membership in a very wide range of industries. Its strongholds were in the
docks, cars and road transport, its original strong manual
orientation complemented by a white collar trade group.
Significant membership loss in the 1980s was scarcely restrained
by amalgamations with the Agricultural Workers and the Dyers
and Bleachers. The GMB was historically the TGWU's rival.
Outstripped in the 1960s and 1970s, it regained ground after
1980 through a number of mergers notably with the Boilermakers'
Union, the white collar union APEX and the Tailor and Garment
Workers' Union. It recruits white collar and manual workers in
local authorities, the NHS, food, leisure industries, textiles,
shipbuilding, manufacturing industry, construction, energy and
engineering.

The AEEU is a 1992 merger of the historic craft unions, the
AEU and the EETPU, both transformed by earlier marriages.
The AEU recruited skilled engineers across industry. It also had
aspirations to be an industrial union for engineering, recruiting by
the 1940s all grades of workers but facing stiff competition,
particularly in the car industry, from the TGWU. Its amalgamation policy in the 1960s and 1970s met with mixed success:
the Foundry Workers were successfully absorbed but merger with
TASS, originally the draughtsmen's union, proved temporary.

Table 1.2 *Britain's major unions, 1992*

Union	Membership
UNISON	1,486,984
Transport and General Workers' Union	1,036,000
Amalgamated Engineering and Electrical Union	884,000
General Municipal and Boilermakers	799,101
Manufacturing, Science and Finance Union	552,000
Union of Shop, Distributive and Allied Workers	316,491
Royal College of Nursing	299,000
Graphical, Paper and Media Union	269,881
National Union of Teachers	213,656
National Association of Schoolmasters and Union of Women Teachers	190,637
Union of Communication Workers	179,266
Union of Construction, Allied Trades and Technicians	157,201
Banking Insurance and Finance Union	153,562
Association of Teachers and Lecturers	152,795
National Communications Union	126,376
Civil and Public Services Association	124,504
National Union of Civil and Public Servants	111,831
Rail, Maritime and Transport Workers	105,146
Institution of Professionals, Managers and Specialists	90,008
National Association of Teachers in Further and Higher Education	75,232

Source: Reports of TUC, Certification Officer.

The EETPU, the result of a merger between electricians and plumbers, recruited electricians horizontally across industry whilst aiming to organise all workers in electricity supply, all production workers in electrical engineering as well as electrical contractors. During the 1980s it absorbed a large number of smaller unions and like the engineers transformed itself into a general union aggressively recruiting in any sector where opportunities presented themselves.

ASTMS, a white collar amalgamation of supervisors in manufacturing industry and scientific workers in education, grew enormously between 1964 and 1979. It became the counterpart of the

TGWU for white collar staff, a general union operating wherever it saw an opening. In 1988 it merged with TASS to create the Manufacturing, Science and Finance Union, recruiting white collar staff largely in private industry but also in sectors like education.

Britain's sixth biggest union the Union of Shop, Distributive and Allied Workers is again more promiscuous than its name suggests. As well as aspiring unsuccessfully to be an industrial union for the retail trades USDAW has members in manufacturing industry, food processing, transport, warehousing, mail order, insurance and the chemical industry. The Royal College of Nursing, the only non-TUC union in the top ten, presents itself in contrast as the professional union for nurses. It competes with UNISON and is discussing whether it should open itself to less skilled care assistants.

The Graphical, Paper and Media Union, established in 1990 through fusion of SOGAT 1982 and the NGA, brings together the historically fragmented, now weakened, printing unions in an aspiring industrial union. The Union of Communication Workers recruits a wide range of post office staff, delivery workers, telephonists and manual workers. Its historical counterpart the National Communications Union organises engineers in the post office and now with the privatisation of telecommunications in British Telecom and Girobank.

In the schools the National Union of Teachers competes with the National Union of Schoolmasters/Union of Women Teachers, the Association of Teachers and Lecturers and a plethora of other unions. The absence of any impetus to industrial unionism in education can be seen by continuing divisions even among teachers. In higher education NATFHE based in the former polytechnics and further education colleges is complemented by the AUT in the old universities and by the non-TUC Association of University and College Lecturers.

The Construction Workers recruits from the traditional crafts in the building industry and across other industries. It competes with the TGWU which traditionally organised unskilled workers in these areas and now with the AEEU. It has gone through a turbulent period in the 1980s and 1990s. The Banking and Finance Union in contrast performed buoyantly, expanding from its base in banking into insurance companies and building societies.

Union organisation in the civil service reflects job structures. The Civil and Public Services Association, the largest union, recruits clerical, secretarial and ancillary staff. It demonstrates yet again the complexity of union structure as it also has members in the post office, air transport and the research councils. The National Union of Civil and Public Servants is a product of yet another merger between the Civil Service Union and the Society of Civil and Public Servants in 1987. The new union organises executive officers, some administrative grades, supervisory and security staff. It also has members in the post office and the police force. The Institution of Professionals, Managers and Specialists bespeaks the changes in trade unionism in recent years. It grew from the Institute of Professional Civil Servants and represents members in government departments, public sector bodies and private companies. Finally the Rail, Maritime and Transport Union is a 1990 merger of the seafarers and the railway workers.

Multi-unionism and mergers

This brief examination further demonstrates the limitations of traditional categories in understanding current union structure. The contemporary situation is characterised by a number of tendencies.

Conglomerates

There is a move away from traditional forms of organisation, independence and closure towards open, hybrid, conglomerate, multi-grade, multi-industry forms of organisation, crossing occupational and industrial boundaries and internalising past distinctions reflected in separate organisation within the conglomerate. By 1992 more than 4 million members, over 40% of the total, belonged to conglomerates. Adaptation to industrial change is demonstrated by the way UNISON and the civil service unions are increasingly involved in public and private sectors. However, the tendency towards general unionism and promiscuous recruitment is still limited by tradition, established boundary lines and fear of the dangers of unrestrained competition.

Rapid change

The 1980s and 1990s have been periods of rapid change in trade union structure. Of the dozen biggest unions in 1982 only the TGWU, GMB, USDAW and UCATT survived a decade later. What stands out is the resilience of the public sector unions since 1979. Having benefited from a major upsurge from the 1960s unions like NALGO and NUPE maintained their membership position in far less favourable conditions. They have nevertheless felt pressure to merge.

Mergers

It has been a period of 'merger mania'. All the important unions have been involved, and further major marriages such as that between the TGWU and the GMB and the UCW and NCU appear likely. Unions may merge legally by **transfer of engagements** which usually involves a takeover or by **amalgamation** which involves formation of a new organisation. In common parlance the term **merger** is used generally but is perhaps best employed to denote the creation of what is basically a new body usually consummated by organisations of roughly equivalent weight. The term **absorption** usually denotes a large union taking over a smaller one. For example, TASS, prior to its merger with ASTMS in 1988, snapped up the National Union of Gold, Silver and Allied Trades, 1981, the National Union of Sheet Metal Workers, 1983, the Patternmakers, 1984, the Metal Mechanics, 1985 and the Tobacco Workers' Union, 1986. Between 1980 and 1991 the Annual Reports of the Certification Officer record 149 amalgamations involving 4.25 million workers. In 1992 and 1993 the pace quickened: there were amalgamations involving almost 2.5 million members.

Fewer unions

There has been significant reduction in the number of unions from 1,000 in 1940 to 560 in 1968 and 268 in 1992 (Table 1.3). The number of TUC affiliates has also fallen qualitatively since 1979.

Table 1.3   *Number of unions, 1979–92*

Year	Total number	TUC unions
1979	453	109
1980	438	108
1981	414	105
1982	408	102
1983	394	98
1984	375	91
1985	370	88
1986	335	87
1987	330	83
1988	314	83
1989	309	78
1990	287	74
1991	275	70
1992	268	69

Source: Employment Gazette; TUC Reports.

The fall in numbers reflects *concentration* of membership: unions have got bigger. After the war the average union had 10,000 members: today it has more than three times that number. But there are still many small unions: 163 out of the 268 unions in 1992 (61%) had fewer than 2,500 members. The Sheffield Wool Shear Workers' Union lives on with just 13 members. The ten biggest unions which brought up the average all had more than 200,000 members and contained 60% of the total membership (Table 1.4).

Table 1.4   *Trade unions: numbers and membership, ending 1992*

Number of members	Number of unions	Membership (000s)	Number of unions % (cumulative %)		Membership of all unions % (cumulative %s)	
Under 100	34	2	12.7	(12.7)	0.02	
100–499	58	14	21.6	(34.3)	0.2	(0.2)
500–999	25	18	9.3	(43.6)	0.2	(0.4)
1,000–2,499	46	79	17.2	(60.8)	0.9	(1.3)
2,500–4,999	25	94	9.3	(70.1)	1.0	(2.3)
5,000–9,999	17	120	6.3	(76.4)	1.3	(3.6)
10,000–14,999	5	58	1.9	(78.3)	0.6	(4.2)
15,000–24,999	10	178	3.7	(82.0)	2.0	(6.2)
25,000–49,999	19	699	7.1	(89.1)	7.7	(13.9)
50,000–99,999	9	627	3.4	(92.5)	6.9	(20.8)
100,000–249,999	11	1,710	4.1	(96.6)	18.9	(39.7)
250,000 and more	9	5,449	3.4	(100)	60.2	(99.9)
All	268	9,048	100		100	

Source: Employment Gazette, June 1994.

Multi-unionism

But Britain still has a large number of unions in comparison with many European countries. Unions competing for the same type of member and multiple bargaining units has attracted criticism. It has been pointed out this criticism is essentially managerial (Hyman, 1975, 68). Jurisdictional disputes are a minor aspect of industrial relations but multi-unionism may impose organising costs on unions; fragmentation and divided strategies may circumscribe bargaining power. Unions have attempted to overcome these difficulties through joint shop stewards' committees, federations (of which the best known is the Confederation of Shipbuilding and Engineering Unions) and the disputes procedure of the Trade Union Congress, the 'Bridlington Rules'. The TUC has encouraged mergers but has never been in a position to exert real pressure.

Figure 1.1   *Union membership 1900–92*
Source: Bain, 1970; Reports of Certification Officer.

The situation in the 1960s when Ford negotiated with 20 unions has been transformed by mergers. But these are often based on conjunctural circumstances and financial and political considerations as much as structural concerns. The growth of conglomerates may reduce multi-unionism, it will not eradicate it. In 1984 33% of all establishments had two or more unions representing manual workers and 60% of all establishments had two or more unions representing non-manual workers. Around 20% of establishments had two or more bargaining units for manual workers and more than 30% had two or more bargaining units for non-manual employees. By 1990 this picture had hardly changed (Millward *et al.*, 1992, 77ff.). This has led employers to look at 'single union deals' and 'single table bargaining' (see pp. 115–6).

Membership and Density

Union membership grew until 1920. Decline followed, bottoming in 1933, after which recovery commenced. The post-war period was one of slow progress followed from 1968 by a decade of explosive growth. By 1979 there were 13.2 million trade union members and 12 million were in unions affiliated to the TUC. The years since have seen severe sustained decline. By 1992 membership had fallen to under 9 million of which only 7.3 million were now in TUC unions (see Figure 1.1; Table 1.5).

In a dozen years the TUC lost almost 5 million members.

Table 1.5   *Trade union membership, 1960–92*

Year	Overall membership (000s)	% change on previous year	TUC membership (000s)	% change on previous year
1960	9,835		8,299	
1965	10,181	+3.5	8,868	+6.9
1968	10,191	+0.1	8.875	+1.7
1970	11,187	+9.8	10,002	+12.7
1975	12,026	+7.5	11,036	+10.3
1978	13,112	+9.0	12,128	+9.9
1979	13,289	+1.3	12,173	+0.9
1980	12,947	−2.6	11,601	−4.7
1981	12,106	−6.5	11,006	−5.1
1982	11,593	−4.2	10,510	−4.5
1983	11,236	−3.1	10,087	−4.0
1984	10,994	−2.2	9,855	−2.3
1985	10,821	−1.6	9,581	−2.8
1986	10,539	−2.6	9,243	−3.5
1987	10,475	−0.6	9,127	−1.3
1988	10,238	−2.3	8,652	−5.2
1989	10,158	−0.8	8,417	−2.7
1990	9,947	−2.1	8,192	−2.7
1991	9,585	−3.6	7,760	−5.3
1992	8,928	−6.0	7,300	−5.9

Source: Certification Officer, TUC.

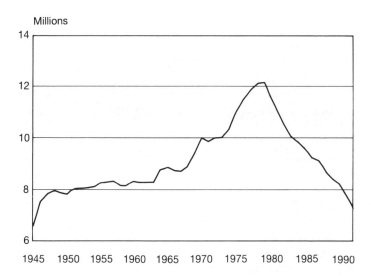

Figure 1.2   *TUC unions 1945–92*
Source: TUC

There is little sign of reversal of this trend. Table 1.5 and Figure 1.2 demonstrate the problem – particularly for TUC affiliates. In the 1970s these 'unionate' unions were threatening to drive their 'professional body' competitors out of business: in 1977 they organised 93% of all union members. By 1992 this had fallen significantly to 80% and some argued 'The whole brunt of the membership decline has been borne by unions affiliated to the TUC' (Metcalf, 1991, 19).

It seems reasonable to deduce that fluctuations are related to changing economic and political trends. Membership may be expected to decrease when there is high unemployment – few retain membership when unemployed and it is harder for unions to bargain – and a hostile political and legal environment. These factors accompanied membership decline in the 1920s and 1930s as well as in recent years. Conversely, low unemployment, rising prices which threaten real wage levels, supportive employers and governments also committed to a strong public sector might be expected to positively affect membership. Unions as active agents of recruitment may also be important in realising or limiting environmental trends.

This does not completely explain why membership stagnated between 1945 and the early 1960s and increased dramatically over the next decade. This leads us to look more closely at changes in industry, the composition of the labour force and specific government policies. It is arguable that faced with periods of wage restraint, rising paper wages and prices in the stable full employment conditions of the late 1960s and early 1970s many, particularly white collar workers, whose wages fell relative to manual workers, looked to unions as potential saviours. Unions were high profiled and legitimised by greater involvement with the state and greater legislative support than in the 1940s and 1950s.

Analysis of union membership which points to differences in occupations, sectors of industry and size of enterprise highlights the limitations of overall membership figures. Unions may have 10 million members but how many *potential members* are there? **Union density** gives us more precision, measuring actual against potential membership and stating membership as a proportion of the workforce. However we can define the workforce in a number of ways. One measure includes civilian employees and the unemployed, another excludes them, giving a higher figure for density for most are not union members. The **Labour Force Survey** uses sampling methods and shows lower density.

Table 1.6 contains two estimates of overall density. Density A is membership as a proportion of employees. Density B is membership as a proportion of employees *and the unemployed*. Both measures show a serious decline in union coverage since 1979. On the first measure density is 41.8%, on the second 36.7%.

If we take a more unionate view, insisting that affiliation to the TUC is the test of trade unionism, the position is worse. Table 1.7 shows a drop of 18 and 19 points on the two measures of density for TUC unions since 1979. Density now stands at just over 30% or just over 34%. The **Labour Force Survey** estimated overall union density in 1993 at 35%, with density amongst people in employment 31% compared with 32% in 1992. We have to

Table 1.6   *Density: all unions, 1979–92*

Year	Union members (000s)	Employees	Unemployed	Total	Density A	Density B
1979	13,289	23,206	1,301	24,507	56.9	54.2
1980	12,947	22,386	2,137	24,523	57.8	52.8
1981	12,106	21,580	2,782	24,362	56.1	49.7
1982	11,593	21,101	2,949	24,050	54.9	48.2
1983	11,236	21,169	2,956	24,125	53.1	46.6
1984	10,994	21,363	3,106	24,469	51.1	44.9
1985	10,821	21,418	3,133	24,551	50.5	41.1
1986	10,539	21,389	3,121	24,510	49.3	43.6
1987	10,475	21,956	2,569	24,525	47.7	42.7
1988	10,376	22,513	2,038	24,551	45.5	42.3
1989	10,158	23,002	1,635	24,639	44.2	41.2
1990	9,947	22,703	1,853	24,556	43.8	40.5
1991	9,585	21,965	2,550	24,515	43.6	39.1
1992	8,928	21,354	2,972	24,326	41.8	86.7

Note: Density A is membership as a % of employees. *Density B* is membership as a % of employees and the unemployed.

Source: Certification Officer; *Employment Gazette.*

return to the early 1930s to find a period where unions only organised a third of the labour force.

Industry and occupation

The **Labour Force Survey** provides valuable information on differences in density between occupations and industries. The big gap in density between industries is clear from Table 1.8. Density declined across categories over the decade but its impact was very variable. Between 1992 and 1993, 4 of the 47 industrial categories registered no change in density, 18 recorded an increase, and 25 experienced a decline.

Traditional strongholds like the railways and the coal industry are still in the lead with 90% density amongst employees although their decline has brought down the overall numbers of union

Table 1.7   *Density: TUC unions, 1979–92*

Year	TUC members (000s)	Employees	Unemployed	Total	Density A	Density B
1979	12,172	23,206	1,301	24,507	52.45	49.67
1980	11,601	22,386	2,137	24,523	51.82	47.31
1981	11,006	21,580	2,782	24,362	51.00	45.18
1982	10,511	21,101	2,949	24,050	49.81	43.70
1983	10,082	21,169	2,956	24,125	47.63	41.79
1984	9,855	21,363	3,106	24,469	46.13	40.28
1985	9,586	21,418	3,133	24,551	44.76	39.05
1986	9,243	21,389	3,121	24,510	43.21	37.71
1987	9,127	21,956	2,569	24,525	41.57	37.22
1988	8,652	22,513	2,038	24,551	38.43	35.24
1989	8,417	23,004	1,635	24,639	36.59	34.16
1990	8,192	22,703	1,853	24,556	36.08	33.36
1991	7,760	21,965	2,550	24,515	35.33	31.65
1992	7,300	21,354	2,972	24,326	34.19	30.01

Note: Density A is membership as a % of employees. *Density B* is
membership as a % employees and the unemployed.

Source: TUC; *Employment Gazette*

members. Also at the top of the league with the public sector are
recently privatised utilities such as gas, electricity and telecommunications although they have suffered some decline. At the
other end of the scale are industries with low density such as
agriculture with 10% density, retail distribution at 13%, hotels
and catering, 10%, and business services, 8%. Comparison with
earlier surveys shows a drop in density in manufacturing from
58% in 1984 to 34% in 1993, in energy and water supply from
88% to 66%, in chemicals from 58% to 34%. Electrical and
electronic engineering 51% to 28% and paper, printing and
publishing 59% to 35% also showed significant falls in density.

The problem is that density is still buoyant in areas where jobs
are being lost, and in the public sector which is also under threat.
It is lowest in areas which are growing such as personal services.

There are *some* hopeful signs. The density in local and national government is holding up well although restructuring may have an adverse impact. Banking and insurance has seen employment growth and a density of almost 50%. However, we have to remember that workers pushing up density on the railways or in the mines are members of TUC unions. Workers pushing up density in banking and finance are often members of non-TUC unions. The low density amongst part-time workers is noteworthy in terms of future trends.

Density also varies between occupational groups. Figure 1.3 underlines again the changing face of British trade unionism. The manual plant and machine operators and craft workers, long conceived as the very stuff of trade unionism, do not differ significantly in density today from workers in professional occupations. If we look at unionateness we have to remember that densities are boosted by members of professional organisations very different from the TGWU. Nonetheless with changes in the composition of the labour force such groups are vital to the future of trade unionism. In the 1990s the average trade unionist is not a

---

Table 1.8a and 1.8b (overleaf)

Notes

[a] % in category who are members of a trade union or staff association. Those who did not report their union status are regarded as non-union members. Those respondents in households which were not contactable in the autumn 1992 and 1993 quarters have been excluded for the purposes of calculating densities.

[b] Includes those who did not provide information on one or more of the dimensions in the table.

[c] Full-time/part-time status is based on respondents' self-assessment, not hours usually worked.

[d] Includes those on government schemes and those who did not state their employment status.

[e] Includes those who did not state their industry.

– No value.

* Cell size too small to provide a reliable estimate.

Source: Department of Employment Gazette, May 1994

Table 1.8a Union density by industry, sector, sex, whether working full-time or part-time, whether non-manual/manual, and by size of workplace

Standard industrial classification	All employees				Autumn 1993, employees							Density (%)[a] workplace size (employees)		
	Spring 1989	Spring 1990	Spring 1991	Autumn 1992	All[b]	Men	Women	Full-time[c]	Part-time[c]	Non-manual	Manual	Less than 25	Less than 50	Over 50
All industries[e]	39	38	37	35	35	38	31	39	21	34	36	18	21	47
Agriculture, forestry, fishing	13	13	11	9	10	12	*	12	*	*	10	7	8	*
All energy & water supply	76	75	73	69	66	70	52	67	52	56	79	54	61	67
Coal extraction, solid fuels	90	92	90	86	79	81	*	80	*	*	82	*	*	83
Coke, oil, gas extraction & nuclear	34	38	38	35	37	40	*	37	*	27	54	*	*	39
Electricity & gas: production & distribution	85	86	82	81	80	84	69	82	62	74	90	*	77	81
Water supply	82	79	74	69	60	67	*	62	*	47	79	*	66	58
All manufacturing	41	40	38	35	34	37	24	36	12	17	45	11	13	43
Metal extraction & manufacture	64	56	55	54	55	58	*	57	*	33	66	*	*	70
Mineral extraction & manufacture	48	49	43	44	45	47	39	47	*	22	55	*	24	56
Chemicals & fibres	38	35	35	35	34	38	24	35	*	19	53	*	*	40
Metal goods	39	36	33	34	28	31	*	30	*	*	37	*	12	39
Mechanical engineering	39	38	36	32	29	31	20	31	*	13	41	12	12	41
Office machinery & data processing equipment	12	11	12	7	13	13	*	13	–	*	25	*	*	16
Electric & electronic engineering	36	34	35	30	28	30	24	29	*	15	41	15	13	34
Vehicles & motor parts	63	60	57	56	51	55	31	53	*	25	63	*	*	59
Other transport equipment	62	64	60	53	56	57	*	57	–	45	65	*	*	61
Instrument engineering	20	16	23	23	16	*	*	17	*	*	*	*	*	*
Food, drink & tobacco	47	44	42	39	38	41	31	40	26	19	47	13	15	46
Textiles	43	37	36	34	38	41	35	40	*	*	45	*	*	47
Leather, clothing & footwear	33	32	34	27	28	28	28	32	*	*	34	*	*	42
Timber & furniture	22	22	21	16	15	17	*	16	–	*	20	*	*	25
Paper, printing & publishing	43	43	40	37	35	44	18	39	*	20	52	21	22	44

Rubber, plastics & other manufacturing	36	*	*	35	9	*	27	13	30	25	29	29	30	34
Construction	41	14	11	31	19	*	27	12	28	25	27	28	29	30
All services	48	23	19	31	37	22	41	33	38	35	35	37	37	37
Wholesale distribution	19	5	4	18	5	*	11	6	12	10	12	14	15	16
Retail distribution	24	7	6	17	12	11	16	13	13	13	14	16	16	15
Hotels & catering	17	8	8	10	10	8	13	10	10	10	9	11	11	11
Repairs	*	5	*	9	*	*	8	*	8	7	6	10	10	11
Railways	84	84	83	90	73	*	85	*	85	84	90	91	92	94
Other transport	57	18	15	50	26	15	43	23	46	40	41	45	44	47
Postal services	87	65	51	87	61	39	88	53	89	80	81	83	84	84
Telecommunications	73	70	68	88	61	*	73	63	76	73	74	73	75	80
Banking & finance	43	62	65	*	53	56	52	57	45	52	50	49	49	49
Insurance	38	41	38	*	38	*	40	30	46	39	39	39	35	36
Business services	11	5	4	14	7	*	9	5	11	8	8	9	9	8
Renting of movables	*	*	*	*	*	*	*	*	*	*	13	11	9	12
Owning & dealing in real estate	61	35	28	38	49	*	50	47	45	46	44	45	41	44
National government	65	60	58	56	64	52	65	61	67	63	63	62	64	63
Local government	64	56	54	58	63	43	67	60	66	62	61	65	64	69
Fire, police, justice, defence, social security	53	56	45	52	66	33	56	53	54	54	53	52	53	49
Sanitary services	42	20	19	26	44	15	42	19	40	30	37	34	38	41
Higher education	49	51	57	42	51	31	55	45	53	49	52	56	56	56
Schools	64	55	56	29	73	30	78	54	76	59	60	60	62	63
Other education	56	31	28	42	50	27	60	42	58	49	47	44	43	53
Research & development	43	*	*	*	35	*	39	*	43	38	37	40	40	44
Hospitals	66	36	36	44	67	53	68	61	64	61	60	66	66	67
Other medical	62	31	26	52	35	28	47	33	68	37	39	37	38	41
Entertainment & leisure	41	24	24	33	28	18	36	26	35	30	32	35	36	38
Other services	48	25	20	24	39	25	35	29	34	30	29	31	32	31

Table 1.8b Union density by industry, sector, occupation and employment status

	Autumn 1993, employees, occupations										Autumn 1993
	Managers & administrators	Professional occupations	Associate professional & technical	Clerical & secretarial	Craft & related occupations	Personal & protective service occupations	Sales occupations	Plant & machine operatives	Other occupations	Self-employed	All in employment[d]
All industries[e]	24	52	50	30	41	30	12	46	32	8	31
Agriculture, forestry, fishing	*	*	–	*	*	*	*	*	11	17	14
All energy & water supply	50	54	60	58	85	*	–	75	70	*	65
Coal extraction, solid fuels	*	*	*	*	92	*	–	*	*	*	79
Coke, oil, gas extraction & nuclear	*	*	*	*	*	*	–	61	*	*	37
Electricity & gas: production & distribution	72	73	78	77	94	*	*	85	*	–	80
Water supply	*	*	*	*	*	*	*	82	*	–	58
All manufacturing	12	25	29	22	44	42	10	47	35	4	32
Metal extraction & manufacture	*	*	*	*	65	*	*	68	*	*	54
Mineral extraction & manufacture	*	*	*	*	60	*	*	50	*	–	43
Chemicals & fibres	*	*	*	23	67	*	*	53	*	*	33
Metal goods	*	*	*	*	36	–	–	41	*	*	26
Mechanical engineering	11	*	*	19	40	*	*	42	*	*	28
Office machinery & data processing equipment	*	*	*	*	*	–	*	*	*	–	13
Electric & electronic engineering	*	23	*	17	41	*	*	42	*	*	27
Vehicles & motor parts	*	*	*	36	60	*	*	66	*	–	49
Other transport equipment	*	50	64	58	65	*	*	63	*	*	55
Instrument engineering	*	*	*	*	*	–	–	*	–	–	15
Food, drink & tobacco	*	*	*	26	40	*	*	51	42	–	36
Textiles	*	*	*	*	53	*	*	38	*	*	36
Leather, clothing & footwear	*	–	*	*	35	*	*	29	*	–	26
Timber & furniture	–	–	*	*	17	–	*	26	*	*	12

Rubber, plastics & other manufacturing	*	*	*	*	28	—	*	38	*	*	23
Construction	17	24	31	17	32	*	*	28	23	5	17
All services	28	58	54	31	34	30	13	44	34	9	32
Wholesale distribution	*	*	*	8	*	*	*	25	*	*	10
Retail distribution	14	*	*	19	10	*	12	24	13	6	12
Hotels & catering	13	—	*	*	9	7	*	*	14	*	9
Repairs	*	—	—	*	*	—	*	—	—	*	5
Railways	16	*	*	86	90	92	*	93	82	—	84
Other transport	85	*	69	24	58	57	*	52	44	12	35
Postal services	62	*	*	43	*	*	*	*	88	*	80
Telecommunications	48	*	*	68	92	—	*	*	—	*	72
Banking & finance	37	53	36	57	*	*	*	*	*	—	52
Insurance	7	*	37	33	*	—	51	—	*	*	37
Business services	*	9	10	4	*	*	*	*	*	5	7
Renting of movables	*	*	*	*	*	—	*	*	—	*	*
Owning & dealing in real estate	29	*	76	56	*	*	—	*	*	*	39
National government	65	59	69	60	*	82	*	*	*	*	63
Local government	65	73	69	56	*	*	*	*	57	*	61
Fire, police, justice, defence, social security	53	51	46	54	58	55	—	*	*	—	53
Sanitary services	*	*	72	*	*	*	—	51	22	*	26
Higher education	*	56	50	31	*	*	*	*	*	—	49
Schools	*	80	37	33	*	28	*	*	33	*	58
Other education	*	57	49	*	*	*	*	*	*	*	41
Research & development	*	37	*	*	*	*	—	*	*	*	38
Hospitals	44	61	79	44	*	46	*	*	54	*	61
Other medical	*	*	69	*	—	42	—	*	*	41	38
Entertainment & leisure	22	44	38	23	50	23	*	*	32	25	29
Other services	36	51	45	26	*	20	*	*	34	7	27

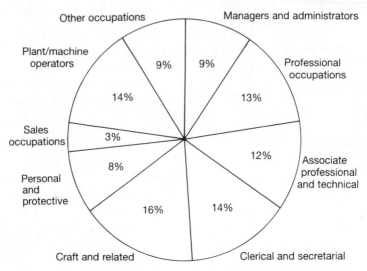

Figure 1.3   *Union membership by occupational group, Great Britain, 1992*
Source: Labour Force Survey 1992

factory worker in overalls but a nurse, a teacher, a local government office worker.

Density is related to *size of workplace*: it is significantly higher in workplaces with 25 or more employees. Density is higher amongst *older* people. Union members are also becoming *better educated* – union density was highest for men with higher education qualifications below degree level. There are also important *regional* differences. The northern region of England has the highest density and the south east outside London the lowest. Scotland, Lancashire, Wales and Yorkshire have strong densities but over most of the country density is well below 50% of the labour force.

Determinants of density
Density, like membership growth, will be influenced by: the business cycle; employment; wage and price levels; the political climate; legislation; and changes in industrial structure and labour force composition. Studies have emphasised the importance of size of establishment and the associated bureaucratisation of work

relations. Impersonal treatment of employees and central determination of general rules strengthen collective consciousness and encourage collective organisation which in its turn reinforces bureaucratisation. Also crucial is employer support or hostility, in itself influenced by the stance taken by the state. Union organisation and leadership is also relevant as an active agent maximising or minimising these conditions. Some argue unions cannot buck the market, increasing aggregate membership when environmental factors are unfavourable. Others claim external structural factors are not determining: union activity can increase density (Bain, 1970; Bain and Elsheikh, 1976; Undy *et al.*, 1981).

These factors have come together in a negative configuration to deflate membership and density in the 1980s and 1990s. There is however little agreement on *precisely how they have interacted* to stimulate decline and which factors have been most influential. It seems clear decline was the product of 'a complex interaction' of the economic situation, state policy, changes in the composition of the labour force, the strategies of employers and the strategies of unions (Metcalf, 1991, 135). Within this broad judgement some claim that employment legislation was the primary explanation for decline in the first half of the 1980s – despite the fact it was largely preceded by economic change and decline in density (Freeman and Pelletier, 1990). Others rely on the mix of real wage increases, high unemployment and government policies. Some argue that changes in the composition of the workforce have played little part (Disney, 1990). It is clear that lack of employer support is a growing problem (Millward, 1994, 24). We discuss explanations for decline further in Chapter 10.

Gender

In the struggle between unity and division, sexism and racism play a role in atomising workers. More than 35% of the membership of TUC affiliated unions now consists of women: in thirteen unions more than half the membership is female. In the biggest union, Unison, the figure is around 65%. The **Labour Force Survey** still shows a gap between male and female densities (see Table

1.9). But this has closed in recent years and the difference lies
largely in the number of women working part-time. Part-time
workers are less likely to be in unions but density is far higher
amongst women part-timers than amongst men. The latter tend to
be older workers over 60 or working part-time on a casual basis
and very young. For women, part-time work is an essential feature
of their working lives. Women moreover, often work in low

Table 1.9   *Union density by ethnic origin and sex*

Density (%)[a]	All	Men	Women
All in employment[bc]	33	36	30
Of which:			
White	33	36	30
Minority groups	32	31	32
Of which:			
West Indian/Guyanese	46	43	48
Indian	33	35	31
Pakistan/Bangladeshi	25	26	[d]
Other minority groups	23	23	22
All employees[c]	37	42	32
Of which:			
White	37	42	32
Minority groups	37	38	36
Of which:			
West Indian/Guyanese	50	49	50
Indian	40	45	34
Pakistan/Bangladeshi	32	34	[d]
Other minority groups	27	27	27

[a] % in category who are members of a trade union or staff association.
Those who did not report their union status are regarded as non-union
members.
[b] Includes those on government schemes and those who did not report
their employment status.
[c] Includes those who did not provide information on their ethnic origin.
[d] Cell size too small to provide a reliable estimate.

Source: Employment Gazette, January 1993.

density industries: with small workplaces, scattered employees, high turnover, lack of employer support, these industries are difficult to organise. If we take these factors into account the relationship between gender and unionisation becomes negligible.

Some unions such as the AEU only admitted women to membership in the 1940s. Unions remain male oriented and male dominated, structured by patriarchal relations. Many women have had to face two jobs – at home *and* in employment – and gender segregation in the labour market. Unions have attempted to encourage greater female representation. By the 1990s change was uneven. In NUPE 70% of the members were women, 46% of the Executive and 38% of full-time officers; in USDAW the figures were 71%, 31% and 20%; and in the TGWU 17%, 8% and 3% (LRD, 1991).

Women officers can have an impact on female participation and issues such as equal pay, child care and maternity – yet there is increasing competition for these posts. In 1993 there were only three women general secretaries of TUC unions, all small organisations – the FDA, NAPO and KFAT. One survey found that only 10% of 3,000 full-time officers employed by the five biggest unions were women (Heery and Kelly, 1988). Domestic responsibilities still constrain participation. Progress in implementing paper policies and genuine aspirations, in reforming union mechanisms to facilitate female involvement at appropriate times and suitable situations, in providing child care and prioritising issues such as equal pay and maternity has often been slow. Yet with continuing discrimination and changes in the labour force women workers are of key importance to unions for both principled and practical reasons.

Ethnicity

Black workers are just as likely to be union members as their white counterparts. Table 1.9 shows densities of 32% and 33% respectively in 1991. Density differs between ethnic groups. It is high amongst those with a West Indian background – at 46% these workers have the highest density of any social group – and lower for those with a Pakistan/Bangladeshi background at 25%.

This is remarkable given the exclusionary stance unions have adopted towards black workers. The 1950s and 1960s saw these workers concentrated in low paid, unskilled jobs, more likely to work shifts, more susceptible to unemployment and more likely to earn less than similarly qualified white workers. They were often the object of racism, the colour bar, even strikes against their employment by white members, problems exacerbated by the refusal of union leaders and activists to accept that racism occurred and required corrective action. The entry of black workers into industrial conflict in well publicised disputes in the 1970s at Imperial Typewriters and Mansfield Hosiery highlighted problems. Growing opposition at Congress to the General Council's 'colour blind' attitude led to a more positive response in the 1980s with unions beginning to monitor black membership, adopt equal opportunity measures and examine how representation could be improved. By the mid-1980s black density was higher than that of white workers but black members were less likely to be stewards and full-time officers. However, unions were beginning to change their structures to facilitate black involvement and combat racism (Brown, 1984; LRD, 1988).

By the 1990s one union, NALGO, had an officer at national level who dealt with race equality issues and specific representation on its executive. A majority of larger unions had developed some mechanisms to deal with these issues and to increase black membership. However, a survey of 21 unions showed that only 9 had any black full-time officers. The election of Bill Morris as General Secretary of the TGWU was widely welcomed but a TUC study showed that much remained to be done. In one union with 100 full-time officers only 1 was black as were 2 out of 132 employees at headquarters. Across the board unions' black employees were concentrated in the lower work grades (LRD, 1993a; TUC, 1991b).

Organisation

British unions have always prided themselves on their democracy but internal arrangements exhibit a wide variety of different forms. A key argument has been about union democracy. Should it be *representative* – having elected or indirectly appointed officials, should members 'leave it to the professionals'? Or should democracy be *participative*, with members actively involved at all levels? Evidence over the years suggest unions have never attracted more than minority participation, even at local level.

The branch – the basic unit of formal organisation – is the starting point for participation (see Figure 1.4). The branch may be geographically based, enrolling members where they work, or workplace or employer based. Its members elect representatives to committees which supervise the day to day work of the unions at **district, area, divisional or regional level**. They also elect a **National Executive Committee** and chief officers termed **General Secretary** and/or **President**. Legislation requires that all such representatives must be elected by postal ballot at least every five years.

In some unions, such as the AEU, District Committees exercised a real influence and area organisation played a key role in the NUM. In the general unions an important locus of control was at the regional level and District Committees wielded far less power than in the former craft unions with their traditions of local autonomy. The National Executive usually consists of lay members elected from branches. But in some unions full-time officers are eligible and successful lay candidates became full-time representatives. The General Secretary and/or President theoretically report to the EU but often exercise a powerful influence upon it. Its role is to execute policy and administer affairs between delegate conferences. Held annually, in some cases bi-annually, **Conference** is normally the governing body deciding policy. Just as the National Executive can vary from less than 20 to over 70 representatives, composition of Conferences varies significantly. The TGWU's Biennial Delegate Conference has involved around 800 delegates, the AEU's National Committee meetings

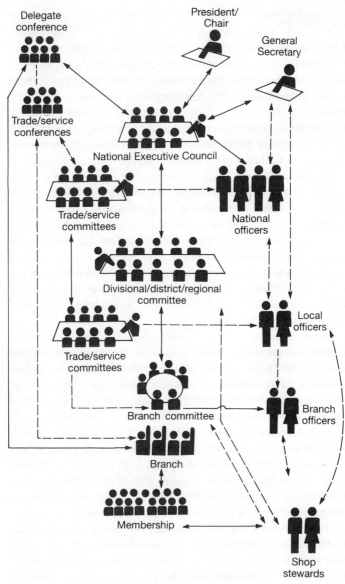

Figure 1.4   *Trade union organisation*

consisted of less than a tenth of that number. In some unions there is a separate **Rules Revision Conference** and **Final Appeal Court**. In other unions this is a function of the Conference.

Superimposed on this geographical structure is often a system of industrial representation. The TGWU exhibits a long-standing dualism in its **trade group structure** with trade group committees overlapping with regional and national structures. Many unions have sought to specifically articulate industrial concerns through the development of industrial and employer based structures. A more recent development has been representation on the basis of gender and ethnicity. Since the 1980s unions have become more self-critical about the effectiveness of organisational structures, employing consultants to recommend improvements.

Whilst strong emphasis has been placed on lay involvement, large scale organisation requires **full-time officers**. In theory they are employed to implement policy. The Webbs long ago noted the difference between aspiration and reality in union democracy: 'The actual government of the trade union world rests exclusively in the hands of a class apart, the salaried officers of the great societies' (Webb and Webb, 1920, 65). In some unions officers are elected; in most, appointed. Historically the bureaucracy of British unions was under-developed with one full-time officer to every 3,800 members compared with 1,800 in West Germany by the 1960s (Royal Commission, 1968, 188). Increased membership pushed up the ratio to 1:4,000 but it then declined to 1:3,500 (Kelly and Heery, 1989, 210). Officers handle a wide range of issues dealing with grievances and disciplinary problems unresolved in the workplace, industrial tribunal and arbitration cases and negotiations over wages and conditions, as well as advising members on union policy, employment legislation, pensions and numerous other problems. Recently there has been a growth in employment of specialists to deal with legal issues, health and safety and recruitment, as well as research and education staff. Unions remain weak in the deployment of strategic resources. And they have always been dependent on **lay officials** to act as initiator, sieve and safety net.

Workplace organisation

A workplace would always have a 'union man' who recruited, collected dues, advised members and provided links with the branch. Apart from areas such as printing where **the chapel** was the workplace branch, workplace organisation was rudimentary. It received a fillip with the introduction of piece work systems and new machinery in engineering in the 1890s. During World War I with scarcity of labour and dilution shopfloor bargaining spread through the munitions industries and beyond. Links between different groups produced the 'Shop Stewards' Movement' emphasising rank and file democracy and socialist change. By 1920 several unions provided for **shop stewards** and works committees in their rulebooks. The onset of recession reduced bargaining power and the stewards were often the first to be made redundant. The revival of the economy in the late 1930s and World War II produced a renewal of workplace organisation which spread from engineering through manufacturing industry.

In the 1960s the number of stewards was estimated at 90,000 and by 1968 at 175,000 (McCarthy and Parker, 1968). By the 1970s, boosted by full employment, decentralised bargaining and attempts to reform industrial relations, workplace organisation had spread from the metal trades to the distributive and service industries and to local government and the health service. The initial thrust came from below and shop stewards' committees sometimes encountered bitter opposition from union leaders who viewed them as a threat to the formal system of union government. By the 1970s unions such as NALGO and NUPE were creating workplace representation and revising their structures to accommodate them. As a response to reform tendencies in industrial relations or a desire for enhanced democracy unions sought to articulate workplace organisation with wider structures and integrate shop stewards.

By 1979 there were more than 350,000 workplace representatives. Shop stewards were as pervasive as trade unionism – 75% of establishments recognising unions recognised workplace representatives for manual workers and 33% for white collar workers (Millward and Stevens, 1986, 80). Their incidence was high not only in traditional strongholds but in nationalised industries, public utilities, clothing, leather and footwear and food, drink and tobacco. Workplace organisation showed similarities across industry and had become increasingly sophisticated (Brown, 1981). The scope of domestic bargaining remained restricted prioritising wages and security. The controls imposed over work were important but fragmented and defensive. The fact that stewards were *responsive* meant they responded to the ordinary, 'bread and butter', parochial concerns of their members.

Stewards elected, often unopposed, on a show of hands and representing on average around 20 members were seen as a token of lay involvement and participative grassroots democracy. At one end of the scale – dependent on the bargaining structure – workplace representatives recruited members and handled grievances with management; at the other they were involved in detailed negotiations over wages. Stewards usually formed a **Stewards' Committee**, and if more than one union was involved, a **Joint Shop Stewards' Committee**, sometimes a **Joint Union Negotiating Committee**. Beyond the workplace, notably in engineering, stewards established **Combine Committees** consisting of representatives from plants in a particular company, a move accommodated by some unions which established employer based advisory committees.

Convenors or senior stewards spending large amounts of working time on union business became common. Management provided facilities with representatives legally entitled to paid time off for their industrial relations functions and for training under the terms of the Employment Protection Act 1975. By the late 1970s there were around 10,000 full-time stewards.

The shop steward was both spokesperson for the work group and official of the union. In some situations, notably large car factories, stewards enjoyed a real degree of independence from full-time officers and formal union organisation although even here there was interpenetration between workplace organisation and the union branch. Taking the unions as a whole the degree of autonomy was sometimes over-estimated. Even in geographically based branches 'stewards were much more frequent in their attendance than were other branch members. Stewards also commonly held positions on their branch committees' (Daniel and Milward, 1983, 284). Obviously 350,000 workplace representatives could not all be closely linked to union structures. But despite antagonism in the 1950s and 1960s from union leaders, relations with full-time officers were often based on a *co-operative division of labour* rather than reflecting an antagonistic distrust of the union bureaucracy on the one side or fear of a militant rank and file on the other (Batstone *et al.*, 1977, 185).

Under an adversarial stance there was, too, often mutual interdependence between workplace representatives and managers. Management sometimes sponsored and often accommodated to workplace organisation, providing resources and relying on stewards to carry out a variety of functions, from raising grievances to facilitating change at work (Terry, 1983). This continued in the 1980s and 1990s when the economic and political climate has undermined workplace organisation. It proved resilient in the early part of the 1980s. Thereafter 'there is little doubt that there was decline across the 1984 to 1990 period and that it was substantial' (Millward *et al.*, 1992, 116). Nonetheless active workplace representatives remain a distinctive aspect of British trade unionism. Without these often maligned voluntary carers who give commitment for little personal reward trade unions would be unable to function efficiently.

Recognition and security

Unions have depended on their own efforts to secure recognition. Apart from a brief period – under the provisions of the Employment Protection Act 1975, abolished in 1980 – they have operated without statutory support. Legal provisions requiring employers to recognise and bargain with unions if certain conditions of representativeness are met are common in other legal jurisdictions but have been absent in Britain. Unions have benefited from public policy supporting collective bargaining, the charters of nationalised industries, the policy of government departments and local government which envisaged union recognition and the mission of ACAS to encourage extension of collective bargaining. These have all come under pressure in recent years.

Key influences on recognition have been ownership (whether the enterprise is public or private, independent or part of a wide corporation), size of establishment, size of enterprise and employment category. Unions found it tougher to get recognition for white collar workers compared with manual employees. The established structure of recognition appears to have been maintained in the early 1980s but to have come under greater pressure over the last decade. What is worrying the unions is that the state's emphasis on union exclusion has found increasing resonance with employers; hostility and derecognition is growing.

If all employees were required to join, a stable membership base and source of finance would be secured, bargaining power might be enhanced and the legitimacy of collectivism powerfully asserted. The **closed shop** refers to the situation where by formal agreement or custom all workers in a grade or category must join the relevant recognised union as a condition of employment. The **pre-entry closed shop** denotes the arrangement operated in the past by craft unions, but also more widely, by which union membership was required as a condition of hiring. The **post-entry closed shop** denotes the more common situation where new employees were required to join the relevant union shortly after hiring.

In the 1960s the closed shop covered 3.75 million largely manual workers concentrated in the union strongholds of engineering, printing, coal and steel. The advent of legal support in the trade union and labour relations legislation of the mid-1970s pushed numbers covered to 5 million with significant increases in nationalised industries and amongst white collar workers (Dunn and Gennard, 1984). Since then decline has proceeded in tandem with debilitating industrial change and consecutive legal restrictions. By 1984 the closed shop covered 3.5 million workers; by 1990 it was a disintegrating landmark covering only some 500,000 workers (Millward *et al.*, 1992, 99).

The deduction of dues at source – **the check-off** – is another

tribute to employer support. On grounds of efficiency this
bureaucratic system came to replace collection of dues by
stewards in the workplace and members attending branch meetings to subscribe. Cash flow is secured on a more reliable basis
with minimal cost. By the end of the 1980s it covered 70% of all
members (Millward *et al.*, 1992, 124). The cost is management
control over union security. Employers such as British Rail and
British Coal used the withdrawal of check-off arrangements as a
bargaining weapon with the unions and in 1993 government
legislation fixed upon it in an attempt to disorganise unions'
operations.

Union finances

Unions seem to be big business: total money income in 1991 was
£620 million. Income from members made up 80% of this figure
and income from investments 7%. However, we have to take
expenditure to service 9 million members into account. Eight of
the 20 biggest unions were in deficit during 1991. Subscription
dependency of all unions was 81.5% but for 15 out of the 23
biggest unions over 90% of income came from subscriptions and
the RCN was completely dependent on membership dues. Some
unions like the RMT or GPMU are relatively well off. Others
such as UCATT or USDAW live hand to mouth. For the big
unions 85% of expenditure went on administration and nearly
12%, a declining figure, on benefits. Unions at the workplace are
also subsidised by employers through facilities and time off. With
decline in membership the object is to reduce administrative
expenditure and increase the real level of subscriptions. In the
early 1990s the unions were having success with the latter; the
former was proving an uphill battle.

   Union dues take up a smaller proportion of annual earnings
than in comparable countries. From 1950 to 1979 they declined as
a proportion of earnings, thereafter increasing from 0.3% of
average earnings in 1979 to 0.35% in 1984 and 0.38% in 1990, a
figure still way below the TUC target of 1% set a decade earlier.
In Scandinavia the figure is well above 1%; it is 1% in Germany.

If the British still get their trade unionism on the cheap – subscriptions to the big unions varied in 1991 from £28.23 in the Schoolmasters/Union of Women Teachers to £100.69 in the GPMU, with a mean of £54.85 – there were signs of a significant increase in the early 1990s. Overall unions are poorer in the 1990s than they were in the 1950s with smaller reserves. Intense competition restrains ability to increase subscriptions which would make all the difference. Despite economies in personnel and structure and continuing mergers, problems remain.

The TUC: the union centre

The TUC is the national co-ordinating centre of British trade unionism. Its affiliates organise more than 80% of trade unionists. **Congress** meets annually. Voting strength is related to membership size. Congress also elects the **General Council** which carries out policy between each congress. In the past it was elected on a trade group basis. Important restructuring in 1983 and 1989 produced a new system. The present procedure groups unions in sections according to size.

Section A   Unions with 200,000 or more members are awarded seats on a proportional basis:

200,000–399,999: 2 seats
400,000–649,999: 3 seats
650,000–899,999: 4 seats
900,000–1,199,999: 5 seats
1,200,000–1,499,999: 6 seats

Unions in this section with 100,000 or more women members must nominate at least one woman.

Section B   Unions with membership between 100,000 and 199,999 are entitled to one seat.

Section C   Unions with membership of less than 100,000 collectively elect 8 members.

Section D   Unions with less than 200,000 members collectively elect four women representatives.

This produces a general council of around 40 members. A key role is played by the General Secretary – since the war a member of the TUC staff. John Monks who succeeded Norman Willis in 1993 was, like his predecessor, formally elected for life unopposed at Congress. He is supported by a Deputy General Secretary and two Assistant General Secretaries. The full-time staff of the TUC, around 120, are organised into departments: organisation, economics, international and so on. The General Council traditionally organised its work on a committee basis. In 1994 a re-launch saw the abolition of all of these except the finance and general purposes committee which became the principle decision-making body. There is an Annual Womens' TUC Conference and a Black Workers Conference. There is a separate TUC for Scotland.

There are eight regional councils in England plus the Welsh TUC with full-time secretaries and in some cases research staff. There are also full-time regional education officers. Like the regional secretaries they are employees of Congress House and ultimately answerable to the TUC. The 300 or so local Trades Councils with delegates from affiliates are grouped into County Associations with an annual conference. The TUC's role has had four major dimensions:

1 It has acted as **regulator** and **supporter** of the activities of its affiliates. This has been based on the Bridlington Agreement of 1939 by which TUC disputes committees adjudicate inter-union conflicts. The TUC can intervene in disputes between affiliated unions and employers, co-ordinate industrial action in support of affiliates and investigate their affairs.
2 The TUC acts as **provider of services** for members. This has been valuable to smaller unions in areas such as education and research. In recent years the TUC has attempted to provide more legal and financial services.
3 The TUC acts as **spokesperson for affiliates to the state**

and other interest groups. For over a century the prime role of the TUC has been to influence the actions of government over a wide range of issues of major concern to union members (TUC, 1983, 12).
4 The TUC acts as a **spokesperson for affiliates in the international arena** forging links in other countries. It has been increasingly preoccupied with developing a role in the EU.

Compared with union centres elsewhere the TUC has possessed completeness, with a majority of trade unionists affiliated to it. Splits have been few and temporary. Competing centres based on political or religious differences exist in France, Italy or Spain, while splits on blue collar/white collar lines are evident in Germany and the Scandinavian states. In the UK they have been avoided. However, the number of members in non-TUC unions has doubled. Moreover, the TUC does not charter unions, and its powers over its affiliates have in general been limited partly because of its inability to form sustained linkage of practical value with the state and employers. Decentralised bargaining has also weakened central control. Having established a stronger role as co-ordinator over incomes policy and industrial relations reform in the 1960s and 1970s the TUC has seen this role challenged and diminished in succeeding decades. Problems afflicting affiliates have led them to question the role of the TUC and their expenditure on it. The TUC in turn has pointed out that it is poorly resourced, comparing affiliation fees in Britain with other countries.

The political dimension

The establishment of the TUC in 1868 represented the unions' awareness of the need to constitute themselves as a pressure group to fight for legislation to organise and vote in elections. The establishment of the Labour Party in embryo in 1900, in more fully fledged form in 1918, demonstrated a need to extend the range of political issues trade unionists could directly influence and deepen control over their representation. The break from the

Liberal Party should not be over-estimated in terms of changes in ideology or vision. The creation of the Labour Party involved a means of better working the system not dispensing with it. Today 25 major unions including 8 of the 10 biggest unions are affiliated to the Labour Party. But many others swim in its orbit. The inescapability of political action is demonstrated by the growth in union political funds. Unions accord primacy to the industrial sphere. But if politics is a second string to their bow it has been a very important string. If political activity can never replace industrial activity it has, given the increasing role of the state, become inextricably interlinked with industrial activity.

Despite increasing politicisation of the industrial sphere unions have operated a division of labour in which political change comes through Parliament not industrial action and political hegemony is granted to the political leadership. This diffidence is part of a general defensiveness. Despite the porous Clause IV of the Party Constitution promising 'to secure for the producers by hand and brain the full fruits of their industry', union politics has been powerfully structured by **Labourism**. The commitment to pragmatic, limited change within capitalism, reform rather than revolution has remained dominant through recent history. Labourism saw the world in terms of 'them' and 'us': 'them' and 'us' had distinct, sometimes conflicting, interests but both sides had a legitimate and enduring role. There was a split in 'us' between male workers, the protagonists of trade unionism and female domestic carers whose territory was the home. Labourism was built around the twin pillars of collective bargaining and parliamentary politics and embodied strong attachment to the institutions of the British state. The state's role in this was important, excluding the market from political regulation, granting autonomy to employers and unions and priority to collective bargaining, it asserted its neutrality and provided the unions with their own private domain. Privileging stability and social order over economic efficiency, state abstention purchased the loyalty of trade unionists to a system and political culture which gave them an autonomous role and underpinned Labourism.

Labourism *was contested*. In the early years of the century it was challenged by what is loosely termed **syndicalism**, a movement based on the industrial militancy of the period 1900 to 1921 which took up questions of power and authority in the workplace and challenged the state with a conception of an 'industrial parliament' in which workers would control their industries through revolutionised industrial unions and workers' councils. The syndicalist challenge was strengthened by the impact of the 1917 revolution in Russia but faltered with the collapse of the economy and defeat of militancy in the early 1920s. That defeat sealed the ascendency of Labourism although domination was only finally confirmed in the climacteric year of 1945. Syndicalism possessed of necessity a strong unofficial and rank and file orientation. When, as in 1919 or 1926, trade unionism presented a challenge to the system its leadership strove successfully to ensure it was short lived and not repeated. Preserving much of radical liberalism they developed instead pragmatic strategies for restructuring the economy through state intervention. Nonetheless industrial politics remained adversarial: the job of 'us' remained to distrust and when required fight 'them', if according to a version of the Marquess of Queensberry rules. Moreover, many trade unionists never fully accepted the economic logic of reformed capitalism so persuasive to their brothers and sisters in Scandinavia or West Germany.

Labourism in Britain has been set in the aspiration and, to a limited extent, the reality of a **Labour Movement** aspiring to embrace all workers industrially and politically. In America the term is usually used to refer only to trade unionism based on collective bargaining. In Britain the Labour Movement more commonly refers to two wings, the industrial and political, hefting together the unions, the party and the co-operative movement, combining industrial protection with a wider social vision. The Labour Movement has been seen as embracing a wide range of industrial and political activists, papers and magazines and cultural, research and education bodies. The decreased purchase of the Labour Movement both as reality and aspiration has been a major problem in recent decades. Some have seen in the years since 1979 the crisis or even the demise of Labourism.

The international dimension

The development of globalisation, world capital markets and, to a lesser degree, integration of production with increasing integration of national economies and intensifying competition, means more than ever that many problems unions seek to control are best confronted at international level. The biggest 100 transnationals own around half of all cross-frontier assets and dominate national economies and world trade. Unions operating on a purely national level will be fighting the losing battle local craft societies fought with the emergence of national markets in the last century. Yet the unions' international organisation has proved inadequate in meeting the challenge.

The TUC is a prominent member of the worldwide **International Confederation of Free Trade Unions**. The ICFTU was established in 1949 as a breakaway under the pressures of the cold war from the **World Federation of Trade Unions** which also embraced union centres in the Soviet bloc. The WFTU continued enrolling not only federations from the communist countries but also African, Arab and South American federations until it became moribund with the upheavals in the USSR and Eastern Europe. The ICFTU has affiliates in more than 120 countries organising some 113 million workers. Having broken from the WFTU on the grounds that many of the latters' affiliates were not free unions the ICFTU was soon the object of criticism that it was funded by the CIA through the American centre the AFL-CIO and was an instrument of US foreign policy.

The TUC also sends delegates to the **International Labour Organisation**. It is affiliated to the **Trade Union Advisory Committee of the Organisation for Economic Co-operation and Development** and the **Commonwealth Trade Union Council**, a body covering some 25 million workers in 40 Commonwealth countries which aims at creating links with governments and providing a range of assistance to unions particularly in the Third World. At the centre of the TUC's international activities in recent years has been the **European Trade Union Confederation**. The ETUC, established in 1973, consists of 36 national centres with a membership of 44 million. It covers union centres in non-EU countries as well as member states. Perhaps its major endeavour has been to bring pressure to bear on EU decision-making processes and co-ordinate EU-wide union policies. For many the TUC's recent work in the ETUC and the CTUC stand in refreshing contrast to the torpor and imbrication with state policy which characterised much of the work of its International Department in the 1960s and 1970s.

Individual unions form links with their counterparts in other countries through the **International Trade Secretariats** which cover groups such as public service workers, metal workers, chemical workers and so forth, many of them linked to the ICFTU. The International Secretariats have been valuable in establishing links between workers in different countries, particularly through councils for large multinationals which have held worldwide conferences, although transnational bargaining has failed to develop. Unions are also represented on the industrial committees of the ETUC and have benefited from the work of the ETUC's research arm the **European Trade Union Institute**. A problem has been the inability of many of the combine committees of workplace representatives established in the 1960s and 1970s to move beyond the role of useful but limited information exchange mechanisms in the 1980s and 1990s.

Conclusions

Trade unions are organisations of employees who combine to protect their interests at work and beyond. The form of organisation and the methods they use depend on their values and structural situation but also on the power, values and strategies of employers and the state. The specific form union structure has taken in Britain represents unbroken, unplanned evolution. The categories 'craft', 'industrial', 'general', 'white collar' are useful in understanding development, less helpful in classifying unions today. The motor of development has been economic and industrial change rather than political influence. Unions have reacted pragmatically: there has been no architect of structure and no blueprint. The result is a kaleidoscope of competing unions with different forms. The present thrust is towards the conglomerate, uniting workers from a variety of grades and industries and articulating specific representation within the organisation. This organic and reactive pattern of development now appears to be accepted; demands for *planned* re-organisation are few. Re-organisation is occurring rather through *ad hoc* mergers.

History has produced a relatively stable, unified movement which operates industrially and politically through collective bargaining, pressure group politics and an intimate relationship with the Labour Party. Unlike other countries it has not seen splits on religious, political or industrial grounds. Industrial unity has been reflected in political unity. In response to changes in collective bargaining, there has been a high degree of decentralisation within the unions, with the power of the centre over affiliates circumscribed and a history of strong workplace organisation. Workplace representatives have at times possessed significant bargaining functions compared with their counterparts in other countries. In international terms membership and density has been high. Growth in the early years of the century terminated in decline until the early 1930s. Thereafter increases in membership and density subsided into stability before dramatic growth between 1968 and 1979. The period since then has seen significant decline. Workplace organisation too has suffered.

In recent years attention has focused on discrimination on grounds of gender and ethnicity in union organisation and practice; a variety of ameliorative measures have been employed. The lessons drawn by unions from long, often bitter, experience has been that gains can be made within the existing social framework. There have been many links with unions in other countries but national concerns have been preponderant and in the post-war period union internationalism was often a pallid reflection of cold war concerns. There has been recent change with developments in the EU.

Further reading

Two books which provide more discussion on the rationale of trade unionism and its goals, from different perspectives, are Colin Crouch, *Trade Unions: The Logic of Collective Action*, Fontana, 1982, and Richard Hyman, *Industrial Relations: A Marxist Introduction*, Macmillan, 1975. Henry Pelling's *A History of British Trade Unionism*, Penguin, 1988, is a good introduction. Tony Lane's *The Union Makes Us Strong*, Arrow, 1974, unfortunately out of print, is an excellent analysis of union purposes set against their historical evolution. H. A. Turner, *Trade Union Growth, Structure and Policy: A Comparative Study of the Cotton Unions*, Allen & Unwin, 1962, provides insights beyond its title and although dated is perhaps the best work on how union structure evolved. You can read more about 'unionateness' and the development of white collar unionism in Robert Blackburn, *Union Character and Social Class*, Batsford, 1967. George Bain, *The Growth of White Collar Unionism*, Oxford University Press, 1970, contains a wealth of useful analysis of membership growth and density.

2

Unions, economy and society

In Chapter 1 we emphasised that trade unions are social and political actors. Any assessment of trade unionism in the 1990s cannot simply focus on unions as bargaining agents at work and in industry. It has to examine the social, economic and political processes which constrain union activity and which unions in their turn seek to influence and control. Unions contribute to social change; in the process they are changed themselves. This chapter examines theories of trade unionism, the role it plays in society and its impact on social change. It then looks at the economic and industrial context vital to union activities.

Theories of trade unionism

Most writers see unions as a normal feature of capitalist society. North Americans particularly have stressed the job-centred nature of trade unionism. Trade unionism is about sectional interest and job consciousness not class consciousness. Trade unions have no transformative mission. They seek simply to protect their members within existing society. In the words of the US miners' leader John L. Lewis, 'Trade unionism is a pheno-menon of capitalism quite similar to the corporation. . .the economic aims of both are identical – gain.' Trade unionists are sometimes led astray by intellectuals – hence the political ideals in many constitutions. Their *practice* is based not on fighting capi-talism but on exploiting it, on the politics of the pork barrel. Trade unionism is thus about bread and butter issues, 'controlling the job' to achieve security of employment, not controlling industry or transforming society. As an unremarkable and unthreatening aspect of the capitalist landscape unions resemble businesses (Perlman, 1928).

The conservatism of Perlman's 'pure and simple' trade unionism was echoed by Tannenbaum who saw trade unionism as restoring the organic life and dignity workers enjoyed before the birth of capitalism. It did not challenge capitalism: it civilised it and integrated workers through collective bargaining and partici- pation in industry (Tannenbaum, 1921). Hoxie provided a detailed classification of union types. **Ideological unions** embraced political action to change society. **Business unions** saw maximising the price of their members' labour as their central mission and limited themselves to economic concerns. **Friendly or uplift unions** sought to improve members' position through the provision of welfare benefits. Like Perlman, Hoxie charac- terised American unions as business or economic unions (Hoxie, 1917).

The Webbs saw British unions rooted in the divorce between ownership and production. Improving their members' working lives centred on collective bargaining. But it also involved wider social change and democratising the workplace through political activities which could gradually transform capitalism. But the unions' central role lay in the regulation of workplace and industry to restrain competition between workers. In this regulation the Webbs discerned the germ of wider social planning (Webb and Webb, 1920).

Allan Flanders, too, saw collective bargaining at the heart of trade unionism. Like Perlman he derived purpose from observed activity. Flanders theorised collective bargaining as a rule-making process through which unions pursued substantive outcomes and job regulation; it provided protection and participation and created rights and obligations in industry. The essential *social purpose* of trade unionism was participation in job regulation, a form of industrial democracy. Political activity was ancillary. Unions were not just economic organisations but neither were

they political parties; too specific or all pervasive political commitment could endanger industrial unity. Affiliation to the Labour
Party was to facilitate industrial ends. Unions acting as 'a sword of
justice' were a distinctive pressure group not just another vested
interest. They had played a role in wider social change and would
continue to do so (Flanders, 1970, 38ff.).

These theorists all place a strong emphasis on trade unions as
bargaining agents intent on securing a bigger slice of the cake, not
the whole cake or the kitchen in which it was produced. Unions
are not only interested in economic ends but in the regulation of
work. Some such as Perlman see the political dimension as
limited. Others like Flanders see it as important but still
secondary, although for Flanders the zenith of job regulation was
participation in incomes policy. All see unions affecting social
change but in gradual fashion.

Marxist alternatives

Marxist analysis provides an alternative tradition sensing in trade
unionism potential for the transformation of capitalism. Marx and
Engels initially saw 'pure and simple' trade unionism as itself a
threat to capitalism. Combination transcending competition
bound workers together and challenged economic stability.
Unions were 'schools of war' which would teach workers their
interests could not be met within capitalism and train them for the
struggle to overthrow it. Later Marx and Engels were concerned
that unions were 'fighting with effects not with the cause of these
effects. . .applying palliatives not curing the malady'. They
explained their failure in terms of the treachery of union leaders
and the **embourgeoisement** of their members.

Lenin stressed the limitations of trade unionism in generating
revolutionary consciousness and social transformation. Working-
class struggle in itself could produce only **trade union consciousness**, understanding of the need to combine, fight the
employers and seek social reform. Understanding of the need to
replace capitalism required socialist theory developed by workers
and intellectuals organised in a revolutionary party. Union activity
was necessary but insufficient: economic struggle could integrate

the working class into capitalism, facilitate the buying off of skilled workers and officials and strengthen the hold of capitalist ideas. This analysis was developed by Trotsky who argued in the 1920s and 1930s that declining monopoly capitalism could no longer tolerate even limited economic gains. The incorporation of the unions and the role of the union bureaucracy in controlling their members was important for capital in 'an epoch of imperialist decay'.

These ideas inform modern analysis. With the growth of conflict in the 1960s Perry Anderson asserted Leninist orthodoxy:

As institutions trade unions do not challenge the existence of a society based on a division of classes they merely express it. Thus trade unions can never be viable vehicles of advance towards socialism in themselves; by their nature they are tied to capitalism. They can bargain within the society but not transform it (Anderson, 1967, 264).

This 'pessimistic' strand in Marxism was contested by Richard Hyman who saw Lenin's position in *What Is To Be Done* as 'inflexible' and argued it was best to view trade union and revolutionary consciousness in terms of a continuum, not a polarity. Following the optimistic early Marx he argued that union activity, particularly industrial action, can educate the masses. The limits of trade union consciousness can vary in different contexts and shift swiftly: there are no general theories or iron laws. Trade unionism is more plastic than Lenin suggests and its leaders more responsive to rank and file pressure than Trotsky suggests. In key periods when the economy is in crisis, where the margin for concessions is slim, union leaders may be unwilling or unable to control their members. Consequent struggles may provide potential for opening members' eyes to the iniquities of capitalism and the necessity and realisability of socialism (Hyman, 1971).

John Kelly returns to these issues in his book *Trade Unions and Socialist Politics*. Basing himself on Rosa Luxemburg's *The Mass Strike* he argues that large scale strikes will produce state intervention. In periods characterised by such strike waves significant numbers of trade unionists will come to understand the need for revolution. The emphasis is on the spontaneous generation of socialist consciousness through industrial conflict rather than the construction of socialist consciousness through the medium of the party. He is opposed to those who argue the need for more gradual encroaching progress through political institutions and industrial democracy. Kelly analyses three periods of militant strike activity in Britain: 1915–22, 1968–74 and 1977–79. In the first he finds an upsurge of political consciousness. The gains in the second period were more limited but there was a general shift to the left. The militancy of 1977–79 showed little growth in class consciousness (1988, 101ff.).

Unions and social and economic change

What is clear from a brief survey is that as a response to capitalism unions change with capitalism; they behave differently at different times *but within the limits of capitalism.* As we saw in Chapter 1 unions in Britain based on skilled craft workers originally approximated to the business union model of Hoxie and Perlman. It was only between 1880 and 1920 that the conception of a movement dedicated to changing society emerged. However this was based upon *gradually* improving conditions and redistributing wealth, pursuing the general interests of workers which were perceived as distinct from those of 'the bosses', through *using the state within capitalism.* British unions rarely allowed their anti-capitalist discourse to interfere with the hard business of collective bargaining, although in comparison with their American cousins they have demonstrated a greater interest in the state and social reform. Flanders's analysis, despite its fuzzy relating of the political to the industrial and its inflation of collective bargaining into democracy, explains better what has happened this century than either the business union model – that there has been a real commitment to social restructuring – or the Marxist model – that commitment has been limited and reformist. Within Marxist analysis the pessimistic tradition summed up by Anderson is most compelling.

There have been strains of rebellion and at times a real, if limited, Marxist influence, just as there have been strains of business unionism. But despite their many insights the existing Marxist accounts falter as *explanations of change*, under-estimating the resilience of capitalism and working-class attachment to its institutions. The militancy of the years 1968–74 was significant and more extensive than at any time since the early 1920s. Large scale confrontations reflected a radical mood of dissatisfaction with the achievements of the post-war consensus and saw the reassertion of the political strike, occupations and 'work-ins', demands for greater control over the workplace and restructuring of the economy in the interests of the working class. But the results of what might be termed the **semi-syndicalism** of the 1960s and 1970s were limited. It produced no revolutionary party of any significance. To see the growth of far left groups, by a few thousand and balanced by the decline of the Communist Party, as a shift left is to deal in fractions of insignificance. It was not reflected as one would expect by socialist change within the unions. No union of significance except possibly the Mineworkers threw up a revolutionary leadership. The left leaders that had emerged by 1968, such as Jack Jones and Hugh Scanlon, were judged by 1975 to have moved to the right. We must surely take what happens in the political sphere as some reflection of changes in consciousness, yet not a solitary parliamentary candidate from the CP or the far left attained more than a derisory vote. The first two years of militancy, 1968–70, produced a Conservative government, the last four a Labour government with less votes than the Conservatives and the smallest Labour share of the vote since the 1930s. The militancy of 1977–79 produced Thatcherism. And the formidable state attacks on the unions since then, as in the 1920s, turned the tide of militancy and witnessed, despite the 1984 miners' strike, a move to the right.

The period 1968–74 was distinctive. Overall the years 1945–79 saw continuing commitment to bargaining within capitalism and a general refusal, despite the brief revival of 'the political strike' of 1968–74, to use industrial power for political purposes. Labourism was underpinned by the relative stability and resilience of the system and perceived success in pressing change within it. That success has been limited. In more than a century of progress to

1980 unions contributed to the civilisation of the workplace and the introduction of the rule of law into industry through the establishment of collective bargaining and the curbing of management prerogative. These developments have been fragile but they have involved an important change in the status of the worker and real material improvements. By the 1970s the difference between what manual workers received when unions determined wages and when they were absent was over 20% and increasing. Studies demonstrated that in periods of union strength the general level of wages increased significantly in excess of what might have been expected through movements in the trade cycle and the market alone (Layard *et al.*, 1978). Yet unions' ability to raise real wages in a sustained way remained limited because of inability to control prices and taxation (Phelps Brown, 1966). In 1974–75 average earnings increased by 27%; but with inflation at 22% and increases in taxes real earnings increased by around 1%. For all the celebration of collective bargaining, it takes place within a framework of decisions on state and employer strategy, investment profit and taxation, already determined. Its scope in Britain remained restricted.

Some economists have argued the impact of unions is real but malign. Union power raises wages in the short term: its ultimate consequence is to deter efficiency, constrain investment and destroy jobs (Minford, 1985). Unions, it is claimed, depress productivity and profitability and threaten economic prosperity (Blanchflower and Oswald, 1988; Metcalf, 1989). This argument is based on neo-classical theories which tend to measure economic activity against an ideal, competitive, market model which glosses over unions and the conflict inherent in the employment relationship which precedes and produces them. It pays little attention to the research of the Harvard economists which sees conflict of interests at work as potentially creative. By giving workers a voice unions may facilitate communications and strengthen morale and motivation in comparison with union free employers. Unions may 'shock' management into improving work organisation and production techniques and stimulate innovation and technological change. By limiting low wages and labour intensification they may energise employers and stimulate more solidly based strategies for efficiency (Freeman and Medoff, 1984; Nolan, 1992). The British evidence for the unions' alleged harmful impact has been criticised as flawed by measurement problems and inadequate investigation of non-unionised firms (Nolan and Marginson, 1990). Other studies question whether unions curb investment and profitability and conclude 'there is no evidence for the view that unions reduce productivity growth' (Wadhwani, 1990, 382). It may be argued that quite apart from their protective and democratic functions, unions are essential in industry because the organisation of production is too important to be left to management. Unless employers are subject to the challenge and stimulus of the organised producers, ultimately dysfunctional routes of sweating and insecurity will deter innovation and consolidate a weak uncompetitive economy (Nolan, 1992). The lesson may be that unions have not been too powerful: they have not been powerful enough and their power has been inadequately addressed and articulated.

Unions have acted as a force for equality, compressing wage differentials between skilled and unskilled men and women, and black and white workers (Metcalf, 1989). But it seems clear that their impact on the overall distribution of income and wealth has been limited. Labour's share of gross domestic product increased from 60% in 1910 to 81% in 1975. Major shifts were associated with the two world wars and the militancy of 1968–74, which produced a declining rate of profit and a reduction of the share of profits in national income. We cannot however attribute all of the change to direct union impact. The limits of union action were demonstrated by continuing concentration of income and wealth whilst, to take one example, 'the unprecedented acceleration of money wages between 1969 and 1973 raised the proportion of income accruing to Labour by 1.35%' (Burkitt and Bowers, 1979, 10). By the 1970s unions had changed society – but within clear limits. They had improved the position of their members: the structural subordination of those members endured.

The unions could point to full employment, the welfare state and, very importantly, their *procedural* rights, their acceptance as part of the establishment. The free rein the limited state gave them in an unregulated system of industrial relations was important even if what they achieved within it remained restricted. Continuing subordination meant aspirations and points of comparison remained limited; there was a strong fatalism and awareness of powerful constraints on change (Runciman, 1966; Marshall *et al.*, 1985). At the workplace and beyond bargaining remained essentially defensive, impeding managerial prerogative but demonstrating little desire to replace it. For the majority Labourism remained the best strategy. Combined deployment of collective bargaining and parliamentary politics had increased living standards and improved the quality of working life, education, housing, welfare, enough for enough people to make the difficult negotiation of radical social transformation unattractive.

Yet the unions were caught up in the contradictions of organisations bearing the banner of sectional interests and the general social good, bargaining agents with a political mission. There can be little doubt that the use of the economic power which the post-war consensus granted unions played a role in undermining it. Unions constituted centres of resistance to hostile change. But they proved incapable, given intra-union power relations and decentralised bargaining, of knitting local power into a national programme, initiating progressive alternatives and supporting them in sustained fashion. When, as with the Social Contract, the TUC did play an initiatory role it was unable to maintain internal cohesion and ensure the Labour Party kept its commitments. The pathos of union power was that it was essentially reactive and negative. The unions were not strong enough or strategic enough to reconcile the different interests of their members, stimulate more imaginative leadership in their political arm and harness the good they did in workplace and industry to positive support for a compelling political and economic programme. From 1945 to 1979 unions proved they were good at stopping things, even at starting them, but not at sustaining them.

We now look in more detail at the factors which have influenced the role of unions and the context in which they operate today.

Britain's economic decline

All the important developments in industrial relations since the late 1960s are rooted in Britain's economic decline. We are talking in relative terms. In the post-war period Britain remained one of the world's richest countries. But it was losing its position near the top of the first division. By the 1960s, the UK was clinging precariously to the top ten and there was growing acceptance across the political spectrum that the UK's progress down the ladder of international competition was accelerating and in the absence of fundamental corrective action, it would continue to do so.

The facts brooked little argument. Between 1945 and 1970, growth in industrial productivity in Britain averaged an annual 1.5%, compared with 3% in the USA and Germany and almost 4% in Japan; its share of manufacturing exports from the advanced economies slumped from 25% to 10%. This was related to a poor rate of capital investment in plant and equipment. The average annual growth of capital stock in the 1950s and 1960s was a little over 4% in the UK, compared with nearly 6% in France, 7% in West Germany and a massive 12.5% in Japan. One study showed fixed assets in manufacturing industry in Japan and Germany as £30,000 and £23,000 per worker respectively, compared with £7,500 in the UK. This problem was exacerbated by the outflow of capital from Britain and by the pattern of inflows, which often redirected production to low wage, labour intensive activities. It took longer and cost more to produce many goods in the UK. Higher production costs and intensive international price competition squeezed the profit margins of British employers (see Table 2.1).

The tight labour markets of the post-war years produced increased labour costs. Passed on to consumers through increased prices, this 'cost plus' inflation produced a further blunting of competitive edge in world markets and further pressure on profits. These problems were softened by the long post-war boom, expansion of world trade and post-war dislocation of competitor economies. Attempts by successive governments failed to trans-

Table 2.1   *Rates of profit for industrial and commercial companies*

Country	% before tax				
	1960	1965	1970	1973	1975
United Kingdom	14.2	11.8	8.7	7.2	3.5
United States of America	9.9	13.7	8.1	8.6	6.9
France	11.9	9.9	11.1	10.2	4.1
Japan	19.7	15.3	22.7	14.7	9.5
Italy	11.0	7.9	8.6	4.5	0.8
Germany	23.4	16.5	15.6	12.1	9.1

Source: Glyn and Harrison, 1980.

form the situation. Rather, decline was cumulative and the economy spiralled into a low investment/low productivity/low growth/low profitability/low investment cycle. In the century to 1979, gross domestic product in Britain had trebled. In the United States of America, Germany and Japan it had grown by a factor of 7, 10 and 50 respectively.

Difficulties were intensified by external problems, particularly the recession of 1973–76. The phenomenon of 'stagflation' emerged as rising unemployment went hand in hand with an annual rate of price rises never less than 8%. Between 1975 and 1980 inflation averaged 13%, compared with 4%, 9% and 8% for Germany, the USA and Japan. Wage levels in Britain were amongst the lowest in Europe. And low wages encouraged low capital and technological intensities in production. Productivity was plunging to around half the levels in major competitors. By 1979, after two decades of sustained deterioration, the UK economy was critically weak (Table 2.2).

Explanations
If there is broad agreement on decline, explanation of its roots has engendered controversy. Much analysis insists on the necessity of a historical view. Britain had the first capitalist revolution and became the first industrial nation. The head start and protected markets that industrial and military power guaranteed produced a

Table 2.2 *Economic performance in the 1970s*

	UK	USA	Japan	West Germany	Italy	France	Sweden
			% changes 1969–79				
Gross domestic product	25	32	80	38	49	49	26
Manufacturing output	7	37	69	31	40	45	21
Gross fixed investment	6	22	76	31	14	35	6
Output per hour: manufacturing	33	34	96	54	54	69	–
Government final consumption	27	11	65	48	65	41	43

Source: Lloyds Bank Review, January 1982.

dominance which bred conservatism and complacency. Competitors were able to industrialise later, utilising more advanced techniques and developing social and political structures better adapted to economic needs. Resistance to innovation in Britain was strengthened by the lack of any major upheaval such as revolution or defeat in war.

Within this framework different accounts give different weight to a diverse range of factors. Some see unions pushing up wages, applying restrictive controls to work and thwarting management's ability to plan and innovate as the prime factor in economic crisis. Others claim that incompetent management, the fragmentation of the economy into small units, or the tendency of capitalists to put consumption before investment, or investment overseas before investment at home, are to blame. Others emphasise a debilitating split between finance capital and industrial capital, so that lending and speculation took precedence over what is really important for a thriving economy: building factories and producing goods. Also cited are: excessive military expenditure; the welfare state; a liberal, elitist system of education, inadequately synchronised with industrial needs; and an antiquated and abstentionist state.

The right emphasise the role of unions in creating inflation and cramping productivity. On the left, many of the causes of economic problems have been laid at the door of greedy and incompetent employers. But there is sometimes surprisingly little consensus amongst those sharing similar ideologies. On the right, criticism of the unions (Joseph, 1979a; Hayek, 1980) has been accompanied by emphasis on the way the economy is organised and the role of government (Bacon and Eltis, 1976). On the left, union strength is cited (Kilpatrick and Lawson, 1980) but so is union weakness (Harris, 1985). Marxist accounts, which underline the role of wage increases in eroding profits (Glyn and Sutcliffe, 1972), have been criticised by other Marxists on technical grounds, notably that such accounts ignore the role of productivity advance as the central lever of capital accumulation, and because this view legitimises an assault on working-class living standards.

There is sometimes overlap between the explanations of those who hold very different views. A Marxist, Perry Anderson, argues, that the conservative aspects of British society which conditioned decline had their origins in the political dominance of the land-owning aristocracy and merchant capital, the victors of the British Civil War, over the industrial manufacturers who developed under their wing and in their image. This constrained the development of an entrepreneurial culture, modern political system and interventionist state (Anderson, 1965; 1987). From the centre, Martin Wiener has argued that an aristocratic disdain for commerce, and the hostility the education system and the civil service held for industry, crippled the entrepreneurial spirit and produced the cult of the gentleman amateur, seriously affecting economic performance (Wiener, 1985). Whilst from the right, we find Sir Keith Joseph, the prophet of Thatcherism, declaring that Britain 'never had a capitalist ruling class or a stable *haute bourgeoisie* . . . bourgeois values have never shaped thought and institutions as they have in some countries' (Joseph, 1975, 501).

The political economy of industrial relations

The second key factor moulding today's industrial relations has been the political reaction to economic decline. From 1940 the major political parties accepted that there should be a significant move away from the *laissez-faire* philosophy, with economic decision-making left to market forces, which was seen as contributory to a slump and two world wars. Instead, the state should take responsibility for the economic and social welfare of citizens. The *post-war compromise* based on technological development, industrial restructuring and high levels of military expenditure represented important concessions to the working class. There was an acceptance that in the prevailing balance of forces a healthier, better educated, better paid labour force could pay dividends for capital. The political and social settlement of 1945 was based on *consensus*. It involved the maintenance of capitalism modified by greater state regulation, nationalisation and the welfare state within a framework of world monetary stability established by the Bretton Woods Agreement of 1944. Government would intervene in the economy, using Keynesian policies of demand management, increasing public spending by using deficit budgeting. The state would spend more than it collected in taxes in a recession but damp down demand in an upturn. This would sustain full employment, economic growth and rising living standards.

In this model, industrial relations could be left largely to self-regulation by employers and trade unions. The **voluntary system of industrial relations** or **collective *laissez-faire*** required the resolution of conflicts in industry through national collective bargaining. Collective bargaining, according autonomy to employers and unions to adjust industrial issues to the wider economic situation, was seen as democratic and efficient; its primacy was approved as evidence of maturity. Few noted the contradiction between the state's economic intervention and its industrial abstention or the underpinning of the system through *gender and ethnic exclusion*. There was a clear division of labour between men and women whilst black workers constituted a specifically exploited stratum in the working class.

This system involved a greater degree of state supervision than its supporters allowed. As the economic situation deteriorated it came under increasing criticism. What happened in industrial relations had an important influence on economic performance and was simply too important to be left to employers and unions. Spending on the welfare state increased and public expenditure took a greater share of gross national product. This was financed by tax increases which bore more and more heavily on those on and below average earnings. To compensate, they looked for wage increases. The power full employment gave the unions enabled them to push up wages which, in turn, pressurised employers to put up prices, stimulating inflation and disrupting the attempts of the state, using Keynesian methods to manage demand. Different solutions were applied, initially within the framework of the post-war consensus. As successive attempts at reform faltered, the search for new solutions led to the post-1945 **welfare compromise** being undermined.

Strategies of reform

The 1964 Labour government, led by Harold Wilson, ushered in an era of reform. An attempt was made to involve unions and employers together with the state in a greater degree of economic planning. A Department of Economic Affairs was established, a National Plan was published and a voluntary incomes policy was agreed with the trade unions. Wilsonian planning crumbled in the face of sterling crises. The government resorted to deflation and incomes policy. Trade unions were increasingly perceived as the major barrier to economic change. A Royal Commission on Trade Unions reported in 1968. The Donovan Report saw the failure of incomes policy as related to decentralised bargaining and the strength of workplace organisation. There was a need for employers and union leaders to re-establish control through a reformed formal system of industrial relations. The Royal Commission urged *voluntary reform* as more effective than legislation. The government was not prepared to wait. It formulated plans for legislation to control union activities. TUC attempts to hold their members in line on wage restraint were increasingly ineffective. From 1968, union membership and militancy accelerated. The plans for legislation were defeated by a coalition of the TUC and Labour Party MPs. By 1970 Britain's underlying economic situation had not been improved and the post-war boom was disintegrating.

The incoming Conservative government of Edward Heath determined on a firmer stance. Trade union power and the new militancy were now to be dealt with by legislation to *regulate collective bargaining*, institutionalise union power and reduce strikes. There was to be no formal incomes policy but a gradually decreasing norm in the public sector. This approach appeared to represent an important break with the pattern of post-war politics. The resurgence of liberal conservatism was temporary. As unemployment increased, the Chancellor Tony Barber turned to expansionary policies and a dash for growth. In early 1972, the government was rocked by a successful miners' strike. The crucial Industrial Relations Act was unmasked as a paper tiger. By the autumn the 'U-turn' was complete as the Prime Minister held talks with TUC and CBI leaders at Downing Street to agree an incomes policy. The endeavour was unsuccessful and the government imposed a wage freeze. The new policy was undermined by the oil crisis of late 1973. When the miners again went on strike Heath called an election on the issue of 'who rules the country'. This produced, in February 1974, a minority Labour government.

The social contract
A decade of intensive assault on the problems of Britain's economic base had yielded few positive results. These problems were now affected by external events: the disintegration of the world system of 1945 was demonstrated in the collapse of the Bretton Woods Agreement in 1971 and the oil price increases of 1973. Attempts to weaken or channel union power appeared to have been counter-productive and encouraged and politicised militancy. The leadership in key unions had swung to the left. The

period 1968–72 saw the biggest outbreak of militancy since 1919 and the rebirth of the political strike. Shop steward organisation spread to new industries. Publicity surrounding incomes policies stimulated aspirations, and erosion of differentials fuelled the growth of white collar trade unionism. Union membership grew from a little over 10 million in 1968, to almost 12 million in 1974. During the Heath years, real take-home pay was increasing annually at 3.5%, several times the rate of the previous decade. There was real pressure on profitability. The disintegration of the boom and attempts to reverse economic decline had stirred up a hornet's nest.

The impact of the radical mood in the unions, as well as the lessons of the decade of government failure, were discernible in the policies of the Wilson government re-elected in October 1974. They represented a more serious attempt to bring off the project of 1964. At their centre was an accord between government and unions advertised as the basis for a new 'social contract'. In return for the TUC exercising restraint in collective bargaining the government was to introduce a wide-ranging programme of legislation which would extend union rights and underpin many of the reforms advocated by the Donovan Commission. There would be a major redistribution of income and wealth, more industrial democracy and a National Enterprise Board which would provide funds for the regeneration of industry. The unions would again be involved in tripartite decision-making through a system of 'planning agreements'. Labour's policies met a similar fate to their predecessors. By 1975 unemployment had broken the 'full employment' barrier. Inflation was a major problem and productivity and profits were being squeezed. The two party system was under strain and the Labour Party's vote had declined in 1970 and significantly in 1974. The radical cutting edge of the industrial strategy was blunted by economic problems. The TUC's attempts to police voluntary incomes policy collapsed in the strike wave of the 1978–79 'Winter of Discontent'.

Thatcherism
The commitment to Keynesianism, full employment and the

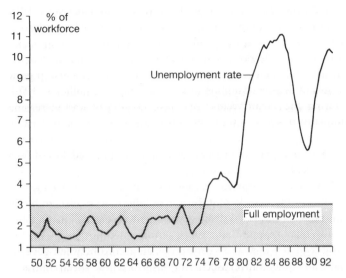

Figure 2.1 *The end of full employment*
Source: Employment Gazette

welfare state had become progressively strained under the
1974–79 Labour government. It was now terminated (see Figure
2.1). Thatcherism, Britain's neo-*laissez-faire*, was in general a
response to the breakdown of post-1945 expansion and the failure
of state planning to shore up the post-war settlement. Specifically
it originated in reaction to the failure of the strategies of *voluntary
reform* and *regulating collective bargaining* and responded to thinkers
of the 'new right' such as F. A. Hayek and Milton Friedman. At its
heart was the belief that the market can do things more efficiently
than the state. State expenditure was seen as cramping initiative
and negating choice. The tax burden it necessitated generated
inflation and reduced profits, investment and growth as economic
actors strove to increase wages and prices to compensate. The job
of government was to restore the free market and limit inflation by
acting on its cause – the too rapid growth of the money supply.
This must be controlled through reduced state expenditure and
higher interest rates to make credit more expensive and pressure

firms to become more competitive, reorganise production, and resist union demands. There was a need to erode the monopoly power of the unions to diminish their interference. State withdrawal from industry also required cutbacks in financial support, privatisation and the slashing of taxes. Crucially the British economy must be opened to the competitive pressures of the world market. These policies bear the name of Mrs Thatcher but their thrust was continued in the 1990s by her successor, John Major.

The neo-Conservative economic experiment was, in its turn, unsuccessful in stemming economic decline. Britain's problems have been intensified by two important factors: greater integration of the world economy and the re-emergence of serious periodic recessions. Government policies exacerbated the impact of the two recessions of the early 1980s and 1990s. If the break with full employment came in 1975 it was institutionalised from 1979. Improvements in productivity and profitability were purchased at a high price. Unemployment doubled between 1979 and 1981 and increased from 2 million to over 3 million thereafter. It fell in the mini-boom of 1987–89, remaining well above post-war levels and

Table 2.3   *Comparative unemployment within OECD countries (% of workforce)*

	UK	USA	Japan	Germany	France	Italy	EC
1979	5.0	–	–	–	–	–	–
1980	6.4	7.0	2.0	3.0	6.3	7.5	6.4
1981	9.8	7.5	2.2	4.4	7.4	7.8	8.2
1982	11.3	9.5	2.4	6.1	8.1	8.4	9.5
1983	12.4	9.5	2.6	8.0	8.3	8.8	10.4
1984	11.7	7.4	2.7	7.1	9.7	9.4	10.7
1985	11.2	7.1	2.6	8.0	8.3	8.8	10.4
1986	11.2	6.9	2.8	6.4	10.4	10.5	10.8
1987	10.3	6.1	2.8	6.2	10.5	10.9	10.5
1988	8.5	5.4	2.5	6.2	10.0	11.0	9.8
1989	6.9	5.2	2.3	5.5	9.6	10.9	8.9

Source: Michie, 1992.

rose again in the 1990s recession. *Neo-Conservatism is identified with high, sustained levels of unemployment and the abandonment of commitment to full employment* (see Table 2.3).

The impact of Thatcherism on inflation and wage increases was inadequate. Increases in wages were curbed in the early 1980s and 1990s. Real wages increased annually at 2.4% all through the 1980s in comparison with a rise of under 1% from 1974–79. The share of national income taken by tax increased from 34.3% in 1979 to 35.3% in 1994. Moreover, as Table 2.4 shows, inflation averaged 7% over the decade compared with 2.2% in Japan, 2.9% in Germany and 5.5% in the USA.

Table 2.4 *Comparative inflation rates (%)*

	UK	France	Germany	Italy	Japan	USA	EC	OECD
1980	16.3	13.3	5.8	20.5	7.1	10.8	12.9	11.3
1981	11.2	13.0	6.2	18.1	4.4	9.2	11.6	9.5
1982	8.7	11.5	4.8	16.9	2.6	5.7	10.2	7.2
1983	4.8	9.7	3.2	15.2	1.9	4.1	8.1	5.5
1984	5.1	7.7	2.5	11.8	2.1	3.8	6.8	4.9
1985	5.4	5.8	2.1	9.0	2.2	3.3	5.5	4.3
1986	4.4	2.7	−0.5	5.8	0.6	2.4	3.2	2.7
1987	4.3	3.1	0.6	4.9	−0.2	4.7	3.1	3.4
1988	4.9	2.7	1.2	5.3	−0.1	3.9	3.3	3.3
1989	5.9	3.3	3.1	6.0	1.7	4.4	4.4	4.3
Mean	7.0	7.2	2.9	11.2	2.2	5.2	6.9	5.6

Source: Johnson, 1991.

Productivity based on job losses improved significantly in manufacturing, less significantly in other sectors. Far from representing 'a productivity miracle' this represented only a return to the levels of the 1960s. Productivity levels remained behind those of competitors such as the USA, Germany and France. Change was fragile: it rested more on labour intensification, job cutting and piecemeal changes in production than on increases in investment, skills and strategic re-development of production (Nolan,

1992). Labour intensification contributed to a recovery in the rate of profit. Manufacturing profits rose sharply by 44%, 1979–89, and the *Bank of England Bulletins* show profit levels remaining buoyant in the 1990s (Glyn, 1992, 81). Table 2.5 demonstrates that in the aftermath of the first Thatcher recession there were six years of strong economic growth. But over the decade it failed to reach the OECD average or attain the levels of Japan or the USA. The real problems of the British economy – poor investment, a weak manufacturing base and a deteriorating balance of payments – remained.

Table 2.5   *International growth comparisons, 1980–90 (% growth in GDP)*

	UK	France	Germany	Italy	Japan	USA	EU	OECD
1979	2.8	–	–	–	–	–	–	–
1980	−2.0	1.6	1.5	4.2	4.3	−0.2	1.5	1.5
1981	−1.2	1.2	0.0	1.0	3.7	1.9	0.1	1.7
1982	1.7	2.5	−1.0	0.3	3.1	−2.5	0.8	−0.1
1983	3.8	0.7	1.9	1.1	3.2	3.6	1.6	2.7
1984	1.8	1.3	3.3	3.0	5.1	6.8	2.5	4.8
1985	3.8	1.9	1.9	2.6	4.8	3.4	2.4	3.4
1986	3.6	2.3	2.3	2.5	2.6	2.7	2.6	2.7
1987	4.4	2.4	1.7	3.0	4.6	3.7	2.8	3.5
1988	4.7	3.8	3.6	4.2	5.7	4.4	3.9	4.4
1989	2.1	3.7	4.0	3.2	4.9	3.0	3.5	3.6
Mean	2.2	2.1	1.9	2.5	4.2	2.6	2.2	2.8

Source: Johnson, 1991.

The state and industrial relations

The strategies adopted by the state since the 1960s to deal with industrial relations boil down to two main approaches. Within these frameworks there may be different emphases.

Corporatism
This strategy is informed by the belief that the 'welfare compromise' broke down because of pressure on unions to maximise

militancy to achieve higher real wages. In response, the state needed to construct new machinery for economic planning which could maintain the benefits of the post-war consensus Keynesianism had failed to sustain. The path taken by the Wilson-Callaghan governments was seen as a move in the direction of **corporatism**. This term denotes a system where the key interest groups, the trade unions and employers' organisations are given a formal role in economic and industrial policy. In return they are expected to take responsibility for implementation of agreed policies by exercising discipline over their members. Corporatism is informed by the belief that politicians should and can regulate market forces.

In place of unregulated competition between interest groups and consequent economic and political disorder, corporatism substitutes the concertation by the state of conflicting interests which are harnessed in the management of the economy. The predictability and planning of corporatism, it is claimed, represents a superior means of allocating economic goods than the hidden hand of the market. Corporatism provides a means by which sectional goals, increased wages or increased profits, can be related to wider objectives such as price stability, increased investment and full employment through state, employers and unions bargaining across the whole economic and political canvas.

Corporatism, it is asserted, avoids the situation where attempts to manage the economy are thwarted by union power in sectional struggles, which undermine long-term economic objectives. Abandoning the *collective laissez-faire* system enables unions to restrain power in return for concessions which, added together, maximise the interests of their members to a greater degree than 'free collective bargaining'. Corporatism, it is claimed, is preferable to 'free collective bargaining' precisely because it gives unions a voice in wider aspects of economic policy which can undermine, or render temporary, the gains of collective bargaining. It can benefit the state *and* the unions.

Others argue corporatism is a ruling class strategy which institutionalises the unions' subordinate position and strengthens capital and the state. Strip away the trappings and all you have left is union-policed wage control, a transfer of income from labour to capital and a demobilising outlawing of class struggle. If in Sweden, under special conditions, it was possible to use con-certation to civilise the subordination of the working class, in most other countries corporatist experiments have served the interests of employers and state, not the unions.

Neo-*laissez-faire*

Advocates of this strategy argue that corporatism failed in the past; it will fail in the future. The welfare compromise broke down because it involved state intervention which stoked inflation and inflated expectations. To deduce from this failure the need for further state intervention is to compound the initial error. The state cannot and should not try to regulate the market. In the new global economy its main function is to energise workers to respond to the demands of the world market.

The pathos of corporatism, it is claimed, lies in its optimistic assumption that unions will be able to restrain their members' bargaining power. Every incomes policy broke down because the internal process of bargaining in the unions, which corporatism demands, was ineffective. The unions were not able to transcend sectionalism; nor should they. Wage deals should depend not upon nationally set norms but upon what the employer and the market can bear. The structures of British unions are particularly ill adapted to ensure that what leaders agree in Downing Street will be delivered in Durham and Devon. Moreover, corporatism legitimises the role of union leaders in political decision-making and increases their appetite for greater involvement in what should be the prerogatives of elected governments.

Supporters of **neo-*laissez-faire*** agree that the problem for the state in industrial relations is the control of union power. This, they argue, can only be achieved by diminished, not increased, state involvement. What makes the economy work is not the intervention of state bureaucracies placating trade unions but entrepreneurs pursuing profits unimpeded in a global free market. The role of the state is to recant on any responsibility for the economic welfare of its citizens and to liberate entrepreneurs from restriction and the market from regulation in Britain and worldwide.

The artificial privileges of unions and the economically debilitating rights accorded by the state to employees must be removed. Employers must be encouraged to make the performance of the firm the touchstone of economic reward and develop a more flexible labour force. This strategy, foregrounding free market and 'residual state', has been pursued by Conservative governments since 1979. Persistence in such policies and their extension, its supporters argue, will ensure a superior context for wealth creation and an eventual solution to the UK's problems.

Changes in capitalism

Recent state strategies have been applied in the context of changes in capitalism important to unions.

Concentration of capital

Most workers are employed by large employers: nearly 5 million work for central government and local government and the NHS. Britain has the largest number of firms employing more than 1,000 workers in the EU. Half of all private sector workers are employed by companies with more than 100 workers, 20% by companies which employ more than 1,000. Until 1979 British industry was characterised by increasing concentration of capital and increasing size of work establishment. Since 1979 there has been significant growth of employment in small firms. By 1986 companies employing less than 20 workers employed 36% of the workforce outside government employment. The average number of employees per plant was halved in the decade to 1988 and the proportion of workers in plants with more than 1,000 workers fell from 29% to 18%. Employers have also sought to decentralise work away from cities and industrial heartlands of union power to low wage, low rent areas, fragment employment and introduce sub-contracting. Yet the larger the concentration of labour, the more work regulation has tended to the impersonal and the bureaucratic, the better the possibilities have been for unions.

Internationalisation of capital

By 1979 some 600 giant multinational companies dominated international investment, technology and production. A mere 160 companies controlled more than 80% of foreign investment in the UK. More than half of UK based enterprises employing more than 2,000 workers had overseas operations and 60% hired more labour abroad than in Britain. By 1984, foreign multinationals owned 402 of the 1,000 largest companies in the UK, nearly four times as many as in 1970, accounting for 15% of total employment in manufacturing and 20% of national output. Economic decline and the pattern of outward investment were underlined by the fact that between 1979 and 1986 the top 40 British manufacturing companies cut their UK workforce by more than 400,000 whilst increasing their overseas work force by more than 125,000.

From the 1970s the world economy became more accident prone, more open to uncontrolled movement of capital, more integrated and more competitive. By the 1990s what stood out was the growth of Japanese and other foreign capital in key sectors of the British economy motivated by moves to the EU internal market, and the economy's new place in a more integrated world market facilitated by abolition of exchange controls and deregulation of financial markets. It was harder for the state to control capital on the 1945 model; deregulation acknowledged and strengthened capital's freedom from the state as the price of inward investment. The British state was explicitly bidding to entice multinationals with cheap labour, low tax policies. As integration of production and finance stimulated mergers and joint ventures and British companies became more involved in both Europe and North America the economy was characterised by increasing internationalisation and autonomy from politics.

This has increased pressure on unions. Multinational companies with integrated development, production and market strategies can mould industrial relations by their economic strength and strategic ability to resist control by governments and unions. Some global companies have a budget greater than many nation-states. They can withdraw investment and transfer production. Sophisticated procedures for accounting and transfer pricing inhibit union bargaining and state planning. In the UK, foreign-owned firms have been credited with an innovatory approach to industrial relations, pioneering concession bargaining, the flexible firm, and single union deals. The state's weakness in relation to capital, the new limits – part real, part ideological preference – to state intervention and the re-emergence of serious recessions directly weakened unions and diminished their broader purchase.

Capital and the ruling class

The power of capital is often less visible than that of the unions. It dominates industrial relations and plays a crucial role in determining the nature of trade unionism.

Ownership and control

As most large enterprises are no longer run by entrepreneurs but professional managers and as shareholding has become more dispersed it is claimed there has been a divorce between ownership and control. In the new 'property-owning democracy' more and more people have a stake in business; the 'managerial revolution' means that managers are less concerned with profits and more with pleasing consumers and employees.

There has been an extension of share ownership. In 1990, 21% of the population, 9 million people, owned shares compared with 7% in 1979. The additional 6 million shareholders were the product of privatisation – 60% owned only one share, 22% only two shares. Through the 1980s the proportion of all shares owned by individuals continued to fall from 28% in 1981 to 20% in 1988 (Johnson, 1991, 168). Ownership of shares remains concentrated and gives little influence to the majority of the minority who directly own them. The pattern of control in large British companies represents control by a small group of shareholders who control substantial blocks of shares and benefit from the dispersal of the remainder. Strategic control over decisions remains in the hands of directors and executives with an important capital stake and is distinct from 'managerial control' (Scott, 1985).

Top managers and directors own more shares than any other

social group. They come from the same background as other important shareholders and share the same ideology, social environment and objectives. Banks and financial institutions may have an input to decisions but are unlikely to pursue different goals. Growth and profit, not 'social responsibility', remain the key performance indicators. Managers must ultimately answer the imperatives of competition and the discipline of capital markets or face takeover or bankruptcy (Nichols, 1969; Westergaard and Resler, 1976). There are differences in the approach and strategy of management in different sectors – with implications for trade unions. But ideas of 'property-owning democracy' and 'managerial revolution' do not hold water.

The ruling class

The most persuasive characterisation of those who own and control industry sees them at the core of 'a socially cohesive, economically dominant class which dominates most significant elite positions' (Bilton *et al.*, 1986, 218). They are part of an *upper class* because they stand at the apex of the hierarchies of wealth, income and power in Britain. But they are also a *ruling class* because their ownership of the means of production, their property and power, is actively used to give them control over the lives and destinies of workers: 'the core of the class consists of those who are actively involved in the strategic control of the major units of capital of which the modern economy is formed' (Scott, 1982, 114).

The ruling class is renewed and bound together through inheritance, education, ideology, networks and material interest. Its capitalist core is part of a wider class inextricably linked to the state apparatus enrolling top civil servants, judges, army officers and politicians firmly bound to the interests of capital. Whilst much remains to be done in documenting its anatomy and personnel,

Britain is ruled by a capitalist class whose economic dominance is sustained by the operations of the state and whose members are disproportionately represented in the power elite which rules the state apparatus (Scott, 1991, 151).

If strategic control over investment and resource allocation in the enterprise is in the hands of a small minority of top executives, operational control of the day-to-day use of resources has to be delegated to technical experts and administrators. This group may own little or no capital themselves but they exercise authority and expertise on behalf of those who do. The exact social characterisation of this 'managerial' or 'service class' has given rise to intense debate (Wright, 1978, 1985; Goldthorpe, 1982). Managerial and technical functionaries have to sell their labour to live. They are different from most workers in the degree of trust, independence, privilege, security and prospects attached to their jobs. This ambiguity has led analysts to argue that this group 'occupy a contradictory location between the bourgeoisie and the proletariat' (Wright, 1978, 63). The degree to which those in contradictory class locations, 'the new middle class', identify themselves with capital or labour will depend on changing economic and political factors.

Wealth and income
Distribution of wealth remains highly concentrated. By 1990 the richest 1% of the population owned more than 20% of the wealth, the richest 5% owned 37% of total wealth, the richest 10% owned more than 50%. The richest 25% owned 75% of total wealth, and the richest 50% owned 94%. Income distribution became more egalitarian in the post-war period but this trend has been dramatically reversed since 1979. By the mid-1980s an unprecedented shift had occurred with the share of income of the better off increasing significantly at the expense of the poorer so that 'income in Britain is now distributed as unequally as that in the United States, which has one of the more unequal distributions of income among industrialised countries' (Rentoul, 1987, 15). By 1991 the bottom half of the population received only a quarter of all income compared with a third in 1979. The bottom tenth saw a decline in real income of 14% between 1979 and 1991. Whilst the top 20% saw their share of income increase from 35% to 41%, a total 13.5 million people, 24% of the population were living on less than half the average income.

Management and unions

British management has been seen as non-professional, non-strategic, under-educated and anti-theory. Industrial relations experts have suggested managers may have different perspectives about unions:

1 The *unitary* perspective views the enterprise as a harmonious, integrated team whose objectives are common and whose interests are shared. The possibilities for structured conflict are limited and when problems do occur they are the product of troublemakers, or the consequence of misunderstandings or poor communications. Whilst managers who operate within this perspective deal with unions, they do so with a mental reluctance which inhibits effective commitment to making the relationship work.

2 More realistic managers regard the enterprise as composed of a variety of groups with different interests and goals. The *pluralist* perspective stems from political theorists who argue that power in society is dispersed between competing interest groups who can bring roughly equivalent pressure to bear on a neutral state to achieve their ends. This perspective accepts conflict as inevitable at work. Trade unions are seen as legitimate representatives of employee interests and conflict between different groups in the enterprise, if channelled through adequate procedures, is considered amenable to resolution satisfactory to all parties.

The pure type of the unitarist is the small owner-manager. The pure type of the pluralist is the personnel manager. But Fox (1966), who developed this framework, argued that many managers oscillate between these two perspectives. Fox later abandoned the pluralist perspective in favour of a *radical* perspective. He argued that the pluralist view of a dispersal of power between management, shareholders and different groups of employees, producing a rough equilibrium of power, distorted reality. Conflicts at work were structural and deep seated and ran along a division between capital and labour with the former immensely more powerful than the latter. The resilience of conflict, despite the pluralists' attempts to institutionalise it out of existence, lay in the subordination employees face at work and in all aspects of economic and social life. Conflict resolution, therefore, depended on a deeper industrial and social transformation than pluralists were prepared to consider (Fox, 1973).

Writers have also characterised the different ways in which management seeks to control the labour process. In *Labor and Monopoly Capital* Harry Braverman argued that history shows increasing attempts by management to control work to extract maximum surplus value. They did this by separating conception and strategy (management) from execution of tasks (workers), breaking down tasks and deskilling work (Braverman, 1974).

Other writers have argued that there is more than one mode of management control. For example, management may exercise direct control or attempt to exploit workers' desire for control over the work process through strategies of **responsible autonomy** which allow discretion within limits and stimulate commitment (Friedman, 1977). Another typology distinguishes **simple control**, close direct supervision; **technical control** where the machine or technological process controls the worker; and **bureaucratic control** where management builds supervision and motivation into the fabric of the organisation through procedures, promotion, ladders, payment systems and fringe benefits (Edwards, 1979).

There have also been attempts to classify different management styles:

1 The **traditionalists**, often managers of small businesses, forcefully oppose unions and, acting within a unitary frame of reference, adopt an authoritarian approach.
2 The **standard moderns** represented until recently the dominant approach in Britain. Unions are recognised and industrial relations specialists appointed. But no great attention is paid to industrial relations unless it intrudes: there is no sustained strategy.
3 **Sophisticated paternalists**, such as Marks & Spencer or IBM, operate within a unitary perspective. They seek to keep

unions out of the enterprise and compensate employees for their absence by participative arrangements and generous rewards.

4 The **sophisticated moderns** are Simon Pure pluralists who foster unions, encourage the closed shop and sponsor strong workplace organisation. They view joint regulation of industrial relations as the best vehicle for management control: Ford and ICI are cited as examples (Purcell and Sisson, 1983).

More recently management styles have been classified on a two dimensional model, 'individualism–collectivism'; 'labour as cost vs labour as resource' (Purcell, 1991) and there has been a growth of interest in **human resource management**, a development of the sophisticated paternalist style. It represents refurbishment of the human relations school often associated with the psychologist Elton Mayo. The enterprise was seen as a community in which workers required reintegrating through participatory management styles. To individualism and integration human resource management adds a harder emphasis on full utilisation of human capital in conditions of increasing competitiveness and an assertion that union based adversarial approaches have failed. Management must become more strategic and initiatory, liquidating industrial relations into strategic corporate planning and maximum utilisation of all the resources of the enterprise. The new *strategic unitarism* asserts the need for market soaked enterprise culture reconciling individual careerism with teamwork through values and goals which reflect a common commitment to the enterprise throughout the workforce. Rewards are skewed towards profit and performance related pay; work organisation involves team building and quality circles; decision-making embraces worker involvement; and communication is sophisticated and direct. There is thus little role for independent collectivism and HRM represents a challenge to trade unionism.

Industrial structure and the labour force

Important changes in the labour force also have implications for the future of the unions although in some cases they represent long-standing trends.

Decline in manufacturing
Decline in manufacturing since 1979 represents continuation of an existing trend; it is still of immense significance. The numbers employed dropped from 7.1 million in 1979 to 4.5 million in 1992 – 22% of total employment compared with 31%. Decline has hit hardest in areas such as metal manufacturing, vehicles and textiles. There have also been significant falls in employment in the non-manufacturing production industries, agriculture, energy, construction and water supply (see Table 2.6).

Table 2.6   *Changes in employment by sector (000s of employees)*

	Primary	Manufacturing	Construction	Services	Total
1979	1,070	7,107	1,201	13,260	22,638
1980	1,068	6,801	1,206	13,384	22,458
1981	1,043	6,099	1,102	13,142	21,386
1982	1,009	5,751	1,038	13,117	20,916
1983	969	5,418	1,015	13,169	20,572
1984	928	5,302	1,010	13,503	20,741
1985	903	5,254	994	13,769	20,920
1986	846	5,122	964	13,954	20,886
1987	802	5,049	983	14,247	21,080
1988	771	5,089	1,021	14,860	21,740
1989	737	5,080	1,056	15,261	22,134
1990	719	5,033	1,044	15,574	22,370
1991	703	4,691	939	15,377	21,710
1992	659	4,492	828	15,260	21,238

Source: Employment Gazette.

Growth in service occupations

Recent years have seen significant increases in employment in business services, banking insurance and finance, distribution and hotels and catering. Today 15 million people work in service occupations. Sainsbury's employ more workers than Ford. In 1979 there were 98 manufacturing jobs for every 100 in private services but by 1992 this had fallen to 56.

Public to private

Privatisation has decreased employment in the public sector. The selling-off of British Telecom and British Gas returned 300,000 workers to the private sector. More than 2 million workers were employed by public corporations in 1979 and 0.6 million by 1992. Nonetheless direct government employment held up well with over 5 million workers in 1979 and 1991.

Manual to white collar

Manual workers, the core of the 'traditional working class', made up 70% of the labour force in the 1950s. Today they comprise less than half, around 46% of the workforce compared with 53% in 1979. The number of white collar workers, in contrast, has almost doubled, fuelled by the growth of service occupations such as financial and business services which employ few manual workers, but also by occupational changes in manufacturing. Nonetheless the manual–white collar distinction is a social construction. Many of the new white collar jobs are 'brain' jobs. Many however are monotonous, repetitive, 'hand' jobs.

Atypical employment

Numbers working part-time increased from under 20% of employees in 1979 to more than a third in 1992. However most of this increase occurred in the years 1979–86 and is connected with the contraction of manufacturing. Workers on temporary contracts have remained a small proportion of employees, around 5%–6%, since the mid-1980s. Those on government work related training programmes declined from 450,000 in 1989 to 316,000 in 1992. There has however been an increase in self-employment described by the Department of Employment as 'unprecedented'. It increased by over 1 million to 3.2 million, 1980–90, before then declining slightly.

Women and men

Between 1982 and 1990 women's employment increased by almost 2 million whilst mens' employment grew by only 1.36 million. By that date women constituted 43% of the employed labour force. This has immense implications. The labour market remained structured by gender with women concentrated in certain industries and at certain levels in those industries. In professional occupations in education, welfare and health, clerical occupations generally, catering, cleaning and hairdressing, women make up 60% of the workforce. In banking and finance women make up 59% of those employed – but only 25% of those in the managerial categories. The number of women in senior positions is increasing, but in 1993 the average earnings of those working full-time, excluding overtime, were 77% of average earnings of males – if we take overtime into account the figure is nearer 72%. Most part-time jobs remain women's jobs – 45% of women work part-time which underpins segregation.

Black workers made some progress in the labour market in the second half of the 1980s. They are however particularly disadvantaged by rising unemployment as was evidenced by higher unemployment rates in the recessions of the early 1980s and 1990s.

North and south

In the 1980s disparities widened between the north, Scotland and Wales and the more prosperous south east which benefited from the growth in service industries. Whilst the 1990s recession initially affected the south more than its predecessor it increasingly affected the north's already weakened base. Whilst parts of London and coastal towns in the south won recognition as assisted areas because of structural unemployment in the early 1990s, the gap still yawned. In 1993 average earnings in Greater London were £4,737 a year higher than for the country as a whole. Outside London differences were limited. Wales was the lowest paid area

with average earnings of £281 a week, the north west highest at
£292 a week – compared with £408 a week in London.

Post-Fordism?

Are these incremental, piecemeal changes or do they reflect
fundamental, sometimes strategic, transformation in the social
organisation of production? Seminal work has argued that a new
model of production is emerging. A response to the fragmentation
of markets for manufactured goods and the crisis of mass production, **flexible specialisation** involves the exploitation of
computer technology to produce particular goods for specific
markets using skilled labour. Flexible specialisation contrasts with
Fordism, specialised machinery and assembly lines used to produce standardised goods for mass markets with unskilled labour.
It facilitates a revival of small enterprise, self-employment, and
craft work (Piore and Sabel, 1984). These ideas were taken up by
the journal *Marxism Today* which amplified the developments we
have been looking at, conflating them with Thatcherism to assert
that neo-Conservatism was the bearer of a *post-Fordist* economy
and *New Times* society based on consumerism and individualism
(Hall and Jacques, 1990).

Post-Fordism has been subject to convincing criticism. There
was never any monolithic system of mass production nor any
simple historical divide between mass production and flexible
specialisation. Fordism co-existed with small batch production
and process production and there have always been segmented
and specialised markets. The 'niche' market is often temporary.
Open to takeover by large producers it simply represents a form of
exploitation of the mass market. Application of new technology
often involves deskilling and intensification of work. Craft production is in decline in advanced economies and expansion is
often resourced by unskilled labour and 'traditional' technology.
Changes in the labour force are limited and piecemeal, with little
evidence of conscious strategic search for modelled change on a
core-periphery basis. Widening divisions do not necessarily entail
dualism; its material basis, guaranteed material benefits for a
privileged core, is absent from government strategy (Hyman,

1991a; Pollert, 1991).

We are witnessing important restructuring. To view this not as incremental but *qualitative*, as 'a transition from one regime of accumulation to another within capitalism' (Hall, 1990, 126), is at least premature in relation to the evidence proponents present. They amplify and lend too much coherence and vision to what are uneven and sometimes tenuously related developments. Fordism is far from dead.

Inequalities at work

The most obvious inequality is pay; disparities are increasing. The average white collar worker earns £100 more than the average manual worker – in 1993 £349.50 compared to £256.60. In 1983 white collar workers earned 20% more than their manual counterparts. By 1993 the differential had widened dramatically to 36% more. The range of difference is greater: a manager in a building society earned on average £551 a week in 1993, a cleaner £174. Despite legislation and changes in the labour market the gap between men and women's earnings remains. Dispersion of earnings is greater. Differentials between earners at the top and bottom of the scale have increased faster under neo-Conservatism than at any other time in recent history (see Table 2.7). But this has occurred whilst *living standards for the majority have increased*, providing a material basis for acceptance of greater inequality.

Of course some white collar employees earn less than manual workers and many are involved in repetitive unskilled work. The real difference lies in the work situation of the mass of employees and those in managerial and professional grades. Inequalities increase as we climb the tree. In 1993 Lord Hanson of the Hanson conglomerate received a salary of £1.35 million, almost £26,000 a week – three times what NHS care assistants were paid for the whole year. Peter Wood, an insurance company executive, received *a bonus* of £18.2 million or £50,000 a day. In 1993, as public sector workers observed a government imposed 1.5% pay limit, *Incomes Data Services* reported that the pay of directors in the top 100 stock exchange companies increased by 12%. Moreover

Table 2.7 Increasing dispersion of earnings in the UK, 1982–92

	1982	1983	1984	1985	1986	1987	1988	1989	1990	1991	1992
				Highest decile point as a proportion of the lowest decile point							
Males											
All occupations	2.61	2.65	2.78	2.82	2.88	2.97	3.02	3.08	3.11	3.16	3.20
Manuals	2.23	2.24	2.35	2.36	2.41	2.46	2.47	2.49	2.52	2.52	2.52
Non-manuals	2.78	2.82	2.97	2.99	3.08	3.14	3.24	3.33	3.31	3.36	3.41
Females											
All occupations	2.52	2.53	2.51	2.50	2.61	2.67	2.80	2.86	2.86	2.92	2.99
Manuals	2.08	2.11	2.11	2.17	2.16	2.24	2.22	2.26	2.31	2.37	2.40
Non-manuals	2.50	2.49	2.49	2.49	2.58	2.63	2.74	2.79	2.78	2.79	2.86

Source: Employment Gazette, New Earnings Survey.

top salary earners draw expenses and perks unavailable to most workers, and dividends. In 1993 Conrad Black of the *Telegraph* received £19.2 million in dividends and David Sainsbury of the supermarket group more than £14 million. Dividends were increasing at an annual rate of 13% and profits at 10%. Since 1979 inequalities have been exacerbated by changes in taxation: the top 10% of households paid 32% of their income in tax in 1992 whilst the bottom 10% paid 43% of their income.

Those higher up the income scale enjoy greater job security. At one end of the scale Ernest Mario of Glaxo received a golden handshake in 1993 of £3 million. In the middle, professional employees receive pay-offs around £50,000. At the other end more than half of all employers have no redundancy agreement and 60% of redundant workers receive the derisory statutory minimum. Almost a quarter of manual workers work shifts compared with 9% of non-manuals. Employees at the bottom of the pile are subject to greater work discipline. They still often have to 'clock in'. The better paid employees are, the better their chances of receiving perks. In the 1980s *Social Trends* found half of all semi-skilled and unskilled manual workers did not have a holiday away from home; 1 in 5 in the professional-managerial category took three holidays. The lower paid suffer discrimination over sick pay and pensions, yet they are more likely to suffer injury at work, retire later and die earlier. Semi-skilled and unskilled workers are six times as likely to die before the age of 64 than those in professional, managerial or administrative categories. They are employed in a more dangerous environment, have less autonomy over their jobs and less satisfaction in their work.

The vanishing working class

Some writers have taken recomposition as indicating that the working class is in terminal decline. In this view, unions do not merely face tremendous difficulties; they are destined to wither away. Different writers use different definitions of class, often based upon people's occupations and whether they do manual or non-manual work. Many define manual workers as 'working-class' and white collar workers as 'middle-class'. Others relate class to income and lifestyle, and argue that when manual workers reach a certain stage of affluence they succumb to **embourgeoisement** and become part of the 'middle class'. Others claim that only 'productive' workers should be classed as working class. Here we assume that the class position of different groups is defined by their position in relation to ownership and control of the production process and their relation to other groups involved in the organisation of production. The working class is constituted by all those who have to sell their labour to live, not simply by those who work with their hands, who are poorly paid or who believe they are working class (Wright, 1978, 17).

Those who believe that the working class is vanishing or declining point to the changes in the labour force particularly the growth of white collar workers. Who are these white collar workers? They are normally divided into two categories, the 'professional-managerial', making up between 20–25% of the employed population, and the 'clerical', making up some 17–18%. The clerical category consists of, amongst others, typists, filing clerks, secretaries, shop assistants, petrol pump attendants and office machine operators. In the past, the traditional 'clerk' was separated off, certainly, from semi-skilled and unskilled manual workers by better pay and conditions, and particularly, by enhanced job security. However, 'by 1978 the average earnings of semi-skilled men have overtaken their clerical counterparts for the first time . . . such income advantages clerical workers enjoyed have been considerably eroded . . . in addition to income relativities, many of the traditionally superior employment conditions of clerks have been gained by manual workers' (Crompton and Jones, 1984, 24, 28).

Moreover, office work has become 'industrialised'. One study found that over 90% of those on clerical grades were in jobs that were 'entirely rule-bound, and required no discretion or autonomy in carrying out job tasks' (Crompton and Jones, 1984, 73). Opportunities for promotion fell largely to the minority of men. The same applies to others in this category. Supermarket assistants working laser-scanning tills have little control over their work. It is increasingly carried out under large scale, factory conditions. Like other employees in this category, they are *workers* in the sense that they live by the sale of their labour power.

The clerical category consists of women – around 70% – who possess few qualifications, come from a working-class background and earn less than the top 30% of manual workers. This, as well as the proletarianisation of the work they do, led to increases in union membership in this group in the 1970s and to the dissolution of 'status superiority'. What's in a term? The majority of these workers are, in reality, manual workers, separated from other workers by their now dissolving *status* rather than by considerations of class. This is not to say that remaining differences, such as the existence of opportunities for promotion, which may predispose this group to individual rather than collective action, are not important.

The professional-managerial category is growing faster than the clerical group. Many are members of the 'new middle class' and exercise a substantial degree of managerial power. But this category also consists of nurses, radiographers, physiotherapists, medical technicians, laboratory technicians and supervisors. The majority possess little control over resources, or the labour of others, '73% of supervisors exercised no control – or skill – in their own work' (Crompton and Jones, 1984, 76). They have nothing to live on but their salary. They are in trade unions. They go on strike. They are, in a real sense, part of the working class, as are the majority of other groups covered by this category, such as draughtsmen or teachers.

The changes taking place are real, not superficial or temporary. What we are observing is not a withering away, but a *reconstitution* of the working class, a remaking which may affect cohesion and unity but which has been continuous since the advent of capitalism. We have to remember that only a little over a century ago there were more agricultural labourers, domestic servants and workers in trade and transport than there were in factories and mines. As the system of production has been continuously transformed, so it has continuously transformed the working class.

The working class has not been transformed by affluence. It is transforming itself by relating to changing technology and employment patterns. It is *expanding, not shrinking*. The divisions between full-time and part-time workers, employed and unemployed, men and women, represent divisions *within* a working class *which has always been divided*. Half a century ago sociologists observed the 'ladder like stratification of the working class with many small rungs' (Zweig, 1948, 84). Continuing changes, together with rising living standards for the majority and a scattering to the top and bottom of the income scale, may be affecting the sense of community, deprivation, cultural difference and identification with the institutions of Labourism. The decline of manual workers, the historic core of trade unionism, poses serious problems. The erosion of the specific weight of dockers, miners and car workers must change the movement. But white collar and service workers have demonstrated a propensity for collective organisation and collective action. What is now required is the construction of a new collective consciousness and solidaristic practice. Class remains as much the basis for material and ideological conflict today as in 1964 (Evans, 1993). Britain remains a class society not a post-class society (Goldthorpe and Marshall, 1992). Whether individualism and consumerism or collectivism wins the soul of the changing working class will depend partly on union strategies and action.

Conclusions

Theorists of trade unions have disagreed over their potential for social change. Proponents of business unionism have seen unions as market organisations, sellers of labour. At the other end of the spectrum some Marxists view unions as agencies in the revolutionary transformation of capitalism. In practice, unions in Britain have contributed to gradually civilising and reforming capitalism. But there were real limits to change and their role in it. Unions have been essentially reactive rather than initiatory. Their position has to be increasingly related to economic decline although evidence for their role in it and their debilitating economic effect is limited. The state has employed a variety of strategies to reverse decline which have affected unions, notably corporatism and neo-*laissez-faire*. Even the rigours of the neo-Conservative experiment since 1979 however have not solved deep seated economic problems.

Important changes in the structure of capital and labour are driven by changes in the world economy increasing international deregulation, competition, integration and the growth of global enterprise. Taken with the re-emergence of periodic recessions and apparent limits on state intervention, trends in global, political economy and Britain's role in it are inimical to trade unionism. Ownership and control of economic resources and income remains highly concentrated with wealth and power in the hands of a small minority. The rich have got richer, the poor poorer.

Whilst some exaggerate the extent and tempo of change, the air is thick with threats to trade unionism although there is as much need for them as ever. Many claim management are moving towards unitary conceptions of employment relations, viewing them strategically and integrating them into corporate planning. Radical restructuring is occurring in industry and the labour force. Moves from production to services; from low-tech to hi-tech; from large to small establishments; from the public sector to the private sector; from full-time work to part-time work and self-employment; from manual to white collar work; put crudely, *from areas of union strength to union weakness*, have immense implications for the future of trade unionism. Particularly important are the growing involvement of women in the labour force and the continuing framing of change by high unemployment. Changes are real and not temporary. But the working class has always been internally fragmented. Unions have always had to face sectionalism and a diversity of perceived interests. On the evidence it is premature to theorise the demise of mass production and the disappearance of the working class. *The class basis for trade unionism, the economic and industrial conditions which bred it still exist.* Nonetheless changes in the world economy, Britain's adaptation to them, developments in the class and industrial structure, innovation in state and managerial strategies and restructuring of work all establish an environment which, in contrast to the post-war settlement, is *hostile to trade unionism*.

Further reading

The two most readily available books on theories of trade unionism are Ross Martin, *Trade Unionism, Purposes and Forms*, Clarendon Press, 1989, and Michael Poole, *Theories of Trade Unionism: A Sociology of Industrial Relations*, Routledge, 1981. David Coates, John Hillard, eds., *The Economic Decline of Modern Britain: The Debate Between Left and Right*, Wheatsheaf, 1986, provides a wealth of contending views on Britain's economic problems. David Coates, *The Crisis of Labour*, Philip Allan, 1989, deals expertly with the development of state policies towards industrial relations from the 1960s.

Jonathan Michie, ed., *The Economic Legacy 1979–1992*, Academic Press, 1992, is an excellent collection of essays on recent economic developments. For recent changes in the class structure read Rosemary Crompton, *Class and Stratification: An Introduction to Recent Debates*, Polity Press, 1993 and John Scott, *Who Rules Britain?*, Polity Press, 1991. Anna Pollert, *Farewell to Flexibility*, Blackwell, 1991, is a good critical introduction to arguments about recent changes in production and much more. John Storey, ed., *New Perspectives on Human Resource Management*, Routledge, 1989, provides an understanding of recent changes in management approaches.

3

Bargaining and the workplace

The future of collective bargaining and workplace organisation are fundamental, interlinked issues facing trade unionism today. Unions have their roots in the workplace: the dynamic of conflict at the point of production ignites the spark of collective organisation. In Britain the coping stone of union strength and stability has been workplace organisation. Expressing itself fully through bargaining with management it has been most workers' primary or only experience of trade unionism. For many years employers sought to exclude bargaining from the workplace, favouring instead national machinery. In the post-war era the state blessed collective bargaining, accepted its internalisation but sought to regulate it more closely. In the era of neo-*laissez-faire* the state sought to expand formal freedom to bargain within the enterprise by eschewing incomes policies whilst weakening the unions and undercutting the economic conditions which made it an effective instrument. Since 1979 governments have sought to de-legitimise and remould workplace unionism and progressively weaken collective bargaining. How successful have such policies been? Is the strike dead as a dodo? Are shop stewards a vanishing species? Is collective bargaining in serious decline? This chapter reviews the evidence.

The bargaining system

A key aspect of union practice after 1945 was domestic bargaining

developed spontaneously by strong workplace trade unionism.
Growing attention to inflation and unconstitutional strikes by the
state produced pressures on workplace organisation. We look first
at how the bargaining system developed.

The growth of collective bargaining
A century ago collective bargaining was still restricted: it was well
established in skilled trades, such as engineering, shipbuilding
and construction, and industries with some form of piecework,
such as textiles, coal and iron and steel. To curb union activity in
the workplace employers sought to establish bargaining at district
level, limit its scope to wages and hours, emphasise procedures for
funnelling disputes beyond the workplace and restrict competitive
pressures by involving employers' associations. Collective
bargaining had developed in the clash between management prerogative and unilateral worker regulation and its rudimentary
external basis continued to be fleshed out by informal rules and
custom and practice in the workplace.

    Before 1914, 'it was difficult to discern a definite trend towards
industry wide pay settlements' (Clegg, 1976, 203). Wartime conditions, inflation, a ban of strikes, compulsory arbitration and state
control of key industries favoured industry-wide agreements.
This tendency was reinforced by the reports of the Whitley Committee (1917–18) which recommended Joint Industrial Councils
and the development of collective bargaining at industry level.
The purpose was to maintain management prerogative in the face
of growing militancy and the spread of shop stewards by conceding controlled bargaining *outside the workplace* to separate
issues like wages and hours from the organisation of production
and limit union impact in the workplace. The Whitley reports had
an immediate impact on national bargaining: by 1921, 73 NJICs
had been established and enduring bargaining structures had
been created in national and local government. The inter-war
depression curbed the progress of multi-employer institutions.
Employers reverted to local bargaining to maximise their power:
by the mid-1930s only 45 NJICs were operating. The basis for
industrial regulation remained intact, developed further during

World War II, and flourished in its aftermath. State support and the extension of the public sector with statutory duties on management to establish bargaining machinery further strengthened the position.

By the 1960s, 65% of the workforce was covered by multi-employer bargaining. There were some 500 industry-wide negotiating bodies for manual workers alone. The agreements they produced regulated hours, overtime and holidays. Some set standard rates of pay, others minima. A state safety net provided for government inquiry, conciliation and arbitration; extension of the terms of collective agreements to other employers; and the stimulation of collective bargaining and protection of the low paid through wages council machinery (see Chapter 6). But in some industries multi-employer bargaining had been undermined, by the 1960s, by the growth of domestic bargaining.

Domestic bargaining

Workplace bargaining developed before and during World War I, declined in the 1920s and grew once more from the late 1930s. In the post-war years shop stewards exploiting piecework, bonus systems and changes in work processes, eroded the impact of national agreements on pay and conditions. Workplace bargaining, 'largely informal, largely fragmented and largely autonomous' grew. It was often *micro-bargaining* based on individual stewards or small groups negotiating on a sectional basis with a proliferation of unwritten agreements and custom and practice. It was rarely strategic and usually outside the ambit and control of higher level management and union officers. In many industries there were arguably two systems of industrial relations:

The formal system assumes industry-wide organisations capable of imposing their decisions on their members. The informal system rests on the wide autonomy of managers in individual companies and the power of industrial work groups (Royal Commission, 1968, 36).

Domestic bargaining spread unevenly. It was strong in engineering and construction, weak in the public sector, far more evident on the shop floor than in the office. Its growth was facilitated by full employment and tight product markets. Its scope was limited and fragmented controls introduced over the work process were essentially defensive. Its symptoms were wage drift and unofficial stoppages. It was increasingly perceived by state and employers as a problem, feeding inflation, inhibiting managerial control and foiling wage restraint.

The Royal Commission on Trade Unions which reported in 1968 recommended integration of the two systems to increase productivity, root out restrictive practices and make British industry more competitive:

effective and orderly collective bargaining is required over such issues as the control of incentive schemes, the regulation of hours actually worked, the use of job evaluation, work practices and the linking of pay to changes in performance, facilities for shop stewards and disciplinary rules (Royal Commission, 1968, 262).

The Donovan Report recommended more comprehensive, formal collective agreements at plant and enterprise level; more effective formal procedures to govern grievances, discipline, redundancy and union organisation; a reform of payment systems; greater integration of stewards within the union and clearer definition of their role. The reform of collective bargaining stimulated by a new Commission on Industrial Relations would strengthen management control, make the labour process more susceptible to efficient planning and thus facilitate the operation of wage restraint and wider economic policy.

Reforming collective bargaining
Developments in industries such as engineering or chemicals were faithfully mirrored in the report. But for much of the labour force workplace bargaining was limited to administering and fleshing out formal agreements, not challenging them. Here there was one system of industrial relations, not two. The orthodox view that workplace bargaining created 'disorder' was related to strategies for the control of wages, and also contentious: wage drift was not a problem for its beneficiaries or many union officers and managers (Goldthorpe, 1974; Batstone *et al.*, 1977). Nonetheless

the TUC accepted the main thrust of Donovan's proposals and reform of collective bargaining from the 1960s led to a further erosion of national bargaining. Productivity bargaining aimed at formal plant and company agreements buying out union controls and encouraging greater efficiency was encouraged by state agencies such as the National Board for Prices and Incomes and the Commission on Industrial Relations, although it met with limited success. These bodies advocated formalisation on the Donovan model with controlled decentralisation. There was an increase in the closed shop, measured day work, the check-off, written procedures, job evaluation and facilities for stewards. By the late 1970s the system had moved further from multi-employer to centralised single employer bargaining. It was reported:

for two-thirds of manual and three-quarters of non-manual employees the formal structure of bargaining has become one of single employer agreements covering one or more factories within a company. Multi-employer agreements . . . cover only a quarter of the manual and a tenth of the non-manual manufacturing workforce (Brown, 1981, 118).

In the private sector employers had succeeded in formalising collective bargaining above the level of the shopfloor but inside the enterprise at plant or company level. They had accepted *internalisation* of bargaining but squared their historic fears that this would cumulatively erode management prerogatives by inserting it in a space which maximised management power. Decentralisation remained; it was now more controlled. Where bargaining took place at plant level it was increasingly controlled through decisions at company level. If management wished to directly undermine workplace organisation bargaining was formally moved from plant to company level as at British Leyland in 1982. Management had gone a long way to formalising and restricting fragmented bargaining and proceduralising and pasteurising workplace industrial relations. In the public sector emphasis on national and regional mechanisms remained; but there was an increase in local bargaining and the development of Donovan-influenced procedures (Terry, 1982). Manual workers in private industry had expanded bargaining by the 1970s so that issues such as changes in production methods, staffing levels and direction of labour were regulated. Capital investment was an issue for bargaining in almost 40% of establishments (Daniel and Millward, 1983, 197). Reform also stimulated coverage: in 1968 around 65% of the workforce had their wages and conditions fixed by collective bargaining but by the mid-1970s the figure was 72% (Brown, 1993, 191).

The shop stewards

By the late 1950s shop stewards, until then weak and defensive, even in what were to become their strongholds, had been stereotyped as a social problem (Tolliday, 1985, 118; Price, 1986, 201). State inquiries, employers and union leaders saw stewards as 'a private union within a union . . . in no way officially or constitutionally linked with the union hierarchy', 'an excrescence on the unions' or in the immortal words of AEU leader Bill Carron, 'werewolves who are rushing madly towards industrial ruin and howling delighted at the foam on their muzzles which they accept as their only guiding light' (quoted in Widgery, 1976, 167ff.). The popular imagination was conditioned by Peter Sellers's 1959 portrayal of a left-wing convenor in the film *I'm All Right Jack*. The shop steward system was condemned or approved because of its spontaneous development, its direct democracy and its independence of official structures. It was viewed as 'a challenge from below' to conventional industrial relations. The right and Labour orthodoxy conceived it as a force of disorder; from the left it was sometimes viewed as bearing 'the seeds of socialism as the self emancipation of the working class' (Cliff and Barker, 1966, 135).

In key industries steward bargaining offered a threat to the 1945 settlement and to management control over the organisation of work. The outcome of key wage bargains passed out of the control of top managers and union officers susceptible to state influence. It was not only money which was in contention but who controlled the organisation of work. However the extent to which shop steward organisation was *an organic part of trade unionism*, albeit an activist, democratic component, dysfunctional to

corporatist strategies of wage-control and management prerogatives, was sometimes overlooked. Workplace organisation, in
terms of any general judgement – outside the docks, where
stewards were only constitutionally recognised after 1967, and
briefly parts of the car industry – was a specific echelon of union
organisation related to other structures. The sense in which it was
sometimes independent, more correctly *quasi-independent* was in
relation to bargaining, not organisation or ideology. Also
minimised was the extent to which its strength was contingent and
flowed from conjunctural full employment policies.

The degree of management accommodation and sponsorship
was also downplayed (Terry, 1983). Yet the extent to which
stewards in the 1960s, even in the areas where they were most
militant, were 'an establishment', 'dependent on management',
'performing a managerial function of grievance settlement,
welfare arrangements and human adjustment' was well documented (Turner, Clack and Roberts, 1967, 212ff.). By the
mid-1960s the steward was characterised as 'an accepted, reasonable and even moderating influence, more of a lubricant than an
irritant'. It was wrong to brand stewards as troublemakers.
'Trouble is often thrust upon them . . . Quite commonly they are
supporters of order exercising a restraining influence on their
members' (McCarthy and Parker, 1968, 56; Royal Commission,
1968, 28). This of course was the view of those who wanted a
consensus based reform of the steward system. Aspiration exaggerated reality, resolving the dialectic between conflict and
accommodation in stewards' activities artificially in favour of the
latter. Some stewards *were* 'troublemakers' in the sense they
challenged what to them was a troublesome *status quo*. Some were
architects of 'disorder' mobilising their members against an
exploitative and oppressive order. Nonetheless state support for
'the lubricant' view spurred extension of the steward system to
areas of previously weak organisation. And state attempts to
mould steward activities through legislation and wage restraint
produced the political strike wave of 1969–74.

Conflict, accommodation and independence varied across
unions and industry. But stewards on the whole were not answer-

able only to those who elected them. Nor for the greater part were they unofficial, 'almost clandestine' (Terry, 1983, 72). There was conflict in some unions and industries; adjustment in structures and culture to accommodate workplace organisation was well in train before Donovan. By the 1970s in many unions stewards were represented at all levels from branch and district to National Executive, providing articulation between the workplace and wider union (England, 1981). Stewards' committees were not factory councils: they were, despite frictions, part of the union. This was generally true of private industry. In the public sector stewards' systems developed because of pressure on management to introduce productivity bargaining and were formally chartered by the unions. Stewards were only recognised in local government in 1969 and in the NHS in 1971. Well into the 1970s, 20% of NUPE branches had no stewards (Fryer *et al.*, 1974). NALGO only agreed to establish a steward system in 1977. In the civil service, too, systems of representation were constructed from above. Distance between workplace organisation and formal union machinery differed but perhaps most typically stewards worked in constructive harness with full-time officers (Batstone *et al.*, 1977). Generally:

Shop stewards as the key link between trade unionism and the lay membership are involved in a two-way relationship of control and dependence with the district officials and committee and more remotely with the national leadership . . . a relationship of interdependence is the norm (Hyman, 1975, 161–3).

The Communist Party exercised a real influence over a minority of stewards operating through its industrial arm, the Liaison Committee for the Defence of Trade Unions. Essentially it placed its faith in the election of left officials and its reach declined from the late 1960s. The International Socialists' (later Socialist Workers' Party) Rank and File Movement proved a temporary development whilst the influence of Militant was limited. Strikes against legislation and support for workers' control demonstrated a contradictory political dynamic not captured by snapshot surveys of political consciousness. But the majority of stewards inhabited a similar political universe to full-time officers but were closer to their members. At the core of commitment was often a limited if militant 'factory consciousness' centred on the need to fight the bosses on the shopfloor (Beynon, 1973). Studies in the vanguard car industry found large numbers of 'leader' stewards with a strong commitment to the wider union and socialist ideas. Even here they were outnumbered by 'populists' and 'cowboys' more responsive to sectional interests and horizons (Batstone *et al.*, 1977). Surveys of white collar representatives in the 1970s found 37% supporting the Conservatives (Nicholson *et al.*, 1981). On the whole, stewards accepted the legitimacy of existing ownership and control of industry. They wanted extended collective bargaining not self-management (Knight, 1979). Even those who exaggerated stewards' political potential sometimes recognised 'the shop stewards' organisations are largely restricted to the narrow horizon of economic trade union demands. They are largely speaking politically apathetic' (Cliff and Barker, 1966, 105). Their roots in the workplace were a strength in terms of responsiveness to members' aspirations. They were a weakness in relation to support for wider political programmes. As *par excellence* exponents of sectional Labourism, stewards constituted an important limitation on attempts by governments to develop corporatism or, in all probability, more left-wing policies.

A natural aspect of the post-war boom, fragmented workplace organisation was not conducive to production of wider strategy and broader organisation necessary as the boom disintegrated and state intervention developed. It is claimed: 'In the 1950s. . .a shop steward movement developed' (Lash and Urry, 1987, 274). Steward organisation never approached the status of 'a movement'. Its ability to build sustained links even across individual employers was limited (Terry, 1985). Its most advanced moment, the identification and linkage which produced the 1972 strike over the imprisonment of the Pentonville Five was not sustained. Within months the Heath government had successfully imposed wage restraint and Labour's victory in 1974 was won on a mere 37% of the vote.

Shop steward militancy was part of the radical mood of dissatisfaction with the limits of the post-war consensus, its enduring low pay, increasing inflation and taxation, most graphically symbolised by May 1968 in France. The security and confidence engendered by full employment eroded as the implications of the oil crisis of 1973–74 gripped. The decline in militancy during the early years of the Social Contract was often ascribed to 'bureaucratisation' and successful integration of stewards into both the wider union and formal industrial relations machinery at the workplace. There was legislative support for time off and facilities for stewards and a special state grant to the unions for training; management responded with concessions. It was argued that this produced formalised procedures, a new layer of full-time stewards, extensive facilities and generous expenses, more hierarchy and centralised control within workplace organisation and a greater distance between many stewards and their constituents. Stewards were less militant bargainers, more operators of procedures. Workplace organisation grew closer to official union structures, and stewards became more amenable to official union policy. A complex system of links stretching from the TUC to the shopfloor was fashioned. It was essential to the success of corporatist policies and increasing moderation at the workplace (Hyman, 1979).

Critics argued this view underestimated the extent to which 'bureaucratisation' had existed before 1974. Integration with the wider union and management support were not novel but continuing influences on workplace organisation. The argument ignores the variety of union constitutions and market situations and rests upon an idealised view of steward organisation in the 1950s and 1960s; hierarchy, extensive facilities, full-time stewards and intimate links with management were long standing. There is nothing automatically corrupting about facilities that may make organisation more effective without impairing democracy. Steward training was more employer influenced before 1970 than after. Union leaders were able to carry their members in the early stages of incomes policy in the 1960s without 'bureaucratisation', and its limits were surely demonstrated by the crumbling of wage restraint from 1977. In as much as integration did occur it had benefits in strengthening and democratising the unions (England, 1981; Batstone, 1984).

As critics point out, the bureaucratisation thesis is empirically flawed. It also privileged organisational factors over politics and economics. Stewards *were* increasingly enmeshed in procedures with less control over bargaining, but they did not lose their independence. They lost confidence and bargaining power in a changed situation. The acceptance of the initial stages of wage restraint in 1975–76 and the consequent downturn in industrial action simply illustrated the weakness of a system of workplace organisation functional for the post-war consensus in the cold douche of its disintegration. Unemployment increased suddenly and substantially by half a million in 1975, growing thereafter. The 30-year-old security of the post-war period was seen as under threat. Confidence in the commitment to full employment and the certainty of job security were fraying. Stewards feared with Labour politicians that 'the party was over'. The leaders of the left, Jack Jones and Hugh Scanlon, were firmly behind wage restraint. They could see no alternative and neither could the majority of stewards. The value of militancy for paper wage increases as inflation approached 30% in mid-1975 was questioned. Internal organisational changes played only a limited role. *Shop stewards on the whole were and always had been pragmatic bargainers*, their behaviour calculative. Aware of new constraints they adopted to them. Wilson and Jones won the battle of ideas, not the battle of integration.

The potential of workplace organisation as a bulwark of resistance to exploitation, as a spur to struggle and as a bridgehead for participative democracy must not be undervalued. But it cannot be *identified*, as it sometimes has been, with rank and file insurgency or the basis for an alternative trade unionism. Unusual when compared with other countries, it remained part of union organisation, not an independent stratum with potential to transcend or circumvent conventional union organisation. Stewards remained subject to similar contradictory pressures to conflict and accommodation as other union personnel. Their nature as pragmatic bargainers meant they constituted a negative threat to state policy. In the end, fragmentation and emphasis on wage militancy meant weakness. Greater involvement in the unions involved the only logical route for a strategy for confronting capital.

Strikes

The immediate post-war years represented a continuation of the industrial peace of the 1930s. Days lost remained low during the 1950s, there was no national stoppage between 1933 and 1953 but the period saw a growth in the number of strikes. Historically the statistics were distorted by disputes in the coal industry which generated a large number of stoppages and days lost. However through the 1960s industrial action spread across industry, partly reflecting greater unionisation: stoppages and days lost increased (see Table 3.1). Strike patterns reflected the rise of domestic bargaining. Strikes were predominantly short, involving a small number of workers, *unofficial*, executed without formal union support and *unconstitutional*, with action occurring before procedures were exhausted.

In the 1970s strikes became longer. Major confrontations and political strikes not seen for half a century reappeared. Industrial conflict as represented by the figures of 1972, 1974 and 1979 was more extensive and more bitter than at any time in the post-war period, moving from the private to the public sector. However strikes remained concentrated in mining, the motor industry, shipbuilding, the docks and in large workplaces generally. If the position was analysed without the coal industry, for example, a very different picture would emerge. From the late 1960s the stereotype of Britain as a strike prone island was continually pressed into service. In reality Britain was placed below the USA, Canada, Australia, Ireland and Italy in international comparisons and its 'strike problem' had to be located in economic decline and its emphasis on voluntary collective bargaining to regulate industrial relations.

Table 3.1   *Strikes in the UK, 1960–79*

Year	No. of stoppages	Workers involved (000s)	Working days lost (000s)
1960	2,849	819	3,024
1961	2,701	779	3,046
1962	2,465	4,423	5,798
1963	2,081	593	1,755
1964	2,535	883	2,277
1965	2,365	876	2,925
1966	1,951	544	2,398
1967	2,133	734	2,787
1968	2,390	2,258	4,690
1969	3,146	1,665	6,846
1970	3,943	1,801	10,980
1971	2,223	1,173	13,558
1972	2,497	1,734	23,909
1973	2,854	1,591	7,173
1974	2,992	1,626	14,750
1975	2,828	809	6,012
1976	2,016	668	3,284
1977	2,703	1,166	10,142
1978	2,471	1,041	9,405
1979	2,080	4,608	29,474

Source: Employment Gazette.

Neo-*laissez-faire*, bargaining and the workplace

From 1975, and more intensively from 1979, the post-war pattern of workplace unionism was under threat. Both the spontaneous, fragmented decentralisation of the earlier period and the later formalised, more managerially controlled, decentralised bargaining were antipathetic to corporatist projects. Incomes policy had become discredited not only because of resistance from workplace organisation but because of failure of governments to realise it as part of a wider strategy of political exchange. No government since 1950 which had operated sustained wage restraint had been re-elected. We now look at the challenges proffered to workplace trade unionism in the years of the alternative, neo-Conservatism.

Macho management?

As recession developed, commentators began to note the emergence of a new breed of managers: old-style co-operation with the unions was out, the firm smack of authority was in. Michael Edwardes at British Leyland and Ian McGregor at BSC were seen as pioneers. Edwardes bypassed the unions, communicating directly with the shopfloor. He drew up a programme involving 25,000 redundancies and extensive changes in working practices, and circulated a copy to every worker's home: 'politically motivated shop stewards could not be relied upon to present a balanced view to employees' (Edwardes, 1984, 93). Management organised its own ballot on the plan and when shop stewards refused to accept the result they imposed it. BL adopted a style in which their first offer was their final offer. They liaised with full-time officers at the expense of shop stewards, took over the platform at union meetings, returned full-time stewards to their jobs and dismissed prominent trade unionists such as Derek Robinson. At BSC, Ian McGregor organised a successful ballot on his 'survival plan' and bypassed the unions by rejecting national bargaining in favour of local deals. A similar approach was taken by Arnold Weinstock at GEC. The mood was that for two decades management had

a buffeting and bashing from government and unions . . . we have an opportunity now that will last for two or three years, then the unions will get themselves together again and the government, like all governments, will run out of steam. So grab it now. We have had a pounding and we are all fed up with it. I think it would be fair to say it's almost vengeance (Beynon, 1983, 9).

The appointment of Ian McGregor to British Coal and the miners' strike strengthened the view that something new was happening. In the wake of the stoppage, the NCB Chair was declaring: 'people are now discovering the price of insubordination and insurrection. And boy, are we going to make it stick!'. Management refused to reinstate those dismissed and imposed a tough new disciplinary code.

Macho management is a misnomer. What was often involved was a tougher and somewhat more strategic reassertion of management prerogative aimed at restructuring industrial relations and undermining rather than frontally attacking the unions. Such a stance continued to dominate the public and newly privatised sector into the 1990s. In steel there was a restructuring of industrial relations and extensive change in the organisation of work (Blyton, 1992). British Airways saw thoroughgoing rationalisation, a reduction of the workforce by over 40% and a more confrontational management style. The Post Office and British Rail witnessed similar aggressive approaches bypassing the unions, breaking up bargaining structures, reducing staffing levels and changing working patterns and job demarcation (Ferner, 1989). In the coal industry the management offensive continued (Leman and Winterton, 1991). A new approach was also evident in local government (Foster, 1993; Colling, 1993) and in central government (Blackwell and Lloyd, 1989; see generally Pendleton and Winterton, 1993).

In the public sector management could be expected to be responsive to state policy. But supporters of the macho management thesis could also point to developments in private industry. On the docks, management combined the use of new communications techniques with a firmer stance towards stewards, withdrawal of facilities and selective derecognition. The removal of the Dock Labour scheme in 1989 facilitated change (Turnbull and Weston, 1993). Critics of management often cited the national newspapers as an example of appeasement. In 1986 Rupert Murdoch took on the unions. His final proposals for the move to Wapping provided for a legally binding agreement and a ban on industrial action. They stated that employees would undertake work with 'complete flexibility. There will be no demarcation lines ... The starting and finishing times of an employee may be changed upon a day's notice . . . manning levels will be determined by the employer . . . New technology may be adopted at any time . . . There will be no closed shop'.

It was argued that it was mistaken to rely on these well-publicised examples: they were publicised because they were the exception. Examples came disproportionally from the public sector and from companies faced with tough product markets. One study found that 'if 15% underestimates the number of "macho managers", 23% is likely to exaggerate it. In about a fifth of the plants in the survey, management has made some attempt to reduce the role of the union' (Batstone, 1984, 258, 260). In another survey 79% of managers said they had made no changes in the way they dealt with shop stewards:

The evidence does not then support the view that the emerging trend of industrial relations is based on an aggressive management attack on established trade unions . . . a more subtle process seems to have been taking place in which firms have certainly been trying to change working practices but in which co-operation and involvement have been seen as important (Edwards, 1985, 35).

These findings, supported in later surveys (Edwards and Marginson, 1988), were questioned on the grounds that they represented the diplomatic response to be expected from direc-tors and factory managers. A study of personnel managers found that they believed that management *had* toughened up. There were constant references to industrial relations improving through fear, and evidence of attempts to bypass the unions (Mackay, 1986). It seemed clear that in the public sector, political and financial pressure hardened the climate and prompted a tougher stance towards unions. A similar approach has been taken by an increasing number of managers in the private sector, impel-led by financial pressures or long-term calculation that industrial relations with weaker unions or no unions at all is more beneficial. Until the second half of the 1980s there was a disjunction between the growing emphasis of the state on union exclusion and the more cautious conservative policy of management. Since then the pace of derecognition and erosion of collective bargaining has increased. As yet *there is no evidence of a large scale attempt to uproot unions but the threat from employers is growing* (Smith and Morton, 1993; LRD, 1993b). In key areas union strength has been scaled down. As Ferner comments, comparing 1979 and 1989, 'the unions in the public and privatised sector had been thrown on the defensive, undermined and bypassed and their bargaining power weakened by a switch from consensual to confrontationist management styles' (1989, 8, 9).

We must not confuse managerial profession with practice: if there is a tendency to more strategic and professional management in some areas there has been no 'managerial revolution'. Even if they restyled themselves as human resource managers there is little evidence that personnel managers have become more powerful in recent years or that across industry industrial relations has become an organic ingredient of managerial planning, still less a major drive in it. Management practice remains varied and opportunistic (Hyman, 1994; Millward *et al.*, 1992, Chapter 2).

Union free

Cases in which companies withdrew negotiating rights remained rare during the first half of the 1980s (ACAS, 1986). In the second half of the decade there was a growth in derecognition. Although it remained a minority trend, it became widespread in shipping and newspapers and spread to other areas (Claydon, 1989; Millward, 1994, 119). By 1990, derecognition was increasing and related to declining density.

The recognition of trade unions by employers – our key indicator of the role of unions in industrial relations – also registered a substantial decline over the decade. This change was concentrated in the period since 1984. It was apparent in the private sector, both manufacturing and services, and the public sector (Millward *et al.*, 1992, 102).

The development of 'union free' areas was particularly driven by failure to attain recognition in new establishments (ACAS, 1989, 1991). Employers in new workplaces less then ten years old were less likely to recognise unions than those in older establishments, and less likely than their counterparts in the 1970s. Employers in new manufacturing sites, private services and hi-tech enterprises were resisting unions (McLoughlin and Gourlay, 1992). Union free areas are a growing factor, perhaps related to removal of statutory support for recognition, and state hostility and strikes for recognition are rarely recorded (ACAS, 1989, 22). In the early 1980s Mrs Thatcher praised the human relations approach taken by union free companies like Marks & Spencer. Some saw in the human resource management of companies like IBM the shape of things to come. They develop careful recruitment strategies, pursue a 'high salary high job security' approach and cultivate a company culture through single status, open promotion and individual negotiations over pay. Overall, in Britain's new low cost, low wage economy 'open shop' is more likely to mean sweatshop with traditional management approaches, no employee involvement, long hours, low pay, reliance on discipline, dismissals and compulsory redundancy (Sisson, 1993). The non-union workplace looks backwards to the last century; it is usually neither a hi-tech nor a HRM workplace. It is likely to be closer to Burnstalls, a Birmingham sweatshop, scene of a publicised strike in 1993, where workers earned £93 a week before tax while handling dangerous chemicals, than to IBM.

Strike-free

Single union/no-strike deals have also been viewed as an ingredient in a new model of company trade unionism. As the Director General of the EEF points out, they enable an employer 'to select a moderate and progressive minded union with which he can agree to operate from the outset an industrial relations culture embracing all the different aspects . . . employee involvement, harmonisation and flexibility of labour' (Bassett, 1986, 87). Employers saw these agreements as ensuring trade unionism would develop within a framework favourable to company objectives: getting the right union committed to company goals is critical. At Yuasa Batteries in South Wales, the TGWU was not recognised. In 1985, the employers felt that their own systems were insufficient to effectively monitor the workforce so they brought in the EETPU to act as a management conveyor belt, to motivate employees and perform the personnel function. Single union deals involve one union representing all employees, selected by the employer. Closed shops are out, and unions have found difficulty in recruiting. Agreements involve 'single status', flexibility and employee involvement. Industrial action is prohibited. In a dispute, both parties agree to **pendulum arbitration**: the arbitrator cannot 'split the difference' but has to choose between the union demand and the employer's final offer. Whilst the EETPU, now part of the AEEU, was identified with this approach, most big unions have been involved.

Single union deals have been particularly associated with Japanese companies – and in them with flexibility and Japanese production systems – but with inward investment generally. They constitute one component in the reassertion of a unitary framework and the right to manage which encompasses human resource management. Their supporters argue that they represent the *only way* unions can recruit in expanding sectors of industry. They establish industrial peace. All employees become single status, monthly paid, salaried staff. The emphasis on training is particularly positive. New company advisory boards provide consultation before key decisions are taken and create a co-operative and productive atmosphere.

Critics argue these agreements involve conceding the fundamental human freedom to withdraw labour; unions emphasise their weakness and become an arm of management. What kind of unionism is possible when the employer picks the union he will negotiate with? Whilst there is sometimes a ballot of the workforce to ratify the employer's decision, this is a managed exercise. Some unions have had to reluctantly accept these deals; the AEEU press them on management. Consequent publicity encourages more managers to consider their adoption. To keep members, other unions are forced to sign on the no-strike dotted line, so that the AEEU are provoking a downward spiral in which basic union principles go to the wall. For employers and employees who support these deals get not a union, but a staff association with the wider union excluded. In Nissan, only around 20% of the workforce is unionised. This modern business unionism works for the employer not the employees.

Single union deals should not be over-estimated. In 1986, the EETPU estimated that less than 20,000 employees were covered by no-strike provisions and the number of 'model' agreements was less than 30 – and strikes have already occurred in enterprises covered by these arrangements. There was no evidence they make workers better off or staunch membership loss. By 1993 it was estimated that less than 220,000 workers were covered by 194 single union agreements – the TGWU and GMB had significant involvement as well as the AEEU. But the majority of these workers were covered by traditional single union recognition rather than 'new model' arrangements. There had been a decline since 1989, probably influenced by union dissatisfaction with the results of beauty contests and recession (Gall, 1993). Single union deals may represent the future, but 'model' deals remain rare in the present: only 1% of workplaces with unions have pendulum arbitration, only 17% with single union representation have company councils; and hardly any have the full single union package (Millward, 1994, 122).

The TUC has pushed **single-table bargaining** as a means of overcoming the conflicts single union deals engender. For employers it produced some of the advantages in minimising the problems of multi-unionism. This mechanism brought together different unions and groups of workers – particularly manual and white collar groups – in a system of co-ordinated bargaining. Employers saw it as reducing disputes and competitive bargaining. Again publicity has outweighed progress. By 1990 there was no evidence of significant moves towards single-table bargaining (Millward *et al.*, 1992, 362).

Shrinking collective bargaining

The coverage of collective bargaining has shrunk significantly and its scope has contracted. This is a major threat to unions. By 1990 less than 50% of employers were covered by collective bargaining compared with more than 70% in the 1970s. Even in establishments of 25 or more employees the *Workplace Industrial Relations Survey* found a highly significant drop in coverage from 71% in 1984 to 54% in 1990. This was:

one of the most dramatic changes in the character of British industrial relations that our survey has measured. The reductions from 64% to 51% in private manufacturing and from 41% to 33% in private services mean that in the private sector as a whole coverage dropped from a majority of employees (52%) to a minority of two fifths . . . In the public sector the fall has been equally stark: from 95% in 1984 to 78% in 1990 (Millward *et al.*, 1992, 93).

The proportion of establishments where unions were recognised for collective bargaining dropped by 20% between 1980 and 1990. Collective bargaining was not becoming rooted in new establishments and thus failing to keep up with structural and compositional change. 'Traditional patterns of industrial relations based on collective agreements' the government argues 'seem increasingly inappropriate' (DE, 1992). By 1994 the CBI was calling for a reappraisal of collective bargaining.

Decentralisation has continued. The number of workers covered by national agreements fell by a third in the decade to 1989. At least 16 major national bargaining groups covering more than a million employees were dismantled between 1986 and 1990 (Brown and Walsh, 1991, 49). In 1990 the end of historic national bargaining between the EEF and CSEU for engineering workers symbolised the trend. In 1991 the government announced termination of six national agreements covering more than half a million workers. Membership of employers' associations declined from 25% in 1979 to 13% in 1990. The move away from multi-employer bargaining led in some cases to enterprise level bargaining, in others to devolution to division, plant or profit centre and in others to employers de-recognising unions. Decentralisation was commonly associated with firm specific economic and organisational policies, attempts to individualise pay and conditions, introduce performance related

remuneration, enhance management control over wage determination and utilisation of labour, and strengthen moves to
internal labour markets. The emphasis has been on reducing the
importance of collective bargaining and relating more to product
markets, less to external labour markets (Purcell, 1991). However
the relationship between the growth of decentralised bargaining,
links between pay and performance and the development of
enhanced   management   control   has   been   questioned.
Fragmentation of bargaining and individualised pay setting
impose costs on management and can produce competitive bidding up and inflation in internal labour markets (Walsh, 1993).

There has, moreover, been a reduction in the scope of
bargaining. In 1980, 54% of managers reported negotiations at
establishment level over redeployment of labour – four years later
the figure had fallen to 29%. There was also decline in negotiations over working conditions, staffing levels and recruitment. By
the end of the decade

fewer issues were subject to joint regulation in 1990 than in 1980
although most of the change appears to have occurred in the early part of
the decade. . .the reduction in bargaining activity overall has been substantial (Millward and Stevens, 1986, 248; Millward *et al.*, 1992, 353).

Wages

A central objective of government policy has been reduction in the
rate of wage increases and a remaking of the processes of wage
determination. As then Employment Minister Kenneth Clarke
put it in 1986:

if we can move to a system where pay increases are based primarily on
performance, merit, company profitability and demand and supply in the
local labour market, we will dethrone once and for all the annual pay
round and the belief that pay increases do not have to be earned . . . At the
heart of our economic problems since the Second World War has been
the problem of paying ourselves more as a nation than we can afford in
higher productivity and output growth.

To achieve these ends the government has sought to deregulate
the market, removing props such as the Fair Wages Resolution

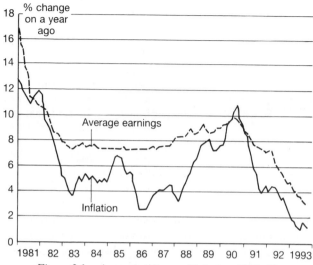

Figure 3.1   *Average earnings and inflation, 1980–93*
Source: Employment Gazette.

and the Wages Councils. An insistent emphasis was on the need to end multi-employer arrangements which curbed downward pressure on wages. Yet as can be seen from Figure 3.1 the 11-year reign of Mrs Thatcher produced a sustained increase in earnings despite unprecedented unemployment and legal restrictions. Average earnings lagged behind price increases in 1979, overtook then in 1980, dropped behind once more, but from 1982 ran ahead of inflation producing a faster rise in real earnings than in the 1970s, falling away again in the early 1990s. Moreover, earnings outstripped productivity in the 1980s producing increases in unit labour costs which undermined the competitive position of UK industry.

The Thatcher administrations were successful in expanding the distribution of earnings (Gregory and Thomson, 1990). There was some evidence that comparability was less important and employer performance more important in bargaining (Gregory *et al.*, 1985). As the second Conservative recession developed, earnings still outpaced prices. The year to March 1991 produced a 9.75% annual rate of average earnings growth. The *Financial Times* editorialised:

The British labour market seems as oblivious as ever to the realities of economic life. The economy is deep in what is now an officially recognised recession following two quarters of decline in gross domestic product; unemployment has been rising for ten consecutive months; and yet pay settlements show no sign of falling. The British labour market seems as inflexible as ever in the face of aggregate shock to the economy (quoted in Beaumont, 1992, 108).

As recession continued, average earnings fell significantly to their lowest levels for 25 years. But they remained ahead of inflation and the annual pay round and comparability remained entrenched. The Major government viewed the situation so seriously that in autumn 1992, with public sector pay outpacing the private sector, they introduced a policy of public sector pay restraint repeated in 1993. Pay restraint was successful but an admission of failure from a market oriented administration.

The vanishing strike?

Statistics demonstrate substantial decline in industrial conflict since 1979 and reflect the changed environment – and the erosion of coal, cars and the docks. The number of strikes declined sharply in the early 1980s and underlying decline continued to 1988. Thereafter an even sharper drop in the number of stoppages occurred (see Table 3.2). By 1990 they were running at 25% of the 1970s average and by 1993 at around 10%, with the lowest number of strikes recorded since statistics began. Working days lost declined more slowly, returning to the levels of the 1960s by the late 1980s and declining sharply thereafter. In the early 1980s there was substitution of overtime bans and other industrial action. By the 1990s all forms of industrial action had declined substantially and the aggressive picketing and secondary action of the 1960s and 1970s was mothballed. The strike was now a service sector – particularly public sector – phenomenon. In the 1980s the figures reflected an international pattern of decline (Brown and

Wadhwani, 1990). The later figures suggest Britain's decline is particularly steep. Britain since 1984 is well below the EU average and decline has continued through recession, upturn and recession. It seems legislation has had some impact (see Chapter 6) and behavioural change in strike prone industries is posited (Bird, 1993). Nonetheless national strikes and successful strikes were still occurring, such as the railway workers and ambulance workers stoppages in 1989. In 1993, 211 stoppages and 649,000 days lost contrasted with an average of 2,462 stoppages and 4.7 million days lost annually in the 1960s and 2,631 stoppages and 12.9 million days lost in the 1970s.

Table 3.2   *Strikes in the UK, 1980–93*

Year	No. of stoppages	Workers involved (000s)	Working days lost (000s)
1980	1,330	834	11,964
1981	1,338	1,513	4,266
1982	1,528	2,103	5,313
1983	1,364	574	3,754
1984	1,221	1,464	27,135
1985	903	791	6,402
1986	1,074	720	1,920
1987	1,014	887	3,546
1988	781	790	3,702
1989	701	727	4,128
1990	630	298	1,903
1991	369	176	761
1992	253	148	528
1993	211	385	649

Source: Employment Gazette.

The public sector

In the public sector governments have sought to cut public expenditure, decentralise and discredit collective bargaining and maximise commercialism. Through a variety of initiatives – the denial of union membership to 8,000 workers at GCHQ in 1984, the removal of teachers' collective bargaining rights in 1987, the undermining of responsibilities on public sector management to recognise unions, continuing pronouncements on the value of individual negotiations – the government has sought in stark contrast to its predecessors to de-legitimise collective bargaining. In the nationalised industries cash limits and political emphasis on reducing staffing and increasing productivity produced general souring in industrial relations. Local government has seen the introduction of compulsory competitive tendering, 'opting out' and local management of schools. In the NHS self-governing trusts have emerged with internal markets and the separation of purchaser and provider roles. Trade unionists in the civil service have seen 'hiving off', the creation of 'executive agencies' and 'market testing'. These measures possess potential for fragmenting and marginalising collective bargaining, individualising contracts and relating them to performance and weakening workplace organisation by isolating it from national organisation and hemming it in with financial controls. More than 1.5 million employees in the public sector are now covered by pay review bodies which marginalise collective bargaining whilst national bargaining structures have been weakened by the withdrawal of a number of local authorities.

The state has been successful in injecting a range of neo-Conservative approaches into public sector industrial relations since 1979. There has been job loss and enhanced management control (Pendleton and Winterton, 1993). Even where, as in local government or the railways, management has attempted to maintain co-operative relations the financial imperatives of government policy have propelled them into restructuring and confrontation. The judgement that industrial relations has become increasingly adversarial in local government (Laffin, 1989, 119) applies more generally across the public sector. Yet by the 1990s trade unionism remained a significant constraint. Average earnings in the early 1990s ran ahead of private sector pay. The unions were unable to foil pay restraint but the government was given a bloody nose over compulsory testing in schools the same year. Density is higher than in the private sector and since 1979 a number of unions – notably the components of UNISON – have maintained their membership. However the 1990 *Workplace Industrial Relations Survey* showed a decline in the incidence of workplace representatives from 84% of workplaces in 1984 to 73% in 1990. Ominously, the number of managers in central government strongly recommending union membership halved between 1984 and 1990.

From the government's viewpoint a major advantage of privatisation was that unions would be flushed out of their strongholds – 90% of public sector employees in 1979 were unionised. By 1982 the government was encountering opposition from NALGO over the sale of gas showrooms and from the unions in British Telecom. There were attempts to organise boycotts on sales of shares to the public and in 1983 the POEU took industrial action. To no avail. Selling-off was accompanied by contracting out. Local authorities and the health service were increasingly required to put services out to tender. A further aspect of restructuring has been the fragmentation of employment units evident in the deregulation of bus services, local management of schools and the introduction of subsidiaries splitting up the Post Office. In central government the introduction of over 50 agencies within the civil service is being linked to separate bargaining units and performance related pay (Smith and Morton, 1993).

Early estimates of the impact on unions were reasonably favourable (Curwen, 1986, 168–9). They have been outnumbered by studies demonstrating that employers have taken the opportunity to reduce the workforce, introduce contract labour and restructure collective bargaining arrangements. Studies of British Steel (Avis, 1990) and the electricity and water industries (Colling, 1991; O'Connell Davidson, 1990; Ogden, 1993) demonstrate the difficulties for the unions. But they have faced similar if not greater problems in non-privatised comparators (Leman and Winterton, 1991).

In certain cases the ability of the unions to threaten the profitability of a private company, particularly if it maintains a monopoly position, gives them more bargaining power than if they were threatening the government (Vickers and Yarrow, 1988, 159). However competitive tendering produces redundancies and intensification of work, sometimes accompanied by cuts in pay (Ascher, 1987, 103ff.). Reductions in pay of up to 50% and inferior conditions have been imposed on NHS ancillaries and school meals workers. It seems unarguable that 'CCT in local government has weakened the bargaining position of manual trade unions . . .', the decentralised bargaining which ensues 'represents a fragmentation of union power and ultimately a weakening of the unions' position' (Foster, 1993, 54). In most cases the unions are unable to influence the situation and resistance has been small scale (Kessler, 1991).

New technology

The introduction of microelectronic technology raises important issues for unions, notably job security, work content, job control, health and safety and remuneration. Its introduction has been more limited and uneven than is sometimes thought (Elger, 1990). From the late 1970s the TUC attempted to provide a concerted framework for union response. Although its overtures to the CBI for a joint approach were rebuffed, the TUC produced its own detailed policy document, *Employment and Technology*, in 1979. It took a neutral view of new technology, accepting its economic inevitability and benefits if its introduction was imprinted with union influence. The TUC perceived the issue as a means of extending collective bargaining into new areas, urging unions to become involved 'at the design stage' or before the decision to purchase and negotiate formal **new technology agreements**, institutionalising joint regulation of innovation. Early surveys demonstrated limited success for the unions: the growth of NTAs was limited, concentrated in white collar areas and already declining (Williams and Moseley, 1981).

It was clear that whilst unions were responding positively to new technology its introduction was largely a matter of managerial prerogative. Unions were informed and consulted, exercising modest influence on managerial goals. In the changed economic situation 'Hopes and aspirations of the late 1970s have not been fulfilled . . . in many cases management have felt that they can use their stronger bargaining power to push new technology through unilaterally' (LRD, 1983, 296). The efficacy of the TUC's formal agreement guidelines and conventional bargaining strategy was doubted and its lack of bite on the ground confirmed (Wilkinson, 1983). A survey of 240 agreements negotiated between 1977 and 1983 noted that both the adoption and content of NTAs had been restricted compared with the original TUC objectives. NTAs had only been actively pursued by a small minority of white collar unions. Whilst other unions might argue that they handled technological change under normal bargaining arrangements, it was the inadequacy of these arrangements in dealing with this specific problem which had prompted the TUC initiative in the first place. Only 11% of agreements provided for mutuality and there was doubt as to the extent to which the often vague procedural rights in NTAs were affecting the process of change in practice (Williams and Steward, 1985).

By 1986 NTAs had tailed off as the climate hardened (Batstone and Gourlay, 1986, 213). It was clear that change was not contingent upon union agreement and that representatives were involved in discussing the tactical detail of implementation rather than negotiating over purpose, job design and work organisation. Such participation often led to little change in management's initial planning (Willman and Winch, 1985; Dodgson and Martin, 1987). Union influence was often comparatively marginal with innovation dominated by management conceptions from start to finish so that managers could conclude: 'participation was a success and helped us in selling the changes we wanted' (Scarborough, 1986, 103). The influence workers had on technological innovation was sometimes exercised informally or by 'stealth' (Moore and Levie, 1985, 513). By the end of the decade such influence was seen as part of the growth of consultation: only 6% of managers negotiated with manual shop stewards over technological change (Price, 1988; Millward *et al.*, 1992, 254).

Union resistance to new technology has been an enduring stereotype. Yet numerous surveys have concluded it is unusual, indeed confined to a handful of industries such as the docks, newspapers and vehicles and generally unfruitful. Northcott and Rogers (1984), found only 7% of managers had encountered opposition. A more detailed study found pay increases in only a minority of cases and concluded: 'commentators should replace their stock phrases with references to *worker support for change* and *trade union support for change*' (Daniel, 1987, 263). New technology may involve the strategic undermining of union power and deskilling, as was the case with the NGA in printing. Alternatively it may provide conjunctural bargaining opportunities although it has potential for longer-term management control. It may diminish the power of some workers and increase employer dependence on others, strengthen management surveillance or worker autonomy. The evidence on deskilling remains disputed (Daniel, 1987; Thompson, 1989).

The evidence generally reinforces the view of unions as reactive and workplace bargaining since 1979 as weak and limited. Unions were handicapped by lack of resources in terms of co-ordinated organisation, research and technical acumen, and imaginative, proactive thinking. They have in consequence been accorded only a minimal role in the management of technical change and have exercised little influence over crucial decisions on the nature, shape and implementation of innovation. This failure has strengthened new technology as a force for control over work rather than its liberation. The lesson would appear to be that if they are to help in realising its liberating potential unions will have to look beyond consultation and collective bargaining.

Flexibility bargaining

Technological innovation is an inseparable part of a more general emphasis on work reorganisation to increase productivity. In the 1980s there was a new emphasis on flexibility bargaining and attempts to change working practices, 'job demarcations' and the deployment of labour while reducing the numbers employed.

Marsden and Thompson examined 137 agreements during 1980–87 which contained flexibility clauses covering 2.3 million workers concentrated in the private sector (Marsden and Thompson, 1990). Ingram reported that through the 1980s 25% of all wage settlements and a third of those involving trade unionists included change in working practices (1991).

Some deals received extensive publicity. 'New Deal at Rover' in 1992 emphasised the company's difficult competitive position and related acceptance to survival. It facilitated new multi-skill teamwork, quality control and continuing redundancies as part of the new 'lean production' system. There remain difficulties in getting a quantitative and qualitative grip on what is involved. For example, Daniel reported under 30% of employers attempting to change craft demarcations, 20% seeking to modify production maintenance demarcations and only 15% introducing multi-skilled craft workers. Only around a third of managers in surveys record changes in 'working practices' (Daniel, 1987, 75; Millward *et al.*, 1992, 334). The main emphasis had been on job demarcations and utilisation of labour; issues such as flexible working time, sub-contracting and temporary working have figured less prominently (Pollert, 1988). Flexibility bargaining seems to be still a minority trend.

But to what extent is *bargaining* involved? Marsden and Thompson distinguish changes in working methods introduced by management which then inevitably posed changes in working practices which were subject to agreement (1990, 85). But agreements may involve a strong measure of imposition and in other cases change in both 'methods' and 'practices' may be unilaterally imposed. It has been argued that companies move through a negotiated approach to a non-negotiated one (Cross, 1988, 9) and that employers took advantage of recession to impose reorganisation. Many flexibility deals were accomplished in the shadow of redundancy and closure. Fear of job loss has played a role as well as cash inducement: 'in many instances management felt that change could be more effectively introduced and employee co-operation encouraged if it were linked to an increase in pay' (Ingram, 1991, 5). In many cases observed change is formally 'by agreement', but union involvement expresses management discretion not union power, the principles of change are 'non-negotiable' and even details of implementation are 'discussed' with the power balance weighed against an 'unconstructive' response. Representatives unable to resist flexibility initiatives have sought to extract what they can. In a position of profitability management have been willing to purchase continuing co-operation as much as initial implementation. It was often opined in the 1960s that a move from consultation to bargaining was a sign of shop steward strength. Are we now seeing a journey in the opposite direction indicating growing weakness? What often seems to be involved is consultation over details rather than negotiation over principles.

Initiatives since the 1980s echo the productivity deals of the 1960s and early 1970s. Now, as then, they appear to involve piecemeal, opportunistic attempts at reform rather than the holistic transformative approach urged by theorists. Nonetheless the impact for many trade unionists this time around has been real. One Longbridge worker claimed he had worked in five different departments over a year and performed 10 different jobs in 3 months:

In the past management couldn't shift you without the agreement of the union; now it's done without consultation . . . it means that you never get to know any of the blokes, it breaks up any unity. In the old days the target was set by timing the operators; now the target is based on the gross potential of the machine. That means they set the machine as fast as possible and you have to keep up with it. They give you targets you can't reach. The gaffer comes to check your counter every hour; blokes have been suspended for failing to have an adequate explanation of why they haven't reached their target (Armstrong *et al.*, 1984, 396–7).

The evidence from the Percentage Utilisation of Labour Index, which measures intensity of labour, and academic studies favours the view that workers are working harder (Bennett and Smith-Gavine, 1988; Edwards and Whitston, 1991). In many cases management has won real concessions. Elger demonstrates that whilst flexibility initiatives have involved a mix of bargaining and

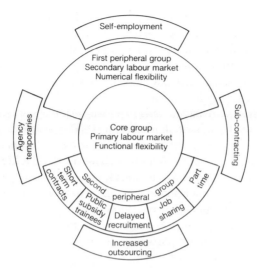

Figure 3.2   *The flexible firm*
Source: Atkinson, 1985.

imposition, the consequence is a reassertion of management pre-rogative, changes in staffing levels, job demarcation and intensification of labour (Elger, 1991). There is no guarantee that these changes guarantee enhanced productivity over the long term. But a repeat of the earlier productivity deals when one set of job controls was 'bought out' only for another set to appear looks unlikely. In the 1990s workplace representatives are weaker and modern initiatives have greater determination behind them.

Core and periphery

An attempt has been made to systematise changes in technology, work organisation and the labour force in the model of the **'flexible firm'** (see Figure 3.2). In this model core workers are motivated by high wages and job security designed to commit them to the organisation. They are skilled, consisting of groups such as managers, designers, sales staff and craft-workers. Their permanent position requires identification with employer goals.

Core employees are subject to **functional flexibility**. They must be ready to adapt to changes in technology, and work organisation, handling different jobs and working in multi-disciplinary teams. This can mean retraining and career change. All core employees have single status and pay systems reward performance and adaptability.

Core groups are insulated from the wider labour market and are analogous to Japan's 'lifetime employees'. The peripheral groups' jobs are not 'firm specific'; they can be resourced from outside. These groups answer the requirement for **numerical flexibility**. This permits the employer to quickly and inexpensively increase or reduce the labour force through part-time and temporary workers. **Flexibility of time** involves shift patterns, flexitime, '9-day fortnights' and 'annual hours'. **Financial flexibility** demands a greater proportion of remuneration linked to performance.

The **first peripheral group** is directly employed, often less skilled workers filling clerical, supervisory, assembly jobs. They may be full-time, but can be hired and fired at limited cost, possess little security and few prospects. The **second peripheral group** consists of part-time workers and those employed on short-term contracts. The jobs of the **external groups** are not firm specific. They may involve accountancy skills or cleaning or catering, and the employers' needs can be met by sub-contracting, specialist employment agencies or self-employed workers. This approach answers the needs of **numeric flexibility** and **functional flexibility** as the outside agency will be competitive, specialised and committed.

Those who developed the concept of the flexible firm insist it is only a model (Atkinson, 1985, 14). It is sometimes advanced as an exciting innovation in the interests of workers generally. Flexibility of time, for example, is extrapolated from its essential context of deregulation and its benefits in terms of greater choice for workers, particularly women, and a richer fit between work and home, foregrounded. It should be embraced and regulated, not resisted. The difficulty, as a range of unions have discovered, is that management believe that to civilise flexibility is to change its

nature: part-time employment is rarely available in pro-rata relation to full-time employment and the means of regulation remain
elusive. For in today's economy flexibility is about deregulation,
low pay, working harder, not personal empowerment. Whilst the
1994 House of Lords judgment that the qualifying period for
unfair dismissal and redundancy pay must be reduced for part-
time workers from 5 years to 2 was welcome it affected only
500,000 out of 5 million part-timers and represented a minimal
improvement (Hewitt, 1993; Huws *et al.*, 1989).

Flexibility has been criticised from a number of angles. Firstly
the extent of empirical change is challenged. Initiatives on 'functional flexibility' have been limited to a minority of enterprises.
They have rarely involved multi-skilling (Cross, 1988), more
often job enlargement with workers working harder on an
extended and sometimes deskilled agenda (Pollert, 1988). The
growth of numerical flexibility, the emergence of part-time work,
short-term contracts, sub-contracting and outworking involves
discrete forms of atypical employment generated in specific contexts, not an integrated category. Studies demonstrate limited
growth in temporary contracts and sub-contracting and establish
that such practices were often used before 1980. Half the establishments surveyed record no change, even a decline in sub-
contracting; more establishments recorded decline or no change
in use of temporary workers than reported an increase
(Marginson, 1991; Wood and Smith, 1989).

Secondly, the nature and provenance of what uneven change
there has been is questioned. Functional flexibility has not
improved skills or employee satisfaction. Its inspiration lies more
in labour intensification than improving the quality of working life.
Numerical flexibility owes more to high unemployment and structural change in industry – which constitute problems for
employees – than to management planning. It is best characterised not by its benign flexibility but by its insecurity and
vulnerability. Even with the core workforce management is out-
sourcing key functions such as research and development. Their
record on training generally questions the core-periphery distinction.

Thirdly, it is clear that the change that has occurred is pragmatic and reactive. There is no new vision. Flexibility is a tactical
survival plan related to recession, harder markets and changes in
the labour force, not a coherent management strategy. What is
usually involved is pragmatic opportunism on the part of management: the flexible firm model lacks conviction. Employers are in
some cases using secondary labour as a supplement to their
existing labour force, not a substitute for it. Temporary work is
often a passport to full-time employment not an alternative to it.
Employers use self-employed workers not to increase flexibility
but to enlist specialist skills. Two recessions in a decade do not
augur well for the establishment of a stable 'core'. In current
conditions few firms can guarantee jobs for life. New forms of
employment celebrated by Thatcherism are not underpinned by
economic stability and remain precarious.

Unions are unlikely to be confronted by the academic model
but more fragmented initiatives: less than 10% of establishments
are core-periphery strategists (Hunter and McInnes, 1992).
These initiatives – as distinct from a regulated worker oriented
flexibility which is not presently available – are not as sometimes
presented pro-labour, but instruments of management control.
Specific innovations may be potentially helpful to unions but
require negotiation, refinement and policing. Again wider
scenarios such as the promise that the AEEU would successfully
pursue restrictionist strategies excluding weaker groups from the
primary work force remain unfulfilled.

Human resource management

The waning of collective bargaining has led to elaboration of new
organisation-specific approaches and suggestions that they are
replacing traditional models. 'No strike/single union' deals, flexibility, employee involvement and alleged greater identification of
workers with the market have been glued together and dubbed the
'new industrial relations'. They are seen as underpinned by
changes in workers' ideology and attitudes: a move from collectivism and independent trade unionism to individualism and

identification with enterprise goals is posited (Bassett, 1986).

Growing attention has been paid to human resource management, re-emphasising the workplace as a unitary enterprise and urging the need to pay greater attention to human resources, engage their commitment and creativity in management goals and integrate them into a more strategic corporate approach. 'Japanisation' is another much touted approach based upon impressions of Japan's industrial success. It is suggested that British managers have much to learn from organisation culture, internal labour markets, group responsibility and total quality management, with an emphasis on 'customer first' and mission statements and 'continuous improvement' and 'drive to excel' attitudes to production. 'Just in time' and 'lean' production methods related to new technology and team and cellular working are all part of the attempt to create a new committed production culture.

If some theories of flexibility have more to do with the business school classroom than the shopfloor, theorists of 'the new industrial relations' and HRM likewise lend too much credence to change. The evidence demonstrates that whilst management is paying more attention to a strategic approach to labour, smoke remains more prevalent than fire: 80% of top personnel managers claimed to have a human resources strategy but less than half could outline it (Marginson *et al.*, 1988). Quality circles remain very much a minority phenomenon – in around 700 enterprises by the end of the 1980s – and by 1990 only 35% of establishments claimed regular meetings of work groups (Millward *et al.*, 1992, 167). Team briefing, central to new communications techniques, is reported in only 400–500 establishments although it seems to be on the increase (Storey and Sisson, 1990). There is, moreover, little evidence that these initiatives are successful. Quality circles have proved of limited value in changing employee attitudes and improving communication (Hill, 1991).

There has been some increase in strategic selection and appraisal (Grint, 1993). Performance related pay is spreading; the merit element remains a small proportion of total pay (Kinnie and Lowe, 1990). Around 45% of establishments had some form of individual pay in 1990 and around a third merit pay (Millward *et al.*, 1992, 262). Such systems are costly to administer, criteria are questioned and extension of the merit component is questionable. They are sometimes related to derecognition, and demoralise and demotivate the workforce (Kessler and Purcell, 1992; Thompson, 1993). Studies of a range of initiatives, profit sharing, autonomous working groups and quality circles suggest that whilst workers may favour them on specific instrumental grounds they make little impact on 'them' and 'us' attitudes or individual–collective distinctions. Workers lack choice over participation and initiatives lack institutional support among senior managers (Kelly and Kelly, 1991).

A detailed study of 15 major employers found many of the components of HRM present but they were not combined in a holistic strategic way (Storey, 1992). Changes in management practice were considerable although what seems to be involved is a series of *ad hoc* human resource responses to particular contexts. This is perhaps because the conditions which have produced the ideal type HRM enterprises – the IBMs and Hewlett Packards – are not readily available or easily constructed. The lack of attention to training and high quality managerial and production systems in Britain may be simply a function of its growing status as an unskilled cheap labour economy. For example, the proportion of income spent on education and training was smaller in 1988 than a decade earlier (Finegold and Soskice, 1988). In the USA the alleged transformation from industrial relations to HRM developed in very different conditions; unions are weaker and had been weaker for longer (Kochan *et al.*, 1986).

Nonetheless, HRM and Japanisation initiatives represent real problems for unions. Some, such as the AEEU, enthusiastically embrace the new trends in the spirit of collaboration and business unionism: this is the only way to attract jobs and keep members. Others, like the GMB, have sought to reconcile them with collective bargaining. The TGWU, impressed with the potency of TQM (cf. Hill, 1991), has changed its policy from 'business as usual' to 'positive engagement' with the new managerialism. Lucio and Weston detect three emphases in the unions' response.

Social partnership stemming from 'realism' characterises the emphasis of the TUC and AEEU on working with management in a human resource framework. **Extending collective bargaining** strongly informs GMB statements whilst the TGWU is seen as a leader amongst unions emphasising **union independence** and regulative surveillance. They discern in the shifting and pragmatic union response a move from opposition to attempted regulation of HRM (Lucio and Weston, 1992). Generally:

there has been a growing understanding that the HRM approach of more directly targetting the individual not just to enhance skills but restructure attitudes to quality of product and service and responsiveness to consumer need (by altering the focus away from the collective) could prove to be the major challenge facing unions over coming years (TUC, 1991a).

Studies have demonstrated new approaches can threaten representation and independence and weaken stewards' bargaining activities. However new information systems, colonisation of the new Company Advisory Council and election of additional stewards in teamworking areas may limit the impact of HRM (Heaton and Linn, 1989; Spencer, 1989). New approaches facing the enormous task of changing low trust culture to high trust culture depend on a complex mix of internal and external factors (Garrahan and Stewart, 1992) – as shown in Nissan's decision in 1993 to cut its labour force. The success of HRM is not predestined; nor is it foredoomed.

Moreover, whilst HRM is intended to displace industrial relations, in Britain it seems to be growing *alongside* workplace trade unionism rather than taking its place. Employers seem to be neglecting the unions in favour of HRM, not using HRM to remove the unions. We can conclude that despite the reverses of the neo-Conservative years for workplace trade unionism:

no new pattern of employee representation emerged to replace trade union representation. There was no sign of a new form of industrial relations system to replace the old. Indeed where new forms were adopted they were more commonly a complement to trade union representation rather than a substitute filling a gap left by its decline (Millward *et al.*, 1992, 350).

But if HRM and the 'new industrial relations' have not become dominant or played a major role in transforming ideology and institutions there can be few grounds for complacency on the part of unions. Success in HRM initiatives can *marginalise or co-opt* workplace unionism. More managements are demonstrating an interest in HRM, and if workplace unionism continues to weaken, its attractions may become more potent. As one survey concludes:

even without the new initiatives trade unions would have experienced a hard time during this period. But the existence of an 'alternative' rendered the situation rather more precarious. The marginalisation of the unions took on a greater significance than it might otherwise have been seen to carry. Bypassing union channels appeared symptomatic of investment in the human resource strategy. In reality that commitment was frequently missing but the possibility that it might come about stoked up union fears (Storey, 1992, 261).

Workplace organisation under pressure

All these changes as well as the extensive legislative change (Chapter 6) have had an impact on workplace organisation. There is less of it. The 1986 *Workplace Industrial Relations Survey* found an increase in the number of shop stewards from 317,000 in 1980 to 335,000 in 1984. This represented an increase of 30% in the public sector and 18% in private services and a decrease of 27% in manufacturing. The 1990 survey did not quantify the number of representatives, but recorded a 'substantial decline' since 1984:

the late 1980s saw fewer lay representatives – the most basic building blocks of local trade union organisation. The fall was widespread affecting workplaces of all types but particularly smaller workplaces and those with low levels of union membership (Millward *et al.*, 1992, 143).

In the early 1980s decline was related to closure and redundancy. Stewards are now disappearing from functioning enterprises; this is related to the fall in density. The changes which are debilitating unions at the workplace are structural and compositional. The decline in areas of union power such as manufacturing and large workplaces generally and the growth of areas of union weakness such as the service sector, small workplaces and part-time workers is sapping trade unionism at the roots (Millward *et al.*, 356). The continuing decline of groups such as dockers, miners and engineering workers, with strong solidaristic traditions means we cannot take quality as constant and simply examine change in quantitative terms. Ominously the survey found that in the second half of the 1980s the decline in density was not simply related to employment trends, legislation or increasing employer hostility but to 'weakening support for unionism among employees' (Millward *et al.*, 102). These trends are likely to have intensified in the recession of the early 1990s.

Where workplace organisation remains it looks as it did in the 1970s and in some cases is more formally sophisticated than in the 1960s. The closed shop is dwindling into insignificance. But there has been little change in size of constituencies; methods of election; time off; facilities; and the existence of full-time stewards and check-off. There appears to be stability in Joint Shop Stewards' Committees and Combine Committees although stewards were less likely to be competitively elected. But new pressures are accumulating. The decline in size of enterprise, and in the public sector deregulation of services, CCT, NHS Trusts and local management of schools are fragmenting cohesion, encouraging commercialism and challenging the role of workplace representatives. Workplace organisation is hemmed in by anti-union legislation and undermined by removal of individual protections.

It is possible to project balkanisation with growing 'union free' areas co-existing with those with stable union organisation under pressure as workplace representatives fail to root themselves in new establishments. The fact that stewards are established in fewer workplaces means that workplace organisation is less of a defining characteristic of British industrial relations. Moreover, full-time officers are more involved than in earlier decades and have 'assumed a larger role in workplace matters than before'. In workplaces, where lay representatives have declined or disappeared, full-time officers now directly represent members to a greater extent. And contact between stewards and full-time officers is increasing across the board (Millward *et al.*, 1992, 114, 144).

If, in general, 'shop stewards have a more defensive role than in the past' (Edwards, 1987, 147) we can still point to examples of thriving workplace organisation (Cohen and Fosh, 1988; Fosh, 1993). Dependent on product markets, reconstruction of production and work organisation can increase employers' need for co-operation and enhance stewards' bargaining leverage. However in the context of survey evidence talk of renewal of trade unionism at the workplace in any general sense seems over-optimistic. Such renewal, it is suggested, 'is possible', 'is always on the agenda', 'may be unfolding in the current period' (Fosh, 1993, 589; Fairbrother and Waddington, 1990, 16; Fairbrother, 1990, 150). Evidence for these broad assertions of what is grandiosely termed 'the workplace renewal-of-unionism thesis' is slender and drawn from a small number of case studies, some of which highlight weak workplace organisation – 3 out of 5 in one study (Cohen and Fosh, 1988). Similarly, the assertion that in the public sector 'increasing workplace autonomy as bargaining has become increasingly decentralised' evidences resilience (Fairbrother and Waddington, 1990, 40, 42) appears mistaken. 'Coercive fragmentation' seems a better way of describing what is happening in the public sector. Apart from the evidence of erosion of organisation, decentralisation diminishes the real utility of national co-ordination and the deployment of external power unavailable in the enterprise. It is a sign of weakness, not strength (Colling, 1993; Foster, 1993).

The strength of workplace organisation has often been related to wage movements and the resilience of real earnings for most of the period since 1979 does not suggest a battered and depleted union movement. We have to note however the burgeoning of concessionary bargaining (Ingram, 1991). Moreover, workers are working harder and workplace organisation has proved unable to resist restructuring and intensification of labour. Engagement between stewards and managers increasingly smacks of consultation rather than negotiation. Employers have been able to exploit the insecurity of workplace representatives and 'the fear

factor' to produce not a fundamental transformation of production relations but piecemeal incremental gains in productivity
(Nolan, 1989, 1992). Despite change in the balance of power at
the workplace, with increasing productivity and rising profits,
employers have been willing to pay for co-operation. However,
workers have financed their own wage increases by working
harder (Carruth and Oswald, 1989). And comparative evidence
demonstrates Britain remains a low wage economy despite rhetoric about 'productivity breakthroughs' (Nolan, 1989).

Economists disagree on the impact unions have on wage
settlements. There is now agreement on the maintenance of the
union mark-up, the differential between union determined and
non-union determined wages, in recent years, although some find
it declined and others associate it with the closed shop (Stewart,
1991, 365; Gregg and Machin, 1992). But some economists – and
the TUC – argue that the crucial push on wages comes not from
unions but from management faced with skill shortages, poor
training and armed with increased profits and cultural pre-
disposition to purchase co-operation. In this view unions are
pushing at an open door. Against this the *Workplace Industrial
Relations Survey* has little doubt that union pressures continue to
have 'a significant impact' (Millward *et al.*, 1992, 354). If it is
difficult to make general judgements about workplace organisation on the basis of wage movements in a situation of buoyant
profitability, the same goes for taking the decline in strikes as
evidence of increasing weakness. In the 1980s it might be argued
that workers did not need to strike as they were achieving satisfactory settlements. However in the 1990s wage increases have
declined – and so have strikes.

Restriction of the scope of bargaining and restoration of
management prerogative over issues like recruitment, staffing
levels and deployment of labour underlines the decline in shop
steward power. For the power of stewards in the past was based
not only on ability to achieve increases in pay but on the control
they exercised over work, on **mutuality**, the ability to negotiate
over staffing, deployment of labour and pace of work (Leijnse,
1980, 68; Coates, 1989, 48). In these areas, as the *Workplace*

Industrial Relations Survey demonstrates, management have regained a measure of control. And 'in many workplaces such an enhancement of managerial prerogatives in redirecting labour has been accompanied by more direct labour intensification' (Elger, 1991, 56).

Managers still recognise unions as a constraint: 14% of managers overall, 26% in workplaces with recognised unions, report agreements with unions as a constraint and 5% overall, 10% in workplaces with recognised unions, cite opposition from stewards as a constraint (Millward *et al.*, 1992). This hardly suggests strong union control. In this situation managers have not attempted to destroy workplace organisation but to manoeuvre and orchestrate it. They have often been willing to avoid the costs of conflict by purchasing co-operation but in this process workplace representatives are 'able to secure only minor modifications in the changes required' (CBI, 1987).

Researchers in the early 1980s found formal continuity in workplace organisation and were reluctant to hypothesise increasing weakness in performance (Batstone, 1984; Terry, 1986; Marginson *et al.*, 1988). Morris and Wood (1991) suggest that some survey questions lent themselves to 'no change' responses and that more intensive examination discloses decreasing importance attributed to collective bargaining and greater management assertion aimed at reducing the influence of shop stewards in this period. The evidence now seems to suggest that on the ebbtide of the 1980–82 recession managers using productivity gains to offset wage increases with higher profits and ability to pay facilitating concessions, began to tighten control over work and performance standards and reasserted the right to manage. There has been readjustment in the balance of power as a consequence of the new political economy of *laissez-faire*. In some sectors it is clear and marked. In others it is limited and tenuous. But it is real even where workplace organisation looks much as it did in the 1970s. Change at work is still usually by agreement. That agreement is often shallow, elicited from stewards in a balance of forces unfavourable to opposition. Under formality lies an element of imposition.

The point is reinforced by case studies which argue that, on a range of issues including wages, the process of bargaining became increasingly ritualistic, with outcomes decided in advance by management (Chadwick, 1983). Terry found continuity in management support for workplace organisation and bargaining, but this provided a vehicle for significant management gains in destaffing, overtime, deployment of labour and pace of work (Terry, 1989). In the public sector, workplace organisation has been outmanoeuvred. As Colling remarks of local government:

The expected diminution of trade union influence was also apparent . . . Unions were weakened by the dramatic decentralisation of decision making away from national level where their power base lay. Union representatives were unable to defend the terms and conditions of their members to the extent that was possible prior to CCT (Colling, 1993, 11).

An in-depth study of 15 employers in 1988 concluded:

the general picture was one of some measure of stability in that there had typically been no covert all out assault on unions or collective agreements. Nonetheless in every case these systems were under some threat. One saw this fairly markedly, for example at Plessey, Austin Rover, British Rail, Bradford Council, Jaguar and Lucas. It seemed that a generally cool if not outrightly hostile stance towards trade unions and industrial relations was characteristic in these mainstream organisations at this time (Storey, 1992, 261).

Some see growing potential for 'enterprise trade unionism'. Shop stewards, it is claimed, are becoming detached from the wider union and integrated more with management.

This does not necessarily mean that they necessarily become more docile but that they identify their interests more with the success of the enterprise and less with the job controls, employment anxieties and concern for the poorly organised of the wider union. The structure of trade unionism originally developed for the strategies of employee solidarity is increasingly being shaped to the needs of employers (Brown, 1986, 165).

The sudden increase in unemployment after 1980 administered a shock to workers. Even if TGWU leader Ron Todd's statement, '3 million on the dole and 23 million scared to death' exaggerated the situation, *the fear factor* was real and enduring. In what has been *not simply a changed market situation, but a changed political economy of industrial relations*, it is plausible that by the mid-1980s calculative stewards were accepting management imperatives to a greater degree than hitherto (cf. Terry, 1986, 177) and that this process has continued. 'Them' and 'us' remain, but 'us' is now on most calculations increasingly dependent on 'them'. In this situation more employers are looking at derecognition. The threat from employers is intensifying in the 1990s (Smith and Morton, 1993). In some cases integration through HRM also threatens workplace organisation. Assimilation of stewards as team leaders and collective organisation to the improvement of production, incorporation rather than marginalisation, would seem the more effective trajectory. Constraints clearly exist – an internal enterprise orientation can make employers dependent on workers and increase union bargaining power; the future of independent workplace organisation will depend on their mobilisation. Overall, the landscape is bleak. There are fewer workplace representatives than at the end of the 1970s. They bargain only for a minority of employees over a reduced agenda in the face of weakening support for trade unionism. Despite differences across industry, trade unionism in the workplace has in terms of any general estimation weakened in the years of neo-*laissez-faire*.

Conclusions

Labour's policies brought inherent deficiencies of workplace organisation to the surface; 1979 represented a real break. The growing movement of state policy from weakening collective bargaining to the exclusion of unions has been reflected indirectly in the workplace but employer hostility is now on the increase. Change was limited in the early 1980s. Since then we have seen a debilitation of workplace trade unionism. Density, the closed shop, the number of representatives, coverage and scope of bargaining, the incidence of industrial action, all declined. Workplace representatives proved incapable of resisting intensification of labour or achieving union objectives over new technology. Collective bargaining has been decentralised, formalised, calibrated to a greater degree with management goals. The evidence underplays the difficulties for it takes little account of the recession of the 1990s. The picture remains uneven. In what was the public sector, the civil service and local government, workplace organisation has found it difficult to respond to government measures. Employment relations have become more adversarial, although unions have maintained density and formal organisation reasonably well. But they have been on the defensive as the balance of power has shifted. We are still unable to take stock of the full extent of change generated by privatisation and deregulation. The picture in the private sector is also mixed. In some areas workplace organisation has declined, in others it looks very much like it did in 1979. But the substance of power has flaked. Management, its prerogatives restored, has made few attempts to uproot it, preferring to neglect or utilise it and willing to pay for the privilege. Whilst new technology and new production methods may increase management dependence and in some cases union bargaining power, management attitudes to unions are becoming more hostile in the 1990s.

Across all sectors there has been significant change but *as yet* not transformation of the system. As calculative bargainers, workplace representatives have come to terms with the new world. But if workplace organisation is more employer dependent no alternative has been installed. The 'union free' concept is a growing, largely sweatshop phenomenon outside the management area. Flexibility is a more limited, less organised trend than some assert. There is little evidence of the rooting of the enterprise culture: adversarial attitudes remain along with adversarial structures. Here the unions can take some encouragement. The buoyancy of wages remains a problem for the state. However decline in groups with strong traditions of workplace power and democracy raises questions about the future quality of workplace trade unionism and its specific weight within unions. From the government's point of view progress has been slow and incremental; its basis in economic and legal coercion, rather than consent and commitment, leave doubts as to its permanency.

Further reading

Eric Batstone, Ian Boraston, and Stephen Frenkel, *Shop Stewards in Action*, Blackwell, 1977, and Eric Batstone, *Working Order*, Blackwell, 1984, have a lot of useful information and analysis of workplace organisation before 1979. Huw Beynon's *Working for Ford*, Penguin, 1973, 1984, is the classic case study, whilst Alan Thornett, *From Militancy to Marxism*, Left View Books, 1987, gives a participant's eye-view. Neil Millward, Mark Stevens, David Smart, Bill Hawes, *Workplace Industrial Relations in Transition*, Dartmouth, 1992, is the most up to date and extensive survey. Richard Hyman, *Strikes*, Macmillan, 1989, is invaluable. Anna Pollert, ed., *Farewell to Flexibility*, Blackwell, 1991, deals comprehensively with this debate. John Storey, *Developments in the Management of Human Resources*, Blackwell, 1992, provides a good introduction to the latest management panacea.

4

Union democracy and equal rights

Union democracy has occupied a key position in recent political debate. From both left and right, it has been argued, unions fail to reflect the interests of their members. Since 1984 Conservative governments have felt the limitations of union democracy required state intervention and thus introduced a rolling pro- gramme intended to 'give the unions back to the members'. The TUC has hit back at critics by arguing that problems are inevitable in a movement of 8 million members continually confronting contentious and complex decisions. The unions, it points out, are more democratic than the city, the civil service or the media. Nobody elects the House of Lords or the judiciary. The Con- servatives ruled Britain from 1979 with little over 40% of the popular vote. The case against the unions is a hollow one. Are unions controlled by their members? Are leaders sincere demo- crats, in the words of the TUC, 'accountable to their members every day of the week'? Or do they merit the scathing opinion of Norman Tebbit who believes that 'by comparison with such trade union leaders the late Duke of Wellington looks like a trendy liberal'? This chapter explores the issues.

Members and their unions

Workers join unions to protect themselves at work – but not all workers join unions. The decision is related to personal beliefs and the employment situation. Some assume joining is calculative: workers perceive organisation as an answer to inflation or job loss, weigh specific benefits of membership or possess a moral or political belief in unions (Bain, 1970; Crouch, 1982). Other research emphasises tradition, significant events and social norms: workers join unions because of family or workplace norms, because they 'feel they have to' or because 'everybody else is in the union'. This is not only because of the closed shop – high proportions join because of social pressures not perceived as coercive (Goldthorpe *et al.*, 1968, 97). A range of surveys over a long period emphasise members' attachment to unions is instrumental but they endorse collectivism, are highly supportive of unions, prioritise benefits from collective bargaining, although in only around a quarter of cases is there strong moral or ideological commitment (Kerr, 1992). Other studies find strong intrinsic beliefs in trade unionism and emphasise the dangers of dichotomising solidaristic and instrumental attachments (Fosh, 1981).

It has been suggested that a change has occurred: 'individualism now outweighs collectivism in what union members want' (Bassett and Cave, 1993, 7). This is based on a survey in which more than 70% cited advice on discipline and legal assistance as reasons for joining, compared with only 62% crediting negotiation of pay. In reality the research referred to found 95% of members characterised the statement 'NUPE negotiates my pay and conditions' as 'very important/important' compared with 98% prioritising disciplinary protection and 56% prioritising financial benefits (Kerr, 1992, 45). Resolution of disciplinary and grievance issues depends ultimately on 'collectivism'. And there is little support for a new individualism in other research. One survey found the two top ranked reasons for membership were: 'To protect me if problems come up' (93%), and 'To get higher pay and better conditions' (80%) (Millward, 1990, 34). Another study commented:

Has a new individualism and new management practices affected the reasons why people join unions? The simple answer is that this does not seem to be the case. Reasons for joining remain in a largely traditional mould dominated by workers' perceptions of a need for support at work

when problems arise. . .the three most commonly cited reasons for joining were pay and conditions, individual support and a belief in trade
unionism (Whitston and Waddington, 1992, 3).

There does not appear to be a gulf between the attitudes of
members and non-members: non-members do not appear to be
anti-union and high proportions cite reasons such as the
unavailability of unions or their inability to help them, as reasons
for not belonging (Kerr, 1992, 49; Gallie, 1989, 2). We should not
under-estimate the degree of 'principled' ideological support for
trade unionism or the influence of custom and tradition (Booth,
1985) but the attachment of most members is still best characterised – it probably always was – as 'instrumental collectivism'
(Goldthorpe *et al.*, 1968, 106). Most members *do* view their union
differently than they view their insurance company. Individual
work benefits and financial packages are largely incidental: 'no
more than a marginal influence on reasons for joining' (Whitston
and Waddington, 1992, 3). If this is so, it is far from clear unions
need 'to rebalance their traditional mix of the individual and the
collective and to meet the new individual demand' by turning
themselves into private service organisations like the AA (Bassett
and Cave, 1993, 8). Nonetheless, the view of members and
potential members as passive consumers has proved influential.

Nor is there a wide gulf between the attitudes of members and
shop stewards, although the latter tend more to collective
orientations (Nicholson *et al.*, 1981; Fosh, 1981). There are
differences in participation. Once again this represents continuity
rather than change. As long ago as the 1940s surveys found only
3% of members attending meetings and only 1% active in the
branch. Most members reacted passively and saw stewards as
their only contact with the union (Goldstein, 1952, 264). Twenty
years later studies found 7% attending branch meetings, 26%
voting in branch elections but 83% voting for shop stewards, and
the picture did not seem to have changed two decades after that
(Goldthorpe *et al.*, 1968, 101; Daniel and Millward, 1983, 85).

The position varied: in the 1970s around 5% of members were
estimated to attend NUPE branch meetings; and around 30%,

NALGO's more infrequent meetings (Fryer *et al.*, 1974). Whilst national elections provided an impetus for periodic participation it remained minority participation. Between 1972 and 1982 the average turnout for elections of officers in the AEU varied between 24% and 38%. In the GMB the figure was nearer 10% (Eaton and Gill, 1983). Voting for the General Secretary of the TGWU produced a turnout of only 40% whilst in the NUM it was nearer 80%. Workplace and postal ballots produced higher involvement than branch ballots but participation outside the workplace remained a minority phenomenon.

Activism is related to quality of commitment to trade unionism, but we should not forget that many members participate in informal ways: reading union literature, talking to stewards, raising and supporting grievances. They demonstrate commitment to collectivism selectively by attending meetings on wage negotiations or taking industrial action. And the view that unions *should be* democratic and open to participation remains pervasive despite increased emphasis on servicing members.

A question of democracy

The outline of decision-making mechanisms in Chapter 1 shows how union democracy works on paper. Practice is more messy and sometimes unedifying, for unions operate in a political culture which legitimises manipulation and pursuit of power without too many scruples. 'Mr Smith might just scrape home', *The Financial Times* explained regarding the 1993 Labour Party Conference, 'if unions such as NUPE, UCW and USDAW all wriggle out of conference commitments to reject reform and instead back him.' Conference is, we are told, the unions' supreme policy making body and USDAW's 1993 Conference voted to oppose Mr Smith's reforms. A few months later its Labour Party delegation disregarded union policy and supported Mr Smith – and they were not alone in ignoring the wishes of their members. All kinds of pressures are sometimes brought to bear to ensure democratic processes produce the right results. A report of the NUJ's 1987 Conference states:

The NUJ came under intense pressure at the TUC to remit its motion criticising the TUC's international department. 'Before it came on the agenda we had pressure put on by Norman Willis and Mike Walsh (head of the TUC's international department). Ron Todd, General Secretary of the TGWU, almost tore my head off. After we remitted the motion other unions did come up and say they would have supported us', TUC delegate Colin Bourne said.

The union's TUC delegation was censured but it was then too late to affect the issue. This is a relatively common occurrence at the TUC. As Hugh Clegg observed of the 1960s and 1970s:

the General Council dominates Congress ... unless the Council is divided it is not easy for Congress to initiate policy for if it were to pass a positive resolution contrary to the Council's wishes the Council could ignore it or make only the smallest gesture towards its fulfilment (1979, 336).

Union conferences can often be managed in similar fashion. They are sometimes too large and unwieldy to exercise much influence on the detail of policy. Real power, some would argue, is concentrated in the Executive. It is difficult if not impossible for branches to influence the Executive on a month-to-month basis. They can interpret conference decisions to their own satisfaction or argue that changed circumstances have rendered their realisation redundant and weather the storm at the next Conference when it is perhaps too late to do anything about the original issue. For example, the 1986 Conference of the NUJ instructed its Executive to instigate disciplinary action against members working at Rupert Murdoch's Wapping plant. The Executive promised to carry out the members' wishes but reported back to the 1987 Conference that it had been unable to do so for 'it had discovered procedural difficulties'.

Or perhaps, particularly where the executive is a lay one, real power resides not in the executive but in the General Secretary or President. The TGWU for decades bore the stamp of its architect Ernest Bevin. He believed, like his successor, that *power flowed downwards*, officers and Executive were there to execute his instructions and 'the lay members must be conscious that there are certain things they cannot do and that they must leave the officers to carry out the tasks in which they are employed to specialise, the lay member supplementing this work and thereby making a very happy combination' (Allen, 1957, 84).

Elections may change things; but they too can be managed. The EETPU in the 1970s and 1980s provided a classic example. Candidates for office were not allowed to distribute literature, give interviews or visit branches for campaign purposes. The Executive exercised tight control over election addresses, and leadership-sponsored candidates, usually full-time officials standing against rank and file candidates, possessed strong advantages. In 1990 the police were involved when 16 mail bags of ballot papers vanished during TGWU Executive elections. In 1993 alone UCATT agreed to reform its system of elections after an inquiry by a QC established abuse. Scotland Yard began an inquiry into ballot rigging in the Seafarers' Union. And the successful candidate for Treasurer in the NUT, an established opponent of the leadership, was barred from holding office, a decision held invalid by the courts.

The majority of full-time officers are unelected. Yet, it may be argued, they possess considerable political power with accountability to the leadership stressed more than accountability to the membership who pay their wages. At the end of the long running Timex dispute in 1993 the strikers, kept under tight control by full-time officers throughout, were informed that if they did not accept the company's terms all support would be terminated. The strikers at Burnstalls in Birmingham were not allowed a vote on ending their dispute – the decision was taken for them by the full-time officers.

We have to examine union democracy warts and all and decide how far the warts infect the all. It can be argued that exceptions prove the rule; well publicised examples, often of *alleged* abuse, highlight that most of the time unions operate democratically. The only major documented scandal since the war concerned ballot rigging in the ETU. Despite periodic scares in the TGWU nothing of any substance has ever been established, and when doubts were raised about the 1986 election for General Secretary it was the successful candidate Ron Todd who insisted on a re-run. There are undoubtedly bureaucratic abuses but these are to be expected in any sizeable organisation and many have more to do with inefficiencies inherent in large and under-resourced unions than chicanery or corruption. The majority of activists are determined to ensure unions operate democratically and that decision-making is fair.

Union democracy: an example

Whether we see constraints on union democracy as endemic or superficial we have to take the measure of its complexity. In 1976 the National Coal Board decided on a new payment scheme. At the 1977 NUM annual Conference the scheme was rejected. Despite this, the National Executive announced a ballot of members. The Kent area, arguing that the NEC was breaking the rules, went to court. The judges declared the Executive was not behaving undemocratically: 'what the NEC is proposing to do is to hold a secret ballot of all members. This is the very essence of the democratic process . . . a far more satisfactory and democratic method than leaving it to the delegates of a conference'.

In the ballot, a majority voted against the scheme. The Executive refused to accept the result, ruling any of the unions' areas which wanted to introduce the scheme could do so. This went against the wishes of the majority expressed in the ballot. Relying on the support the judges had given to the ballot, three areas went to court asking for a ruling that the Executive were behaving undemocratically. The court upheld the Executive's action: 'the result of a ballot, nationally conducted, is not binding upon the NEC in using its powers in between conferences'. Mr Justice Watkins stated, 'It has no great force or significance.'

The local incentive scheme was introduced. Was this as a result of a democratic decision? Or was it as a result of an Executive which had already made up *its* mind imposing its will upon the membership? Were the judges who thought a national ballot was the essence of democracy right? Or was the judge who believed it was 'of no great significance' on firmer ground? Was it right for the Executive to go against the decision of a more representative gathering of delegates, the Conference *and* a national referendum of members?

In early 1984, the Executives of the Scottish and Yorkshire areas voted to support strike action against closures. The NEC supported the action and sanctioned area strikes under Rule 41 of the NUM constitution. This allowed individual areas to call strikes without a national ballot. Rule 43 required such a ballot for *national* action, but was not this just playing with words? Were not the proponents of Rule 41 trying to manipulate a national strike without allowing the membership a national ballot? Was not the national ballot the guarantee of united action in a fragmented union? Had not the national ballots in 1972 and 1974 laid the foundations for successful action? Would it not now be fatal to enter upon a prolonged struggle without ensuring that the rules were followed?

Not at all, replied the Executive: if each area calls out its own members, even if that means in aggregation a national strike, the rules have been followed. A national ballot could mean that areas which wanted to take action to oppose closures could be stopped by miners not facing the same problem. Individual areas should have the right to take action and the right to try to convince other areas to support them. Democracy should protect the rights of minorities to take action. And look at what the courts said in 1977 about the lack of importance of the national ballot.

The problem for the supporters of Rule 41 was that most areas were required by their own rules to ballot before approaching the Executive under Rule 41. Moreover, South Wales and Nottingham held ballots which went *against* industrial action. Moreover, when dissident miners took cases to court the judges now ruled that the national ballot was the foundation stone of democracy. Executive and Conference had no power to call what was really national action in the absence of a vote of all the membership. The controversy continued through the strike. The procedural arguments were intimately related to issues of substance: where one stood on the issue of job loss and what should be done about it. The ballot issue had a vital impact on the fortunes of the strike and the legal judgments eventually produced the state takeover of the NUM's assets.

This example illustrates that democracy in unions is a far from straightforward matter. The NUM, with its different areas and traditions, illustrates the problem in heightened form. But all unions experience similar difficulties in reconciling competing interests. Moreover, as this example underlines, union democracy is not some scholastic exercise: it goes to the root of union activity.

Why union democracy?

Most people believe unions should be democratic. Only a minority argue: 'The end of trade union activity is to protect and improve the general living standards of its members and not to provide workers with an exercise in self government' (Allen, 1954, 15). This view is sometimes accompanied by the assertion that trade unionism with collective bargaining at its heart requires expertise and professionalism. Union officers are like managers and democracy can constrain efficiency. The difficulty with such business union arguments is that there may be disagreement amongst members as to *which* policies best protect and improve living standards. Some may oppose, some may support diminishing differentials between members. Some may demand political involvement, others reject it. There may be differences over the qualities required for leadership positions. Groups inside and *outside* the unions will have different ideas on what the interests of the members are, and how they should be pursued. Employers will take an interest in organisations exercising influence on the enterprise. They may seek to limit union goals and view the union as a means of impressing management purposes upon the workforce. The state may in similar fashion see unions as a conveyor belt for its policies.

For unions are not debating societies. Policy requires *implementation* as well as formulation. Unions are *agencies for action*, ultimately dependent on members' participation and 'willingness to act' (Offe and Wiesenthal, 1985). Unions encompass antagonisms of interest and ideology. Yet as agencies for applying power they require mobilisation which necessitates unity and control. Only by acting in a disciplined fashion can unions deploy power. When they join a union, workers give up some freedom to act individually. Union democracy provides the sinews of unity. It is a means of reconciling differences and some guarantee that members will have a voice before they are called upon to take action, that collective power will be used in the interests of those it is intended to serve rather than internal elites, employers or the state. These considerations are stronger in a society where leaving the union has often not been an option. Union democracy moreover may be viewed as enhancing democracy in civil society, repairing the deficiencies of parliamentary democracy and training a working-class leadership.

The rules of democracy embodied in union constitutions are therefore formulated to regulate the struggle of competing groups and the mobilisation of collective action. Some see union democracy as valuable *per se* or as educating activists but it is ultimately a means to an end – organised action over agreed policies.

The problem of bureaucracy

Both left and right place tremendous faith in union democracy. If the members' words were made flesh, democracy would produce satisfactory left-wing/right-wing policies as the case may be! The problem is seen as the union coming between the members and their aspirations. We saw in Chapter 1 that unions may develop their own institutional interests. At times such interests may diverge from those of members. Union leaders may wish to terminate an expensive strike because of pressure on funds. They may be more willing to trade wage restraint for employment legislation than many members. In his famous book *Political Parties* (1911) Robert Michels, a German sociologist, argued that conflict between divergent interests set limits to democracy in working-class organisations. It was *inevitable*, he argued, that leaders developing a monopoly of skills and expertise assimilated to the middle class and became distanced from the lives and interests of their members. An **iron law of oligarchy** existed by which privileged officers sought to advance their own interests against the more radical interests of the membership so that policies moved remorselessly in a conservative direction. Similar views were found in the classical Marxist analysis of Lenin and Trotsky which developed the idea of 'the trade union bureaucracy', a social stratum with a vested material interest in the maintenance of collective bargaining with management and the capitalist system which produced its privileges, and hence the control of the rank and file whose interest lay in challenging their exploitation and union leaders and in the abolition of capitalism. The incorporation of union leaders as junior partners was portrayed as a calculative strategy of capital and the state.

This approach found little resonance in conventional analysis. For the most part pluralists treated union democracy as unproblematic and unimportant. Workers' interests lay in the reasonable pursuit of higher wages and job security. Officers supported these interests, and conflicts over what might be possible at a certain time or the need to look beyond immediate aspirations to future union security were minimal and functional. Union government generally worked well (Batstone, 1984, 25ff.).

Radical and Marxist theorists, notably Richard Hyman, revived conflict analysis in the 1970s. In his view bureaucracy is a *social relation* permeating union practice, stemming primarily from conflict between accommodative and oppositional tendencies in trade unionism and the collaborative impact of collective bargaining, rather than articulation of the material interests of a particular stratum. Bureaucratisation may affect shop stewards as well as the full-time custodians of union security and survival, who are impelled to placate the state and capital for organisational ends. Conflict in unions centres on struggle between bureaucratic accommodative tendencies on the one hand and autonomous tendencies on the other. The objective goal of the rank and file, the removal of the capitalist system, is facilitated by direct democracy and thwarted by attenuation of goals to collective bargaining facilitated by pressures from employers and the state. In this view a more democratic movement would be a more radical movement. Moreover Michels is wrong to see the triumph of bureaucracy and oligarchy as inevitable, for *countervailing tendencies* are strong. The interests of the rank and file interact with formal commitment to democracy, leaders' socialisation as shop stewards in its values, and members' expectation of democracy to constitute an important restriction on oligarchy. Unions which become simply an arm of state or employer forfeit support and provoke opposition and challenge. The relative autonomy of the shop steward system constitutes a major barrier to oligarchy and accommodation (Hyman, 1971, 1975, 1979).

The development of the new right saw a new emphasis: against theories of **bureaucratic conservatism** they asserted **bureaucratic militancy**. They believed that what motivates bureaucratic circumvention of union democracy is not so much material interest as ideology. Put succinctly by Norman Tebbit the argument is that: 'arrogant misuse of the wealth and power of the trade unions to serve the political ambitions of unrepresentative leaders has been a growing cause of public concern. Trade unions should become more democratic institutions responsive to the views and wishes of their members'. At least one professor of industrial relations claims that Marxist philosophy and a belief in using the unions to further its imperatives characterises many union leaders (Roberts, 1988). **Bureaucratic militancy** argues that union leaders intimidate or manipulate members into compliance with the left-wing policies they espouse. In this view radical conceptions are inverted: the conflict line in unions runs between an insurgent leadership and a moderate rank and file whose interests lie in compromise and partnership with employers.

A major difficulty with theories of bureaucratisation as an explanation of relations within unions is the simple dichotomy of conflicting interests attributed to officers and rank and file. There are clear problems in *demarcating* these categories. However we do so we end up with differentiation *within them*. First level full-time officers are in a different structural position and exercise different functions than general secretaries or TUC staff: within each grouping, values, political beliefs and approach to union policy will differ. The same is true for shop stewards and members. Differentiation in pay, jobs and industries between members creates **sectionalism**. The existence of political factionalism illustrates that position does not determine practice, and conflict within unions is not necessarily structurally based. In certain cases officers urge action and passive members do not support them – or rather some do and some do not. In other cases leaders undoubtedly restrain the militancy of members. During the 1984–85 strike, miners in Nottingham behaved more moderately than their local and national leaders. Leaders in the TGWU, NUR and ASLEF, who at various times urged members to take action to back the NUM, received inadequate support. Evidence demonstrates union leaders often seek to respond to members' wishes, not deflect them. We cannot simply read off behaviour from structural position. We need to examine all the specifics of the situation and the actors' relation to it before making a judgement.

The radical who ascribes militancy at all times to the members, disregarding problems of prevailing consciousness and particular circumstances is just as mistaken as the Conservative who ascribes consistent militancy regardless of tradition, time, place and balance of forces to the union leader. But it would be just as erroneous to ignore or downplay structural position and union function which can generate distinct interests, meanings and strategies. The general secretary who is a member of the same left-wing party as a steward may be constrained by his or her position to behave differently, as history teaches. If we cannot erect a general theory of bureaucratisation it would be just as simplistic to state that the major conflict lines which run through unions are based *only* on values and political attitudes. Individuals' values and politics interact with structure and function in different situations. We cannot ignore bureaucratisating pressures related to certain functions any more than we can predicate essential antagonism between the interests of professionals and members, nor ascribe all the problems of trade unionism to this antagonism.

In certain circumstances officials' commitment to long-term relationships with employers, orders from above, desire for pro-

motion or the financial position of the union may lead them to
oppose action supported by members who possess a direct interest
in the outcome. At times institutional interests or a wider view may
prompt officers to aggression, whereas the members are Conservative or see the possibilities in a more limited fashion. As they
stand, theories of bureaucracy are flawed instruments. But we
cannot return to the simple world of the pluralists where the
absence of any deep-seated problems breeds complacency about
union democracy. For example, we can only understand episodes
such as the struggle over incomes policy in the 1970s or employment legislation in the 1980s if we accept the reality of the
constraints placed on TUC leaders. But we could also explore the
fact that TUC staff were pursuing their own institutional interests
which were sometimes in conflict with those of affiliated unions,
and which were themselves subject to internal conflict and politically and structurally based. Simplistic theories of bureaucracy are
often linked to simplistic conceptions of democracy. If there was
more direct democracy, radicals erroneously assume, there would
be a move to the left. Moreover enhanced democracy is sometimes on the left too easily identified with enhanced power of
which it is only one ingredient. Theories of bureaucratic militancy
assume in contrast there would be a move to the right. Both views
mistake the nature of union members who, whatever objective
interests we ultimately impute to them, anchored in capitalist
society in the here and now, demonstrate to different degrees in
different situations a complex and varying mix of militant and
reactionary ideas.

What kind of democracy?

The Webbs noted that early craft unions attempted to realise the
literal meaning of democracy, 'rule by the people' on the model of
the city-states of Ancient Greece where all citizens participated in
decision-making. All members had access to the general meeting
which tried to deal with as many issues as it could. Responsibilities
were delegated with reluctance. Each branch took its turn as head
office and there was regular rotation of official positions. Even

when growth in size and the development of collective bargaining necessitated more elaborate organisation the craft unions were keenly aware of the need to control officers and develop mechanisms to involve lay members.

The Webbs believed direct democracy was irreconcilable with efficiency. There was a tension between the parochialism of members and the wider vision, expertise and consistency professional officers could bring to activities. Once organisation became sophisticated, devices such as the mass meeting, referendum and delegation would produce incompetence or dictatorship. They prescribed instead a version of parliamentary democracy, government by representative institutions. Like MPs, free from constraint from citizens until the next election, union leaders should be representatives insulated from direct control rather than delegates carrying out a mandate. Participation should be partial and centred on the branch as a link between leaders and constituents. This retreat from direct democracy however said little about party and opposition (Webb and Webb, 1902).

This was discussed in a detailed study of an American print union which argued that democracy could be practised in unions and that the party system played a healthy role, just as it does in parliamentary democracy. It enabled issues to be organised and presented to the voters with a choice between alternative programmes and personnel. It ensured that government was open to effective scrutiny, criticism and challenge by experienced judges. This system provided extended opportunities for members to participate in decision-making and gain valuable skills and experience. However, this union was seen as untypical and perhaps an anachronism. Its members were highly skilled and homogeneous, the beneficiaries of a long-established tradition. Nonetheless it was democratic: both parties accepted the results of elections, eschewing attempts to entrench themselves in power by changing the rules (Lipset *et al.*, 1956).

In Britain writers emphasised the reality of democracy, but its limited operation. Factors which influence participation and control, the size and dispersion of membership, skill, education and occupational identity, were analysed. Unions were classified as

exclusive democracies – with a homogeneous and cohesive membership and participation, like the traditional craft unions; **aristocracies**, in which one group dominates the union apparatus, like the face workers in the NUM or Co-op workers in USDAW; and **popular bossdoms**, unions with strong leadership control based on full-time officials and little rank and file participation, like the general unions, typically the TGWU. It was argued that it is essential to look at the actual working of the political process in unions rather than simply measuring constitutions against conceptions of political democracy, and that we should not neglect the extent to which passive members can identify union policy with their own interests (Turner, 1962).

More recent studies have seen the guarantee of democracy in the 'survival of faction', examining factors which make for this, such as the traditions and political culture of the union, the type of technology, its members' work and the strength or weakness of workplace organisation (Martin, 1968; Banks, 1974). The growth of party and faction in British unions has been demonstrated for a range of different unions (Undy and Martin, 1984). It has also been asserted that the common emphasis on union democracy has obscured the fact that there may be different means for taking decisions at local and national level. Unions have different channels for decision-making for collective bargaining and non-bargaining issues. Different systems require specific scrutiny (Undy *et al.*, 1981). Critics have argued that we need a broader, not a narrower, canvas. In their concentration upon internal arrangements many observers fail to relate them to external pressures. It is impossible, for example, to study union democracy in isolation from government policies, which have attempted to limit its scope. What is required is re-assertion of popular democracy rooted in the workplace (Hyman, 1975; Fairbrother, 1984).

On the whole writers in the pluralist tradition follow the Webbs in supporting **representative democracy**. Like the Webbs they have been uncertain as to the desirability of factionalism. Traditionally they supported union autonomy: within broad limits the nature of democracy was a matter for union members not the state. Pluralists have generally thought implicitly and benignly of union democracy in representative terms without pondering over-much the applicability of this model. They have rarely for example called for what is a fundamental of representative democracy, election of full-time officials. Radicals have supported more participation, more accountability and more decentralisation of decision-making. They have called for election of officials and an educating leadership cast in the delegate rather than representative mould. Their model is one of **popular democracy** with trade unionists as *active citizens* directly controlling events and little room for state intervention. The recent emphasis has been more on the workplace than the wider union.

Conservatives, diagnosing 'the union problem' as exploitation of the individual by leaders and activists, have advocated plebiscitary forms of democracy to facilitate participation by inactive members and institutional safeguards for the individual. They have been prepared to use the state to a greater extent than ever before to impose a uniform model of democracy on unions. Essentially the model is one of **business unionism**: the individual member is conceived as a *passive consumer contracting for services*. The member is not intended to *participate* in activity but to judge and if necessary reject results. However the continuing flood of legislation loaded toward consumer protection and individual rights of members raises questions as to the *responsibility* of members to the minimum *activism* necessary to mobilisation; and whether the increasing burdens placed by the state on the union as business are such as to impede its core activities. Nonetheless key leaders in the TUC and unions like the GMB have taken up the model of the union as a business with full-time staff as managers and members as clients. Their example has been followed by many other unions such as the TGWU which, in the wake of the Klein Report, commissioned from US consultants in 1992, appointed a highly paid chief executive and sought to encourage full-time officers to perceive themselves as managers. The key link here is between full-time staff and individual members. The emphasis is on professionalism and passivity. The importance of workplace representatives and activism is diminished.

Workplace and union

The well-springs of union strength and democracy lie in the workplace and are channelled through workplace organisation. Issues which arise are vital to members; their energetic pursuit and successful resolution builds confidence, participation and commitment. Shop stewards are fellow workers who experience similar problems and their closeness to the membership makes for responsiveness, accountability and a strong element of direct democracy. If 'bureaucratisation' can occur it is more easily countered in the workplace than outside it. Several guides to democratic organisation exist (Campbell and McIlroy, 1981). Cohen and Fosh provide a useful model which stresses the need for democratic leadership, effective communication, accessible meetings, commitment to membership interests and a strategy of enhancing participation which encourages a collectivist approach (1988, 11, 12).

A surprising absence in some recent literature is the relation of the workplace to the wider union and the need to approach democracy *in and beyond the workplace* – a need recognised to some degree in the activist based conceptions of democracy supported in the 1960s and 1970s by leaders such as Jack Jones. The functioning of democracy at other levels of the union is intensely relevant to the workplace, both practically in terms of progressing workplace interests, and in countering parochialism, 'factory consciousness' and bureaucracy. In his classic study, *Working for Ford*, Huw Beynon demonstrates the imperative for strong workplace organisation to drive beyond the workplace to secure influence in external structures. 'They *used* the union at Dunlop's. If they were in a position where they needed support they had people on all the committees who would argue for them' (Beynon, 1973, 72). The problems faced by workplace organisation which has little purchase outside its own confines have been graphically detailed (Thornett, 1987).

Really democratising the workplace requires a unified simultaneous concern for membership involvement and control *throughout the organisation* securing a presence on district, area and executive committees, seeking to democratise the whole union. This is particularly so when the model of non-participative business unionism is gaining ground and pressures towards decentralisation in bargaining and centralisation in mobilising industrial action and union government require new forms of co-ordination. Tendencies towards plebiscitary decision-making and managerial trade unionism may be seen as threatening the democratic role of the lay activist. They suggest reassertion of a mode of articulation between workplace and union which sees stewards as the emissaries of the apparatus, not its controllers, a relationship long established in some unions. In these circumstances supporters of activist-based democracy need to widen their horizons. A programme for *union democracy* is essential. To draw a line between workplace trade unionism and wider decision-making and electoral processes, or between 'active unionism' in the workplace and 'bureaucratically effective unionism' outside it, is artificial and self-defeating for those who wish to strengthen union democracy (for an example, see Fairbrother and Waddington, 1990, 16, 17).

Patterns of union democracy

We cannot ultimately judge how different aspects of union democracy operate in isolation. It is not very helpful for trade unionists to be told that the system of employer bargaining, through shop stewards, is very democratic and efficient, if the members of their union's TUC delegation – over whom they have minimal democratic control – inform them that they have just voted for a wage freeze. There is an intimate relationship between a union's industrial and political, organisational and bargaining activities, and we need to try to see how the branch, stewards' committee, executive and full-time officers interact in practice and respond to external pressures. We must also remember that the structures of unions illustrate their different histories but are continually evolving. The structure of former craft unions reflects their origin amongst skilled workers and their suspicion of centralised authority. A union like the TGWU still bears the marks of its forerunners, the general unions, which, recruiting a wide range of unskilled workers susceptible to high turnover, were built from the top, depending on professional organisers and strong central leadership. But just as the internal framework of general unions was modified by the amalgamations of the 1920s, so today we are seeing important restructuring.

The large lay member Executive of the TGWU was viewed as very democratic in terms of the direct relationship of its members with those they represent. However, when we add a full-time General Secretary, elected by the whole membership for life, to a large conference meeting only every two years, the structure provides *opportunities* for the exercise of domination by the General Secretary. With the resources of the head office and the advantages of permanent tenure, he was able to control the changing non-professional Executive. Through direct influence over the appointment of full-time officials, the General Secretary achieved a high degree of autonomy and attained a mastery over a large and heterogeneous conference.

This was the pattern of control in the TGWU until the late 1970s, with powerful General Secretaries dominating the union through links with the regional and trade group secretaries and ensuring the succession through their choice of deputy. But these structures provide opportunities and constraints which may be utilised in different ways. In the early 1960s Frank Cousins encouraged gradual devolution involving shop stewards on union committees and extension of workplace bargaining. This process was accelerated by Jack Jones who urged the move away from an officer led union whilst remaining dominant himself. The consequences in terms of enhanced democracy were symbolised by the defeat of the leadership over incomes policy at the 1977 Conference and the relative weakness of Jones's successor as General Secretary, Moss Evans. From the late 1970s executive members with rights to time off, and later often unemployed, became full-time officers in all but name. With their own legitimacy – they were elected, not appointed – they were in a better position to assert themselves. The broad faction which had supported Jones was replaced by the early 1980s by right wing and broad left groupings.

The TGWU's competitor the GMB remained in contrast a one-faction leader-dominated union with powerful regional secretaries sitting *ex officio* on the executive, strongly influencing lay representation to it from regional councils and supporting one of their number as General Secretary. Reforms in the 1970s such as the introduction of industrial conferences were intended not to change the pattern of control but to make it more effective. The union entered the 1980s still cast in a traditional top-down mould.

The AEU provided a contrast to this popular bossdom displaying the endurance of the craft model. Its constitution reflected the model of separation of powers with the policy-making conference, the National Committee, legislating, an Executive carrying out its decisions and an elected Final Appeal Court adjudicating on contentious issues. The judgement that this was an extremely democratic organisation was strengthened by the argument that the compact full-time Executive of seven could control the Executive officers whose functions were, in any case, divided between a President and a General Secretary. The small National Committee met annually. It could, thus, claim to play a stronger role than the TGWU conference in limiting the power of Executive and officials. Power was further dispersed by the strong role of district committees and election of full-time officers. The rosy picture was completed by the fact that shop stewards were strong at the workplace and active on district committees. Democracy was facilitated by the existence of a two party system which provided for a choice of policies to be presented to the electorate in a way traditionally impossible in general unions. Its success could be demonstrated by the passing of power from right to left in the mid-1960s and from left to right in the mid-1970s.

However, the position changed as the leadership manipulated and modified this structure to maintain dominance. In response to the left's success, based upon strong branch organisation, the right wing, which had retained control of the rules' revision committee, pushed through postal balloting. They believed that this would mobilise right-wing support more effectively. Postal balloting was gradually extended and, in the early 1980s, applied to the election of TUC and Labour Party delegations and the Final Appeal Court. The right controlled the Executive and National Committee and were determined to limit the influence of the latter, a bastion of the left. It attempted to erode the powers of district committees and its hand was strengthened by the reorganisation and amalgamation of districts and branches after 1980. The economic situation has eroded the ability of workplace organisations to act as a restraint on the central leadership. The devolved structure of the AEU has cloaked increasing concentration of power.

Reform of the constitution to secure such centralisation was taken further in the AEU's traditional sister union the EETPU, historically organised in similar fashion. In the 1960s, after the Communist Party leadership was removed as a result of ballot-rigging, a new right-wing group took control. They changed the rules to replace the lay Executive elected every two years with a full-time Executive elected every five years; replaced membership election of full-time officers with Executive appointment; abolished area committees; replaced the rank and file Appeal Court with an appeal body consisting of Executive members; gave increased power to the Executive to close and amalgamate branches; barred Communist Party members from holding office; and declared that conference decisions were not binding on the Executive.

The leadership justified restructuring in terms of the dangers of Communist subversion and on the grounds that members are interested in success in collective bargaining, not in attending meetings. It claimed that the right-wing majority on the Executive and the election, by wide margins, of Eric Hammond as General Secretary in 1982 and again in 1987, demonstrated membership support. Opponents argued leadership domination was maintained by control over appointments, internal media and discipline. Branches were suspended because of opposition to the Executive and elections declared invalid. Several left-wingers underwent surprising political conversions in a union described as 'an elective dictatorship'.

Such essays in remoulding constitutions to centralise and sustain control are not the prerogative of the right wing. An interesting phenomenon is the dominance of left-wing leaders in unions whose members reflect centre or right political tendencies. TASS, the draughtsmen's union, which amalgamated with ASTMS in 1988 to form the giant Manufacturing, Science and Finance Union, has traditionally combined a conservative membership with a high degree of union consciousness and organisation. Until the early 1960s the lay member Executive was dominated by the right wing, but by 1963 the broad left led by Communist Party members succeeded in taking control. Their strategy was to gain as many full-time officer posts as possible, and full-time officers came to play an increasing role in the broad left.

By the early 1970s, divisions had opened up within the broad left. The opposition was gradually removed from the Executive and Divisional Councils. Delegates to conference were no longer elected from branches but from divisions. The system by which full-time officers were appointed for life – a base for leadership power – was maintained. There was hostility to combine committees and, political opponents argued, a reluctance to mobilise the union to defend militants who were not supporters of the majority line. Left-wing policies on political issues were combined with caution over industrial policy. The opposition saw this as motivated by a desire not to make too many demands upon the membership: members will tolerate left-wing policies as long as they are not required to do anything active to implement them. The leadership's trajectory was justified by reference to the need not to get too far ahead of the rank and file. By the 1980s it was estimated that more than 90% of conference delegates, the entire National Executive and all the full-time officers were supporters of the broad left.

In the public sector during the 1960s and 1970s NALGO was pulling away from its professional association moorings. Its federal nature, representing different services, a disparate lay Executive and a large if formally powerful Conference meant that the Executive often prevaricated over translating conference policy into action. In practice a powerful role was accorded to branches with activists participating through the committee structure at all levels. The full-time officers at times met the stereotype of professional civil servants and the steward system was only developed from 1978. NUPE's rules provided for an executive elected in the branches every two years and a complex District, Area, Divisional Council and Conference structure. By the early 1980s the steward system was reflecting a more assertive rank and file, but NUPE remained a union in which full-time officers, in contrast with previous decades recruited from within the union, played an important leadership role in day-to-day decision-making.

The remodelling of the TUC in 1994 also had implications for union democracy. The new Executive Committee which would meet monthly and play a key leadership role involved only 26 members from 16 of the TUC's affiliates. The larger, more representative, General Council would now only meet five times a year not monthly. Congress was increasingly perceived as possessing a public relations rather than policy-making function and the scrapping of the issue based and industry committees further reduced participation and increased the potential for professionalisation and centralisation of decision-making. Overall, evolving patterns of union democracy reflected traditional theories in a variety of forms without fully meeting the norms of any of them. Supporters of representative democracy never explained, for example, why opposition was not legitimised but denounced and if necessary prohibited. Elements of direct democracy remained, particularly at the workplace, but the representative process in unions remained a pallid reflection of models of political democracy. There was also some change in the internal anatomy of democracy. Overall, groups with powerful traditions of grassroots collectivism such as miners and dockers were depleted. In a union like the TGWU the declining power of dockers and car workers represented in the election of past General Secretaries from these backgrounds was an important development. Some felt that together with the weakening of workplace organisation this was producing a shift in the internal locus of power from workplace to union office.

It has been argued that the necessities of recruitment and the ethos of the age are now bringing managerial service conceptions of trade unionism to the fore. The post-war years saw the dominance of professional negotiators servicing the members, the 1960s and 1970s participative relationships, with the emergence of the lay activists, and the recent period has witnessed the growing ascendancy of managerialism (Heery and Kelly, 1994). The evidence for this trend cannot be ignored, although variations persist. It has been complemented in some unions by a growth of factionalism so that different groups compete to manage the organisation, recruit and service members on platforms often unclear to many members. However the disruption factionalism can cause to managerialism has been recognised by leaders such as Bill Morris of the TGWU who has attempted to reverse its progress. Mergers may strengthen this approach – such as the influence of the professional dominated GMB on its potential partner the TGWU. The new consumer based approach does not deny democracy but provides a more limited role for both participation and political contention. Members are viewed as clients rather than activists with an impetus to influence the destiny of the organisation. Power is centralised at the top of the union and exercised with the benefit of specialist expertise. It is a trend the state has supported and one which has been facilitated in some unions by the weakening of shop steward organisation.

The state and union democracy

The industrial unrest of the 1970s convinced Conservatives that a majority of passive, moderate members were being manipulated by an activist minority of extremists. If the silent majority were able to participate through postal ballots, insulated from the 'intimidation' of union meetings there would a move to the right and improved industrial relations. Moderates could not be expected to attend meeting after meeting, so a means had to be developed to limit the influence of militant activists. Governments moved from legislation over ballots to legislation protecting dissident members against union discipline and from there to providing state aid for members to take action against unions (see

Chapter 6). What has been involved, in sum, is a qualitative increment to state regulation of trade unionism and a diminution of self-regulation by union members.

Legislated democracy: the argument for

1 Unions are involved in activities vital to economy and society with 'important legal immunities and privileges not afforded to other organisations' (Department of Employment, 1983, 1). Left to themselves their decision-making mechanisms are profoundly unsatisfactory. In 1980 more than 40% of General Secretaries were unelected and never had to face the voters.

2 The closed shop provides a cameo of the lack of democracy in unions. Until Mrs Thatcher acted, many workers were forced into joining a union without any right to vote in a ballot. The closed shop interferes with the freedom of the individual and the right to work. By constraining management's right to hire and fire and deploy labour in the most effective fashion, it can inhibit the efficiency of the enterprise. Those press-ganged into membership are unlikely to become loyal, let alone active, members.

3 You cannot improve participation if you insist on members attending meetings. Mass meetings are open to intimidation. They can be 'arranged at times and locations which are inconvenient. The vote may be taken at the end of a long meeting. In these ways members can be discouraged from voting. Furthermore, there are clear risks of manipulation' (DE, 1983, 9). Voting by show of hands is not good enough in parliamentary elections and should not be good enough for union elections. Even if members are allowed to vote by workplace ballot, 'an elector may be unduly influenced when being given his ballot paper. He may be afforded insufficient privacy when recording his vote' (D.E., 1983, 9).

4 The secret postal ballot overcomes these difficulties. It brings practical difficulties, such as the need for increased finance. These problems can be overcome. It is in the unions' interests to compile a register of members and utilise the services of an independent scrutineer.

5 The advantages of the postal ballot outweigh the disadvantages. When unions voluntarily introduced such systems 'The numbers voting have immediately and significantly increased' (DE, 1983, 4). The extension of this system will make unions more democratic and produce more moderate leadership.

6 Individuals who wish to exert their democratic right not to participate in industrial action require specific protection from union leaders. The new Commissioners are essential to aid intimidated members in pursuing their legal rights against unions. Conservatives are reluctant to intervene in the internal affairs of voluntary organisations and have done so only as a last resort. But union leaders ignored every opportunity for self-reform, even refusing state funds for ballots under the 1980 Employment Act.

The argument against

1 Postal ballots produce decreased turnout compared with workplace ballots. In NUM leadership elections there was around 75% turnout, and in the workplace ballot held for the first General Secretary of the GPMU a 70% turnout. This is far higher than the levels registered in postal ballots required by the 1988 legislation. There is no evidence that postal ballots produce more moderate leaders. In fact they have produced defeats of sitting General Secretaries by right-wing (NUJ) and left-wing candidates (NATFHE).

2 The closed shop is justified by imbalance of power between employer and employee. Members give up freedom to opt out to increase their general freedom, by building an organisation which can challenge decisions dictated by the management. 'Free-riders' should be regarded in the same way as tax dodgers. They use their individual rights to enjoy the benefits fellow workers' efforts make possible. Why should not those fellow workers use *their* individual rights not to work with that free-rider?

3 Governments have produced no evidence of intimidation or manipulation. Postal ballots are not immune to manipulation as the ETU affair in the 1950s demonstrated. Neither MPs nor

the electorate vote by post which facilitates 'outside intervention' from the media and limits the discussion which can take
place at work. Politicians declare opposition to government by
referendums yet this is exactly what legislation prescribes for
union government.

4 Unions' vitality depends on members acting collectively. Postal
   balloting can minimise the quality of participation. Members
   are in a better position to take decisions when they have listened
   to the arguments. If workers vote at the workplace they are in a
   better position to consider collective interests than if they vote
   as isolated individuals at home. Workers are at their weakest as
   atomised individuals. If important decisions are taken by postal
   ballot, democracy will suffer. If members become more
   inactive, what guarantee is there that they will take the field
   when called upon by their union? A union which has lost the
   ability to mobilise its membership in action is a broken reed.

5 Rights to ignore strike decisions arrived at by state-imposed
   ballots emphasise that the purpose of legislation is to
   disorganise and demobilise trade unionism, not make it more
   democratic. There is no legal aid for unfair dismissal and
   Conservatives have been critical of the Commission for Racial
   Equality and the Equal Opportunities Commission, established
   to aid litigators only after voluminous evidence demonstrated
   widespread discrimination. The establishment of the two new
   Commissioners to aid anti-union litigants on the basis of a
   molehill of evidence highlights the partisanship of state intervention.

6 State intervention weakens the roots of democracy in society by
   restricting the scope of legitimate self-government of social
   organisations. The Conservatives have not simply sought to
   impose a contentious model of democracy on unions. As the
   1993 Act requiring ballots on check-off demonstrates, the
   project is about demobilising the unions and impeding every
   effective aspect of their activities. It is not about democratic
   mechanisms but political outcomes. It is therefore fitting that it
   has had less impact than the Conservatives envisaged.

The state and restructuring

The main pressures towards internal restructuring and greater uniformity have stemmed from legislation, membership loss and mergers. Declining membership has foregrounded a further factor, *business efficiency*, and strengthened full-time officers, specialists and consultants against the activists. In many unions this has proceeded through the new ethos operating on existing structures. Both the TGWU and GMB adapted to mergers during the 1980s with minimal disturbance. The TGWU's trade group structure facilitated absorption of textile and agricultural workers. In the GMB mergers stimulated adoption of a trade group structure essential to an adventurous takeover policy. The existing two section General and Municipal Workers and Boilermakers possessed their own representative bodies. Mergers with the NUTGW and APEX produced Clothing and Textile, Professional/Executive and Clerical and Craft Trade Groups, providing an alternative focus of power to the regional baronies. The AEEU established in 1992 will maintain the existing structures of the EETPU and AEU for four years with the joint executive as the supreme decision-making body. The marginalisation of opposition in both organisations and the similar political complexion of their leaderships make it more likely that the fused organisation will adopt an EETPU-like structure with power at the centre and the AEU model of democratic craft control will fade from the scene.

MSF's move to a joint rulebook in 1989 produced conflict along ex-ASTMS, ex-TASS lines. In dispute were the right of branches to be represented at conference and retain funds, the more open working of ASTMS with power devolved to industrial groups, divisions and branches compared with full-time officer control and centralised decision-making in TASS, as well as political differences. ASTMS had been strongly oriented towards the Labour Party in contrast to the Stalinist leadership of TASS. The consequence was the establishment of rules limiting branch involvement without reproducing the TASS model, a factional split between the revamped TASS broad left, and the new 'MSF for Labour', and a victory for the latter centred on the former ASTMS leadership.

Restructuring via merger has interacted with legislative pressures to produce wider change. In the TGWU, elimination by the 1984 Act of indirect elections meant trade group representatives on the executive had to be elected by the members, not the trade group committees, whilst the General Secretary was a five-year not a lifetime appointment. The new cycle of elections stimulated factionalism and made the General Secretary more dependent on the Executive. During 1986–88 it produced right-wing control of the Executive – which became more activist than ever before – and caused friction with General Secretary, Ron Todd. The broad left regrouped and established tighter, more effective, organisation. From 1989 they controlled the Executive and their candidates for General Secretary and Deputy, Bill Morris and Jack Adams, were installed. The introduction of postal ballots recast but did not end the role of lay officials in mobilising support. Branch nominations became increasingly important in elections as activists utilised them as a platform to muster the postal ballot.

Legislation required the GMB to end branch block voting, introduce electoral addresses and end indirect elections to its Central Executive Council. Moving to workplace ballots under the 1984 Act and postal ballots under the 1988 legislation meant an increase and then a sizeable decrease in participation but little change in the nature of the union's government. The regional secretaries remained entrenched, factionalism was again held at bay and attempts by the union's modernisers to introduce further change, such as ballots for delegates to biennial conference, were defeated. Legal innovation had little impact on the AEU and EETPU which already possessed postal ballot arrangements. The exit of left-wingers to form the EPIU after the EEPTU's expulsion from the TUC further entrenched leadership control. Branch reorganisation in the AEU in 1990 reflected right-wing domination undisturbed by external change.

It is also difficult to discern any specific impact on the policies of the unions which formed UNISON in 1993. From 1984 NALGO moved to the left in policy and leadership. It strongly opposed the legislation and dragged its heels over implementation. Legal impact on its government seemed slight, although direct election seemed to have enhanced the profile and legitimacy of the General Secretary. NALGO continued as a coalition union with strong branch autonomy and relatively weak central leadership. NUPE in contrast moved to the right. It became a model Kinnockite union led from the centre by full-time officers. The introduction of workplace organisation produced a relatively integrated network of full-time officers and lay activists articulated with a cohesive leadership. Its progress was undisturbed by the balloting requirements and the same could be said for the third partner in the merger, COHSE. Further restructuring induced by the merger seemed likely, particularly in view of the different structures and culture of NALGO and NUPE.

In most unions legal change reduced electoral participation but acted minimally on outcomes. The most visible development was perhaps the growth of factionalism, mild in NALGO, still unknown in one-faction NUPE. The CPSA maintained its reputation as market leader: the broad left was split by the emergence on the right of Broad Left 84 and on the left the Socialist Caucus. In 1993 Broad Left 84 split into two factions. The left proved less able than its TGWU counterpart to deliver the postal vote and the fall in turnout coincided with a period of control by the moderate faction in the 1990s. In the NUT a moderate broad left group controlled the Executive but a split left organised in the Campaign for a Democratic Union and the Socialist Teachers' Alliance advanced in the early 1990s. In UCATT however the introduction of postal ballots produced left control with George Brumwell's election as General Secretary and a left majority on the Executive. Perhaps the most dramatic refutation of 'the postal ballots produce moderate leadership' thesis was in the NCU where the broad left swept back after defeat by the 'Members First' and 'Clerical Group' faction to control of the Executive in 1993. In recent years factions have been more sophisticated organisationally, but essentially electoral machines with minimal attention paid to external politics and in some cases limited internal democracy.

State intervention has therefore interacted with the overall climate, pressures on recruitment and specifically mergers to produce restructuring, a new business ethos and a growth in factionalism. Change in process has not produced the substantive transformation governments intended. Since 1988 when legislation demanded postal ballots for executive positions the fall in turnout has been general and significant. There has been no swing to moderates in elections. The number of cases referred to the CROTUM and Certification Officer have been derisory. The provisions for ballots before industrial action have strengthened central control over the mobilisation process but reinforced its legitimacy (see pp. 262–3). Unions have demonstrated ability to adapt. What must be worrying is the continual need to respond to new changes which leaves union democracy in a state of perpetual motion. Its nature will undoubtedly be further transformed by legislation, the consolidation of mergers like UNISON and future mergers, such as that between the TGWU and GMB.

Equal rights

The reflection and reinforcement of the social disadvantage of women and ethnic minorities in unions constitutes a central restriction on democracy. Unions have accepted existing divisions of labour structured by gender and ethnicity, embodied them in their policies and strengthened them by practising them. Any development of union democracy will require specific attention to exclusionary factors.

Women members
Women's lower participation rates are related to their domestic role and support for it in union behaviour. Through collective bargaining unions directly restricted employment of women, negotiated arrangements on pay, conditions and job security which favoured 'male breadwinners' and ignored equal pay, child care and sexual harassment. The time, place and style of meetings, women's double burden as breadwinner and domestic carer,

and their interrupted careers at work militated against activism (Beale, 1982; Hunt, 1982). Unions have been permeated by male concerns and male culture. This continued even as women's role in the labour force significantly increased. Often working part-time, in scattered workplaces with high turnover, women are sometimes perceived as costly to recruit and retain. In certain areas structural difficulties which have constrained recruitment and women's activism became stereotyped, reinforcing initial difficulties (Yeandle, 1984).

In the early 1980s two of Britain's three biggest unions with more than 700,000 members between them had no women members on their Executive. The Tailor and Garment Workers' membership was 90% female, yet only 7% of its Executive were women. In the National Union of Teachers, 66% of the membership, but only 9% of the Executive, were women. The picture was similar in other unions. In NUPE, for example, 63% of the membership were women but only 8 of 30 places on the Executive and only 7 out of 150 full-time officer positions were filled by women.

Since then the question of changing structures and culture to encourage membership and involvement from women has become an important item on union agendas from a mixture of principle, opportunism (unions need to attract more women), and tokenism (existing male leaders need to attract and placate women members and this has chimed with 'the new consumerism's' emphasis on targetting specific groups of members). Unions have reformed structures to involve women members. They have attempted to stimulate activism by emphasis on equality, child care, confidence building and 'women only' bodies. They have appointed national and regional women's officers, organised special women's conferences and women-only education courses. Whilst full-time officer positions remain male dominated there are signs of a shift: more women are being appointed although they still encounter serious problems and even harassment from lay members and male officers (Heery and Kelly, 1988).

A number of unions have practised positive discrimination through reserved seats on committees: NUPE, a pioneer in the

1970s, was able to report that by 1987 a majority of its Executive were women and the GMB introduced a similar mechanism in 1988. Nonetheless, progress has been mixed (Table 4.1). The 1991 *Labour Research* survey showed only 23% of Conference delegates, 20% of union National Executives and less than 20% of full-time officers were women (LRD, 1991). Despite reserved seats men still outnumbered women more than 2:1 on the TUC General Council and a majority of unions failed to meet targets for increasing the proportion of women on Congress delegations. However, agreement that women would hold a minimum of 44:67 seats on the first Executive of UNISON highlighted the progress that was possible. Yet in UNISON, which has a good record, only 20% of senior national officers are women, who constitute 68% of the membership. In many unions despite changes in structures the inner sanctum of senior management remains a male preserve.

Changes in mechanism can go only some way to combat deep-seated problems which impede their efficient operation. Studies

Table 4.1 *Women's participation in the ten unions with the largest female membership*

Union	No. of women members	% women members	% on National Executive	% TUC delegation	% full-time national officers
NUPE	430,000	71.3	46.1	36.1	38.5
NALGO	398,660 (1989)	53.1	42.0	41.7	31.6
GMB	267,894	30.8	29.4	19.8	11.8
USDAW	251,371	71.3	31.3	26.9	20.0
TGWU	210,758	16.9	7.7	20.6	3.4
COHSE	156,900	79.0	50.0	31.6	54.2
MSF	140,000	21.4	21.6	25.5	21.4
NUT	133,675	72.0	28.6	40.0	42.9
AEU	105,022	14.2	0.0	7.4	0.6

Source: LRD, 1991.

of NALGO and USDAW show how men of the same age have more experience, more expertise and more confidence than women because their work careers are not interrupted by domestic commitments. Minorities of branches provide child care for meetings, which cause problems in terms of timing, location and transportation, but also at a deeper level because of constraints imposed by patriarchal relations in the home and the difficulty of adding a third commitment as union activist to what is already a double burden (Rees, 1992). A report produced by USDAW found large numbers of women members encountered branch meetings as clique dominated, jargon ridden, irrelevant gatherings (USDAW, 1987).

Black representation

The election of Bill Morris as General Secretary of the TGWU in 1991 marked an important step forward for anti-racism in the Labour Movement. He remained the sole representative of the ethnic minorities on the TUC General Council. Unions remained passive as members adopted policies of exclusion and neglect towards black immigrants in the post-war years and did little to change the subordinate position they were assigned as replacement labour in the industrial structure. The TUC supported immigration control and failed to demand anti-racist legislation. They urged black workers to ignore their colour, even if white workers were not prepared to do so, and employed an idealistic image of trade unionism in which black and white were already indissolubly united to conjure away the realities of sometimes bitter divisions. The response of numerous black workers demonstrated, in contrast, loyalty and commitment to the unions with high density figures recorded from the 1960s. Unions only changed as interventionist state strategies developed, and under pressure from black workers and the rank and file.

Change has gathered impetus since 1980 but still has limitations despite recruitment pressures. The 1994 decision by the TUC General Council to set aside three seats for black trade unionists represented another landmark. Black workers represent a small minority of trade unionists compared with women and unions have been far more reticent in using positive discrimination to encourage involvement.

A growing number of unions – but still a minority – have established committees which, like that in the GMB, advise the Executive on 'the recruitment, retention and representation of black and ethnic minority workers' and many of these have committees at regional level. Some of these however are general Equality Committees. Only NALGO, and to a lesser extent NATFHE, developed integrated black worker involvement. NALGO established equality officers and black workers' groups at branch and district level with black representation on the Executive and an annual black members' Conference. A national officer dealt specifically with anti-racist issues and it was hoped this would be carried over to UNISON. The TUC established a black workers Conference in 1988 and it first took motions in 1993. Nonetheless unions remain handicapped in dealing with these issues as a minority monitor new members (LRD, 1993a).

There has also been a new attention to the barriers constraining activism, from shiftwork to meetings in pubs and community culture. Participation by some black workers at workplace or branch level is vital to extending involvement to others in the community, particularly involvement in recruitment activity (Commission for Racial Equality, 1992).

An emphasis on 'black issues' in particular campaigns, such as NUPE's support for regrading in the health service or BIFU's successful campaign over the wearing of saris in the Midland Bank, can be important in breaking down barriers. So can emphasis on the needs of black women members who are specifically disadvantaged in terms of pay, conditions, employment security and cultural subordination. NALGO set quotas for black women in its representation system. MSF has emphasised the need for women's and anti-racist committees to work together and members have created a Black and Ethnic Minority Women's network.

Positive discrimination
Strategies of positive discrimination have caused controversy.

Proponents justify them on the grounds that women and black workers suffer specific discrimination; specific action is required to deal with this. Without special measures the problems these groups face would constitute too great an obstacle to participation for all but a tiny minority. Special conferences are required for confidence-building and strategy creation. They help oppressed workers into the union mainstream where they act as an example to the next generation. Many of the changes introduced to help women should now be applied to black workers.

Opponents of positive discrimination argue it is divisive and ineffective: women and blacks should look upon themselves as trade unionists, not *black* trade unionists or *women* trade unionists. All workers have similar problems, whatever their gender or skin colour. Special bodies separate groups out from the mainstream, constituting an assertion that they cannot compete on equal terms. This undermines those who already operate adequately and inhibits newcomers who could emulate them, if they did not constantly have their alleged inferiority rammed down their throats. Beneficiaries of reserved seats will be treated as second rate representatives. Gays have joined disabled people as recipients of positive discrimination. What about Irish people or Jews? The working-class movement is supposed to be about unity, yet it is becoming increasingly fragmented. Whatever happened to *class*? Trade unionism is about emphasising what the members have in common, not what divides them.

A real concern is the extent to which the discourse and practice of anti-racism and anti-sexism develops beyond apparatus and activists to influence members and permeate mainstream activity. Or alternatively it remains a style tolerated by the majority as long as its impact on the real world – who gets this job and who does not – is minimal. It is incumbent on union activists to both avoid counter-productive approaches which fail to relate to the prevailing consciousness of most members and thus help to change it and mount strategies which attack the material roots of oppression not just its symptoms. A real criticism of positive discrimination strategies is that whilst they have provided an alternative ladder for some, there is little evidence as yet that they have contributed to significant improvement of the position of women or black trade unionists as a whole.

Conclusions

Members' attachment to trade unionism remains based on 'collective instrumentalism', there is little evidence of the growth of 'individualistic consumerism'. Participation remains limited but is more marked at the workplace. As agencies of collective action unions require democratic mechanisms to reconcile competing interests and legitimise mobilisation. Union democracy is bound up with questions of conflict, politics and power. It is inherently complex, with formal mechanisms mediated in practice through the development of bureaucracy and struggles between interest groups, where process sometimes takes second place to outcomes. Institutional goals may conflict with membership objectives in a conservative fashion. But oligarchy and bureaucratic conservatism cannot be seen as centred on a permanent conflict between a bureaucratic, conservative apparatus and a radical, democratic rank and file. The structural location of actors is important to explanation, but is in itself complex, intersecting with values, tradition and political beliefs.

Historically, unions adopted a wide range of decision-making arrangements reflecting different conceptions of democracy. Recent important influences on change have been membership loss, amalgamation and legislation. Analysis and prescription has to examine democracy at all levels of the unions, ignoring neither the workplace nor the wider union context which constrains what happens at the workplace. Competing conceptions of democracy emphasise direct democracy, representative democracy and plebiscitary, consumer democracy and are related to radical, pluralist and conservative, business conceptions of trade unionism. Since 1979, in a break with the past, the state has intervened to impose a specific, detailed form of decision-making. Legislation on the 'business' model has eroded the ability of members to make their own rules and rendered them more uniform. It has not produced greater participation or more moderate leadership but has centralised control over mobilisation. Changes in the labour force and union membership together with changes in workplace organisation also have implications for union government. The replication of gender and ethnic oppression within unions has seriously limited democracy. Despite the lack of evidence behind it, key union leaders have lent support to the individual consumer-managerial model. Driven by membership loss and a hostile climate they have re-asserted a professional-client view of links between member and union. The union is seen as less a school for democracy, more a business providing services. Jack Jones's emphasis on lay activists has given way to John Monks's emphasis on consultants, facilitated internally by the difficulties of workplace organisation and externally by state policy.

Unions are far from self-governing utopias. Democracy is restricted both by internal conflicts and external pressures on oppositional agencies operating in a society which sets firm limits to democracy. But compared with other institutions unions provide an important measure of democracy in society. It can be deepened, and extension of popular democracy in and beyond the workplace is an important aspiration. But there appear to be real limits today to qualitative change. Unions are likely to continue to reflect in a limited way a variety of conceptions of democracy.

Further reading

There are no comprehensive up to date surveys of union democracy. Roger Undy, Roderick Martin, *Ballots and Trade Union Democracy*, Blackwell, 1984, gives the picture in the early 1980s and Peter Fairbrother, *All Those in Favour: The Politics of Union Democracy*, Pluto Press, 1984, discusses issues of the same period from a more radical perspective. Patricia Fosh, Edmund Heery, eds., *Trade Unions and Their Members*, Macmillan, 1990, is a more up to date collection of valuable essays. Indispensable generally are Richard Hyman, *Marxism and the Sociology of Trade Unionism*, Pluto Press, 1971, and *Industrial Relations: A Marxist Introduction*, Macmillan, 1975. Specific studies include Seymour Lipset *et al.*, *Union Democracy*, Free Press, 1956, and Herbert Turner, *Trade Union Growth, Structure and Policy*, Allen and Unwin, 1962. Jenny

Beale's *Getting It Together: Women as Trade Unionists*, Pluto Press, 1982 is a good introduction to feminist critiques of union democracy. Teresa Rees, *Women and the Labour Market*, Routledge, 1992 contains more recent contemporary material. The Labour Research Department has produced a number of useful pamphlets on unions and ethnic minorities.

5

Unions and the state

Are trade unions too involved in politics? Do they exercise too much political power? These are perennial questions whenever trade unions are discussed. Yet unions have been involved in politics since their earliest days. The American political scientist Harold Lasswell summed up politics crudely, if effectively, as, 'who gets what, when, how'. Since unions are essentially involved in the same process we can regard some commitment to politics as inevitable. What is often at stake in debate is the *kind* and *quality* of the unions' political engagement rather than whether they should be involved at all. For the unions politics has grown organically and unavoidably from economics rather than being essentially a response to attacks on legal status and bargaining function (Crouch, 1982, Chapter 6). It has been increasingly difficult to talk of collective bargaining as an autonomous process sealed off from politics.

Even in the unfavourable climate since 1979 unions have played an extended, if unfruitful, political role struggling to defend the achievements of the post–war settlement. The view that unions 'had a limited political role before 1966 and virtually no such role since 1979' (Marsh, 1992, 240) runs the danger of confusing achievement with activity. The unions' intense, if sterile, political engagements with the new Conservatism, their continued involvement in the Labour Party, their attempt to develop a new role in the EU illustrate the continuing political imperative of British trade unionism.

Politics is ultimately about *the organisation and administration of the state*. Unions adopt a variety of means of influencing the state through direct campaigns, through the TUC and through the Labour Party. The next three chapters look at different aspects of the unions' political role. We scrutinise attempts to influence the state through the TUC, the framework of law the state imposes on union activities and the unions' changing relationship with the Labour Party, bearing in mind these areas are intermeshed in practice.

Influencing the state

Attempts to influence the state are as old as trade unions. After the disillusion with direct action engendered by the 1926 General Strike they assumed greater coherence. TUC General Secretary Walter Citrine, aided and abetted by Ernest Bevin, the leader of the TGWU, was determined to establish a close relationship with governments of whatever political complexion and to make the TUC the major vehicle for transactions between the unions and the state. A major breakthrough came with World War II. Bevin's appointment as Minister of Labour in 1940 epitomised the new relationship. Union representatives were appointed to a range of government bodies and tripartite committees, and were involved in discussing productivity, price control and rationing. The Prime Minister ensured union leaders were given direct access to Ministers. The need to involve workers in the war effort and the energy of Bevin led to a range of concessions on issues such as union recognition. The relationship between the TUC and the 1945 Labour government was very different from the 'arm's length' approach of Ramsay MacDonald and the 1924 and 1929 Labour governments.

Another landmark year was 1951: the incoming Conservative government confirmed the corporate bias of the state and the position of organised labour as the 'fifth estate' in society. And the TUC affirmed its pragmatic desire for state involvement:

It is our long–standing practice to work with whatever government is in power . . . to find practical solutions to the social and economic problems facing the country (TUC, 1952, 300).

Forty years later union leaders recalled with nostalgia the close constructive relationships they had enjoyed with Churchill's Minister of Labour, Sir Walter Monckton. The response of Citrine's most influential successor at the TUC, George Woodcock, to the growing economic difficulties of the 1960s was to prescribe a new urgency, a more enthusiastic approach to participation in the corporate bias of the British state. Woodcock eagerly supported the establishment of the National Economic Development Council in 1962 and nominated the 'top six' union leaders to serve on it. He increasingly favoured incomes policy and sought to control shop stewards, with minimal success. Woodcock was the most coherent strategist of non–partisan political integration since Citrine, urging against those who pointed to the diminution of the movement's powers of **mobilisation** that the TUC had 'left Trafalgar Square a long time ago'. Its natural environment now was 'the corridors of power'.

The TUC's relationship with Labour was seriously shaken by the failures of the 1964–70 Wilson governments and *In Place of Strife*. They greeted Ted Heath's Conservative government in 1970 – despite its radical proposals – in what were now traditional terms:

the TUC does not sing one song when Conservative Governments are in power and another when Labour Governments are in power. We deal with governments strictly on the merits of the issues (TUC, 1970, 631).

The ensuing confrontations with the Heath government produced a change of emphasis in TUC strategy. The shock of renewed conflict and the need to reassert partnership rights with Labour after *In Place of Strife* led to a new relationship between the TUC and the Labour Party. The Trade Union – Labour Party Liaison Committee, initiated in 1972, with representatives from Labour's parliamentary leadership, its National Executive and the TUC General Council exerted strong influence on the ensuing Social Contract (Hatfield, 1978). The Liaison Committee was a tribute to the enhanced power of the TUC; through it the unions contributed to policy outcomes. However, they were now increasingly politically identified with the Labour Party. They had moved some distance from Citrine's dictum, that they should not base their fortunes on one political party.

Corporatism and union power

By the mid-1960s, it was argued, the unions had become the country's most powerful pressure group overshadowing organised capital (Middlemas, 1979, 396–400). The intensity and scope of relations with government had grown; so had the importance attached to them by ministers and the ease and informality of relationships. There had been 'a literally colossal expansion in the frequency and range of the TUC's access to government, a great and sustained rise in the primary effectiveness of the TUC'. Success in terms of substantive policy, *secondary effectiveness*, had increased but still remained limited, particularly over contentious issues (Martin, 1980, 338–40). Under the facade the internal decay of national bargaining, with its correlative promise that union leaders could control their members, one of the key components of the post–war consensus, was stoking up problems for enduring political exchange.

Union leaders themselves believed that their political influence was not only substantial but part of the natural order of things:

In a highly industrialised and economically vulnerable society no decision can be taken by government without first hearing and heeding the voice of the organised trade union movement (TUC, 1974, 335).

By 1974 the unions had seen off Wilson's attempts at legislation and contributed to the downfall of Heath. They were represented on an ever growing range of bodies. They had access to top politicians of all major parties and were seen as having written the script for the incoming Wilson government. By 1975 Jack Jones of the TGWU was caricatured as 'leader of the Labour Party' and opinion polls showed a majority of respondents stating he was 'the most powerful man in Britain'. This period was widely characterised as corporatist and the unions were seen as 'running the country':

[The TUC] overshadowed the potential of employers, owners and management to influence the organisation of the state and however negatively the General Council may transmit the inchoate political will of its membership, trade union hegemony has broadened out further than in any comparable western nation profoundly to alter the nature of the state (Middlemas, 1979, 451–2).

Yet the degree to which the state institutionalised direct representation of capital and labour and the degree of success this period yielded union politics have been exaggerated.

Labour, the unions and corporatism
Against the conventional view, it can be argued:

1 Corporatism requires the involvement of capital. This occurred minimally. Bodies such as the NEDC were discussion bodies, not instruments for directive planning. The system of planning agreements between governments and companies never really got off the drawing board. The National Enterprise Board fell far short of its initial objective of controlling a leading company in each key sector of industry, and failed to act as a stimulus to private investment. The lack of progress on industrial democracy summed up the limits of Labour's attempt to plan capital.
2 The Social Contract was basically an agreement between government and unions, not a mechanism of concertation between the state and the two 'social partners'. It increasingly became simply an instrument for the control of wages. There was no open and formalised bargaining between the state, capital and labour, where broad social objectives were articulated and bargained over. There was no national economic forum, no national economic assessment and no national economic plan. Instead, the economic crisis of June 1975 was utilised to 'bounce' the TUC into agreeing the 'voluntary' £6 pay policy. The temporary, imposed, fragile nature of the process was underscored when one year later, in September 1976, the TUC voted for a phased return to free collective bargaining.

3 The distance from corporatism is highlighted by the lack of agreement within the unions to the wage restraint that was their part of the bargain. From the start, there was opposition from prominent leaders. Others saw it as a temporary, piecemeal expedient, not as the germ of a more comprehensive system of long–term planning. The conditions for political exchange simply did not exist, given the decentralised nature of collective bargaining and union organisation. The TUC was incapable of overcoming this fragmentation.

4 The history of the 1974–79 government was not a history of a growth of corporatism, but of gradual *breakdown* of what was initially little more than a corporatist *tendency* or *inflection* in a policy increasingly conventional and focused on wage control. After two successful years, wage restraint was disrupted. The period 1977–78 produced challenges from the Leyland toolroom workers and the fire–fighters – and the TGWU ceased to support the policy. When James Callaghan attempted to enforce a 5% limit for 1978–79, the dam burst as a wide range of groups sought to compensate for three years of belt–tightening. Companies like Ford were not prepared to abide by government norms any more than their employees.

5 The lessons for any future corporatist experiment include the need for tripartite bargaining across the economic spectrum and the necessity for the government to deliver on *its* promises. Whether this is possible in a situation of economic decline and whether such formalised bargaining stimulates a heightening of aspirations are arguable issues. A key question is whether the CBI and the TUC, given their traditions and Britain's devolved and fragmented system of collective bargaining, which since 1979 has become *ever more decentralised*, are in any position to undertake the orchestration of intra–organisational bargaining required for meaningful and enduring concertation. A further problem is the unions' relationship to the Labour Party.

6 Another fundamental criticism contends that corporatism, even of the very limited type practised in the 1960s and 1970s, compromises union independence, weakens links between leadership and rank and file, and undermines activism. The

withering of the sinews of mobilisation, the extinction of the *Daily Herald* and the educational body the National Council of Labour Colleges, the weakening of trades councils and links at local level between the Labour Party and union activists – have been noted (Minkin, 1991, 486). Union leaders spending their time on quangos would, it is argued, be better occupied building up the strengths of their unions. Their influence on these bodies is limited; they become increasingly estranged from their members and any conception of activist trade unionism. The results unions achieve in corporatist arrangements do not justify the price.

Running the country?
It is often claimed that the election of the 1979 Conservative government marked a sudden decisive decline in the fortunes of the unions who, 1974–79, dominated government policy making. This view is open to question on the following grounds:

1 It is difficult not to agree with the assertion that 'the year 1975 marked a high point of union influence as rare as it was brief' (Coates, 1980, 71). The employment legislation provided means for extending union membership. There were soon more than 2,000 nominees installed on tripartite bodies at national and local level. There were high hopes of the Industry Act. And the TUC leaders were, it seemed, never out of Downing Street.

2 After this it was downhill. By early 1975, Callaghan was already stating: 'Britain must now accept lower average wages or face mounting unemployment.' By the summer, it was clear that acceptance of the £6 maximum would involve a fall in living standards for many trade unionists. The real power the unions were able to demonstrate lay in delivering 24 months of tight wage control which reduced real earnings. Moreover the trade–off did not work. By 1977, unemployment had more than doubled, and the government had traded off the maintenance of public expenditure they had promised the TUC to the International Monetary Fund in return for a large loan.

3 Corporatist bargaining involves unions in restraining the economic power of their members in return for the maintenance of full employment and welfare expenditure. Yet under Labour, school–building programmes were cut by 60%, hospital–building was reduced and fewer council houses were built than under the Heath government. Moreover, it was Labour, in defiance of union policies, which ruptured the post–war commitment to full employment and Keynesianism. As James Callaghan told the 1976 Labour Party Conference: 'We used to think that you could spend your way out of a recession by cutting taxes and boosting government spending. I tell you in all candour that this option no longer exists.'

4 If Labour was not converted to monetarism, they increasingly utilised, from 1976, a monetarist approach, cutting public expenditure as a proportion of gross national product, reducing the budget deficit and introducing monetary targets. They differed from monetarists in their reliance on incomes policy, in the large subventions to firms in trouble, in their limited programme of nationalisation, and in their close links with the trade unions. Nonetheless, scrutiny of Labour policies illustrates the need to see in Thatcherism continuity as well as change. The reluctant acquiescence of the unions in a modified monetarism, designed to placate the IMF, demonstrates the distance between the rhetoric of power and the more limited reality.

5 It is clear that the unions did not get what they wanted: union power was used to secure members' acquiescence in a policy very different from that which union conferences advocated. However, the limits of the unions' power of restraint were also evident. Any corporatist–style strategy requires a reconciliation *within* the key interest groups of competing demands and interests. Until 1978, Labour's incomes policy favoured semi–skilled workers in the private sector and manual workers in the public sector. This eroded differentials which created growing *intra–union conflict* and support for Mrs Thatcher's promise of free collective bargaining.

6 What trade union leaders gained under the Labour government was not so much 'the power to determine the substantive drift of policy, as the ability to participate in a new set of *procedural* rights which created the very impression of influence that the resulting drift of policy so often belied' (Coates, 1980, 203). The negative dispersed power of trade unionism was demonstrated in the Winter of Discontent. Its positive power was essentially demonstrated in deference to Labour's leaders rather than domination of the party.

Union power before Thatcher

In the 1960s and 1970s the unions used economic and industrial muscle to halt key government initiatives and, more positively, play a role in policy formation in the years 1970–74. Their access to government was so well established as to be termed 'a constitutional convention if a newly minted one' (Kingdom, 1991, 35). But if the unions' power was real, it was negative rather than creative, and it was restricted. Their role was based upon *their position in the economy and the leverage this gave them*. But the unions' economic power was clearly limited, in terms of the resources available to them (Coates, 1983) and could not be easily translated into purchase on the political process. The strength of a fragmented movement requires harnessing and articulation. Moreover, their economic power was fragile, dependent on continued state commitment to the post-war consensus, crucially to **full employment**, and to union involvement in government. The unions did not have their hands directly on the levers of power in Whitehall or the boardrooms. Union power was *contingent and reactive not primary and inherent*. It had been *given*; it had not been *taken*. Its fruits were limited by the difficulties confronting the Labour government and the unions' inability to provide viable alternatives and influence economic policy (Artis and Cobham, 1991, 266–77). The limits of the political reach of the unions were noted by Martin:

for major policy issues possessing a special importance for either TUC or government, or both there is something to be said for the commonplace conclusion of other pressure group studies: a determined government carries the day in the event of direct conflict (1980, 340).

The fragile basis and secondary nature of union power had been urged at the start of the 1970s:

These trappings are a facade and create an illusion of power . . . involvement is not power . . . The concrete reality of power involves the class conscious use of the economic strength [of the unions] and, in a capitalist society this strength varies with the level of employment. In so far then as the TUC has any real power it is determined by the employment situation. A sudden change in the level of employment would alter its power situation irrespective of the extent to which the TUC was involved in the formal decision-making process (Allen, 1971, 208).

The situation in which the power the state granted unions was perceived as being misused against it could be resolved by the state taking away what it had given. Even in the late 1970s most people believed a return to mass unemployment simply could not happen here. The idea that a government would combine this with significant political exclusion of the unions seemed improbable. But it came to pass.

Thatcherism and the unions

It would be mistaken to view Conservative industrial relations policy as the implementation of imperatives graven in stone in the 1970s. We should not underestimate the influence of 'new right' ideas: a strong ideological orientation developed, influenced by thinkers such as Friedrich Hayek, stimulated by the failure of previous attempts to stem economic decline and obstructive union power, particularly the failure of Heath. It was complemented by a strategic approach to undermining the unions. The Carrington Report, commissioned in 1975 by Mrs Thatcher, sought to learn the lessons of Heath's downfall. The Ridley Report of 1978 suggested buying off workers in key industries, fighting the weaker groups first, changing the law to restrict strikes and picketing, and greater use of a stronger police force in major disputes. *Stepping Stones*, produced by Sir John Hoskyns, later the

Prime Minister's political adviser, saw the unions as the key barrier to economic regeneration and emphasised the importance of union reform and the exclusion of their leaders from the corridors of power (McIlroy, 1991, 12–21).

However, the extent to which these ideas became a formal part of Conservative policy before 1979 was limited. Policy documents such as *The Right Approach to the Economy* were far from the pure milk of new right ideas. Jim Prior still supported the ideas of Heath's post–1972 experiment and looked to a revision of the Social Contract. Mrs Thatcher was wary of him, paying lip service to his ideas whilst supporting the New Right behind his back (Young, 1989, 117). The amplification of the events of the Winter of Discontent into myth strengthened the view that the unions were the major problem – and a vote-winning issue (Marsh, 1992, 59–64).

But Mrs Thatcher's first cabinet remained 'unThatcherised'. Prior was Secretary of State for Employment and he, like Sir Ian Gilmour and others, remained corporatists *who wished to work with the unions* (Gilmour, 1983, 190–2). What gave the Thatcherites confidence was the confused reaction of the union leaders. They appeared men of straw compared with the recollected invincibles of the early 1970s:

The Prime Minister and Sir Geoffrey Howe were 'amazed' by that session. Union leaders seemed surprisingly docile and confused . . . Having lived through the Heath decade they were surprised by how easily Mrs Thatcher dominated the meeting (Dorfman, 1983, 220).

Central was the Prime Minister's ability to keep her nerve and sit out the 1979–81 recession. It was estimated that three-quarters of the increase in unemployment could be attributed to government policies (Layard and Nickell, 1985). Yet in the context of an unexpected world downturn this was far from calculated. Mrs Thatcher did not *engineer* mass unemployment: prioritising control of inflation, she did little to stop it and grasped the opportunities it proffered with both hands. The 'achievement' in breaking from *state maintenance* of full employment, the consequent devastation of manufacturing industry and its impact in reducing union membership and disciplining those in work, the continuation of sustained high levels of unemployment – as well as public apathy to it – these were key to the success of policy. After 1982 the impact of the Falklands War and rising real wages for those in work eased Mrs Thatcher's way. She had successfully dispensed with incomes policy and provided 'free collective bargaining' under conditions where it meant pay increases for some and for others the dole queue. The ensuing increased fragmentation provided sufficient beneficiaries to ensure electoral success.

This was not easily achieved. As unemployment increased Mrs Thatcher was more unpopular than any previous Prime Minister. There was desperation within a cabinet still 'dominated by men with a different viewpoint to her. Sir John Hoskyns asked her to at least consider a 'U-turn' (Young, 1989, 149, 211). After the cabinet reshuffle in 1981 which saw the leadership 'Thatcherised' and Jim Prior dispatched to Belfast and replaced by her own man, Norman Tebbit, matters improved. But until the 1983 election deployment of policy remained cautious. Some in the Conservative leadership still:

feared that increasing unemployment and the monetary and fiscal squeezes which, in part at least, caused it would provoke strident union militancy. In consequence the need to deal with and, if necessary placate, the trade unions was an important part of their argument at various points during the first term (Cosgrave, 1985, 164).

Mrs Thatcher's statecraft was important. She used Prior and then discarded him. She took on the weakened steel workers in 1980 but overruled Ministers who wanted to take on the miners in early 1981. As one of her Ministers John Biffen noted then: 'the spectre that frightened the government was the very clear evidence that there would be massive industrial action' (Cosgrave, 1985, 226). Through the 1980s the Conservatives were careful to avoid a public sector alliance, backing off from confrontation with the water workers in 1983 and placating the railway workers during the 1984–85 miners' strike. Each case was examined in power terms. Those who could cause disruption got a better deal than those with weaker bargaining power. Opportunism was never far away: public sector pay increased by 10% in the year before the 1992 election.

Thatcherism was a new if developing approach to political economy. But we should not view it as too planned or coherent. The monetarism of 1980 for example had run its course by mid-decade. Luck played a role, as with the report of the Clegg Commission which prompted an increase in public sector pay in the difficult early period and the healthy exchange rate which facilitated increases in real wages. Policy *developed* through the influence of ideology *and* reaction to events, design *and* circumstance, statecraft and the political negotiation of support. It was bolstered by electoral success. Thus by the mid-1980s it acquired its own impetus; its appetites grew. The government was prepared to take on the NUM. With the work of excluding the unions politically and basic remedial legislation completed, there was a new emphasis on excluding, regulating and disorganising the unions. Themes unrehearsed in the 1970s were now heard. Each victory provided a new fillip and new additions to the agenda. As the ability of the unions to respond diminished, policy increasingly represented a reaction to events. Despite important changes and the succession of John Major essential continuities mean the approach is still usefully characterised as **Thatcherism**.

Conservative policy: the key components

Conservative policy has demanded the transformation, restriction and exclusion of unions. The models of apolitical US business unionism and Japanese enterprise unions were periodically referred to. A key factor has been the relationship of industrial relations policy to economic policy. The attack on the unions was viewed as an essential ingredient of economic regeneration based upon galvanising industry, making it more efficient by opening it to the pressures of international competition and integrating it more completely in the world market. Conservative policy has involved a number of emphases developed gradually and unevenly.

1 The decisive weakening of union bargaining power through the restriction of *workers' power to act collectively* was central. There were to be legal limitations on union organisation and industrial action. With diminished ability to act collectively, the scope and coverage of collective bargaining would be weakened. Employees would be pushed towards the individually 'negotiated' contract. This would strengthen the power of employers and reduce union membership.

2 These policies would restore the market, re-inject competition into industry, enhance profit levels, reduce wages and further the development of new enterprises, free from unions in the traditional mould and from strikes. The public sector should be restructured, deregulated and privatised. The state would stimulate the restoration of the *competitive entrepreneurial individual* by acting as a role model, introducing local bargaining and performance related pay. This would facilitate competition between employees and erode identity of interest. Wages, no longer based on comparability, would find their market level.

3 The state could make a key contribution by tight monetary policy, acting in the spirit of Sir Keith Joseph's injunction: 'full employment is not in the gift of government. It should not be promised and cannot be provided' (Joseph, 1979b, 2). Matters must be left to market forces. Higher unemployment would be accompanied by accelerating change in the industrial structure and employment practices. Legislation would increase tendencies to more flexible working which could strengthen the individualisation of industrial relations and assert the irrelevance of trade unions.

4 The government wished to stimulate business unionism. This required not only a weakening of links with the Labour Party but the erosion of trade unionism as a *movement*, a loosening of solidaristic bonds across industry and a greater identification of the union with the needs of the enterprise. 'In the nineties,' Norman Tebbit stated, 'I believe that managements and work forces will have to come closer together, seeing that their common interest is in the firm – not the national union.'

5 These objectives required attenuation of concepts of unions as

a 'fifth estate' in society. Union leaders were to be excluded
from the corridors of power. They should show themselves
more responsive to members at the expense of the concerns of
irresponsible activists, a change to be facilitated by the introduction of systems of plebiscitary democracy.

6 Some trade unionists had a stake in the old system of Labour
Party links, a swollen protected public sector and state aid to
industry. Instead employers should offer employees a stake in
the new system – introducing employee shareholding, profit
sharing and employee involvement.

7 The precursor of a residual state complementing a free market
must be an activist state, intervening in the labour market to
prepare the conditions for final withdrawal. A number of
set piece confrontations between government and unions were
budgeted for. Andrew Gamble's formula 'free economy, strong
state' aptly characterised the Conservative approach. Government would never again back down before mass picketing but
would use the full force of the state to quell the use of disorder
from which the unions had benefited in the 1970s.

Out in the cold

In 1979 the leaders of the unions had direct access to Ministers
and were meshed into social decision-making via a network of
industrial and economic bodies such as the NEDC; the Industrial
Training Boards; the Advisory, Conciliation, and Arbitration
Services; the Health and Safety Executive; the Manpower
Services Commission; and the National Enterprise Board. They
were well represented on the boards of nationalised industries.
TUC nominees also sat on bodies such as the Schools' Council,
the Health Authorities, the two Equality Commissions and Industrial Tribunals.

The corridors of power

Direct contact with government decreased but continued links
with the TUC were initially manipulated not terminated. The
Chancellor Geoffrey Howe refused to meet the TUC before his

first budget which launched the tight monetary and fiscal squeeze vital to the future of Thatcherism. Instead the TUC Economic Committee was granted a meeting with the Prime Minister a fortnight later in which:

[Mrs Thatcher] seized control of the session right at the outset. The TUC's plans and strategies went out the window as she held the floor for virtually the entire hour the meeting lasted . . . they listened passively as the Prime Minister lectured to them (Dorfman, 1983, 110, 111).

This formative episode demonstrated the new reality. Access was now to be 'after the event' access. Encounters would involve transmissions in which government briefed the unions on how to live with decisions they had played no part in. Nonetheless, a wide range of contacts took place – the TUC were 'beered and sandwiched' in the 1980 steel dispute just as in earlier decades. Meetings between Prior and the TUC over employment legislation in 1979 and 1980 were extensive. But the union leaders felt they were unproductive and their comments were having no discernible impact. Meanwhile in the primary area which influenced union activities an economic policy was being put in place which ended the post-war consensus and which would decisively sap union power.

Contact continued even when Prior was replaced by Tebbit. If Ministers were still prepared to talk they were not prepared to trim, for, in Mrs Thatcher's words, 'there was no alternative'. Also involved was a removal of the unions' *legitimacy* as participants in social decision-making. The restoration of individualism and the free market required government and management to address citizens directly, not through the good offices of bureaucrats which legitimated collectivism. The unfruitful nature of those contacts there *were* further cooled the atmosphere. As Conservative policies achieved success, there was less need to seek co-operation. The government only talked formally with TUC leaders if they smelt trouble, as over the 1981 inner-city riots and over GCHQ. Contacts in 1984 and 1985 included two meetings with the Prime Minister and with Ministers not only at Employment but at the Foreign Office, Energy, Trade and Social

Security. If what was achieved was negligible links were maintained even after Labour's 1987 election defeat. Intimate informal contact was, however, exploited by government through 'the cold war'. Frank Chappell dined with Tebbit and Nigel Lawson. Murray advised Tebbit on MSC appointments whilst ex-NUM President Joe Gormley discussed his successor's strategy with Ministers (Tebbit, 1988, 184; Lawson, 1992, 148). It is therefore mistaken to think that 'the 1980s have witnessed the virtual rupture of relations between the unions and the Conservative Government' (Longstreth, 1988, 415).

The full range and level of contacts to 1984 can be seen in Table 5.1. There is little difference in terms of overall number of contacts between the Labour 1970s and the Conservative 1980s. However, contact is increasingly initiated by the TUC, not the government, it occurs at a lower level, and it increasingly involves a move from harder face–to–face contact to weaker contact by writing. And, as Table 5.2 demonstrates, there is a significant decline in the *effectiveness* of TUC contacts with government.

However, it may be argued that the definition of contact adhered to here is too diffuse. An exchange of letters may involve only good manners, rather than even minimal acceptance of the significance of the TUC as a pressure group. An agreement to meet at Ministerial level denotes more serious acceptance. Moreover, the differences between the TUC's relations with the Conservatives as compared to the last Labour government are minimised if we measure matters only by formal contact. Such was the intimacy between the TUC and the 1974–79 government that many contacts would not show up in TUC Reports. If it is difficult to measure access, it is even harder to gauge the importance and value of relationships when 'contacts' covers – as it does – a bewildering range of problems from those vital to the unions, the economy and employment legislation, to those of less significance. **Effectiveness**, the degree to which the TUC got what it wanted from the government, is even harder to calculate. Many meetings are barely consultative. Where there is genuine consultation or negotiation, to what degree are the TUC's arguments or pressure an important influence in a change of government position?

Table 5.1 *Levels of policy contacts of the TUC (%)*

	Labour				Conservative					
	1976	1977	1978	1979	1979	1980	1981	1982	1983	1984
Prime Minister	7	4	7	9	4	1	1	3	1	2
Minister	67	66	65	65	65	64	61	58	64	66
Official	4	2	2	1	0	0	1	0	1	2
Advisory Committee	7	4	2	5	2	3	2	3	4	3
Quango[a]	10	11	15	10	15	15	12	11	13	14
Select Committee	1	1	2	1	0	4	6	5	4	3
Royal Commission	1	2	1	2	0	0	0	1	1	0
MP	1	1	0	1	0	2	5	6	2	1
Public Opinion[b]	1	0	1	1	10	5	4	5	7	8
Unknown	1	9	6	6	4	6	7	9	4	1
Totals	279	205	242	187	48	252	281	280	248	264

[a] Quangos: The MSC, HSC, ACAS, Equal Opportunities Commission, Commission for Racial Equality were most important, NEDC contacts are also included.

[b] Influencing public opinion takes the form of demonstration, days of action, strikes and advertisements in the media, also counted were appeals against the government to the International Labour Organisation (1983).

Source: Mitchell, 1987.

Table 5.2 *The effectiveness of TUC contacts with government*

| | Labour | | | | Conservative | | | | | |
	1976	1977	1978	1979	1979	1980	1981	1982	1983	1984
Successes	42.5	43.0	47.0	40.5	4.5	18.5	22.5	22.0	14.0	18.5
(As % of contacts)	(15)	(21)	(19)	(22)	(9)	(7)	(8)	(8)	(6)	(7)
Tripartite success	10.5	6.0	9.5	4.0	6.5	6.5	9.5	9.0	4.0	10.5
(As % of contacts)	(25)	(14)	(20)	(10)	(22)	(35)	(42)	(41)	(29)	(57)

Source: Mitchell, 1987.

Accepting the fallibility of this approach, we have updated Mitchell's findings, looking only at the harder measure of face-to-face contact with Ministers. In 1985 there were 23 meetings with Ministers and one with the Prime Minister. The difficulties of measuring effectiveness can be seen from a meeting with the Employment Secretary over proposed legislation on Wages Councils. The TUC argued that they should not be abolished, nor should young people be removed from protection. The government proceeded with the latter not the former. But it is questionable how serious the government was about implementing the former. In only 1.5 of the 1985 contacts is it possible to discern any TUC success in influencing policy. This is not to suggest that exchange of information and consultation are not valuable in themselves. In 1986 there were no meetings with the Prime Minister and 10 at Ministerial level and, in 1987, 11 meetings, again all at Ministerial level. The decline in frequency and effectiveness of meetings continued and in both these years there was no meeting in which the TUC clearly achieved modification of government policy.

There is also an increase in simple refusals to meet – for example registered by Nicholas Ridley over the Poll Tax and Norman Fowler over EU directives. As Table 5.3 illustrates, the government is still willing to maintain relations with the TUC over a wide range of important issues. But it is far from willing to accord it the level or degree of access of the 1970s, still less to take the TUC's advice or change pre-established positions.

The advent of John Major made little difference. A meeting between top TUC leaders and the Chancellor of the Exchequer in 1993 was the first since 1988. When TUC General Secretary Norman Willis met John Major the same year it was indirectly as part of a joint delegation of European trade unionists. The TUC can still often get access to government but rarely today at the highest level. And *results* are quite another matter. In the 1990s the TUC is still an active pressure group – but an increasingly unsuccessful one.

Table 5.3   *TUC meetings with Ministers*

1985	Level	Subject	Outcome
October	Home Secretary	Shops Bill	U
November	Energy Secretary	Energy industry	U
November	Sec. of State for Transport	Transport Act	I
December	Sec. of State for Health & Social Security	Government Social Security Review	U
1986			
January	Under-Secretary for Employment	Repeal of protective legislation	U
January	Sec. of State for Transport	Transport Act	I
January	Minister of Trade	Multi-fibre agreement	I
February	Minister of Social Security	1986 Budget	I
March	Minister of State: Home Office	Public Order Bill	U
March	Sec. of State for Employment	MSC community programme	U
March	Minister of Trade	Multi-fibre agreement	I
April	Sec. of State for Health & Social Security	Social Security Bill	U
May	Arts Minister	Public spending on arts	I
May	Energy Secretary	Gas Bill	U
May	Paymaster General	Wages Bill	U
July	Treasury Minister	Public expenditure	I
July	Minister of Agriculture	Agricultural issues	I
July	Sec. of State for Health & Social Security	Public expenditure	U
July	Home Secretary	Prisons	U
September	Sec. of State for Foreign Affairs	South African sanctions	U

Table 5.3 continued

November	Sec. of State for Employment	Deregulation	U
December	Minister of State for Foreign Affairs	South African sanctions	U
December	Sec. of State for Education	Teachers' pay machinery	U
1987			
February	Sec. of State for Education	Teachers' pay machinery	U
February	Home Secretary	Public inquiry into police at Wapping	U
February	Chancellor of the Exchequer	TUC submission on Budget	U
February	Minister of State for Industry	Steel industry	I
April	Sec. of State for Employment	Manpower Services Commission	I
June	Sec. of State for Employment	Green Paper on employment law	U
July	Minister of State for Transport	GATT and textiles	I

Notes
S: TUC successful in objective.
U: TUC unsuccessful in objective.
I: Meeting largely in nature of exchange of information.

Source: TUC Reports.

The decline of tripartism
The picture of significant loss of political influence is sustained if we turn to the tripartite bodies. Only a shadow of corporatism remains, its substance sucked dry by administrations hostile to the insertion of collective intermediaries between individual citizens and the state.

Again change was far from immediate and sweeping. The unions maintained rough parity of representation on ACAS. But ACAS's legal role in securing union recognition and the extension of collective bargaining was removed by the first Thatcher government. In 1993 its mission to *encourage* collective bargaining was terminated. Whilst many training boards were quickly abolished – together with fulcrums of corporatism such as the National Enterprise Board – the MSC on which unions maintained equal representation with employers continued to play a significant role until the mid-1980s. However its successor, the Training Commission, established in 1987, gave employers the right to 9 representatives compared with only 3 from the unions. When the Employment Training Scheme was boycotted by the unions in 1988 the government replaced the Commission with the Training Agency and Training and Enterprise Councils. Two-thirds of the members of the new bodies were to be employers and senior figures in industry. In 1992 only 58 of the 1,136 directors of the 82 TECs were trade unionists – around 5%. In the key area of training the corporatist emphasis sustained since the Industrial Training Act 1964 was replaced by privatisation and employer dominance. Where vestiges remained, as with state finance for shop steward training, the system was under close government scrutiny and, as banning of TUC materials on courses demonstrated, ultimately controlled by the state (McIlroy, 1993).

The unions maintained representation on other bodies such as industrial tribunals and they were asked to nominate to the new quangos established through the complex contradictions of government policy. By the mid-1980s they were still represented on around 140 different bodies and key coping stones of corporatism such as the NEDC were still functioning. But the influence union representatives exercised on these bodies and the influence these bodies exercised on government was negligible. Mrs Thatcher pronounced the NEDC 'a waste of time'. After the 1987 election the government announced that the NEDC would in future only meet quarterly instead of monthly and there would be a severe reduction in staffing. In 1992 the NEDC was abolished. The removal of this major landmark demonstrated beyond all doubt that corporatism was a corpse. The axing of relics of the Social Contract, such as the state grant for shop steward training, in the same year finally wrote *finis* to the role the

TUC had developed so painstakingly since 1926.

The unions' response

There was undoubtedly an element of disorientation and demoralisation in the aftermath of the Conservatives' 1979 electoral victory. Some have argued the latter evoked despair in Congress House. In this view TUC staff had at least a good inkling of the threat Thatcherism represented (Dorfman, 1983, 20, 97–8). Against this was the fact that Thatcherism was not dominant in 1979; in some ways its overt programme was less radical than that presented by Heath in 1970. There is, moreover, the recollected view of Len Murray:

We thought that this was another Conservative Government and we had had plenty of Conservative governments in the past and we'd got on with them, you know, reasonably well. And we saw no reason why we shouldn't get on with Mrs Thatcher reasonably well (McIlroy, 1992, 149).

There were problems of leadership. Moss Evans of the TGWU and Terry Duffy of the AEU were poor replacements for Jack Jones and Hugh Scanlon. By May 1979 the economic situation was already deteriorating. The unions would find themselves facing major threats with the ground falling from under them in the worst recession for half a century. The response was to stimulate a return to the post-war consensus and the kind of 'U-turn' in macroeconomic policy executed in 1972 through pressure which would simultaneously frighten the Thatcherites, bolster the wets in the Conservative Party and prepare the way for a Labour government. The TUC saw their task as criticising government policy, organising their affiliates into a posture of antagonism and involving themselves in the detail of policy-making against the day when Labour was returned to power. The pendulum would swing, Thatcherism would turn the electorate leftwards. The TUC's hopes were shared by the Conservative wets who believed 'the Thatcherite phase would be no more than an intermission after which those to whom the Conservative Party historically belonged would resume command' (Young, 1989,

139). And would then rebuild links with the unions. To encourage this as Thatcher's unpopularity increased the TUC implemented a tactical withdrawal of goodwill and boycott of talks:

they would not seek a meeting with the Chancellor as this would serve no useful purpose. The focus had to be on presenting to the public the TUC's alternative to the monetarist deflationary policies of the present government (TUC, 1980, 389).

This was complemented by campaigning. In the early 1980s the TUC seemed to have a campaign for everything. There were the TUC/Labour Party demonstrations on unemployment, the 1981 and 1983 People's Marches for Jobs and Days of Action over legislation and the NHS dispute. A variety of initiatives, such as the Campaign for Economic and Social Advance were launched. The TUC dallied with the notion that a movement from below might accelerate the demise of Thatcher. Such a movement was unlikely: fragmentation had increased since the early 1970s and shop steward militancy was now coming up against a sudden unprecedented increase in unemployment. The leadership which had developed in the post-war years, more confident, less cautious than their predecessors, were now facing the challenges trade unionism had confronted in the 1920s and 1930s. Moreover, the militancy of 1978–79 had frightened many union leaders who were also worried at the electoral implications of any mass mobilisation. They were, therefore, determined to exercise hands-on control over campaigns. The TUC called off the unemployment demonstrations when the Labour leadership felt they might be electorally counter-productive. They supported the second People's March under extreme pressure from the TGWU and TUC Regional Councils. And they were careful not to call for industrial action against the government. The TUC remained within the parameters of Labourism. There was never any intention of *replacing* links with government with campaigning in the streets. Len Murray was at one with George Woodcock's dictum that the TUC had left Trafalgar Square a long time ago.

The unions' policy response to Thatcherism centred on the Alternative Economic Strategy which went hand in hand for many with support for constitutional change in the Labour Party to ensure future implementation of agreed programmes (see Chapter 7). Different versions of the AES proposed more direct-ive planning of industry, foreign trade and financial markets; greater state investment and control over key enterprises; import controls; withdrawal from the EU; workers' participation and aggressive redistribution of income and wealth. Against Thatcher's international economic policy it posed a national siege economy approach at the very time trends towards world economic integration, deregulation and globalisation were rendering such approaches redundant. In all probability it would have met a similar fate to the approach of the 1980s Mitterrand government in France. But the unions' alternative to Thatcherism never left the drawing board.

For the promise of a Labour government like the promise of a 'U-turn' proved insubstantial. The wets refused to organise:

We felt that it would be dangerous for us to form ourselves into a cabal since we would run the risk of being castigated immediately as conniving together against the leadership (Prior, 1986, 140).

In September 1981 when the cabinet was reshuffled accounts were settled with the wets. The massive industrial action Mrs Thatcher feared never came. Declaring 'Turn if you like. The Lady's not for turning', Mrs Thatcher proved more obdurate than Heath. *Unlike her predecessor she really wanted to end the post-war consensus* and she was willing to confront the problems this would throw up.

The new realism

By the time of Labour's worst post-war defeat in 1983 the unions had lost over 2 million members and, in retrospect, decisive battles. At the 1983 Congress Len Murray personally led the opposition to a hardening of the union position and a formal break with government. Supported by right-wing leaders such as Frank Chappell of the EETPU he outlined plans for 'a new realism'. Accepting the world had changed dramatically since 1978, unions had to come to terms with the new world and their weakened position in it. What was involved was an adaption to Mrs Thatcher's success. New realism took various forms. For the new Labour Party leadership of Neil Kinnock it meant breaking Labour from the lurch left and accepting key points of Thatcherism. For the EETPU it involved a move to business unionism and no strike deals. For Len Murray it meant attempting to turn the TUC once again into a pressure group which accepted it was not entitled to a seat in government. The post-1979 strategy of antagonism had failed. The unions had to acknowledge that they were not, in Murray's words, 'some sort of alternative government, Brother Bonnie Prince Charlie waiting to be summoned back from exile'. The electorate was against them. Unions had to represent their members' interests now and this required holding out the hand of co-operation to the Conservatives. This would involve the TUC distancing itself somewhat from Labour.

In one sense this represented few difficulties. The new Labour Party leadership wanted a less intimate relationship with the TUC which it viewed as less than an electoral asset. However, there were some on the General Council who opposed Murray. Opposition was underpinned by a very strong argument. There was no way into Downing Street: even the tradespersons' entrance was bolted and barred. For Murray and his supporters the insuperable problem was that the political basis for a new accord in which the TUC would play a subaltern role, was non-existent. Mrs Thatcher had never wanted the unions, even as junior partners. By 1983 she did not need them. Murray's refusal in December 1983 to support the NGA in its dispute with Eddie Shah was a clear signal that 'Barkis is willing'.

Murray co-authored a charter for the new approach, *TUC Strategy*. Whilst it reasserted TUC opposition to Conservative legislation, it also stressed the utility of unions in increasing efficiency. Unions accepted 'the need to sustain the enterprise as a thriving concern'. Employers and government, in their turn, 'have to take note of unions because they are the vehicle for winning the consent of individuals, as workers, for policies employers and governments wish to pursue and that they need the co-operation of workers if they are to succeed'. The document recalled the historic links between the unions and the Tories: 'TUC involvement in government owes much to Churchill's war-time coalition government and to the Conservative governments that established the NEDC and the MSC'. If the TUC, since 1979, had criticised Conservative policies, it had 'drawn a clear distinction between the use of industrial action for industrial purposes, and its use for political purposes insisting that governments, no matter how distasteful their polices, are to be changed through the ballot box, not industrial action'. Governments, whatever their complexion, had to involve the TUC because of the important section of society it represented.

Cogent and conciliatory as this offer of partnership was, Mrs Thatcher wasn't having any. The storm in January 1984 over her attempts to ban trade unions at the GCHQ signals centre in Cheltenham produced the TUC's clearest gesture yet. If the government withdrew the ban, they promised a *voluntary* 'no strike' agreement. Mrs Thatcher met the TUC leaders and turned them down flat. In the face of such intransigence, Murray was unable to hold the line for 'new realism'. The TUC withdrew its representatives from the NEDC and, whilst this proved temporary, the miners' strike then dislocated the situation for some twelve months.

Murray had spent himself on constructing support for the new realism. He resigned as General Secretary. His subsequent elevation to the House of Lords as the miners went down to defeat highlighted the contradictions of British trade unions in the 1980s.

Alternatives: the great miners' strike

Asked in late 1977 how she would deal with a miners' strike Mrs Thatcher replied that she would call a referendum. By 1984 she was better prepared. This was a political strike and its political nature on the government's side was demonstrated by its willingness to bear the costs – over £2.5 billion – to defeat what it saw as the most politically disruptive section of organised labour. By 1984 unemployment had been around 3 million for two years. The TUC had lost 3 million members and the strike figures were down. Moreover, real pay rises in 1982 and 1983 suggested a 'feel good factor' might be operating for many of those in work. This might have suggested unprepossessing prospects for militancy: many felt there was little alternative given the limitations of 'new realism'. The only thing that could change the government, they argued, was direct action and in this context attention turned to the miners – victors in two recent confrontations with government. As recently as 1981 Mrs Thatcher had backed away from a re-run because as the Secretary of State for Energy David Howell later observed:

neither the government, nor I think society as a whole, was in a position to get locked into a coal strike . . . I don't think the country was prepared and the whole NUM and the trade union movement tended to be united on one side.

By 1984, as urged in the Ridley Report, coal stocks were high and the police were ready to deal with mass picketing. The price of coal had tumbled. The government had assumed such a confrontation could occur, particularly since the election of Arthur Scargill as NUM President in December 1981. Nonetheless the failure of the miners' leadership to secure a majority for action in two subsequent ballots demonstrated divisions in the miners' ranks. The time of year and stockpiles of coal at power stations and throughout industry made a strike unlikely in the spring of 1984.

The failure to secure the support of the Nottingham miners who worked through the year-long stoppage and the failure to hold a national ballot on action constituted a running sore debilitating the impact of action mounted in very difficult objective circumstances. Into this context of division and an unfavourable power situation, the state stepped in in a fashion not seen since 1926.

In the 1972 miners' strike, notably at Saltley Gates, the police had backed down before mass picketing. Now the restraint of the post-war consensus went overboard. *If mass unemployment was key to the impact of Thatcherism so was taking the gloves off the power of the state.* The union leadership was monitored by MI5. A large mobile police force was used on an unprecedented post-war scale, deployed *en masse* to outnumber pickets and used aggressively to break picket lines. By the second week of the strike 20,000 police drawn from 43 different forces were available, on the basis that on any picket line the police must possess overwhelming superiority. Pickets were stopped from entering Nottingham through roadblocks, and operations were co-ordinated by the Association of Chief Police Officers through the National Reporting Centre at Scotland Yard. Nearly 10,000 people were arrested during the 51-week strike and the cost of police overtime was put at £140 million (McIlroy, 1985). The extensive use of civil law against the union was an essential complement to criminal actions against activists in disorganising and eventually breaking the strike.

Yet as in any such struggle the outcome was not inevitable. There were key moments, as when NACOD threatened strike action which would have closed all the pits, when the state faced defeat. What ultimately ensured Mrs Thatcher's victory was not coercion but the absence of solidarity. The TUC sat on the sidelines: no 'contribution was forthcoming from either the TUC or the national leadership of the Labour Party. The NUM attracted only vestigial support of a token kind' (Coates, 1989, 131). For the most part, TUC and Labour Party leaders wished the strike had not happened and would end as quickly as possible for it disrupted the real work of building bridges to government and recasting Labour Party policy.

The consequences of the miners' defeat were mixed. It was rather catastrophic to describe it as Norman Tebbit did as 'the last battle in the struggle against the unions' (Goodman, 1985, 45). Nonetheless, the miners' strike was a watershed: if the strikes of 1972 and 1974 symbolised the surge of union power, the strike of 1984–85 demonstrated its ebbing. Thatcher had revenged Heath's defeats and faced down the praetorian guard of the Labour Movement. *The miners' defeat was a watershed* which facilitated the resurgence of the now not so new realism. Unions such as the GMB under John Edmonds and even, under a posture of defiance, the TGWU now followed a similar 'realist' line to that of Norman Willis, Murray's successor as TUC General Secretary. Its direct impact in demoralising other groups or workers is questionable. But as an exemplar of the new state response to mass action the defeat meshed with the economic situation and the ever-increasing web of legislation to strengthen caution and constitutionalism in industrial action.

The TUC: organisational stress

The TUC's political influence requires reconciliation of the differing interests of affiliates to represent them effectively to the state, a degree of unity and cohesion. Yet its authority with its members is influenced by its success with the state. State hostility has thus undermined the TUC internally and externally, the two dimensions interacting in debilitating fashion. In the years of Conservative rule the TUC has been seen as conflict ridden. Again closer examination discloses a more complex picture.

The statistics do not support the stereotype of internecine turmoil. Table 5.4 shows an overall decline – indeed a collapse – in the number of disputes entering the TUC disputes machinery in the 1980s compared with the previous decade and also a decline in what might be perceived as the more intractable problems, those which resist earlier conciliation and proceed to adjudication. In the years 1975–79 there were on average 96 complaints each year and on average 25 of these proceeded to a formal decision. Between 1980 and 1987 the figures dropped to 74 and 12. Since 1987 the Disputes Committee has heard on average only 9 complaints a year. Whilst these figures could be explained, at least to some degree, by decreases in union membership and/or a loss of faith by unions in the efficacy of the TUC machinery they gave no credence at all to the popular view of a large scale growth in union strife.

What seems plausible is that inter-union conflict became more fundamental and explosive. Eric Hammond's comment to Congress delegates 'Hitler would have been proud of you lot' (TUC,

Table 5.4   *The TUC and inter-union disputes*

Year	Disputes reported to TUC	Disputes committee hearing	Independent review committee
1975	78	28	–
1976	52	33	4
1977	111	25	16
1978	130	23	12
1979	111	16	13
1980	99	11	2
1981	91	17	2
1982	80	16	0
1983	68	8	2
1984	65	14	1
1985	55	13	0
1986	68	13	0
1987	70	14	0
1988	65	17	0
1989	61	8	0
1990	53	5	0
1991	49	7	0
1992	41	4	0

Source: McIlroy, 1992.

1984, 403) expressed the flavour of the in-fighting. This was because of enhanced perceptions of divergent interests and the different conceptions of purpose unions developed as the 1970s consensus flaked in the face of membership decline and unfavourable political and economic circumstances. The failure of the campaign against legislation prompted a greater tendency towards 'every union for itself'. The EETPU and AEU's embracing of a strong variant of 'new realism' acted to stimulate divisions. These crystallised in different attitudes to employment legislation and single union 'no strike deals'. As divisions strengthened, the TUC's desire to avoid splits at all costs in itself contributed to the most significant post-war split in the British Labour Movement.

Inter-union struggles

The gravity of the problem was highlighted in 1984 by the Hitachi case. In adjudicating on the complaint by six unions against the EETPU the TUC agreed that the EETPU should not have signed a single union agreement, but the electricians were not instructed to return to the *status quo*. The TUC compromise – new employees would be informed of the right to join other unions and officials of other unions would have rights in procedures via the EETPU – gave the electricians most of what they wanted and encouraged the view that aggression paid. This was reinforced by their success at the *Today* newspaper where Eddie Shah handed the EETPU jobs which would normally have been performed by members of the print unions. Aggrieved unions successfully sought revision of the Bridlington principles at the 1985 Congress. Now 'no affiliated organisation should enter into a single union agreement or union membership agreement under any circumstances . . . where other unions would be deprived of their existing rights except by prior agreement of the other unions concerned' (TUC, 1985, 429). However this still left the question of 'greenfield' sites open.

The dispute over taking state funds for union ballots further soured the atmosphere (see p. 258). However the TUC maintained its conciliatory attitude during the Wapping dispute. When, in February 1986, the EETPU were found guilty of 5 out of 7 charges arising from the involvement of their officials in recruiting labour to work at Rupert Murdoch's new plant their response was cautious. TUC full-time staff exercised a strong influence in limiting disciplinary action against the electricians. Deputy General Secretary Ken Graham successfully opposed instructing the EETPU to direct members at Wapping not to work with non–unionists, on the now familiar ground that this would bring the TUC into conflict with the employment legislation.

The 1986 Congress rejected this position; it resolved that the EETPU should be directed to 'instruct' its members. Nothing was done. The General Council reported to the 1987 Congress it had felt unable to reverse its decision: the EETPU could not be tried twice on the same charges. The 1987 Congress laid the ground for progress by voting to establish a special review body which would examine the whole field of recruitment and inter-union relations. Subsequent new evidence, demonstrating the EETPU had misled the General Council over involvement with Rupert Murdoch and continued to have dealings with News International, meant that Norman Willis was once more forced to mount rearguard action to avoid the EETPU's suspension. The General Secretary's activities over the Dundee affair further weakened TUC authority. No less than 11 TUC affiliates had established bargaining rights at Ford. Yet, in mid-1987, the AEU announced it had signed a single union deal with the company covering a new operation in Dundee. Although this seemed to be in clear violation of the 1985 amendment to Bridlington, the TUC placed more emphasis on new jobs. The matter was resolved only when, in the face of strong opposition from the TGWU and MSF, Ford announced it was shelving the scheme.

By 1988 matters were reaching crisis point. At the April General Council, the EETPU was strongly censured for its behaviour over Wapping, the General Secretary again arguing that stronger measures were precluded by the danger of legal action by the EETPU. The union's failure to comply with disputes committee awards at Orion Electronics and Christian Salveson was also noted. In both these cases the EETPU had signed single union agreements in violation of TUC policy and without consulting other unions with membership.

The consequent expulsion of the EETPU for failure to accept TUC directives in these two cases provided the opportunity for a new beginning. The 1988 Congress accepted the inadequacy of the Bridlington principles in dealing with new challenges and gave the TUC new powers as a union regulator. Principle 5 of the TUC Disputes Principles and Procedures was modified and a new Code of Practice introduced. In future unions discussing single-union agreements should notify the TUC giving details of other unions with interests in the situation. The TUC would then offer advice. Unions should not sign recognition agreements which removed rights to take industrial action and when negotiating recognition should be careful not to undermine the 'general level of terms and conditions of employment' already the subject of agreement with the employer concerned.

The split wrecked the 'completeness' of the TUC. Much hot air was expended on likely conflicts over recruitment and the establishment of an alternative TUC. Apart from a handful of cases, such as the EETPU's recruitment of UCATT officials, competition for members remained bitter but muted although in 1990 the EETPU played a role in the Council of Managerial and Professional Services with 28 other non-TUC unions. Matters were complicated in 1992 when electricians and engineers merged to form the AEEU. However, negotiations produced a compromise. The new organisation successfully balloted on TUC affiliation in 1993 and a conciliation procedure was established to ease the former EETPU's readmission to the fold.

Into the 1990s

It would be wrong to over-emphasise fragmentation and conflict. From 1987, mergers and closer links demonstrated that co-operation over political fund ballots was not an isolated event. The EETPU's exclusion was brief. With the establishment in 1987 of the Special Review Committee the TUC made a positive contribution in a series of strategic documents to analysis of the unions' ills and the promotion of a union revival based on more efficient recruitment. It continued nonetheless on the downward slope. Membership loss and collapse in political influence continued as the economic situation improved. Its internal authority was diminished and it failed to etch a new role as a recruiting agency for its affiliates (see Chapter 10). The TUC *had* consolidated and developed many of the organisational gains of the two previous decades, such as regional machinery, and for much of the decade maintained provision of services to affiliates which in quantity and quality surpassed its performance during most of the post-war period (McIlroy, 1992, 172–7). It had developed as a 'think tank'. However its pursuit of a wider role was undermined by the unelectability of Labour and the reduced role the TUC now played in Party decision-making.

In the 1990s weaknesses became more apparent. The development of 'mega-unions' such as UNISON, the AEEU and possibly a merged GMB–TGWU raised questions as to the TUC's future relevance if the bulk of affiliated membership was concentrated into a handful of unions, themselves capable of carrying out functions hitherto the prerogative of Congress House. Financial strains were never far away. By 1992 the General Council had agreed in principle to cut the TUC wage bill by 20%, reduce the number of departments from 9 to 7 and cut the number of regional secretaries and education officers from 9 to 6. Plans to limit the operation of trades councils encountered opposition but the role of the TUC was under serious review. In 1993 its annual income was £10 million – around a tenth of UNISON's. The year 1994 saw a relaunch with TUC organisation remoulded in recognition of its reduced functions. The system of committees shadowing government departments was scrapped; the General Council would meet less frequently with a new Executive meeting monthly. Under its new General Secretary, John Monks, the TUC accepted that the days of extended influence over all aspects of government policy were finally over. There was a healthy emphasis on key campaigns and the need to concentrate on full employment. However the dominant stress was on business unionism and partnership with employers: 'in the past the British industrial relations system has focused on conflict resolution rather than consensus building. This must change if our economic performance is to match the best in the world' (TUC, 1993, 2). Relaunch conferences were addressed by Ministers – and boycotted by the TGWU. There was renewed emphasis on building bridges to the Conservatives and Liberal Democrats, with former Liberal Democrat Des Wilson appointed as PR Consultant.

The major development of the late 1980s, the turn to Europe, continued (see Chapter 8). The other card was incomes policy. Britain's entry into the ERM in October 1990 prompted intensified discussion on the role of wages and the TUC were determined to get in on the act. Flavour of the month was 'co-ordinated bargaining' as advocated by the GMB and UCW. Related to Labour's proposals for a national minimum wage and National Economic Assessment the argument was that if the majority of wage deals could be compressed into the three months following the Chancellor's autumn statement wages could be restrained. This was viewed as a step towards an incomes policy under Labour. But the opportunism of some union leaders bred impatience. At the NEDC they offered a 'responsible stance on pay' in return for tripartite talks on pay, productivity and investment in the aftermath of ERM entry. Peremptory rejection of the offer by government and CBI underlined the desperation of the TUC: even *talks* about pay restraint would represent a small step forward. But it was clear they could not deliver – both exclusion from political representation and decentralisation of bargaining had undermined their authority. Even if they could, the government was not prepared to re-legitimise the unions. As the consequent abolition of the NEDC demonstrated, John Major represented much the same as Margaret Thatcher. When Major did introduce formal wage restraint in the public sector the TUC were simply not consulted. Instead, they had to make do with inviting Howard Davies of the CBI to address the 1992 Congress – another first.

The 1992–93 dispute over government plans to close 31 pits with a loss of 20,000 mining jobs provided a cameo of the differences between the early 1990s and a decade earlier. In 1982 there were 300,000 miners; in 1992, 30,000. Instead of balloting for an all out stoppage the NUM balloted for one-day strikes. It was now the unions not the employers who sought to use the law on the grounds that proper procedures for closure had not been followed. Instead of being sidelined, the TUC was given control of the campaign over pit closures and secured a moratorium on industrial action. It mounted instead a protest campaign highly successful in mobilising public opinion and embarrassing the government. The changed climate was demonstrated by the support accorded the miners. However, a plan to reprieve 12 pits for two years defused the movement although it was clear that with impending privatisation the mining industry was finally heading for death row. It was only in April 1993 after seven months of protest that the NUM mounted a one-day strike in conjunction with the railway workers. However, the TUC refused to support wider action and the UDM stayed at work.

The government had overreached itself but once again it regrouped and by 1993 was moving to close pits it had reprieved only months before. Despite the new 'people power' approach and significant public protest it was, in the end, yet another defeat for the unions.

Conclusions

From 1940, the TUC increased its power as a spokesperson for affiliates. This process accelerated from the 1960s as the state increasingly sought to involve the unions in solutions to economic decline. Some saw the translation of the TUC from Trafalgar Square to Whitehall unproblematically, as a voyage to acceptance and power. Others viewed it as a more questionable journey to increasing procedural influence. The social and economic position of union members was improved but far from transformed; policy leverage remained limited, even on Labour governments. Critics noted the fragility of links to the state and the extent to which success as a pressure group was dependent on state economic intervention and full employment. Nonetheless, the political influence unions wielded was real, if susceptible to exaggeration and structurally limited. Unions had made good their right to involvement in government and their claim that organised labour was the fifth estate of the realm 'a firm tenet of British political culture' (Martin, 1980, 327). But even with Labour governments they were never involved as principals in the *primary determination* of economic policy; only as agents agreeing and implementing the delivery of objectives through mechanisms such as incomes policy. The view that the unions related to government as master to servant (Barnes and Reid, 1980, 222) is caricature.

From 1975 to 1976 decline set in. Since 1979 the unions have suffered a severe loss of political power: there has been only the most limited role for an independent voice for working people in the processes of government. The significance of this cannot be under-estimated. It may be argued that exclusion was always in the gift of government, given the preponderant power of state and capital. But in pursuing it Mrs Thatcher was rebelling against the conservatism of the British state and the self-interest of sections of its personnel in the context of four decades of consensus. In using coercive powers mothballed since the 1930s she was taking real political risks. Her achievement should not be under-estimated.

Some of the key structures of incorporation remained in place. But their power to affect policy was reduced and the influence on them of the unions increasingly insubstantial. Having failed to achieve their objectives under Labour, the unions have been pushed out of the centres of power onto the margins. If British unions never became such a firm fixture in the political firmament as their Swedish counterparts, their fall is no less dramatic. Their political arm has been excluded from power. Overtures to governments have produced no response. Economic and industrial relations policy has been implemented without union participation. Contacts with ministers have been limited. Measuring TUC performance against the key criteria of access, quality, methods of communication, quality of communication, effectiveness of access and outcomes (Martin, 1980, 2–4) we see in clear definition the decline of the TUC as an effective pressure group. Loss of political voice has interacted with loss of authority within the movement. The irony is clear. The Conservatives have been successful in political exclusion. Yet the economic policy of which exclusion was a subordinate ingredient has singularly failed.

Finally, the TUC has been unable to develop any viable alternative. When George Woodcock defined its essential contemporary purpose as 'to deal with affairs of the moment in committee rooms with people who have power' (TUC, 1961, 35) critics pointed to the dangers of compromising independence and ability to mobilise. Certainly in the years of Conservative rule some might see the rancid harvest of corporatism being reaped. The unions' political alternative to Thatcherism, the AES, never got off the ground. Since then they have supported but played little part in creating political initiatives which have involved a retreat from radicalism and from social democracy. The unions have been unable or unwilling to mobilise their membership and have been reliant on the broken backed strategy of offering and re-offering their services to governments which simply have no use for them. The other persisting ingredient in the accommodative tendencies which flowered in the new realism and became dominant by the 1990s was the mistaken view that the employers could be won to an anti-Conservative partnership. In fact they remained resolute supporters of the government. By 1994 John Monks's relaunch appeared to suggest the TUC was accepting a role as one of many pressure groups with greater emphasis on business unionism, although the basis for a partnership with employers still seemed elusive.

Will things change? To pose the question shows how dependent the unions are on events beyond their control. By 1994 it was claimed that a number of meetings between the TUC and Ministers heralded the end of the cold war. But the TUC's representativeness has been undermined by decline and decentralisation. Some believe that having lost their virginity on incomes policy the Conservatives will find themselves compelled by the logic of EU developments to call on the unions for help with their problems. The failure of Mrs Thatcher's 'economic miracle' will prompt more state involvement in industry and training and provide an opening. It is possible. But it looks unlikely. The Conservatives remain suspicious of the unions and cynical about their ability to deliver. Real change still seems predicated on the possibility of a Labour administration.

Further reading

Robert Taylor's *The Trade Union Question in British Politics: Government and Unions Since 1945*, Blackwell, 1993, is a good general survey. Ross Martin, *TUC: The Growth of a Pressure Group 1868–1976*, Clarendon Press 1980, contains a mass of useful information on the TUC although its model for understanding its activities is over-developed and under-applied. There are some splendid insights into the operations of the TUC bureaucracy in the late 1970s and early 1980s in Gerald Dorfman, *British Trade Unionism Against the Trades Union Congress*, Macmillan, 1983. Despite criticism, Keith Middlemas, *Politics in Industrial Society*, Deutsch, 1979, remains a classic of political analysis and fully discusses the corporate bias of the British state.

David Coates, *Labour in Power*, Longman, 1980, is a powerful, well argued critique from the left of the last Labour government. The volume of essays edited by Michael Artis and David Cobham, *Labour's Economic Policies, 1974–79*, Manchester University Press, 1991, is more sympathetic and contains a wealth of detailed analysis of all aspects of policy. The best short analysis of Thatcherism is Andrew Gamble, *The Free Economy and the Strong State: The Politics of Thatcherism*, Macmillan, 1988. Longer, more journalistic, but excellent is Hugo Young, *One Of Us*, Macmillan, 1991.

6

Unions and the law

In the 1980s there was a revolution in labour law. The tradition of state abstention has been ruptured and the enduring framework for union autonomy erected between 1870 and 1906 has been remodelled. Conservative governments have carried through a programme of change unparalleled this century. Intellectual influences on the new Conservatism, such as F. A. Hayek, argue that unions distort the working of the market, oppress the individual and create beliefs in social justice which cannot be fulfilled. 'They are the main reason for the decline of the British economy in general' (Hayek, 1980, 58). Law is at the root of the union problem: 'There can be no salvation for Britain until the special privileges granted to the trade unions . . . are removed' (Hayek, 1980, 52). The Conservatives' 1979 manifesto took up themes of individualism, disequilibrium of power and its misuse. It asserted that 'by heaping privilege without responsibility on the trade unions Labour have given the minority of extremists the power to abuse individual liberties and to thwart Britain's chances of success'. The Conservatives acted upon these ideas and others gradually and creatively with legislative initiatives increasingly related to institutional measures to weaken collective bargaining and exclude unions in the public sector. Before examining changes since 1979 it is important to scrutinise the background; and the view that, at the core of labour law, lay artificial privileges requiring drastic surgery if constitutional and economic vigour were to be restored in Britain.

Labour law and history

When trade unions emerged they faced illegality under both criminal and civil law. The Combination Acts of 1799 and 1800 were only part of a battery of more than 40 statutes which criminalised workers' organisation. Combination was viewed not only as a threat to the free workings of the market which guaranteed the well-being of society but, with the French Revolution sweeping Europe, as a threat to the social and political *status quo*. The penal legislation outlawed agreements or organisation to influence terms and conditions of employment; prosecutions were common. The Master and Servant Acts made a breach of contract by an employee a criminal offence, whereas an employer had to be sued in the civil courts. As late as the 1870s there were more than 10,000 prosecutions each year. Legislation also made most forms of industrial action and picketing criminal 'intimidation' or 'molestation'. When, in 1824–25, the Combination Acts were repealed, the new legislation re-enacted a list of criminal offences. Under both criminal and civil law, the unions were **conspiracies** and under the civil law they were associations in **restraint of trade**.

For the judges, regulation of work began and ended with the market and the contract of employment, which was the legal manifestation of *laissez-faire*. Ignoring the fact employers dictated terms rather than negotiated them, judges deemed illegal any combination. Collective bargaining was anathema to the common law and its custodians. When they were forced by Parliament to recognise unions they cavilled at their methods. The 1859 Molestation of Workmen Act ushered in a period of gradual, if grudging, reform. The unions and their middle-class supporters pressurised the Liberal and Conservative Parties. The 1871 Trade Union Act and Criminal Law Amendment Act protected unions from criminal liabilities. They were immunised from actions 'in restraint of trade' and given civil status. The resilience of the judiciary was soon reflected in *R* v. *Bunn* where the organisers of a gas strike were successfully prosecuted for conspiracy. Union pressure led to the 1875 Conspiracy and

Protection of Property Act repealing the Master and Servant Acts and protecting unions from conspiracy where they were acting 'in contemplation of furtherance of a trade dispute'.

The judges turned to the civil law. Union activities were now branded as civil wrongs or torts. The courts held that a strike to secure 100% membership and dismissal of non-members was a civil conspiracy to injure; and instructing or urging workers to withdraw their labour could constitute the tort of inducing breach of contract. In 1901, the decision of the House of Lords in the *Taff Vale* case opened union funds to attack. A campaign by the unions led to the enactment of the 1906 Trade Disputes Act. Unions were to be protected against the torts of civil conspiracy and inducing breach of contract, so long as they acted in contemplation or furtherance of a trade dispute. Their funds were to be protected against civil actions by employers.

Trade union privileges?

The argument against the Edwardian legal settlement is simply put. Companies, or individual citizens, cannot go around committing civil wrongs such as inducement to breach of contract. If trade unions are allowed to do so they are the subject of special privilege, which enables them to bring business to a halt, inflate wage levels, featherbed jobs and debilitate the economy. Yet it is difficult to see how the argument that the protections place unions above 'the ordinary law of the land' can be sustained.

The 'ordinary law of the land' is not a fixed category. It develops to take account of economic and social change. It is the product of political pressure by different interests. In the early 1800s factory owners mounted a successful campaign against wage fixing by magistrates. Did the resultant system of free market regulation give employers special privileges or raise them above the general law of the land? Did the creation of limited liability for companies give *them* special privileges and put *them* above the ordinary law of the land on debt which applies to all individual citizens? Few adherents of the new right would accept that this was so. Yet unions, urging legal change to protect their activities, were simply asserting the legitimacy of working-class self-activity against *laissez-faire*, just as the supporters of that creed had sought to break down older structures of economy, property and law. If capital could not develop effectively under the absolutism of the monarchy, unions were unable to function efficiently under the legal ordinance of *laissez-faire*. If the 'ordinary law of the land' had continued to govern activities, unions would have had a twilight existence.

The argument is ultimately a political one. If one is for trade unions then one must be for their exemption from 'the ordinary law of the land'. The argument can only be about the degree of exemption. When, before the 1906 Act, Lord Justice Lindley commented that 'you cannot make a strike effective without doing more than is lawful', he was summing up the fate of trade unionism if the common law was *not* overridden by the legislature. As the government pointed out, the 1906 legislation was not intended 'to confer any exceptional immunities, far from it; it was in order to remove exceptional disabilities imposed on those trade unions, disabilities which are contrary to the general spirit of our law' (von Prondzynski, 1985, 192). *Lumley* v. *Gye* (1853), which introduced the civil wrong of 'inducement', involved an impresario seducing an opera singer to break a contract. The courts did not hesitate to press union support for industrial action into the same mould. But there was no compelling reason why *Lumley* v. *Gye* should have been applied to the very different situation of a union procuring industrial action. The 1906 Act, which protected unions from inducement to breach of contract simply accepted that what was good for impresarios was not good for unions and that without protection from the fallacious analogies of the judiciary, unions could not fulfil their legitimate social and economic roles.

The interim injunction continued to cause problems. If an employer could make out a *prima facie* case judges were prepared to restrain industrial action until full trial if they felt that 'the balance of convenience' favoured the employer. Invariably the courts decided that this was the position. It was more convenient to halt the action than allow economic loss to continue, leaving the employer to later recoup it in damages. The courts also failed to accept that granting an injunction could be inconvenient for the union. Yet if the strike was over a dismissal, the injunction did not restore the *status quo*. It did not reinstate the dismissed employee. If the strike was over wages, an injunction normally ensured that the trade unionists had to bargain, deprived of the strike weapon.

The system of immunities

Despite its lack of substance the 'privilege' argument gained colour from the *form* protections took. Parliament did not give the unions *rights*. There has never been a code of 'positive rights' – to organise, to bargain, to strike – as in other countries. In Britain, unions sought 'exclusion' or 'immunity' from the common law doctrines created by the judges. The doctrine of conspiracy, the tort of inducement to breach of contract, continued in being. Unions were exempted from their jurisdiction *under specific circumstances*.

The British working class, the first in the world, lacking previous exemplars and an alternative philosophy, made their way in the same piecemeal, pragmatic fashion as capital had. Their leadership was cautious and accommodative, more interested in *ad hoc* compromise than the creation of a new economic or legal order. The empiricism of British society was reflected in the lack of a written constitution. The unions, in their key formative period, with universal suffrage some way off, had no political party to articulate an alternative legal framework. They were dependent on middle-class reformers and the Conservatives and Liberals who believed in a limited role for the state. Given their experience with the law, trade unionists wished to protect themselves by retreating beyond its reach, rather than positively penetrating the legal universe. The result was a compromise with the common law, not its transformation (Fox, 1985a; Wedderburn, 1986).

The system of immunities was, therefore, simply a method of insulating the unions from judicial law-making. Its content was in many ways extremely limited. Strikers had no protection against dismissal. Pickets had no right to stop a driver to put their case. Industrial action to oppose government policies was not protected. Moreover, the fact that 'conspiracy' and 'inducement to breach of contract' continued to apply outside industrial relations gave sustenance to the view that unions were a special case. The fact that the common law doctrines still existed meant that they could still be developed by the judges.

The judges

In the conventional view, judges are neutral referees, deciding disputes by impartial reference to an established body of law. Their autonomy enables them to mediate between individuals and the state and restrain excessive deployment of political power. Marxists, in contrast, have long argued that the judiciary is an integral part of the ruling class, that 'the judicial elites, like other elites of the state system, are mainly drawn from the upper and middle layers of society and those judges who are not have clearly come to belong to those layers by the time they reach the bench' (Miliband, 1969, 138). The apparent independence of the law, whose content is influenced by class struggle, but which is ultimately an instrument of capital, strengthens illusions in the neutrality of the state.

A recent distinctive critique notes that over the last century the dominance of the upper and middle class 'is overwhelming . . . four out of five full-time professional judges are products of public schools and of Oxford or Cambridge' (Griffith, 1991, 34). Legal training, practice and remuneration constitute conservatising factors. Judges cannot be neutral because they are often placed in situations where they have to make political choices. In reality:

their interpretation of what is in the public interest and therefore politically desirable is determined by the kind of people they are and the position they hold in our society . . . this position is a part of established authority and so is necessarily conservative and illiberal. From all this flows the view of the public interest, which is shown in judicial attitudes such as tenderness towards private property and dislike of trade unions, strong adherence to the maintenance of order, distaste for minority opinions, demonstrations and protests (Griffith, 1991, 319).

The judges themselves have periodically been willing to gnaw at these problems. In the 1920s, Lord Justice Scrutton mused that:

the habits you are trained in, the people with whom you mix, lead to your having a certain class of ideas of such a nature that when you have to deal with other ideas you do not give as sound and accurate judgements as you would wish . . . Labour says 'where are your impartial judges? They all move in the same circle as the employers and they are all educated and nursed in the same ideas as the employers. How can a labour man or a trade unionists get impartial justice?' It is very difficult sometimes to be sure that you have put yourself in a thoroughly impartial position between two disputants who are of your own class and one not of your own class (Abel–Smith and Stevens, 1967, 117).

Half a century later, the Lord Chancellor, Viscount Hailsham, observed that 'there is no such thing as a value-free or neutral interpretation of the law'. A prominent judge, Lord Devlin, observed that 'Judges are inevitably part of the establishment and the establishment's ideas are those which are operating in our minds . . . I think the law has to be part of the establishment' (McIlroy, 1983, 15, 16).

The history of judicial law-making in relation to the unions provides grist for the critical mill, whilst also supporting the view that 'the avoidance of outrageous bias is much more likely in periods of relative social calm than in periods of acute social conflict' (Miliband, 1969, 141). As the class conflict of the early years of the century gave way to the enforced quiescence of the inter-war period, the judges, in cases such as *Reynolds* v. *Shipping Federation* (1924) and the *Crofter Case* (1942) accepted as legitimate union objectives earlier deemed unlawful. The post-war boom, too, produced few confrontations between the unions and the courts. As its disintegration led to a renewal of class struggle, judicial activism re-emerged.

When the 1974 Labour government firmed up the 1906 legislation, judicial concern reached an intensity unprecedented since 1914. The judges began to pick apart Labour's legislation. Lord Salmon was early to speak out against the introduction of legislation he might later have to impartially interpret:

there are groups very small numerically, but extremely cohesive and tenacious, who have infiltrated the unions with the intention of seizing power if they can. Their objectives and ideas are entirely different from those of the trade unions which we all know and respect. Their avowed purpose is to wreck the social contract and the democratic system under which we live (Griffith, 1991, 56).

The 'moral panic' which was to culminate in the Winter of Discontent was already on. Lord Justice Lawton likened the NGA to 'a political commissar in a communist state'. 'Parliament', Lord Denning, said, in *BBC* v. *Hearn*, 'has conferred more freedom from constraint on trade unions than has ever been known to the law before. All legal restraints have been lifted so that they can now do as they will.'

Although, as Lord Scarman pointed out, in *NWL* v. *Woods*, the law was simply 'back to what Parliament had intended when it enacted the Act of 1906', the Court of Appeal, in judgments such as *Express Newspapers* v. *McShane* (1979) and *Duport Steels* v. *Sirs* (1980), rendered the immunities meaningless. In 1979–80, these cases were reversed by the House of Lords: the creativity demonstrated by the Court of Appeal could bring the legal apparatus into disrepute. Nonetheless, Lord Diplock noted that seventy years after the Trade Disputes Act, the immunities still 'tended to stick in judicial gorges'. The conclusion in *Duport Steels* that they applied to secondary action was:

intrinsically repugnant to anyone who has spent his life in the practice of the law or the administration of justice. Sharing these instincts, it was a conclusion that I, myself, reached with considerable reluctance, for, given the existence of a trade dispute, it involves granting to trade unions a power which has no other limits than their own self-restraint to inflict, by means which are contrary to the general law, untold harm.

Lord Salmon stated ominously that the time had come for the law to be altered. Mrs Thatcher and the 1980 Employment Act were at hand.

Collective *laissez-faire*

Most of those who studied British industrial relations until the 1970s termed the system a 'voluntary' one. Unions supported legislation to ensure they could bargain and strike. They feared more extended enactment would, because of the plasticity of statute in the nimble fingers of the judges, produce more restrictive regulation. Reliance on law could sap independence and pave the way for restrictive legislation. If the state played too great a role in providing rights, workers might question the rationale for union membership. What the state had given it could legitimately remove.

Employers too accepted collective bargaining as the preferred means of regulation. Voluntarism emphasised employer autonomy in a culture resistant to state intervention: employers preferred to solve their own problems, even at the cost of industrial action. The law could not succeed in forcing large numbers of strikers back to work and its intervention could sour future industrial relations. From the state's point of view, autonomy nurtured belief in its neutrality and purchased loyalty from the unions. There was no need for the state to overload itself with functions which could be left to unions and employers and the workings of the market. The judges' brief as secondary legislators underpinned 'the limited state', providing a system for fine-tuning existing law to the problems of the moment and drawing attention to any need for legislation.

An examination of British industrial relations certainly seemed to justify its description as collective *laissez-faire*. Until the 1970s legal landmarks were few. There was no law giving trade unionists rights to recognition or requiring employers to bargain. Collective agreements were not legally enforceable. Health and Safety legislation provided a minimum floor of civilised working conditions. The Fair Wages Resolutions and the Terms and Conditions of Employment Act (1959), provided limited machinery for extending terms and conditions arrived at in industries regulated by collective bargaining. Wages Council legislation, dating from 1909, laid down minimum wages in weakly organised industries.

Taken together with the immunity statutes, they made the British system one of the most minimally legally regulated in the world. By the post-war period, 'collective *laissez-faire*' was seen as *prescriptive*: it represented the best way of ordering industrial relations in an advanced economy. The 1971 Industrial Relations Act was a passing cloud. Even the deluge of labour law under the Wilson and Callaghan governments was not viewed by some as striking at the roots of voluntarism (Kahn–Freund, 1979).

The limitations of voluntarism

Others have noted the *limits* of state abstention and self-regulation. The state introduced in both world wars powerful measures to control trade unions, such as the Munitions of War Act, 1915, and Order 1305, 1940. The latter legislation lingered on until 1951, when its use against members of the TGWU provoked its repeal. The Attlee and Churchill cabinets considered the introduction of strike ballots, legal control of unofficial strikes, and bans on strikes in essential services. The Emergency Powers Act, 1920, and 1964, and the Trade Disputes Act, 1927, were not inconsiderable statutes. The latter limited union membership for public employees, imposed criminal penalties on political strikes, restricted picketing and replaced 'opting-out' of the political levy with 'opting-in'. The 1920 Act and its 1964 successor gave the state extensive powers to intervene in strikes and use the military to do the work of the strikers. Its role in the General Strike and large scale disputes demonstrated it was far from neutral.

Between 1965 and 1968, and 1972 and 1974, incomes policy legislation controlled the price of labour. This legislation provided for criminal penalties but, dealing with wages, it went to the root of collective bargaining and can only be ignored at the expense of a most restrictive definition of labour law. Moreover, the 1963 Contracts of Employment Act, and the 1965 Redundancy Payments Act, marked the mid-1960s as the end of an era. Since 1964, every government has aspired to greater legal regulation and by 1975 this trend appeared irreversible.

If voluntarism is used in the sense of abstention of the law, its proponents appear to be correct in analysing the situation in these

terms, until the 1960s. If we are talking more broadly of voluntarism as a shared set of values, centred on a neutral state, it
only adequately described limited periods with its maintenance
conditional upon a power balance favourable to capital. As 'an
ideological belief common to both sides of industry' voluntarism
was largely a brief post-war phenomenon (Lewis and Simpson,
1981, 9, 16). The state intervened through Whitleyism when
union power increased. It did little to support collective
bargaining when it declined. The inter-war period saw abstention
of the law, but the weakness of the unions left management with
an open field. They did not need state intervention; the unions
lacked the power to impose it. The fact that growing expectations
by workers, underpinned by full employment and disintegration
of economic stability, went hand in hand with disintegration of
voluntarism raises the question of whether collective *laissez-faire*
represented, from a union point of view, the best means of regulating industrial relations.

By its emphasis on the procedures of collective bargaining and
the value of legal abstention, voluntarism obscures questions of
power and substance. The kind of law available as an alternative is
a key issue. The absence of one kind of law may help trade unions.
The absence of another kind may handicap them. A system of
favourable legal rights administered by a reformed judiciary may
further union purposes more efficiently than a voluntarist system.
Can we favour self-regulation against legal regulation without
some assessment of the *outcomes* of collective bargaining? Self-
regulation by collective bargaining did not cover all workers as
legislation could; it depended for its efficacy on the mobilisation of
union power which varied across industry. The state itself did
little to foster collective bargaining and where it took root the
standards it achieved in curbing employer prerogative and protecting employees against victimisation and discrimination were
limited – as illustrated by equal pay. The assertion of the necessity
of a more civilised and just work regime by employees, the EU and
the ILO, as well as the inflationary consequences of autonomy,
stimulated between 1960 and 1975 the end of collective *laissez-
faire*. In this light, state abstention may be seen as acquiescence in

a distribution of power which strengthened the existing social order in industry and reinforced the subordination of workers through providing an element of autonomy. And the growing state intervention from the 1960s, when unions were stronger, may be seen as the state attempting to re-order a situation capital could no longer control.

Collective bargaining redresses inequality of power between employer and worker; it does not significantly affect the structures of power, ownership and control (Fox, 1985b). Voluntarism can, therefore, be seen as shaped by both the needs of capital and pressures from the labour movement. Its acceptance represented a defensive compromise, organic to the unions' separation between economics and politics, which left existing structures of ownership, wealth, income and law intact. It gave workers some control and some means of civilising their subordination, but by *de-politicising* industrial relations it played a role in distracting attention from the structures of power and domination which might have produced more fundamental change. Immunities ultimately solved little. The terms on which the judiciary were excluded from intervention premissed their periodic re-entry into the field to the detriment of trade unions. Had this unsatisfactory compromise been rejected in favour of a more comprehensive reform, a positive code of rights and democratised judiciary, it is at least possible unions might have had a greater impact on the disequilibrium of power. It is by no means certain that voluntarism was the best way for the unions – or that a return to voluntarism today would represent the optimum solution.

The Donovan Report and *In Place of Strife*

The Report of the Royal Commission on Trade Unions – the Donovan Report, 1968 – represented a strong defence of the voluntary system. Collective bargaining was still the best method of giving workers a voice in decisions; problems could be solved by voluntary reform. Donovan wished to keep the legal wolf from the door, opposing new restrictive obligations on unions. Nonetheless, the report argued that if voluntary change failed, penalties on strikes should be considered. The extension and renovation of collective bargaining could also be immediately stimulated by the enactment of legislation on union recognition and unfair dismissal, as well as provisions for the registration of collective agreements plugging in to the Contracts of Employment and Redundancy Payments legislation and the Prices and Incomes Acts.

This recipe was not to the liking of Harold Wilson. The 1969 White Paper, *In Place of Strife*, proposed legislation covering many of Donovan's proposals. There was to be new law on dismissal, recognition and disclosure of information. However, the unions bitterly opposed plans to allow the government to suspend uncon- stitutional stoppages for 28 days and trigger compulsory ballots before official strikes. The government sought to rush through a short bill covering 'the penal clauses'. This was opposed by the TUC, by members of the cabinet and by backbench MPs. After a special conference gave the TUC new powers to intervene in unofficial strikes, the government withdrew the Bill in return for a 'solemn and binding undertaking' that the TUC would pursue a more forceful line.

The Industrial Relations Act

By the mid-1960s, the Conservative Party was converted to 'legalism'. The philosophy of their 1968 policy document, *Fair Deal at Work*, was clear; extensive legislation was required to *restrict trade union power and to remould collective bargaining*. The parties themselves were incapable or unwilling to reform indus- trial relations without a greater degree of legal intervention. The 1971 Industrial Relations Act marked a clear rupture with vol- untarism, attempting to replace collective *laissez-faire* with legally regulated collective bargaining on the US model.

The provisions on registration were crucial. Unions which registered would be subject to a certain degree of state super- vision. In return, they could avail themselves of a range of rights to recognition, bargaining and disclosure of information. Reinforcing this 'reform' emphasis were clauses *presuming* collective agreements to be binding, a series of unfair industrial practices, limiting unions' right to take secondary action and to picket, and powers granted to the Secretary of State to apply for orders prohibiting industrial action harmful to the economy. Compulsory ballots on industrial action and 'cooling-off periods' could also be ordered. A National Industrial Relations Court was established to deal with the collective provisions of the legislation. Individual rights, such as unfair dismissal, were enacted.

The legislation was attempting to achieve an awful lot with one toss of the dice. Not only was it comprehensive to a fault, it was also contradictory. At one and the same time it attempted to *reform industrial relations* which required union co-operation and to *restrict the unions* – a move likely to limit that co-operation. Titbits such as unfair dismissal and recognition procedures were offered to the unions. But this approach was undermined by provisions allowing workers to opt out of union membership and seeking to make unions responsible for industrial action. There were problems in the drafting of the act – crucially, there was uncertainty as to the unions' legal responsibility for the activities of shop stewards. In certain areas the government was given an enforcement role. The legislation provided employers with an opportunity for provoking a widespread confrontation with the unions. Some, indeed, saw the act as informed by incompatible philosophies embodied in two phantom draftsmen: one 'a civil servant concerned mainly to bring order and a tidy structure into collective British industrial relations; the second is quite different, a Conservative lawyer imbued above all else with doctrines of individual rights' (Wedderburn, 1972, 270, 282).

The government's refusal to consult over the fundamentals of the legislation strengthened opposition. What was central, however, was the relatively powerful position of the unions and the confident belief, confirmed by the *In Place of Strife* furore, that legal initiatives could be defeated. A series of one-day strikes and a co-ordinated campaign by the TUC built opposition. However, several important unions refused to accept the TUC's instruction to de-register under the Act. Some had to be expelled. Whilst the policy of withdrawing union representatives from industrial tribunals was largely observed, the fact that unions still took cases limited its rationale. Moreover, as soon as the boycott of the new court posed problems, the TGWU appeared before it.

Nonetheless, employers were reluctant to use the Act. Rank and file opposition was reinforced by the TUC's posture and by the success of the miners in punching holes in the Heath government's wage restraint policies. The government's use of the pre-strike ballot against railway workers in early 1972 produced an overwhelming vote in favour of strike action. The imprisonment of five dockers in Pentonville gaol in the summer of 1972 provoked a major political confrontation. The TUC called the first one-day general strike since 1926 and a rolling strike movement began. The House of Lords published, with unprecedented haste, a judgment reversing the decision which had led to the dockers' contempt of court. Although they had not purged their contempt, they were released.

By 1974 even the CBI supported repeal of the Act. Its impact on day-to-day industrial relations was minimal, 'the central analysis about the nature and causes of industrial conflict upon which the Act was based was often not shared by management, unions or workers'. Management connived in exclusion clauses which kept collective agreements non-enforceable and in maintaining the closed shop. Only 31 applications were made to the NIRC, largely by small employers in conflict-ridden industries:

Employers generally refused to see their industrial relations as a problem and the 'disorder' described by others was often defended by managers because it gave them flexibility . . . Management seemed anxious to avoid the loss of control to outsiders which they felt the use of the new legal institutions implied . . . the Act had little influence on the general practice of industrial relations (Weekes *et al.*, 1975, 223, 232).

The lessons drawn were the old lessons. The law should be kept out of industrial relations: it could not defeat union opposition. Others saw the mistakes as strategic and tactical. Heath had gone about things the wrong way from the start and backed down ignominiously when the going got tough. The real lessons, however, were not just problems of enforcement and compliance in the abstract. What was crucial was *the economic and political context* in which compliance was sought. The context of wider policy could strengthen tendencies to compliance or non-compliance. As Moran points out:

in turning to more interventionist economic policies after 1972 Mr Heath and his colleagues destroyed the original economic assumptions on which the Act was based ... the legislation was part of a more general prescription involving injection of greater market influences into the economy (Moran, 1979, 42).

The main reason for the failure of the Act was the unions' refusal to accept it (Fosh *et al.*, 1993, 24). But the more fundamental reason for failure was the unions' ability to successfully realise that refusal. A central problem with Edward Heath's efforts at reordering was that, at least by 1972, they were part of a strategy for maintaining the post-war consensus. The conditions of that consensus strengthened union power and boosted their ability to successfully refuse acceptance to legal restriction. As unemployment increased to 1 million through 1971 Heath saw the Thatcherite future: he retreated before it. It was only in the following decade that economic change and union reform were synchronised – with devastating effect for the unions' ability to deny acceptance.

Social contract and employment protection

In its evidence to the Donovan Commission, the TUC reaffirmed support for voluntarism. But conversion to a more detailed legal framework had been proceeding through the 1960s. For its part, the incoming 1975 Labour government saw legal concessions as an inexpensive means of purchasing acquiescence in wage restraint and as a means of speeding up Donovan-style changes in industrial relations. There was to be no simple return to the pre-1971 position. But new legislation would support, not restrict, union activities.

The Trade Union and Labour Relations Act, 1974, and the Trade Union and Labour Relations (Amendment) Act, 1976, refurbished the immunities. Employers were protected against unfair dismissal actions where they dismissed non-union members in a closed shop. The Employment Protection Act, 1975, placed the Advisory, Conciliation, and Arbitration Services on a statutory footing. A Certification Officer was established to adjudicate on whether trade unions met the criterion of independence, a prerequisite for receipt of many of the new legal rights.

ACAS was given a brief to extend collective bargaining. Unions could refer disputes over recognition and disclosure of information to ACAS which would follow a statutory procedure, culminating in compulsory arbitration. Employers had new duties to provide information to unions and to consult in redundancy situations. There were new provisions for the extension of 'recognised terms and conditions of employment'. Union representatives were given time off for union activities and facilities to help them in their work. The unfair dismissal provisions were extended. There were new rights for employees laid off and rights to itemised pay statements. Wages Councils were strengthened and new Codes of Practice produced by ACAS on discipline, time off for shop stewards and disclosure of information.

The Health and Safety at Work Act of 1974 was an enabling act intended to stimulate renovation and codification of the whole field of welfare legislation. It provided, moreover, for a new system of workplace safety representatives and safety committees. Pensions were dealt with by the Social Security Pensions Act, 1975, and equal rights by new provisions on maternity leave and maternity pay, the Sex Discrimination Act, 1975, and the Race Relations Act, 1976.

This legislation was seen as an important increment to union power. The Conservatives complained in their 1979 manifesto that 'between 1974 and 1976 Labour enacted "a militant's charter" of trade union legislation. It tilted the balance of power in bargaining throughout industry away from responsible management and towards unions and sometimes towards unofficial groups'.

But the TUC did not have it all its own way with legislation, as the failure over protection for pickets and the fiasco about industrial democracy demonstrated. Its value to the unions was restricted by inability to maintain a strong grassroots movement capable of enforcing it against employers, and failure to develop complementary measures such as the proposals for industrial democracy. What strikes us today is its limitations. It lagged behind standards set in EU countries. The legislation on unfair dismissal, for example, failed to give tribunals powers to *enforce* reinstatement. By 1980, reinstatement was the remedy in less then 1% of cases. The median award of compensation was £375 in 1978, £410 in 1979 and £963 in 1981. In that year, more than half of the awards were for amounts under £1,000 and workers had less than a one in four chance of winning a case. The situation was even more limited in relation to discrimination. By 1983, 46% of successful applicants under the Sex Discrimination Act and 62% of successful applicants under the Race Relations Act received less then £500. There were only 575 applications under both jurisdictions. Tribunals became increasingly legalistic (Dickens *et al.*, 1985; Hepple, 1983). If many of the new rights were limited, the courts deprived them of the efficacy they possessed:

The law of unfair dismissal has been sterilised to such an extent that, it is reasonable to conclude that far from controlling managerial discretion and, therefore, protecting the interests of workers in job security, the law generally endorses and legitimates a strong conception of managerial authority (Collins, 1982, 170).

Much the same could be said of the 'collective rights'. The recognition procedure was lengthy and lacked teeth, guaranteeing only compulsory arbitration of certain terms and conditions of employment. ACAS made recommendations for recognition in 158 out of the 247 cases under the procedure; in only 58 cases did ACAS know of compliance. Moreover:

although the sanction was weak in intention and weaker still in operation it was perceived differently by the judges. They compared it with the powers of compulsory acquisition of property and described it as 'as interference with individual liberty' which 'could hardly be tolerated in a free society unless there were safeguards against abuse' (Dickens and Bain, 1986, 92).

Just as they whittled down the revived immunities, so judges turned their attention to the new rights. By 1979 a series of judgments in the Court of Appeal, *Grunwick* v. *ACAS, UKAPE* v. *ACAS* and *EMA* v. *ACAS* led the chair of ACAS to inform the government that the recognition procedure was no longer operable to any satisfactory degree.

Labour's legislation was far from 'a militants' charter', particularly if set in the context of the Social Contract. It should be seen, rather, as part of the project of reforming and formalising industrial relations, which started with the Contracts of Employment Act and continued through the Donovan proposals. The Redundancy Payments legislation, for example, was described by Labour Minister Ray Gunter as having 'an important, necessary part to play in allaying fears of redundancy and resistance to new methods and economic change . . . our object is to increase mobility of labour by reducing resistance to change' (McIlroy, 1983, 25).

Unfair dismissal legislation was intended to stimulate disciplinary procedures and increase management efficiency and legitimacy, avoiding industrial disputes, as well as providing compensation for dismissed employees. The procedures for recognition and disclosure of information were intended to extend and professionalise collective bargaining, as were the provisions on the closed shop and time off. If employment protection aimed at purchasing union compliance in incomes policy and responding to developments in the EU, it was also a weapon in restoring and modernising management control.

Here the legislation met with some success. It encouraged growth of procedures and professionalisation of shop steward organisation. Change is highlighted by one survey reporting that only 8% of private sector establishments had a formal written disciplinary procedure in 1969, and 80% in 1980 (Dickens *et al.*, 1985; Daniel and Millward, 1983; Daniel and Stilgoe, 1978).

By 1980, there was a clear trend 'towards the juridification of individual disputes . . . Matters once entirely within the sphere of managerial prerogatives or left to collective bargaining are now directly regulated by positive legal rights and duties' (Hepple,

1983, 393). If the degree to which the conduct of industrial relations was regulated by the law was still limited compared with other countries, it was substantial compared with 1960. Some observers drew a distinction between individual protective law and the law relating to collective labour relations. The growth of the former category, it was argued, was consistent with traditional policies of voluntarism. The 1974–79 Labour government had been careful not to intrude into the latter. The rupture with the past occurred in 1980, not in 1974 or 1964 (Clark and Wedderburn, 1983). Others argue that the Social Contract witnessed enactment of a substantial corpus of collective labour legislation. Had traditional philosophy applied in 1974, the trade unions would have demanded a small act restoring the immunities. They would not have supported legislation on recognition, disclosure of information, the closed shop or rights for shop stewards (von Prondzynski, 1985). If by 1979 collective *laissez-faire* had been overthrown, it was left to Thatcherism to undermine collective bargaining.

Neo-*laissez-faire* and the law

Major employment legislation

1980 Employment Act
- Abolished recognition rights
- Restricted picketing and secondary action
- Ballots required for new closed shops
- State funds for union ballots

1982 Employment Act
- Ballots for all closed shops
- Definition of 'trade dispute' tightened
- 'Union labour only' clauses unlawful
- Unions liable for unlawful acts

1984 Trade Union Act
- Union executives, General Secretaries and Presidents with

voting rights to be elected by secret ballot every five years
- Ballots required before industrial action
- Ballots required on political funds every ten years

1988 Employment Act
- Unlawful to enforce post-entry closed shop
- Political fund ballots must be postal
- Unfair to discipline members refusing to participate in industrial action after a ballot
- Ballots for union elections extended and now postal
- Members given rights to inspect union books
- Commissioner for the Rights of Trade Union Members (CROTUM) established

1989 Employment Act
- Time off for union representatives limited
- Industrial tribunal procedure tightened and applicants to pay deposits
- Restrictions on employment of women and young people lifted
- Training Commission abolished

1990 Employment Act
- Union liable for unofficial action unless written repudiation
- Unofficial strikers can be selectively sacked
- All secondary action unlawful
- Unlawful to enforce pre-entry closed shop

1992 Trade Union and Labour Relations (Consolidation) Act
- Consolidates collective employment law

1993 Trade Union Reform and Employment Rights Act
- Strike ballots and ballots on mergers to be postal
- Written ratification of check-off required every three years
- Right to join union of choice undermines Bridlington Agreement
- Citizens' right to sue if damaged by industrial action
- New Commissioner for Protection against Unlawful Industrial

Action to finance cases
- Seven days' notice required for industrial action
- Wages Councils abolished
- Employers allowed to offer inducements for non-union contracts
- EU required extension of employment protection rights

The Conservative approach was influenced by the new right. Mrs Thatcher admired and had read Hayek whose doctrines she pronounced 'supreme' (Ranelagh, 1992, ix). It has, however, been argued that the new right philosophy was less important than pragmatic response to the events of the 1970s and 1980s (Auerbach, 1990, 230ff.). The growing influence of the new right before 1979 was, of course, itself a reaction to events, to the 'corporatist' failure of the Heath and the Labour governments and the need for a powerful alternative to the rejected incomes policy. Successive attempts to reform collective *laissez-faire* had been based upon and reaffirmed the unions as the fundamental problem. New right analysis chimed with the reality of union resistance and the 'common sense' of the suburban saloon bar, providing for many, compelling explanation and prescription. The legislation of the 1980s was in its precise content and timing a reaction to the events of that decade. Nonetheless, it is clear that the *influence* of new right ideas provided inspiration and guide to the Thatcherite thinking which informed it (McIlroy, 1991, 10–16). There were other influences – for example, US legislation (Fosh *et al.*, 1993, 209). However, the fit between *some important aspects* of the legislation and the ideas of the new right is evident. As Wedderburn points out, Hayek did not dictate the legislation. The provenance of all its provisions cannot be tracked to his work but we would be 'juridically tone deaf' if we did not see the influence of his thought on it (1987, 15).

The fact that immunities have been curtailed, not abolished, simply illustrates the difference between Hayek the political philosopher and Thatcher the practising politician, required to moderate endorsement of ideas with a feel for practical barriers to their translation. To expect the pedigree and detail of every legislative measure to be traceable to Hayek is to misunderstand the constraints on parliamentary politicians. Moreover, neither guiding ideology nor political practice were frozen; they changed over time in relation to changing political events. The 1990 and 1993 acts were produced in very different circumstances from their predecessors of 1980 and 1982. The emphasis changed gradually from facilitating a new balance between employers and unions to making unions and collective bargaining marginal to industrial relations. The legal framework today is a unique, complex and, in its detail, eclectic and sometimes contradictory structure. It is doubtful if Hayek would support the state intervention involved in creation of the two commissioners (see p. 253). If collective *laissez-faire* had been marked 'for removal' since the 1960s either corporatism or legally regulated collective bargaining appeared likely to replace it. Instead, a hybrid framework maintains British exceptionalism in relation to other countries. That framework is very much the product of the unfolding industrial and political events of the 1980s and 1990s as perceived by practical supple politicians utilising the new right, not as infallible dogma, but an important repository of ideas, some of which could be deployed, some of which could not.

Conservative thinking in 1979 was based upon a reading of where Heath had gone wrong and a belief that after the Winter of Discontent restrictive legal action was not only necessary but possible and popular. Key sections of the state wanted change: the judges' views were shared by top civil servants (Barnes and Reid, 1980, ix). Yet healthy respect for the unions dictated gradualism and the synchronisation of legislation with an economic policy which would weaken union resistance. There would be no one major Act, no new labour court, no devices such as registration which the unions could exploit, no direct role for government which could politicise matters. Sanctions would lie against unions, not individuals, minimising the mobilising impact of martyrs. Yet, with incomes policy ruled out, legislation was central. Jim Prior expressed a consensual position in the cabinet. He wanted:

to bring about a lasting change in attitude by changing the law gradually, with as little resistance and therefore as much stealth as possible. There were also dangers in having tougher legislation which employers might in practice be afraid to use. It would be wrong to pass legislation which the courts could not enforce as happened with the 1971 Act (Prior, 1986, 158).

The divisions were about the first steps, the overall scope of change and its speed. The 1980 Employment Act was a cabinet compromise. It attracted backbench opposition but essentially satisfied Mrs Thatcher: 'All the evidence is that she was quite content with the pace of things even if she was also quite content to have Prior blamed for that pace' (Cosgrave, 1985, 166).

Prior was prepared for further legislation on the closed shop but wanted his measures on industrial action to be given time to be tested and accepted (Prior, 1986, 170–1). Like Heath, Prior believed in collective bargaining. His successor Tebbit was more dubious. He was prepared to go further and introduce the crucial *Taff Vale* clause making unions and their funds responsible for breaches of legislation, although he claimed he only got this through cabinet committee with the Prime Minister's support (Tebbit, 1988, 184, 188). The 1982 Act and the ensuing general election success represented a first watershed. After the *Stockport Messenger* dispute, particularly after the miners' strike, fear of non-compliance and, consequently, caution were reduced. With the acceptance of the 1984 Act the government had set the foundations in place. Subsequent legislation involved their extension, reaction to industrial events, whether the miners' strike or the 1989 'summer of discontent', a desire to extend or curb case law developments, 'the principle of legislating for the last dispute' (Auerbach, 1993, 47).

The 1980 Employment Act was classic, piecemeal, restrictive legislation aimed at restoring a 'proper balance of power' between employers and unions. Its limited erosion of the immunities owed more to Lord Denning than Hayek. The 1982 and 1990 Acts – the gap between them illuminates the Conservative approach – seriously eroded the immunities and sought to undermine, not regulate, collective bargaining. By 1983 it was clear that collective bargaining as well as union organisation and industrial action was under attack. Moreover, a growing emphasis was on arming the individual as well as the employer against union power. Legislation increasingly restricted union activities not through erosion of immunity but through internal regulation protecting member against union through mandatory ballots and individual rights – notably to opt out of industrial action. The late 1980s saw a new phase of intervention to support individualism with the creation of the Commissioner for the Rights of Trade Union Members. Erosion of employment protection, removal of support for collective bargaining and deregulation of the labour market were themes accompanied, after 1988, by 'throwing law' at almost every aspect of union practice. The freedom of British employers qualitatively increased. British unions became the most regulated independent institutions in the world.

The dynamic of legislation was increasingly erosion of collective bargaining and its replacement by the individual contract of employment: 'collective bargaining and collective agreement seem increasingly inappropriate and are in decline . . . [workers] want the opportunity to influence, in some cases to negotiate, their own terms and conditions of employment' (DE, 1992, 45). Whilst Employment Secretary Michael Howard suggested the legal attack might cease after the 1990 Act – the most radical since 1984 – John Major's government demonstrated continuity with the 1993 Trade Union Reform and Employment Rights Act. Legislating to restrict union activities had taken on its own momentum and autonomy. By 1990 it had little at all to do with the economic or industrial problems which had launched the project in 1979.

Conservative employment legislation, 1979–93

The Conservative legislation consists of seven major acts as well as important legislation dealing with specific issues such as the 1986 Sex Discrimination Act and the 1986 Wages Act. This legislation has been set in a web of ancillary measures. The overall thrust has been dramatically restrictive, although some protective measures have been required by EU membership.

Undermining protection, increasing flexibility
A range of measures were intended to lubricate industrial restructuring, replace collective bargaining by individual contracts and intensify competition. The qualification for unfair dismissal increased, from 6 months' to 1 year's continuous employment and was eventually raised to 2 years, removing millions from legal protection. The minimum length of a fixed-term contract under which the employer may exclude employees' rights was sliced from 2 years to 12 months. The onus of proof in tribunal cases which favoured the employee was neutralised. In determining fairness of dismissal, tribunals now had to consider the size of the enterprise and the employer's administrative resources. The 'basic' award of compensation was reduced. A 'pre-hearing assessment' to scrutinise the validity of an applicant's case was introduced. Security of tenure was weakened from the docks to the universities. Guarantee payments were cut, arrangements for maternity leave and maternity pay were made more complex and the Redundancy Payments Fund abolished.

The government ignored studies which demonstrated that employment protection burdens were minimal (Evans *et al.*, 1985; Clifton and Tatton-Brown, 1979; Daniel and Stilgoe, 1978). However, membership of the EU forced the government to introduce measures such as the Transfer of Undertakings (Protection of Employment) Regulations, 1981, the Equal Pay (Amendment) Regulations, 1983, and the Sex Discrimination Act, 1986.

Weakening collective bargaining
To facilitate 'deregulation', the 1980 legislation abolished the procedure dealing with trade union recognition and axed Schedule 11 to the Employment Protection Act, which provided for the extension of recognised terms and conditions to comparable workers. In 1983, the Fair Wages Resolution was rescinded, in 1986 young workers were removed from the protection of wages councils and in 1993 the councils were abolished. The Truck Acts were repealed and the restriction in the Factories

Act of women's hours of work removed. In 1989 the rights of workplace representatives to time off were limited. Legislation supporting collective bargaining has been dismantled and statute law replaced by the common law. A range of measures from the removal of teachers' bargaining rights to undermining of management obligations to encourage union membership and termination of the 60-year-old arbitration agreement with the civil service unions have weakened collective bargaining and pointed towards atomised, individual, self-help.

Limiting the immunities

The definition of *a trade dispute* – the gateway to union protection – has been restricted. To attract protection, disputes must now not merely be *related* to the list of employment issues contained in the formula, but they must be *wholly or mainly* about these issues. Disputes must now be between employers and *their workers*. Disputes between *workers and workers* are no longer protected and support for disputes outside the UK minimally so.

Protection was narrowed to workers picketing their own place of work and a restrictive Code of Practice promulgated. Protection for secondary or sympathetic action was severely restricted in 1980. Immunity was withdrawn in 1990. The aim has been to confine industrial action to *the workers' own employer*, foster enterprise isolation and employee identification with the enterprise and minimise solidarity. Industrial action to pressurise employers to recognise unions, the closed shop and 'union only' practices has been severely circumscribed, whilst the 1990 Act imposed penalties against unions which failed to disown unofficial strikers.

Unions now lose immunities if they fail to repudiate industrial action initiated without a secret ballot. In 1988, the government legislated to protect workers who refused to take action called after a successful ballot under the 1984 Trade Union Act. Social security measures have also been utilised: a sum deemed to have been paid by the union as strike pay is deducted from benefit whether or not such payment actually exists.

Disorganising the unions

Under the 1980 and 1982 Employment Acts, closed shops were only protected if approved in a ballot by over 80%. In the 1988 Act the government cynically removed all statutory support for the closed shop, making dismissal for non-membership of a union automatically unfair. The 1990 Act hit at the *pre-entry closed shop* making it unlawful to require membership as a condition of employment.

The protection given to unions after the *Taff Vale* case has been revoked so that union funds are now open to legal action. Legislation remoulded unions' internal practices with new balloting requirements for the election of executives, and political funds. The 1993 legislation extended postal ballots to industrial action, outlawed the Bridlington agreement regulating union spheres of interest and required members to sign regular forms for deduction of dues at source. To strengthen individualism a Commissioner for the Rights of Trade Union Members was created in 1988 to help members bring legal action against their union. In 1993 members of the public were given rights to sue strikers and a Commissioner for Protection Against Unlawful Industrial Action established to fund actions.

The union response

Four factors influenced the TUC's initial response. The first was Prior. He was able to present himself as resisting demands for more ambitious measures giving the impression the 1980 Act was a 'once and for all' measure. The more Tory MPs urged that the legislation was not tough enough the harder it became for the TUC to mount a major response (Prior, 1986, 158–9). Secondly, the TUC were frustrated by the piecemeal nature of the Bill and the absence of easy targets. Thirdly, they had little idea of the potential and stamina of Thatcherism, believing an eventual return to consensus politics would mean that this was the beginning and end of the legislative programme. As Len Murray put it:

We didn't believe a lot of what she was saying. . .We just didn't believe it.

Our major error was that we didn't believe that she was committed to a very radical reorganisation in the industrial relations field (quoted in McIlroy, 1991, 49).

Fourthly, the economic situation was already militating against a successful response. As Table 6.1 demonstrates the recession was developing in ways unfavourable to the unions. What was emerging, partly through dogma, partly through muddle, was a policy which would facilitate the legal offensive by sapping the bases of union power through a sudden unprecedented rise in unemployment.

Table 6.1   *The background to union defeat*

	Strikes			Unemploy-ment %	Inflation %	Union membership
	Number	Workers involved	Days lost			
1979	2080	1,001,000	9,405,000	5.0	13	13,289,000
1980	1330	830,000	11,964,000	6.4	18	12,947,000
1981	1338	1,512,000	4,266,000	9.8	12	12,106,000
1982	1528	2,101,000	5,313,000	11.3	8	11,593,000

Source: Employment Gazette.

Organised defiance

In consequence, the TUC campaign against the 1980 Act, centred on a Day of Action in May 1980 and an educational campaign, was limited. It took the 1982 Act to prompt a major response. A Special Conference at Wembley in April 1982 supported a programme intended to draw the teeth of the Conservative measures. Unions would not participate in ballots on the closed shop, or accept public funds for internal ballots. Union representatives would withdraw from tribunal hearings of closed shop cases. The TUC would establish a campaign fund. Crucially, the TUC General Council, when requested by a union faced with legal action, would have the power, if satisfied that assistance from other unions was justified, to 'co-ordinate action by other affiliated unions in support of the union in difficulty, including, if necessary, calling for industrial action against the employer concerned, or more widely' (TUC, 1982, 20). Talks between the TUC and Prior had produced nothing, whilst Sir Geoffrey Howe had set in place economic policy which could determine how the legislation worked. Now there was a need for action.

Despite statements from senior figures such as David Basnett of the GMB that the unions would break the law, TUC staff privately cast doubt on this. The TUC was wishfully thinking of 1972-style scenarios where shop stewards would take the lead. But the conditions which had underpinned the 1970s response were now vanishing. As unemployment reached new heights, confidence, security and the belief that aggression paid were on the wane. Workers were worried about their jobs. The initial response was cautious. When, in August 1982, the branch secretary of the Fleet Street electricians was brought before the courts for breaching an injunction, the judge contented himself with a small fine for contempt. Only a handful of employers – Chloride and the Mersey Docks and Harbour Road were amongst the most notable – took legal action, in small disputes, and only after careful calculation. But it soon became clear that the union officials against whom injunctions were directed under the 1980 Act were anxious to comply, as the recession took its toll on union membership (Evans, 1985).

A change was discernible after the 1983 general election. As part of its campaign against privatisation the Post Office Engineering Union instructed its members not to connect the private Mercury network with British Telecom. Mercury, a new company with a lot to lose, took the union to court. The High Court judge refused an injunction on the grounds that, under the new legislation, the action was related *wholly or mainly* to workers' concern over their jobs and, therefore, fell within the new definition of a trade dispute. This decision was reversed in the Court of Appeal. The Master of the Rolls, Sir John Donaldson, accepted the predominant element in the dispute was not concern over employment but political opposition to privatisation. The union's inducement to its members to break their contracts was, therefore, not protected. The POEU was informed by TUC General Secretary Len Murray that the TUC's policy was not intended to encourage breaches of the law and they withdrew their instruction.

The next union in the firing line, the NGA, was made of sterner stuff. Eddie Shah, who ran Messenger Group Newspapers, attempted to establish an open shop at his Warrington plant. The NGA instructed all its members to boycott the Messenger Group and began to picket the Warrington plant. Mr Shah was granted an injunction because the unions were in breach of the 1980 Act – the members were picketing a workplace other than their own – and the 1982 Act – they were pressurising advertisers and suppliers of Mr Shah in order to obtain a closed shop. When the union ignored the injunction it was first fined £50,000 then £100,000 and eventually a further £250,000. At the end of November 1983, the High Court ordered its total assets sequestered – taken over by court-appointed accountants. In December 1983, the Employment Committee of the TUC General Council voted to support the NGA's stance. They were repudiated by Len Murray and a subsequent meeting of the full General Council voted, amongst much bitterness, to leave the NGA to its fate.

From defiance to acquiescence

It was now clear the TUC was not prepared to attract legal penalties by carrying out the mandate of co-ordinating solidarity action that it had requested at Wembley. Its position now was that it could not support law-breaking. Co-ordination would, in itself, breach the new laws. It could, therefore, never be justified. And the example of the NGA showed how unlikely it was that any individual union would be able to stand up to the full might of the law.

There were cases, such as the dispute at Shell in 1983, where the courts issued injunctions and the workers ignored them. In the dispute between Dimbleby and Sons Ltd and the NUJ, the union

– which instructed its members to boycott copy to the new printers of Dimbleby's newspaper, an anti-union company, T. Bailey Foreman – initially defied the injunction. But, in the end, the NUJ was forced to accept its terms. This case also showed the wide ambit of the legislation. The NUJ, the courts held, had a dispute with T. Bailey Foreman which refused to employ their members. It had no dispute with TBF Ltd, who did the printing, a separate company under law, even though both were corporate entities controlled by the same company and had the same directors and shareholders.

The *Messenger* dispute witnessed the use of a mass police presence against the pickets. The miners' strike which erupted in March 1984 was characterised by cautious use of the civil law. In the first days of the strike, injunctions were granted to the NCB restraining the Yorkshire Area NUM from organising members to picket beyond their own workplace. When the injunction was ignored, the NCB refused to raise the issue of contempt and adjourned the proceedings. They were concerned at the impact the use of the legislation might have in uniting a divided union. Other big state corporations such as BSC and the CEGB failed to use the law, leading to wide-ranging criticism that government influence was inhibiting the use of the new measures against the kind of situation that they had been expressly designed to deal with.

In April 1984, however, Reads, a small transport company, were awarded an injunction against the South Wales NUM who were unlawfully picketing their lorries. In July, the area was fined £50,000 and, in August, its assets were sequestrated. Nonetheless, the primary legal influences on the miners' strike were not the employment legislation but the criminal law and the age-old breach of contract actions based on the union's rule book brought by working miners and their advisers, actions which eventually led to sequestration of the national union's assets (Beynon, 1985; Fine and Millar, 1985). After the defeat of the miners it was clear, if it had not been before, that the new legislation would not be defeated by direct union action.

The TUC accepted the 1984 Trade Union Act. Despite a

TUC interdict, officials of all affiliates closed their eyes as their shop stewards participated in ballots on the maintenance of closed shop arrangements. A major breakthrough for the government in grafting secret ballots onto the process of industrial action came in the Austin–Rover dispute in late 1984. Six unions called a strike after votes at mass meetings. Whilst the EETPU refused to officially sanction the action until a secret ballot was held, the other unions continued support in breach of a High Court injunction. The TGWU's £200,000 fine for contempt and the eventual disavowal of the strike by the other unions represented another milestone.

The disintegration of defiance was being demonstrated meanwhile in a struggle over the boycott of state funds for union ballots. Both the AEU and EETPU, because of their support for secret postal ballots and their financial difficulties, were by 1983 determined to take advantage of this financial aid. In 1984, the government announced that unless claims for money spent on ballots since 1980 were received by February 1985, they would not be met. Both unions resolved to act.

An AEU ballot saw members vote 12 to 1 for acceptance of the state subsidy. Although the AEU's National Committee ordered a re-run of the ballot, the union, in June 1985, took delivery of more than £1 million to cover costs of balloting since 1980 and the EETPU also lodged an application. The General Council voted to discipline the AEU, but the 1985 Congress produced a compromise by which the re-run ballot would explicitly refer to the TUC policy that government money was not acceptable. Despite this provision, the re-run ballot showed an 8 to 1 majority in favour of taking the money and the EETPU voted 9 to 1 in favour. In February 1986, the TUC convened a Special Conference which voted to drop the boycott. This Conference set the final seal on the demise of any TUC defiance of the new legislation.

At the same time, the Wapping dispute was sounding the knell of active opposition and illustrating how useful the new legislation could be to employers. The law protected Rupert Murdoch as he sacked his workforce and transferred production to a new plant. The picketing and secondary action that the unions had historically used to deal with this kind of situation were now unlawful. In the space of a few weeks, News International initiated a dozen legal actions against the unions. This time the NGA was more prudent but SOGAT went to the brink. Its assets were sequestrated and it was fined for contempt. It now did something a union had never done before: it quickly took steps to purge its contempt and gave the court assurances that, in future, it would operate within the law. The unions were, henceforth, severely impeded by the existence of the legislation in efficiently running the dispute. It seemed that where Heath had failed in the 1970s, Thatcher had succeeded in the 1980s.

Living with the enemy
By the time of the Conservative election victory in 1987 any pretence of TUC co-ordination of union opposition had vanished. The government had demonstrated that compliance could be elicited by coercion. Without widespread solidarity action there was no way round sequestration. Two of the most powerful sections of workers – the miners and the printers – had fought the law on their own and lost. The unions had failed to successfully confront the law. Now they had to attempt to manoeuvre around it, bobbing and weaving to minimise its impact on their activities. The extent to which the legislation could control the direction of industrial disputes and influence their outcome was demonstrated in the dispute between P & O Ferries and the National Union of Seafarers in 1988. P & O wished to change working practices and make workers redundant as did other employers in the industry. When in January 1988, the Isle of Man Steam Packet Company sacked workers fighting redundancies the NUS called a one-day national strike. Despite the similar position workers faced throughout the industry, the undermining of national agreements and the fact that P & O owned 40% of the Isle of Man Steam Packet Company, the courts granted P & O and Sealink injunctions against unlawful secondary action. The strike was eventually called off though not before the union had been fined for contempt.

P & O employees however continued their own stoppage and

were dismissed. In response, the NUS balloted for a national stoppage against what was seen as co-ordinated cost-cutting. In March the High Court granted P & O an unprecedented order *prohibiting the union from holding a ballot*, as a successful outcome could produce unlawful secondary action. The union called off the ballot but when further talks were unsuccessful and P & O withdrew recognition they again called for national industrial action. The judge fined the NUS £150,000 and ordered sequestration of its assets. The union was fined further sums and the industrial action gradually lost momentum.

The ability of the judges to develop the legislation was seen again in 1989 when London Underground was granted an injunction against industrial action because the wording on the ballot paper was too broad. The union had to mount a second ballot and when this produced a 'yes' vote, fend off further legal actions by employers on the grounds that some members had not received ballot papers. As NUR leader Jimmy Knapp observed: 'We are rapidly reaching the position in this country where it is not possible to call a strike and remain within the law' (McIlroy, 1991, 167).

This was an exaggeration. But the difficulties were tested when the TGWU attempted to run the 1989 dock strike by sticking to the letter of the law only to discover there was no letter of the law. Dockers voted 3:1 for industrial action, to find the employers requesting an injunction on the grounds that the ballot papers were improperly worded. Unsuccessful, the employers appealed, and the Court of Appeal upheld the view that a new argument – that the Dock Labour Scheme imposed a statutory duty on dockers not to take industrial action – required further scrutiny. They awarded an injunction: the damage a dock strike could inflict on the public interest required its prohibition pending appeal. Time was vital in this dispute as a bill was being rushed through Parliament abolishing the Dock Labour Scheme. None-theless, legal proceedings begun in early May were not completed until the end of June when the House of Lords overruled the Court of Appeal's novel and sweeping decision. By then the damage had been done. With delay, elements of disorganisation and division developed in the union. As the four week period in which the result of a ballot was operative had now passed a new ballot had to be held. It was 14 July before the ultimately unsuccessful strike could commence.

This dispute demonstrated, if in exceptional fashion, the way the legislation could strengthen the strike strategy of employers and state and weaken the sinews of union mobilisation. Judicial creativity continued. In 1992, for example, NALGO successfully balloted members in Newham in dispute over local authority cutbacks. When industrial action commenced the employers were granted an injunction in the High Court ordering employees back to work on the grounds that a union had to be neutral once a ballot was called and could not campaign for a 'yes' vote! Whilst this extraordinary judgment was overturned in the Court of Appeal it underlined again the difficulties unions faced from an apparently never-ending legal offensive. The TUC argued that the changes they managed to introduce into the 1993 Trade Union Reform Act were greater than the concessions gained from all the previous bills put together. They were nonetheless marginal. And the unions were faced with a simultaneous body blow with the government announcement that state funding for ballots – £4 million in 1991 – would be gradually cut, with the unions having to carry the bill themselves after 1996.

The impact of the legislation

We can examine the evidence under a number of headings.

Union security

There is little evidence that the 1980 Act directly undermined union recognition. The weaknesses of previous legal support were evident. The CBI reported no significant change between 1979 and 1986 in the immediate aftermath of the repeal of supportive legislation. Increasing derecognition since the mid-1980s seems to have had more to do with employer reappraisal of the sustained changes in employment patterns and the cumulative erosion of union power since 1979 rooted in economic changes, than belated realisation that the recognition legislation was repealed as long ago as 1980. We might hazard a connection between the decline of the recognition strike and prohibitions on secondary action but this too is likely to be related to growing union weakness located in economic change. By 1990 the closed shop covered only half a million employees (Millward et al, 1992, 102). Again it is difficult to relate this to the legislation rather than closure, redundancies and changes in industrial structure and the workforce. ACAS estimated that by 1986 only 30,000 of the then 3 million workers in closed shops had held ballots, which argues the limited reach of the law. There were only ten legal cases between November 1983 and July 1985 and several of these were financed by the Freedom Association. The problems of estimating impact can be seen in conflict between studies claiming legislation was responsible for almost the entire decline in density 1979–86, and others which claim its impact was minimal (Freeman and Pelletier, 1989; Disney, 1989). The latter view is far nearer the mark. Density had already crumbled significantly by 1983, the very earliest we can grant the legislation any impact. At best legislation had a mild effect in reinforcing the key factors: changes in employment levels and composition (see Chapter 10).

Industrial action

There has been a qualitative decline in industrial action (see p. 120) but again it is difficult to ascribe a particular impact to legislation, except as one part of a web of economic and political circumstance. It is clear that prohibitions on secondary action and unofficial strikes and the constraints balloting imposes on all strikes may curb bargaining power. The legal changes to 1986, particularly the balloting requirements, introduced a greater element of caution into industrial action (Brown and Wadhwani, 1990).

Strike ballots

These have affected the conduct of industrial action. The number of ballots gradually increased from 79 in 1985 to 196 in 1986, 251 in 1987, 331 in 1988, and 359 in 1989. By 1987, 53 different unions had participated in ballots and between 1987 and 1989 over 90% of the votes were in favour of industrial action (ACAS *Annual Reports*). As the number of strikes fell, the number of ballots increased but it is noteworthy that ballots were only held in around a third of disputes in 1987 and around 50% in 1989. Ballots encourage caution, centralisation of the conduct of disputes in the hands of full-time officers and formalisation of decision-making. They can strengthen the union's hand in negotiations or weaken it if unsuccessful. They prompt more calculation and planning but legitimise any eventual industrial action. Until the 1993 legislation most ballots were held at the workplace and there is little evidence of decollectivisation of decision-making (Martin *et al.*, 1991).

Union government
The legislation has been successful in securing compliance and the remoulding of unions' internal procedures. However, postal ballots for internal elections produce lower turnout, not more moderate leaders and more 'responsible' policies (see Chapter 4). The dysfunctional impact of legislation for the government can be seen from the political fund ballots (see Chapter 7). Only a handful of cases have been brought involving the new array of rights union members were given. The broader cultural impact of legislating plebiscitary democracy, which couples the union apparatus with the members at the expense of activism and redefines members in the direction of consumers of services rather than active citizens, has been important. It may interact with centralisation of control over mobilisation induced by legislative requirements to strengthen the role of full-time professionals (Chapter 4).

Employment protection
Conservative governments have been cumulatively successful in eroding, if not removing, individual protections such as unfair dismissal. The number of industrial tribunal cases fell but then increased in the early 1990s (McIlroy, 1991, 192). Research offers little support for the idea that legislation 'interferes with good

employee-employer relations in the small firm or has inhibited employers from creating jobs. . .managers do not find employment legislation a major consideration in their day-to-day management of the enterprise' (Curran, 1989, 13). A range of studies has questioned the utility of abolishing Wages Councils: it will not increase employment as the government believes – it will increase low pay (Standing, 1986; McNeil *et al.*, 1988). Nonetheless the 1990 WIRS survey found that managers consulted lawyers more and the changed environment was certainly influencing individual issues at work: 'the law had come to exercise a more significant role than ever before in the day to day conduct of employment relationships' (Millward *et al.*, 1992, 356).

Use of the law

In the key area of industrial action and ballots employers use the law to a greater extent than before 1979. But they take legal action in only a small number of cases. The most detailed study traced 77 cases between 1984 and 1987 and later surveys demonstrate no great change. Through the 1980s the emphasis shifted from cases on picketing to secondary action and then to ballots. In more than 90% of cases employers seek injunctions and in more than 90% of cases they succeed. In only three of the 77 cases above did employers go on to seek damages. Cases were concentrated in certain sections such as printing, shipping and public services (Evans, 1987; LRD, 1989). It is difficult to measure the impact of *threats* of litigation. What is missing from the statistics is the degree to which, because the legislation is there and has been successfully used elsewhere, unions modify their methods, accept offers they would otherwise reject and follow paths that, in the absence of legislation, they would ignore. The purpose of the legislation is, after all, not to provide work for lawyers but to transform the behaviour of unions. A survey in 1990 found that whilst legal action remained rare, in 1 in 3 workplaces employers had threatened to use the law in negotiations and in 1 in 5 workplaces unions had called off industrial action in response to such threats (LRD, 1990). A later study similarly found that legislation had a strong influence on the conduct of industrial action, strengthening the employers' hand, structuring and inhibiting union behaviour (Elgar and Simpson, 1993).

General assessment

The law has been influential in restricting and weakening unions *as part of the wider economic and political context*. The problem of isolating its impact remains insuperable. Of course in the Conservative project the law was not intended to be isolated: it was organically related to achieving wider economic objectives. Mrs Thatcher was successful in guiding important legislation onto the statute book, seeing it used and complied with. In this she surpassed her predecessors, Wilson and Heath. Crucial to success was rising and sustained unemployment, which weakened resistance. However as the mirage 'economic miracle' dissipated, fundamental questions were raised about the positive effect of legislation intended as a contribution to economic regeneration. The unions had been weakened, their immunities severely curtailed, their activities regulated in detail unheard-of in comparable countries, the employment protection of their members eroded, the prerogatives of employers unfettered. Yet Britain's economic problems remained. Particularly after 1988 the economic logic of legislative change was not apparent and an important drive appeared to be internal regulation of union activities. The Hayekian theme that unions, not employers, were the exploiters of the workers emerged through a battery of rights given to members against their unions as rights against employers were reduced.

The present framework is, in consequence, remarkably lopsided. It contains many of the limitations on unions enacted in other jurisdictions although it far surpasses them. It lacks the correlative individual and collective rights of other systems although it is here under continuing pressure from the EU. In as much as it is effective the new system increased the power of employers constraining democracy and weakening civilised standards at work.

To deregulate the labour market Britain has denounced four International Labour Conventions since 1979. The International

Labour Organisation has delivered nine judgments against Britain for breach of its Conventions. In 1989 and again in 1992 the ILO Committee of Experts found Britain's employment legislation in violation of Convention 87 on Freedom of Association and the Right to Organise. In 1991 the ILO Freedom of Association Committee took up the cudgels. Criticised were employers' freedom to dismiss strikers as exemplified in the Wapping and P & O disputes, the restrictions on secondary action, the manipulation of company ownership in the Dimbleby and Wapping affairs and the restriction on unions' rights to discipline members refusing to participate in balloted industrial action. The ban on unions at GCHQ and the denial of teachers' negotiating rights came in for particular comment. Despite all this the future, if it is a Conservative future, appears likely to involve further additions to what is already an unbalanced legal labyrinth.

Alternatives

The detailed alternative on offer is the Labour Party's programme. There would be extended employment protection, new rights to recognition, but the *status quo* on the closed shop and picketing. Looser restrictions on secondary action and sympathy strikes would be maintained as would union responsibility in tort. Ballots would continue but unions would have more choice over method and only members would be eligible to take legal action. There would be a new labour court. Important aspects of the Conservative framework would remain, refined and balanced by new protections, a mix of immunities and positive rights.

If change comes it is likely to take this form: Labour's proposals cut with the grain of EU developments and have been grudgingly accepted by the unions. A more radical approach has urged a recasting of legislation in the form of positive rights. Jim Prior's 1981 Green Paper on trade union immunities raised this issue and some academics supported replacement of immunities on the grounds that rights would be less susceptible to judicial misinterpretation. Given that 'it is scarcely possible to discover in the long history of the "golden formula" an important reported judgement which advanced the collective interests as such of workers effectively and unequivocally on a critical point of law' (Wedderburn, 1985, 513), such an approach is appealing. To positive rights to strike could be added rights to organise, bargain, security of employment and participation in decision-making.

A change in form will not of itself solve problems. Positive rights are unlikely to be unqualified and would be open to judicial scrutiny. We have to examine which formulation of content will best resist restrictive interpretation. Emphasising problems, Lord Wedderburn notes that few systems consist of all rights or all immunities, that there is a need to relate legislation to national traditions and that 'the root problem is not the form of the law, it is its administration' (Wedderburn, 1992, 1983, 521). Content of legislation and who interprets it are vital. The judiciary still represent a problem. Any system in which a leading judge can, as Sir John Donaldson did in 1983, advise the government on legal issues he will have to adjudicate upon, is open to question in terms of independence. When the same judge plays a part in reversing the important High Court ruling in the *Mercury Telecommunications* case on debatable criteria, and is then reported as holding shares in Mercury's parent company, the gravity of the problem is highlighted.

Any substantial programme of reform will have to involve reform of the judiciary or a more democratic labour court. From the union viewpoint it will have to counter attempts to create a framework in which rights are hedged around with qualifications which limit their utility. In several countries, such as Germany, there are rights to strike and labour courts. But these are inserted in a web of checks such as exhaustion of procedures, permission from the equivalent of the TUC and prohibitions on political strikes. And just as vital as the overall shape of the legal framework is the *context* in which it operates. A political and economic situation must be created which enables unions to utilise rights effectively in practice.

Taking into account all these difficulties, a move to a charter of rights may be the unions' best move. It could mesh with demands for general constitutional reform and greater commitment to the

EU as well as critical reaction against the present legal framework and an acceptance that there can be no return to the past. Embracing positive rights could represent a new beginning for trade unions and the new form aligned to wider changes could embody a new legitimacy for trade unionism.

Whatever form it takes, a greater degree of legal regulation of industrial relations is certain. A retreat to voluntarism seems unfruitful and impracticable. The challenge for the unions is to reject the withdrawal into their own private sphere, which the immunities symbolised, in favour of a positive programme of social renovation which would involve a new legitimacy for trade unionism. If realisation of these objectives appears distant today they are objectives the unions cannot lose sight of if they are to forge an equitable and enduring framework for their activities.

Conclusions

The traditional shape of labour law in Britain was the product of the specific historical evolution of the first capitalist nation. What was distinctive was the autonomy and space rather than the power accorded to unions by the state, the absence of both restrictive and supportive legislation, but also the resilience of a hostile, unmodernised judiciary committed to common law conceptions and Victorian values. Nonetheless, there were always limits to collective *laissez-faire* and from the 1960s revision proceeded in tandem with economic change. The changing landscape of labour law has been increasingly influenced by political reaction to economic events, the scapegoating of the unions and the failure of alternative solutions, crucially incomes policy. The first limited steps to refine the 1906 settlement from 1963 were conditioned by moves towards wage planning, deploying law at the margins to reform collective bargaining. By 1969 Labour was converted to ending legal abstention. The more ambitious 1971 Industrial Relations Act which sought to legally regulate collective bargaining and to control inflation as an alternative to a formal incomes policy, recognised the legitimacy and centrality of unions and collective bargaining. In this, Heath stands in contrast to

Thatcher. The innovations of the 1974–79 Labour government involved qualitative extension of legislation in the field of employment protection and bargaining rights. It brought Britain more into the mainstream by increasing legal support for union organisation and activities whilst maintaining abstention in key areas such as industrial action. The corporatist Social Contract legislation represented a break with voluntarism and a new emphasis on the use of law to extend and reform collective bargaining to facilitate its control. While valuable to union operations the new framework was more limited than sometimes suggested.

The Conservative years saw incomes policy cast aside and the triumph of full-blooded restriction with the legitimacy of collective bargaining and unions now in question. The new approach involved new right ideology, state craft, learning from experience, and success in opening up new vistas. The most sustained revolutionary programme of employment legislation ever has sought to undermine trade unionism, deregulate the labour market, undermine employment protection, encourage individualism and diminish collective bargaining. The impetus has shifted from controlling to eroding collective bargaining and trade unionism. The only countervailing pressures have come from the EU. The front of assault has been extensive, with unions facing challenges over almost all aspects of their activities, including political funds and the check-off, as well as the more traditional concerns of labour law. Growing emphasis on the rights of individual members against the collective organisation has combined with erosion of the immunities to threaten internal cohesion, mobilisation and efficiency. An unbalanced legal framework now exists, more unlike that in comparable countries than its voluntarist predecessor and far more inequitable. Unions prickle with responsibilities regulated in detail by the state; correlative rights are conspicuous by their absence.

The Conservatives' legal counter-revolution has been a formal triumph for government. TUC defiance intended to send it the same way as the Industrial Relations Act passed from co-ordinated defiance to defiant acquiescence to reluctant acceptance. Campaigning faded into impotent protest. State abstention was perceived as a means of integrating unions into the body politic and fostering labourism. The disintegration of collective *laissez-faire* and the passing over of the state to assault collectivism itself has not produced any compelling new labour movement ideology. The legislation has made an undoubted contribution to weakening the unions. It affirms and legitimises their reduction. Its role in economic regeneration, its avowed ultimate end, is highly questionable. The future will turn on political change. A Labour government is likely to maintain key landmarks of the Thatcherite landscape while seeking to place them in a more balanced union-favourable setting. As far as the unions are concerned there can be no return to 1979. Legal regulation is here to stay and the future argument will be over its content and form.

Further reading

Lord Wedderburn, *The Worker and the Law*, Penguin, 1986, is a classic and readable introduction to the framework and issues of employment law. Alan Fox, *History and Heritage: The Social Organisation of the British Industrial Relations System*, Allen & Unwin, 1985, is essential for the historical context of legal development, and John Griffith's masterly *The Politics of the Judiciary*, Fontana, 1991 is indispensable for understanding the judiciary.

Paul Davies and Mark Freedland, *Labour Legislation and Public Policy*, Clarendon Press, 1993, provides a detailed and authoritative exploration of the history of labour law since 1945. Bill McCarthy, ed., *Legal Intervention in Industrial Relations, Gains and Losses*, Blackwell, 1992, is a good collection of essays on the Conservative legislation.

7
Unions and the Labour Party

Many who concede the unions a necessary and legitimate role in politics question their identification with the Labour Party. In other countries unions play the field or support a Social Democratic party in more flexible fashion. What is questioned in Britain is the intimate nature of the relationship, the key role accorded the unions in the party's organisation and financial arrangements. This, it is argued, stereotypes the party as the creature of a sectional interest group and restricts its ability to adapt to new political imperatives, modernise and shed antiquated socialist rhetoric. The unions are, in their turn, saddled with an unsuccessful party which cannot deliver in the required currency – winning elections. They are expected to foot the bill and demonstrate loyalty to leaders with little sympathy for organised labour. In the 1990s the relationship between unions and party is the subject of contention and proposals for reform. It is likely to develop in new ways; it is unlikely to terminate in divorce. In this chapter we examine the nature of the marriage.

The political activities of the unions

Unlike the activities of employers, the political involvement of unions is closely regulated by the state. Until the early 1900s there were no legal restraints: unions supported Liberal and Independent candidates. The birth of the Labour Representation Committee in 1900 and the development of the Labour Party with the election of 30 MPs in 1906 transformed the situation. The threat to the Conservatives and Liberals attracted attention. Whilst some unions contributed to the party by means of a special Parliamentary Fund others contributed money from their general funds. W. V. Osborne, a branch secretary of the Railway Workers, went to court to stop his union levying money to be spent on the Labour Party. He was a member of the Trade Union Political Freedom League, a forerunner of today's Freedom Association. The case progressed to the House of Lords and the *Osborne* judgment, 1910, held that unions were only entitled to spend money on purposes laid down in the Trade Union Acts, 1871–76. This legislation accepted that unions' only lawful purposes were industrial purposes: to spend members' money on *political* aims was *ultra vires*, beyond their legal powers.

The unions mounted a campaign to reverse the *Osborne* judgment. Companies met no legal obstacles when they wanted to finance the 'big two' parties. The unions, it was urged, should be in the same position. The Liberal government arranged a compromise: the 1913 Trade Union Act allowed unions to spend money on politics, but on certain conditions. Political objectives had to be laid down in union rules. The 1913 Act defined 'political objectives' as the expenditure of money on expenses of: Parliamentary candidates; MPs; local government candidates and councillors; registration of voters; holding of political meetings; and distribution of political literature. Cash spent on these purposes had to come from a **political fund**, separate from the union's general funds. This fund had to be financed by a **political levy** on members, distinct from ordinary dues. Unions could only introduce this system after agreement in a secret ballot. Individuals would still have a right to contract out of paying the political levy. If the legal requirements were not followed, members could complain to a special ombudsman – today the Certification Officer – and eventually to the courts.

The policy of the TUC and the party was restoration of the position prior to *Osborne*. Nevertheless, the 1913 settlement endured until the 1980s. There were two important changes. In 1927, in retaliation for the General Strike, the Conservatives introduced a Trade Disputes Act. Instead of trade unionists having to **contract out** of paying the political levy, they now had to **contract in**. Partly because of this change, the percentage of members of unions paying the levy dropped by more than 30% between 1927 and 1946. In the latter year, Clement Attlee's Labour administration restored the 1913 position – members once more had to opt out.

Political funds

The establishment of a political fund is legally *quite separate from affiliation to the Labour Party*. The importance of this was underlined before the 1983 General Election when NALGO, which did not have a political fund, mounted a campaign against cuts in public spending. Ministers argued that the impact of NALGO's advertisements would be to influence an anti-Conservative vote. The 'Put People First' campaign, they complained, fell within the political objectives of the 1913 Act or demonstrated the need to extend them. In response, the government changed the definition of political objectives in the 1984 Trade Union Act. Expenditure on the production or distribution of literature, films or advertisements 'the main purpose' of which is 'to persuade people to vote or not to vote for a political party or candidate' must now come from a political fund, not from general funds.

These events and the success of the political fund ballots of 1985–86 (see p. 296) prompted creation of political funds by more trade unions. By the 1990s, however, there were still sizeable unions such as the NUT and the Royal College of Nursing which did not have political funds. In 1993, 47 unions had political funds with 6 million members contributing £15.5 million to them (Table 7.1). Around 20 of these were white collar unions such as NALGO, CPSA, IRSF, AUT, NATFHE and NAS/UWT, which now saw that political involvement was essential, although they wished to eschew Labour Party affiliation. All these unions engage in political activity through direct campaigns as well as parliamentary activity. Some unions which are not affiliated to the Labour Party employ MPs as consultants. NALGO and the AUT

Table 7.1   *Political funds of trade unions, 1992*

	No. of members contributing	No. of members exempt
Amalgamated Engineering and Electrical Union	621,110	214,452
Associated Society of Locomotive Engineers and Firemen	17,869	743
Association of Her Majesty's Inspectors of Taxes	2,412	113
Association of University Teachers	30,106	894
Bakers', Food and Allied Workers' Union	30,371	1,851
Broadcasting, Entertainment, Cinematograph and Theatre Union	39,903	45
Ceramic and Allied Trades Union	22,601	521
Civil and Public Services Association	–	–
Communication Managers' Association	14,930	307
Confederation of Health Service Employees	180,220	15,299
Educational Institute of Scotland	44,945	1,758
Electrical and Plumbing Industries' Union	2,040	–
Fire Brigades' Union	37,188	11,782
Furniture, Timber and Allied Trades Union	27,293	4,349
General Union of Association of Loom Overlookers	342	188
GMB	687,236	55,602
Graphical, Paper and Media Union	120,796	149,085
Inland Revenue Staff Federation	54,804	2,256
Institution of Professionals, Managers and Specialists	78,521	2,316
Iron and Steel Trades Confederation	27,810	6,933
Manufacturing, Science and Finance Union	225,691	326,309
Musicians' Union	31,935	1,832
National and Local Government Officers' Association	631,889	45,054
National Association of Colliery Overmen, Deputies and Shotfirers	4,775	36
National Association of Colliery Overmen, Deputies and Shotfiters (Durham Area)	360	–
National Association of Schoolmasters and Union of Women Teachers	108,583	82,054

National Association of Teachers in Further and Higher Education	65,262	2,888
National Communications Union (Engineering and Clerical Groups) – Engineering Group	71,268	17,661
National Communications Union (Engineering and Clerical Groups) – Clerical Group	26,407	3,026
National League of the Blind and Disabled	1,009	75
National Union of Civil and Public Servants	110,714	1,117
National Union of Domestic Appliances and General Operatives	650	6
National Union of Insurance Workers	13,468	2,623
National Union of Knitwear, Footwear and Apparel Trades	49,458	798
National Union of Lock and Metal Workers	3,925	47
National Union of Mineworkers	28,271	65,413
National Union of Public Employees	512,962	11,941
National Union of Rail, Maritime and Transport Workers	103,411	1,735
National Union of Scalemakers	3	1,051
Power Loom Carpet Weavers' and Textile Workers' Union	1,970	80
Rossendale Union of Boot, Shoe and Slipper Operatives	2,218	21
Scottish Carpet Workers' Union	831	–
Society of Telecom Executives	12,149	9,997
Society of Union Employees (NUPE)	164	–
Transport and General Workers' Union	909,530	14,405
Transport Salaried Staffs' Association	35,168	5,706
Union of Communication Workers	172,601	6,261
Union of Construction, Allied Trades and Technicians	110,673	24,695
Union of Democratic Mineworkers	10,997	81
Union of Shop, Distributive and Allied Workers	290,088	26,403
Union of Textile Workers	1,644	60
Total for the 52 unions with political funds for 1992	*5,578,568*	*1,119,869*

Source: Certification Officer.

have had links with MPs from several parties.

The Labour Party

For most big unions establishment of a political fund and affiliation to the Labour Party have gone hand-in-hand. In 1992 45 of the 70 unions affiliated to the TUC had political funds and 30 were affiliated to Labour (see list below). Unions affiliated to the Labour Party still represented 75% of TUC membership. Of the TUC top ten, however, NALGO was not affiliated and the NUT as well as growing unions such as BIFU still had no political fund – a worrying position for Labour. Outside the TUC the biggest union without a political fund was the Royal College of Nursing. Unions such as the Broadcasting and Entertainment Trades Alliance and the Amalgamated Society of Textile Workers had voted in the 1980s for political funds *and* party affiliation. Party supporters hoped that the merger of NALGO with COHSE and NUPE to form UNISON would lead to that union's adhesion. This could turn out to be a crucial issue for the future of union–Labour Party links. The changing occupational nature of TUC affiliates and the move towards public sector white collar composition promises a weakening of the marriage unless there is a breakthrough with important unions such as NALGO affiliating to the party.

Unions affiliated to Labour
Amalgamated Engineering and Electrical Union
Associated Society of Locomotive Engineers and Firemen
Bakers', Food and Allied Workers' Union
Broadcasting, Entertainment, Cinematograph and Theatre Union
Ceramic and Allied Trades Union
Confederation of Health Service Employees (COHSE) (now part of UNISON)
Electrical and Plumbing Industries' Union
Fire Brigades' Union
Graphical, Paper and Media Union

GMB
Iron and Steel Trade Confederation
MSF
Musicians' Union
National Association of Colliery Overmen, Deputies and
Shotfirers
National Communications Union
National League of the Blind and Disabled
National Union of Domestic Appliance and General Operatives
National Union of Knitwear, Footwear and Apparel Trades
National Union of Mineworkers
National Union of Rail, Maritime and Transport Workers
National Union of Public Employees
Power Loom Carpet Weavers' and Textile Workers' Union
Transport and General Workers' Union
Transport Salaried Staffs' Association
Union of Communication Workers
Union of Construction, Allied Trades and Technicians
Union of Shop, Distributive and Allied Workers
Union of Textile Workers

Source: Labour Party.

The political levy

Trade unions collect a political levy varying from £4.30 annually
in the GMB to 80p in UCATT. They then pay an annual sum –
£1.70 in 1993 – for each member they affiliate to the Labour
Party. Affiliation is broadly governed by the number of members
paying the levy. In the past some unions affiliated more than those
contributing to their political fund. Others, notably the TGWU
and the EETPU, affiliated less. Relevant considerations were
desire for power within the party, the union's financial position
and the Labour Party's need for income. During the 1980s as
membership fell unions failed to adjust affiliations downwards; by
1986 around 20 unions affiliated on more than their number of
levy payers. Over the years, however, affiliations have approxi-
mately reflected the number of contributions to political funds.

More worrying for a party which aims to be representative of trade unionists has been the decline of union membership, its changing composition and the impact on affiliation. Affiliations were 6.45 million in 1980, 5.8 million in 1986 and 5.3 million in 1990. White collar unaffiliated unions had performed better in the membership stakes than those affiliated to the party. The TGWU, for example, cut its affiliation from 1.25 million in 1990 to 750,000 in 1994 with consequent financial loss to the party.

The block vote

Unions have close links with social democratic parties in other countries but they are not represented so closely in decision-making. There are some similarities between the British party and Labour parties in Australia, Canada, New Zealand and Ireland. But the *organic links* at every level, the block vote and electoral college structures, the open two-way channel between both wings of the Labour Movement, made the British party distinctive. Votes at the party's annual conference were awarded to unions on the basis of the number of members on which they affiliate to the party. In consequence, the unions have held 90% of votes compared with around 600,000 allocated to constituency delegates. By 1990 the dozen biggest unions still had over 80% of the conference vote and the four largest unions nearly 60%. The TGWU with more than a million votes could easily outvote all the constituency delegates (Table 7.2).

The block vote always attracted critical attention as it did not necessarily represent *members* or even levy payers, but *affiliations* decided upon by the union leadership. Moreover, many of those paying the levy are not members of the Labour Party. Some vote Conservative or Liberal. Criticism was sharpened by the *concentration* of the union vote in fewer hands as the number of affiliated unions declined from 99 in the 1950s to 30 in the 1990s. The growing gap between the number of trade unionists affiliated to Labour and the numbers voting for Labour also attracted comment. The form of voting, with union leaders showing a card representing the union vote regardless of minority opinion, provoked hostility.

Table 7.2   *Trade union voting weight, 1990 Labour Party Conference*

TGWU	1,250,000	
TGWU: Agricultural Workers	41,000	
TGWU: Dyers and Bleachers	37,000	
	1,328,000	1,328,000
GMB	650,000	
GMB: APEX	54,000	
GMB: Boilermakers	75,000	
GMB: Textile Workers	11,000	
	790,000	790,000
NUPE		600,000
AEU		540,000
	Four largest	3,258,000
USDAW		366,000
MSF		304,000
COHSE		200,000
UCW		188,000
UCATT		160,000
NUR		120,000
EETPU		102,000
NCU		95,000
	Twelve largest	4,793,000
	All other unions (22)	554,000
	Total union vote (34)	5,347,000
	Total conference vote	6,038,000

Source: Minkin, 1991.

The unions' position was strengthened by formal domination of the party apparatus. They are allocated 12 of the 29 seats on Labour's National Executive and held a majority of the votes for the 5 seats allocated to women and the election of the Treasurer. They thus had a dominant say in 18 seats on the 29-person executive. Electoral arrangements between unions ensured that many places were filled in advance of elections. The unions had the biggest say in the election of the leader and deputy: 40% of the votes compared with 30% for MPs and 30% for the constituencies. Branches of unions affiliated to the party can affiliate to constituency parties in which their members live. The unions were thus often perceived as controlling the general management committees, historically involved in selecting parliamentary candidates. Even when the system was reformed in 1988 they still had a key role in the electoral college which replaced selection by committee.

Union decision-making

In most unions voting decisions at party conference are the prerogative of delegations taking account of union policy and sometimes advice from the executive. Delegations usually consist of a mix of full-time officers, executive members and elected lay officials. In some unions the nature of the relationship between executive advice and delegation voting is open to interpretation. But the idea that conference voting is dominated by general secretaries is exaggerated. When in 1984 the General Secretary, Moss Evans, attempted to cast the TGWU vote in favour of 'one member one vote' he was overruled by his delegation. In 1982 NUR General Secretary, Sid Weighell, successfully cast the vote against union policy but this forced his resignation. The 12 union representatives on the NEC are often minimally accountable and in recent years key figures such as Tom Sawyer (NUPE) and Eddie Haigh (TGWU) have been able to operate on a very long leash.

The election of the party leadership has provoked most controversy. In the first test of the electoral college, the deputy leadership election between Tony Benn and Dennis Healey in 1981, the large majority of unions left the decision to their executive or conference. A small number – NUPE, NUM, COHSE, POEU and NATSOPA – balloted their members. The TGWU carried out 'consultation' at regional level which went in favour of Healey. This was not binding on the Executive which voted for Benn. The delegation then voted first for the third candidate, Silkin, before a second ballot produced a tie between

Benn and Healey – with the vote eventually being cast for Tony Benn! Progress in forging more efficient democracy has been slow.

By the time of the 1992 elections for leader and deputy leader 4 of the 10 largest affiliates held full ballots of levy payers, 3 aggregated votes held at branch meetings, 1 organised a mixture of branch consultation and a postal ballot of a random sample and 2 left the decision to their annual Conference. NUPE held a postal ballot of all levy payers, the GMB organised a mixture of workplace and postal ballots. But unions such as the TGWU and the AEEU argued that the cost of full postal ballots of levy payers, estimated at £300,000 and £110,000 respectively, prohibited such an exercise. The way the unions cast their votes can be seen from Table 7.3.

Table 7.3 *How Labour's votes were cast, 1992 leadership election*

Leader	CLPs%	MPs %	Unions %	Total %
John Smith	29,311	23,164	38,518	91,016
Bryan Gould	0,689	6,816	1,482	8,984
Deputy leader				
Margaret Beckett	19,038	12,871	25,394	57,303
John Prescott	7,096	9,406	11,627	28,129
Bryan Gould	3,866	7,723	2,979	14,568

Sponsorship

Unions may seek more intimate influence by sponsoring MPs. Sponsorship entails payment of a maximum of 80% of a candidate's election expenses, plus an annual payment to the constituency party. If the constituency employs a full-time agent the union may contribute to salary. Unions selected or elected candidates for sponsorship through internal mechanisms. A growing practice has been adoption of a sitting MP. Sponsorship has declined since the early days when 80–90% of Labour MPs were union supported. But it has undergone a resurgence (see Table 7.4). In 1992 almost 60% of the PLP was sponsored – a return to the levels of the 1930s – and the shadow cabinet has been effectively colonised (see Tables 7.5 and 7.6). Exclusion from the corridors of power seems to have convinced unions of the virtue of having their people in Parliament. Unions utilise sponsorship to generate information on policy, amend legislation and lobby Ministers – with the emphasis on economic and industrial issues. A group of sponsored MPs, particularly in the shadow cabinet, provides a union with a further instrument of influence. This renewed emphasis has been part of a more professional approach. Throughout the 1980s more unions appointed political officers. Research officers were increasingly involved in political developments whilst other full-time officers, many of whom later became MPs, had a specific political brief. This went hand in hand with more regular meetings of unions' parliamentary groups and improved communications with sponsored MPs.

Table 7.4   *Sponsored MPs*

Election	Labour candidates	Union sponsored	Labour MPs	Union sponsored	Union sponsored as % of total MPs
1945	603	126	393	121	30.8
1950	617	140	315	110	34.9
1951	617	137	295	105	35.6
1955	620	129	277	96	34.6
1959	621	129	258	93	36.0
1964	628	138	317	120	37.9
1966	622	138	364	132	36.3
1970	624	137	287	114	39.7
1974	627	155	301	127	42.2
1974	626	141	319	129	40.1
1979	622	159	268	132	49.5
1983	633	153	209	114	54.5
1987	633	146	229	130	56.8
1992	633	199	271	157	57.9

Source: Labour Party.

Table 7.5 *Sponsored Labour candidates, 1992*

Union	Total	Elected
Transport and General Workers' Union (TGWU)	44	38
General Municipal and Boilermakers' Union (GMBU)	22	17
National Union of Mineworkers (NUM)	14	14
Analgamated Engineering Union (AEU)	15	13
Manufacturing, Science and Finance Union (MSF)	13	13
National Union of Public Employees (NUPE)	15	12
National Union of Rail, Maritime and Transport Workers (RMT)	13	12
Confederation of Health Service Employees (COHSE)	6	6
Graphical, Paper and Media Union (GPMU)	7	5
Electrical Electronic Telecommunications and Plumbing Union (EETPU)	10	3
National Communications Unions (NCU)	4	3
Union of Shop, Distributive and Allied Workers (USDAW)	3	3
Transport Salaried Staffs' Association (TSSA)	2	2
Associated Society of Locomotive Engineers and Firemen (ASLEF)	2	1
National Association of Colliery Overmen, Deputies and Shotfirers (NACODS)	1	1
Iron and Steel Trades Confederation (ISTC)	1	–
Union of Communication Workers (UCW)	1	–
Trade Union sponsored	*173*	*143*
Co-operative Party	*26*	*14*
All sponsored candidates	*199*	*157*

Source: Butler and Kavanagh, 1992.

Sponsorship breeds frontier disputes. Whilst several NUM MPs lost sponsorship in the aftermath of the 1984–85 strike, threats of withdrawal of sponsorship have usually produced inaction or withdrawal when referred to the Committee of Privileges. It is questionable what exactly some unions have gained in recent years apart from prestige from the sponsorship of key figures – the TGWU's sponsorship of Neil Kinnock and Tony Blair comes to mind.

Table 7.6   *Sponsorship and the shadow cabinet, 1993*

John Smith	GMB
Margaret Beckett	TGWU
Gordon Brown	TGWU
Tony Blair	TGWU
Robin Cook	RMT
Frank Dobson	RMT
John Prescott	RMT
Bryan Gould	none
Harriet Harman	TGWU
Mo Mowlam	COHSE
Chris Smith	MSF
Ann Clwyd	TGWU
Ann Taylor	GMB
Jack Cunningham	GMB
Michael Meacher	COHSE
Donald Dewar	RMT
David Blunkett	NUPE
Jack Straw	GMB
Tom Clarke	GMB
David Clark	NUPE

Source: The Guardian.

Party membership

The number of those willing to pay the political levy far exceeds those willing to commit themselves to party membership. Individual membership increased until the mid-1950s, peaking at over a million in 1953. Decline since then has been continuous. But it has been particularly serious since 1974 and there are today well under half the 690,000 members recorded in that year. If the years of the 1945 Attlee government represented the zenith of working-class participation, the decade from the mid-1980s represents a low point. Of the 279,000 members with which the party started the 1992 general election year 130,000 were up to three months in arrears and another 18,000 up to a year in arrears. Party officials calculated that the real membership was under 200,000, around 2% of Labour voters. It was difficult to see Labour – in terms of activism – as the party of the traditional working class. The majority of members are drawn from the salariat: 2 out of the 3 unions with the largest numbers of party members, NALGO and the NUT, are not affiliated. The AUT has more members than the NUM, NATFHE as many as NUPE; only 2% of the GMB's 650,000 levy paying members were members of the party (Seyd and Whiteley, 1992, 34–5). Moreover, the Conservative Party has in recent years claimed a membership three times that of the Labour Party.

Funding

In 1979 the Labour Party appeared totally dependent upon union finance. Union affiliations contributed 95% of the General Election fund – in the context of a large overall deficit. Against this background *Trade Unions for a Labour Victory*, an umbrella organisation established in 1978 by a number of unions across the political spectrum to co-ordinate support and fund raising for the Party, became more prominent. An admission that existing structures were working inadequately, TULV came under criticism as an unaccountable club of union bosses intent on outflanking democratic mechanisms. In response, it stressed its financial and organisational role and funding was undoubtedly at the centre of its operations. Labour's financial position was improved by increasing affiliations and establishing a new voluntary levy fund to channel money to the party from those unions with buoyant political funds.

In 1986 TULV was replaced by Trade Unions for Labour (TUFL) which was specifically excluded from policy issues. The Levy Fund was continued, supplemented in 1988 by a Business Plan. By the 1990s the percentage of party funds paid by the unions had dropped to the 50% mark. From 1984 national fund raising activities had been more successful and CLPs now received only around 20% of their financial support from unions (Fatchett, 1987). If the share of union financing was declining, Labour would still find it difficult to survive without it.

The trade union electorate

The future of the Labour Party as a party of government is central to the question of the unions' political *and industrial* fate. Since

1979 Labour has not won an election; that in itself has made a major contribution to the debilitation of the unions. Moreover a significant decline in Labour's working-class vote not only puts the credibility of the union-party connection on the line: it saps the strength of both organisations.

Table 7.7 illustrates various aspects of the problem. In the past the basic determination of voting behaviour was social location. The majority of manual workers voted Labour and the majority of white collar and professional workers voted Conservative. Moreover, large numbers of those voting Labour saw themselves as *supporters* of the party *identifying* their own views with its politics. This social alignment was not complete. A quarter to a third of the manual groups voted Conservative and around a fifth of the 'middle-class' groups voted Labour. It was in this overlap that Labour's prospects were decided. Deviations from class voting were usually analysed in terms of age, with more older people voting Conservative across social groups; working-class deference; gender, with more working- class women voting Conservative than men; *embourgeoisement*, with increased affluence allegedly impacting in voting behaviour; regionalism, with Wales and Scotland favouring Labour more; and the attraction of left-wing ideas to those in professions such as teaching or social work.

This pattern, with nearly 90% of the vote being shared between the two big parties, began to disintegrate in the 1970s. Since then each party's share of the vote has declined. Labour received almost 49% of the vote in 1951 and the Tories 48%. Even in 1970 the two parties split 89% between them. Yet by 1983 the Tories won a massive majority with only 42% of the vote against Labour's 28%. Labour lost more votes than the Conservatives and it has only been able to close the gap gradually in 1987 and 1992.

To some degree – in 1983 and 1987 – it is plausible to relate problems to the split in Labour and the emergence of the Alliance and later the Liberal Democrats. This does not fully explain why so many voters have deserted Labour. The party has suffered, as Table 7.7 demonstrates, a loss of its majority amongst trade union members. Decline is gradual until 1979 but Labour's union vote collapses in 1983. Even after a comeback in 1987 and 1992 less

Table 7.7 The decline in the Labour Party vote

A How the electorate voted (%)

Party	1964	1966	1970	1974 (Feb.)	1974 (Oct.)	1979	1983	1987	1992
Labour	44	48	43	37	39	37	28	31	35
Conservative	43	42	46	38	36	44	42	42	43
SDP/Liberals	11	9	8	19	18	14	25	23	18

B How trade unionists voted (%)

Party	1964	1966	1970	1974 (Feb.)	1974 (Oct.)	1979	1983	1987	1992
Labour	73	71	66	55	55	51	39	42	46
Conservative	22	25	28	30	23	33	31	30	31
SDP/Liberals	5	4	6	15	16	13	30	26	19

C How social groups voted (%)

	Professional/managerial					Office/clerical			
Party	1974	1983	1987	1992		1974	1983	1987	1992
Conservative	63	62	59	56		51	55	52	52
Labour	12	12	14	19		24	21	22	25
Liberal/SDP	22	26	27	22		21	24	26	19

	Skilled manual					Semi-skilled manual			
Party	1974	1983	1987	1992		1974	1983	1987	1992
Conservative	26	39	43	39		22	29	31	31
Labour	49	35	34	40		57	44	50	49
Liberal/SDP	20	27	24	17		16	27	19	16

Source: Crewe and Harrop, 1989; Butler and Kavanagh, 1992.

than 50% of trade unionists vote for the party of the unions. Labour's problems are rooted in the decline of its vote in manual groupings, particularly in the C2 skilled worker category. Historically Labour claimed around 65% of this group. Yet in 1983 its share was only 35%. Despite all the efforts since, the party still gained less than 50% of the skilled manual vote in 1992.

The stabilisation of the Conservative share of the vote at a minority 42% has, under Britain's 'first past the post' electoral system, rendered a Labour Party which cannot crack the magic 40% barrier electorally impotent. The 'two party system' has been replaced by a **dominant minority party system**: the Tories winning a minority of votes gain a majority of seats. How do we explain this transformation which has been crucial to the weakening of the Labour Movement?

Some look to the changing class structure. The manual working class is still the biggest single group but it is declining. In contrast, the white collar groups, particularly the managerial–professional category, have grown fast. It has been argued that the drop in the number of manual workers in itself largely explains Labour's electoral plight. The percentage of manual workers has declined from 47% to 34% whilst the managerial categories have moved from an 18% to a 27% share of the electorate. There is still a correlation between voting Labour and being in a union, even if it is a weaker one than existed in the past. Yet in the 1990s their are 4 million fewer trade unionists than in 1979 (Heath, Jowell and Curtice, 1985).

Against the **declining working class** explanation some have emphasised *politics* to a far greater degree, suggesting a **divided incompetent Labour** model. From different parts of the political spectrum the following are cited: the Winter of Discontent, the party's identification with incomes policy, the splits and divisions of the early 1980s, the years of Kinnockism producing a diluted Thatcherism and an SDP Mark 2 party, and ineffective, unimaginative leadership. Some note that Labour and Liberal Democrats together possess a majority of votes and underline the importance of the defection of the SDP in 1981 in upsetting the balanced coalition Labour was previously able to present to the electorate.

A key strand in analysis has argued that a process of class and partisan **dealignment** has taken place over the last two decades. Books such as Rose and McAllister's *Voters Begin to Choose* (1986) and Sarlvik and Crewe's *Decade of Dealignment* (1983) documented the importance of a loosening of class attachments and a growing instrumentalism amongst voters. Rather than bestowing allegiance on one party they are more fickle and prepared to shop around.

Other work suggested that whilst class remained important the social position of voters needed to be addressed more *specifically*. Voting decisions were not simply influenced by the fact you were a skilled, manual worker but also whether you worked for Nissan or the local council, owned your own house, or used public transport as against your own car. The social situation of voters in relation to consumption as well as production was vital; so too was perception of how the parties' policies impacted on an individual's view of society and economy through media transmission (Dunleavy and Husbands, 1985). By the late 1980s a split working class divided along north–south, private–public sector housing and employment, non-membership or membership of a union, was seen as important in explaining Labour's decline. The voters in the first category, crucially those in the skilled manual category, were seen as having moved away from Labour and realigned with the Conservatives or Liberal Democrats.

The 1992 General Election demonstrated that the problems of the 1980s still dogged Labour. In 1987 Labour did better amongst white collar and semi-skilled, manual groups; the Conservatives kept their edge amongst the skilled, manual category. The Conservatives maintained dominance in the south and saw their majority reduced from 144 to 102 seats. Neil Kinnock required a massive swing in 1992. With problems over the Poll Tax, the EU, the fall of Mrs Thatcher and the recession, the Conservatives still scrambled home with a 20-seat majority. Labour had improved – but not enough. Labour did better in the south but the Conservatives improved in the north. Labour increased its vote amongst trade unionists and in all categories except the semi-skilled manual, but insufficiently to make up the ground lost in

1983. Winning only 35% of the vote, despite an unpopular government and a recession, the party remained in its post-1983 trough. Accepting the meat of post-1979 change, eschewing an alternative political logic and staking victory on the claim to superior, more civilised management of the new consensus proved unsuccessful. Allowing for unfavourable factors, such as the winner-takes-all nature of the system and government manipulation of economic levers in the run up to elections, there remained something seriously wrong with Labour's appeal. Analysis of the election suggested it was not so much Labour's image as the party of high taxation which did the damage but rather its failure to successfully project itself as the party of economic competence. It failed to convince sufficient voters who had deserted in the 1980s that it could run the economy efficiently enough to deliver on its social policy (Heath *et al.* 1994). The aftermath of the election promised much: the tide was running against new right theology, the Conservatives were unprecedentedly unpopular over tax increases and divided over Europe and, in Tony Blair, Labour had a new, presentable leader. Questions remained as to its credibility when the chips were down.

Unions and the Labour Party: the arguments

From the 1970s the unions' involvement in politics became a major political issue and with the advent of the Thatcher government in 1979 the argument intensified.

The case for the prosecution

1 Trade unions are industrial organisations. Whilst they have the right to act as a pressure group, their financial control over a major party of state is questionable in constitutional terms. A Labour government cannot serve the national interest but is at the beck and call of union paymasters with disastrous consequences. There is little evidence of the link improving wages and conditions. The Labour Party may do something for union leaders; it has done little for their members.
2 If you put all your eggs in one basket and that basket has holes in

it you have problems. One study found that almost half of Labour's union funds in the late 1980s came from just two unions – the TGWU and the GMB (Pinto–Duschinsky, 1989, 20). The excesses of the union leaders moreover have made Labour unelectable. Dependent on decisions taken by its union paymasters, the Labour Party is rendered politically volatile. Strong political parties are vital to democracy yet with unions in terminal decline Labour's problems will intensify. The party must look for more secure sources of support.

3 Support for Labour is a classic example of unions misrepresenting their membership. Even in 1992 Labour was unable to win a majority of members. Should not the preferences of the majority of trade unionists who are *anti-Labour* be reflected in support for other parties? A system by which, in the 1980s, 3.5 million trade unionists voted Labour but up to 6 million contributed to its coffers is inequitable. The millions unions spend on politics should be reduced. The residue would be better spent on employing more full-time officers and perhaps contributing smaller amounts to both Labour *and* the Liberal Democrats.

4 The political levy is indefensible: only half the members paying the levy realise they are doing so (Moran, 1974, 90, 91). The TGWU claims that 90% of members pay the levy. In MSF the figure is only around 30%. Such differences can only be explained by inflation or manipulation. Some unions deliberately make it difficult for members to contract out; industrial and political payments are often compounded into one subscription fee and deducted at source. Opting-out requires application, time and courage. Membership application forms obscure the fact there is a right *not* to pay the levy.

5 The block vote is indefensible: it gives members of other parties a voice in Labour Party policy. Union bosses can buy in as many votes as they require to further their political ambitions regardless of how many members pay the levy. Union votes represent not members but pound notes. In reality the party conference is as lacking in democracy as a meeting of company shareholders. The CLP activists who do the hard political slog

– as well as paying three times as much in party subscriptions as levy payers – are disenfranchised by the union cuckoos.

6 The system has clear implications for participatory democracy. In the 1970s the Houghton Report on Financial Aid to Political Parties estimated that the Conservatives had 1.5 million individual members, three times as many as the Labour Party, and the gap has widened since. The obvious deduction was that citizens were not prepared to pay to be active in an organisation which *fails* to empower them. This is backed by recent research: 8 in 10 individual members believe the party leader should be elected on a 'one member one vote' basis and 72% of members agree that 'the trade union block vote at conference brings the party into disrepute' (Seyd and Whitely, 1992, 50, 51). Union domination inhibits political involvement. This is not redressed by participation within the unions. In the 1992 leadership elections the TGWU Executive rejected the recommendations of General Secretary Bill Morris for a ballot. The GMB did hold a ballot but only around 140,000 of the union's membership voted, a turnout of only 21.5%.

The case for the defence

1 The industrial and political purposes of unions are indivisible. Unions need MPs just as much as full-time officers. Government policies affect the state of the economy, the position of employers, the power of unions and the livelihood of their members. Unions which operated only through collective bargaining would be walking on crutches when they had two good feet. The industrial/political split reinforced and developed by the 1913 Act is artificial and unhealthy. If union involvement in politics *is* essential, then having their own party represents the logical form of involvement. Union domination is exaggerated. A survey in 1987 found that only 18 out of 202 constituencies had a majority of union delegates on their management committees (Fatchett, 1987, 54).

2 Conservative criticism represents a chronic case of the pot calling the kettle black. The unions are required to provide details of their political expenditure; the Conservative Party

refuses to do so. Less than a fifth of the Conservatives' £26 million annual budget can be traced, although at least a quarter of Britain's top 200 companies directly fund that party (Scott, 1985, 52–3). The laundering of funds through fronts such as Aims (formerly Aims of Industry), and the network of dummy companies named after English rivers makes calculation difficult. Regular *Labour Research* surveys demonstrate the extent of employer backing. What price the Conservatives' criticism of union sponsorship of MPs when, in 1993, 135 of their backbenchers held 287 directorships and 146 held consultancies? In 1993 revelations of donations of more than £7 million from foreign capitalists such as millionaire Asil Nadir rocked the government. In return donors expected and got access to Ministers. Industrialists are ten times more likely to be awarded honours if they contribute (LRD, 1993c). *The party of capital, in return for funding, carries out policies in the interests of capital.*

3 It is more difficult for employees to halt their bosses' donations to the Tories than it is for Conservatives to secure a revision of union rules. There is no right to opt out of the employers' political levy. The policies of other parties are less satisfactory to the unions: neither would allow the unions a major role. The attack on Labour Party democracy is rich: there is no democracy at all in the Conservative Party! Members play no role in the election of the leadership. The unions are not a cohesive, homogenous block who always agree on politics for the Labour Party. There are big differences between them. And for most of Labour's history, the parliamentary party has maintained a sturdy autonomy from direct union influence.

4 The political levy is indeed indefensible. Why should unions have to meet obligations to ballot, whilst companies have to meet no such criteria? If critics were consistent, they would support legislation to ensure that companies held ballots to get shareholder support for a political fund. The only obligation companies have is to disclose donations in their annual report.

5 Perhaps unions *should* do more to raise the question of political expenditure and exemption. But the system of exemption is,

itself, undemocratic. Democracy is about the wishes of the majority. If the majority of members support political expenditure, why should those who disagree be able to opt out? There is a devastating dearth of evidence about abuse of the political levy. In 1982, when Frank White, MP, asked the Director-General of the EEF whether he possessed evidence of allegations, he was told: 'not anything that I think you would recognise as evidence, no'. Discontented union members possess rights to complain to the Certification Officer. During 1993 one complaint was received from 5.9 million levy payers!

6 Perhaps there *should* be more frequent ballots – as long as they are binding on *all* participants – and perhaps there *is* a need to review the internal procedures of the Labour Party. It is certainly arguable that the block vote inadequately rewards the efforts of constituency activists. But the Labour Party has changed its internal arrangements periodically. Voluntary change – through self-government, not state intervention – is what true participatory democracy is about. But if there is legislation it should embrace companies as well as trade unions.

The recent history of a marriage

We can break down the recent history of the union-party link into five main episodes:

The extension of the union role

In the atmosphere of dissatisfaction with the leadership after the 1979 General Election constitutional reform came to the fore. There were proposals for mandatory re-selection of MPs, broadening of the franchise for leadership elections, and for control of the manifesto to lie solely with the NEC. The unions did not take the lead. Reform was initiated by constituency activists, the Campaign for Labour Party Democracy and later the Rank and File Mobilising Committee. Unions responded to channel the reformists' demands to restore stability and became the beneficiaries of them only partly by design (Minkin, 1991, 193–205).

Left-wing unions such as the TGWU, ASTMS and NUPE were instrumental in carrying mandatory re-selection in 1980 against the opposition of the GMB, AEU and EETPU. At the 1981 special conference to decide the make-up of the electoral college for leadership contests the final outcome was the product of division amongst right-wing unions. The AEU supported a resolution which would give 75% of the votes in the college to the PLP. They then refused to support a GMB resolution which would have given MPs 50% of the vote because of a mandate which pledged them to support a majority for the parliamentarians. The left, in contrast, united behind the successful USDAW resolution (which the USDAW leadership were sure would be defeated) giving the unions 40% of the votes, with the CLPs and MPs each taking 30% (Seyd, 1987).

This surprising *denouement* strengthened the unions' role in the party and gave a fillip to the left. Nonetheless union leaders left and right were concerned at internal factionalism. After the Benn–Healey deputy leadership contest in 1981 they moved to orchestrate the Bishop Stortford concordat. There would be no further constitutional changes and no further challenges for the leadership. The unions used their increased influence to steady the Party and support the leadership, later embracing the Kinnock–Hattersley unification of left and right.

Breakaway from Labour

Disillusion with the unions over their role in the downfall of the Callaghan government combined with horror at constitutional change to motivate the establishment of the SDP. 'A handful of trade union leaders, they observed, can now dictate the choice of a future Prime Minister' (Stephenson, 1982, 185). There was talk of unions defecting to back the new party. *SDP Trade Unionists* was established. High hopes were held of the EETPU when General Secretary Frank Chapple endorsed SDP candidates, appointed SDP memberer John Grant as a union officer and urged the TUC to open talks with other parties. However the SDP's hard line on anti-union legislation won few converts.

The SDP's excellent performance in the 1983 election

provided a new platform. But its advocacy of the 1984 Act and a 'no' vote in political fund ballots created insurmountable barriers. New SDP leader David Owen's flirtation with what Roy Jenkins labelled 'sub-Thatcherite' economic policies and his open admiration for the government position over the miners' strike did little to endear him to the TUC. Labour, led by Neil Kinnock, was now moving to accept key elements of SDP policy. The stability of the marriage had proved powerful; the inept courtship of the unions by the SDP ensured that by 1985 the possibility of union defection had evaporated.

But for the government there was still the legal card to play. As Norman Tebbit mused, legislation could be used:

to encourage a split in the TUC which could bring Social Democrats and right-wing Labour people together with backing from the same trade unions. I hoped that if the ballots for Political Funds were accompanied by a real national debate led by the media it might precipitate a questioning of why the funds were wasted on support of an unelectable muddled semi-Marxist party. The idea of creating an electable rival to the Conservative Party, I agreed sounded crazy but it could set the scene for a long lasting consensus on Thatcherite terms (Tebbit, 1988, 207).

In the wake of her 1983 election victory Mrs Thatcher moved to take action to drive a wedge between unions and the Labour Party.

The 1984 Trade Union Act and ballots on funding
Initial ideas of changing contracting out to contracting in were dropped in return for agreement that the TUC circulate affiliates with information on rights to exemption. In keeping with its philosophy of giving the unions back to their members the government focused instead on ballots. The *form* of the legislative requirements was important. It has been suggested that TUC persuasion influenced the government to go for ballots on the political fund rather than replacing 'opting out' with 'opting in' (McInnes, 1987, 143; Pelling, 1988, 291). The decision appears rather the product of government calculation that the ballots would go against the unions in important cases. Political expenditure would thus be undermined by the self-activity of the

union rank and file, not by government fiat. To minimise accusations that it was acting in partisan fashion to bankrupt its main competitor, the government addressed political expenditure, not political affiliation. Too crude an assault might, it was felt, draw attention to the position of companies. And the Conservatives did not wish to raise the question of state funding of parties.

The 1984 Act, therefore, required unions to ballot members every ten years, not on whether the unions should affiliate to the Labour Party, but on whether they should *maintain a political fund*. All unions with political funds had to hold such a ballot within twelve months of March 1985. In future, these ballots should have to be held every ten years. If no ballot was held, or if no majority was attained, then political expenditure had to stop. There were teasing glimpses of the other agenda. 'What would please me immensely,' Mrs Thatcher was quoted as saying, 'would be if the TUC were not and the unions were not a part of the Labour Party, or the Labour Party a part of the trade union movement.' Later she went even further and stated that she favoured a US-style system where both major parties operated 'within the same framework of free enterprise'.

The unions were aware that one or two major reverses could set in train a dynamic of disintegration. Four important factors influenced the outcome of the ballots. Firstly, a Trade Union Co-ordinating Committee was established to oversee progress. It was effective and imaginative. Secondly, the decision that the ballots should be *phased*, with unions most likely to win going first, to establish momentum, proved excellent strategy. It exploited the government's miscalculation in allowing ballots to take place over 12 months. A fickle media, with a limited timespan of attention, soon lost interest. Thirdly, the decision to play down the link with Labour worked, with political figures sidelined and 80% of CLPs playing no role (Fatchett, 1987, 78). Fourthly, the government was over-confident and misread the signs. Most of the polls found majorities favouring ending links with the Labour Party not political activity itself. Confident they were on a winner the Tories' campaign was limited. By 1985 there was some recovery in the unions' popularity.

There were differences in emphasis. Whereas NUPE and
TGWU, at least in several regions, did argue for the Labour party
link, ASTMS was more muted. There was little discussion of
specific political policies. The central theme was the unions'
ability to successfully protect their members and the need for a
political dimension to this. A key to success was the emphasis on
reaching members where they worked. The limited nature of the
campaign, its peaceful co-existence framework – 'if you don't
want a political voice, OK, but vote "yes" to let other members
have a political fund' – and its efficiency, contributed to its
success.

In one of the few unquestionable union success stories of the
1980s, Mrs Thatcher was handed a 38–0 drubbing. Overall, 83%
voted for political funds, as against a derisory 17% who opposed
them, on a very reasonable 51% turnout. In unions like the NUM
and the TGWU, singled out for criticism by the government, the
'yes' voters were more than 90% and more than 80% respectively.
Even in unions like ASTMS, where a minority paid the levy, there
was a 'yes' vote. Nonetheless the Labour Movement could not get
completely carried away: 'Seventeen unions including all the
purely white collar unions and ten out of the eleven unions with
200,000 members failed to secure a "yes" vote of over 50% of
their members' (Minkin, 1991, 570).

Employment Secretary, Tom King, branded the campaign a
'blatant example of deliberate disinformation and misleading
propaganda'. His complaint was that the vote should have been
about the union links with Labour. Perhaps it should. But it was
pointless crying foul when his administration had clearly established the rules of the game. Within the movement, some felt that
the unions had been excessively coy over the link and lost an
opportunity to re-argue the need for a trade union party. Nonetheless, it was an important triumph. By 1992, 20 unions had
established political funds for the first time and around 80% of
union members were in unions with such funds. From the Conservatives' viewpoint the ballots had misfired: white collar unions
were becoming more political. However, as subsequent general
elections affirmed, these ballots demonstrated support for a

political voice not for a particular party. This was underlined by the failure of Labour to attract more trade unionists to membership. Workplace branches, the hope of the early 1980s, declined. In 1985 there were almost a hundred. In 1988 only a handful were functioning and by 1992 'the Party had forgotten that workplace branches ever existed' (Heffernan and Marqusee, 1992, 186). Moreover the unions were faced with a further round of ballots in 1994–95.

The subordination of the unions

Under the 'dream-ticket' leadership of Neil Kinnock and Roy Hattersley, seen as unifying left and right, the party began taking on board some of the baggage of Thatcherism and the SDP. The new project involved developing a social market party with a subordinate role for the unions, purging the hard left and domesticating the soft left. Motivated by the calamity of 1983, arrested by the miners' strike, this strategy progressed after 1987. The emphasis on electoralism and realism made Kinnock determined to curb militancy and maintain key aspects of the Tories' legal framework. He was adamant no future Labour government would involve the unions as between 1974–79. He viewed links as an electoral embarrassment and a channel through which opposition to the policies of a future Labour government could flow. He was determined on reform. Socialist rhetoric, at which union leaders excelled, played a legitimising role for Labour, particularly in opposition. It was now perceived as counter-productive. Its impact on an electorate which Kinnock believed had invested in Thatcherite values was negative. It mobilised the wrong kind of people, projected the wrong kind of image, alienated capital and middle of the road supporters and raised false hopes of radical social change. Kinnock wished to rid Labour of its image as a party dependent on the unions. His aide Peter Mandelson reputedly remarked in 1989: 'Neil is to the right of Margaret Thatcher on the unions' (Heffernan and Marqusee, 1992, 147).

Having established control of the NEC through support from unions like NUPE and acquiescence by others such as the TGWU, Kinnock used it to limit the rights of CLPs in selecting parliamentary candidates. 'Unsuitable elements', from Sharon Atkin in 1987 in Nottingham East to Lol Duffy in Wallasey in 1992, were replaced by the NEC nominees. The purge of Militant was deepened after Kinnock's 1985 conference attack on Liverpool City Council; by 1991 two MPs Terry Fields and Dave Nellist had been expelled. Planning and public ownership were explicitly disowned. Public spending would be kept under a tight rein if Labour formed a government, with redistribution of income within sharply defined limits. Individualism replaced collectivism as a key emphasis in policy-making; unilateralism and opposition to the EU were junked. Through the Policy Review process policies intended to refine the changes of the Thatcher years were developed under leadership control. Advisers in Kinnock's private office were increasingly influential. Policy seemed aimed more at pleasing the city and the media than the party's working-class base.

Whilst Kinnock used the apparatus to push change through there was minimal opposition. Union leaders and CLP activists alike were trapped in the logic of an electoralism which, eschewing alternatives to the new consensus, insisted that moderation and image would secure victory. The Kinnock revolution was achieved largely by consent. Within both the union leadership and the web of union-party activists the majority tendency was to subordinate everything to regaining power.

In the development of industrial relations policy the unions were sidelined and accepted major concessions. From 1986 the Labour Party–TUC Liaison Committee, the unions' instrument for contributing to policy-making in the 1970s, was marginalised. The commitment to repeal the anti-union legislation was dropped. The Conservative framework of ballots would be retained and Labour would not remove legal responsibility for industrial action from unions as organisations – a situation it had been brought into existence to oppose. To redress what were seen as the mistakes of the 1970s the emphasis on partnership was now on partnership with industry; the emphasis was on efficient management not industrial democracy.

Policy-making was *party dominated*. It flowed from the PLP

leadership to be accepted reluctantly by the unions on the basis that there was no alternative. By 1989 Kinnock was observing: 'We have already made it abundantly clear to our trade union colleagues that in government we will be no soft touch'; and Employment spokesperson Michael Meacher was stating, 'Trade unions will not have unjustifiable covert influence on the Labour Party's policy-making in or out of government.' How far things had gone was demonstrated when Meacher's successor, Tony Blair, announced the party's new policy on the closed shop on a television programme with no prior consultation with the union leaders (McIlroy, 1991, 221). The transformation was nurtured by advice and support from TUC officials:

they were often privately supportive of the Parliamentary leadership sometimes playing a brokerage role between the political and industrial leadership in an effort to produce change on sensitive issues . . . And they needed little encouragement to seek a new formula that would edge the unions gently in the direction of some form of incomes policy (Minkin, 1991, 457).

Some leaders, such as John Edmonds of the GMB, had no doubt as to the need to take their medicine. But even leaders of unions whose policies were more antagonistic, such as Bill Morris of the TGWU, sought to bring their flock into line. There were differences between the politics of unions such as the AEEU, normally characterised as on the right, the GMB in the centre and the TGWU and MSF on the left. But differences were often differences of emphasis and coherence. The TGWU has fought hard over maintenance of the universality principle in welfare benefits and for some element of redistributive taxation, and together with the GMB sought to keep the aim of full employment alive. It has been accepted that the party leadership has the last word. It would be fair overall to say that since 1983 *the general trajectory has seen the unions follow the party to the right*. Even the broad left organisations which are strongest possess little opposi-tional *élan*. Whether the return of a Labour government would change this is another matter. By 1992 the unions had clearly accepted a new subordinate role. They had given over to the party

leadership the cherished private domain of employment legislation. Such was the hegemony of the party leadership that they
were able to intervene in the industrial sphere, as in the railway
and ambulance disputes in 1989–90, impressing upon union
leaders the need to conduct themselves in a fashion which would
not endanger Labour's electoral prospects. The 1990 Conference
voted to end the electoral college for candidate selection, a
decision was taken in 1992 to reduce the block vote to 70% of the
conference votes and attempts were made to limit the policy-
making role of Conference.

Restructuring the relationship

The union issue had been of minimal significance in the 1987
election: the percentage of voters believing unions had 'too much
say' in the Labour Party declined by 1990 to 50% of all voters and
35% of Labour voters. The union question played no role at all in
the 1992 contest (Butler and Kavanagh, 1992). Nonetheless, new
leader John Smith determined to reform the links. Labour would
become like other social democratic parties, giving the leadership
greater autonomy and policy greater predictability. Related to
adaptation to the Conservative constructed consensus, the project
could been seen as shedding Labour's inheritance to make it a
modern capitalist party.

A Mori Poll before the election showed only 4% mentioning
the unions as an obstacle to voting Labour. Yet in the election's
aftermath a survey by the Shadow Communications Agency was
taken up to urge reform and by early 1993 Smith had come out in
favour of abolition of the block vote. Even previous supporters of
modernisation such as John Edmonds claimed that at stake was an
attempt to distance party from unions on the European model.
Intrinsic to the modernisers' strategy was an attempt to emulate
the Conservatives, concentrating power at the top and insulating
the leadership from the unions *and* constituency activists.

Many trade unionists had felt from 1987, 'there were few if any
people around the leader who even know much about the unions
let alone cared about them or respected them' (Bassett, 1991,
313). The union leaders felt with justification that they had been

the bedrock of Labour in the difficult years. They had halted the infighting of the early 1980s and supported the Kinnock–Hattersley ticket. There were few more concessions they could have made to Kinnockism 1987–92. Now they were being scapegoated by a less than impressive leadership.

Despite strong opposition from the two largest affiliates, the TGWU and GMB, the party leadership was able, through forceful manipulation of the block vote they criticised, to push change through. The 1993 conference agreed to end union participation in selection of parliamentary candidates. Henceforth only 'registered supporters', union members who agreed to pay a £3 top-up to the political levy, would be represented. The unions would have a third of the votes in leadership elections – the same as MPs and CLPs. They would no longer be able to cast them *en bloc*. Membership ballots would be mandatory, with only those declaring they were not supporters of other parties eligible to vote. The union vote would then be split on the basis of the ballot result. The unions' 70% of the conference vote would be reviewed with the intention of downward revision. In future it would be divided equally between delegates and cast on a split basis.

These changes represented a substantial blow against traditional collective involvement. It was clear however that unions could absorb them in some ways as they had the balloting requirements of employment legislation. Their implementation underlined again how far union leaders were prepared to move to support party chiefs, and how misconceived many criticisms of the relationship have been. The Conservative Party's relations with capital and the shadowy nature of its party democracy make it a far more obvious, though far less frequent, candidate for stricture. The union–Labour Party relationship has been conducted within a web of conventions and self-accepted constraints through which the unions have ceded precedence to the party. The use of the unions' potential control over party policy has been utilised with diffidence and inhibition (Minkin, 1991). Their stabilising role is clear from recent history. The advantages this gives the political wing are powerful ones. The link has provided the party with an electoral base, institutionalised funding, intimate entry to the concerns of millions of workers and powerful political and organisational ballast. The electoral problems the relationship poses are presently minimal – indeed after four successive election defeats and a great deal of sacrifice it might appear more fitting that the unions rather than the party should question the relationship.

Nonetheless there were good reasons for reform of the block vote. It has all too often made union leaders in Gramsci's phrase 'bankers of men'. However we cannot take at face value the democratic credentials of a leadership which has sought to limit the rights of CLPs to select candidates and Conference to make policy, showing little hesitation in attempting to manipulate the block vote in its own favour to control the constituencies. It is unlikely that the leadership would welcome an active mass membership and likely that reduction of union influence will be followed by continuing limits on the rights of individual members who have historically been to the left of the leadership and in many ways still are (Seyd and Whitely, 1992, 118ff.).

The new system underwent its first test in the 1994 ballot for John Smith's successor. With the vote now split equally between constituency members, MPs and MEPs and trade unionists, on a 'one person one vote' basis, Tony Blair won easily. He polled 57% against 24% for John Prescott and 19% for Margaret Beckett to become the new leader. Amongst trade unionists Blair performed slightly worse, taking 52% against 28% for Prescott and 19% for Beckett. In only two of the larger unions, the RMT and GPMU, was Blair pipped by Prescott. But turnout amongst trade unionists – only 19.5% of the 779,000 eligible voted – compared unfavourably with the 69% turnout in the constituency section. The new rules were strictly applied: the NUM and UCATT were ruled out because they wished to avoid the cost of postal/workplace ballots by voting at the branch. Any many votes were ruled out because trade unionists failed to tick the declaration that they were supporters of the Labour Party. In his first statement as leader Blair warned trade unionists they would have no more influence over a future Labour Government than employers.

Thatcherism triumphant?

Some commentators seeking to explain Conservative success since 1979 emphasise the radical nature of Thatcherism as a novel and compelling set of ideas. Stuart Hall claims that Thatcherism sought to organise support on the basis of **authoritarian populism**. Using resentment against the state, and collectivism, it took up popular concerns such as inflation, crime, the failures of the education system and union power. Thatcher orchestrated these concerns in a politics which fused together a centralised, coercive state with a return to the market. By responding to people's anxieties Thatcherism won over key sections of the electorate and gripped the imagination of many working-class voters (Hall and Jacques, 1983; Hall, 1988).

Critics have questioned the novelty and success of Thatcherism. Many of its preoccupations were inherent in the politics of Heath before 1972. There is a continuity with the policies of the Callaghan government. Moreover, Hall, it is argued, exaggerates the coherence and reach of Thatcherism. Its period of ascendancy was limited. Before 1982 Mrs Thatcher was insecure; after 1987 she was unpopular. Her ultimate failure can be judged by the fact that she became the first Prime Minister to be formally removed by her own party. The Conservative vote in 1979 was scarcely a major endorsement. Thereafter it declined, bobbing around the 42%–43% mark in 1982, 1987 and 1992. The 1992 election was 'the fourth consecutive election in which a majority Tory government was elected with a lower share of the popular vote than any such government since 1922' (Butler and Kavanagh, 1992, 327).

Hall later asserted he had not suggested that Thatcherism was hegemonic, having securely installed a new regime of accumulation and social consensus, only that it was dominant. The Conservatives *have* been dominant but they have been a dominant *minority* party acquiring power only through the quirks of the electoral system and the split in the Labour Party. If only 1,241 electors in key marginal seats had voted Labour in 1992 there would have been a hung Parliament. Grand theory often possesses slender empirical ballast. Conservative success owes more to the failings of Labour than popular endorsement of Conservative ideas.

Hall's view that authoritarian populism represents 'an exceptional form of the state' is particularly wide of the mark. Mrs Thatcher may have taken a strong line on law and order and shown little respect for civil liberties but Britain is still a parliamentary democracy. If there was more of a 'strong state' under Mrs Thatcher than there was under Stanley Baldwin (and that is arguable) the change is one of *quantity* rather than quality. Essentially, it is argued, Hall over-emphasises ideas, building a strawperson Thatcherism that does not exist. As early as 1984 surveys such as *British Social Attitudes* demonstrated strong continuing attachment to the social democratic values of the post-war consensus. In 1988 a MORI survey found large majorities opposing reduced welfare spending, supporting action to combat unemployment as against inflation, and claiming that the gap between incomes was too great. When asked to choose between a society based on socialist or capitalist values 54% picked the former, 39% the latter. By the 1990s what struck many was 'the limited extent to which a decade of Conservative government had helped Thatcherite values to take hold among the public' (Butler and Kavanagh, 1992, 46–7).

The better view is that Conservative success related more to canny political strategy, material changes and the weakness of alternatives on offer than *positive endorsement by the electorate of new right ideas*. Skilled workers voted Tory in 1979 in reaction to wage restraint, to put more money in their pockets. By 1983 many of them got it at the price of greater unemployment and greater dispersal of earnings. Rising living standards led many to opt for the *status quo* in 1983 and 1987, given the alternatives. In reality, what success Thatcherism had was based upon *material* not *ideological* factors. It was difficult to see mass support for the Conservatives in Liverpool, Glasgow, Newcastle or Manchester. And the differences in voting between north and south was to be explained in the end by material differences.

We are talking, remember, about minorities and fractions, with elections and power turning sometimes on a few thousand votes. The majority of voters did not vote Conservative in 1979 or later. All Mrs Thatcher required was not a revolution in ideas but the construction of a *just enough* coalition of 'winners' in terms of her economic policies to construct the 43% of the vote which provided, in terms of three party politics, a massive majority. Once economic difficulties began to emerge after 1989, Mrs Thatcher was unmade by economic change working through in terms of political unpopularity just as she had been made by it. Yet in 1992 Labour *still* lost. Despite the replacement of Mrs Thatcher the electorate blamed the Conservatives for economic problems. Yet they lacked faith in Labour's ability to provide better management even in the depths of a recession. The political situation since 1979 is better characterised as the crisis of Labour rather than the hegemony or dominance of right-wing ideas.

The forward march of Labour halted?

Eric Hobsbawm argued in the book, *The Forward March of Labour Halted?*, and in a series of articles, that the Labour Party's problems are part of an historic crisis. The advance of party and unions halted between 1948 and 1951. Important changes since that time have centred on the decline of the manual working class, the disintegration of traditional communities and common lifestyles, and levels of affluence undreamt of in the past. These developments have produced a growth of sectionalism and a militancy focused on sectional wage demands, symptoms of a decline in class-consciousness which has produced a diminished attachment to unions and the Labour Party. From his analysis Hobsbawm concluded that there was a need for Labour to adopt policies acceptable to middle-class voters, and attempt to win back the SDP. He suggested electoral arrangements with all those opposed to Mrs Thatcher, on the model of the Popular Fronts of the 1930s (Hobsbawm *et al.*, 1981; Hobsbawn, 1989).

Hobsbawm's 'march' metaphor unhelpfully simplifies the historical ebb and flow in the fortunes of a Labour Movement, going forward at one time on one front, being driven back on another.

The unions were severely defeated in 1926, yet Labour was elected three years later. The collapse of the 1929 government and the retreat of the Labour Movement in the 1920s and 1930s, moreover, shows how questionable Hobsbawm's idea of a forward march until the 1950s is. It was only in Hobsbawm's period of decline that many of the strengths of British trade unions, such as the edifice of workplace trade unionism, surely for all its flaws and limitations a vital expression of working-class self-activity and combativity, was constructed.

It was, after all, in 1966 that Labour won 48.8% of the vote, almost equalling its all-time greatest performance of 1951. How, 16 years into the reversal of 'the forward march' did Labour do better than it did in 1924, 1929 or 1935? How, in the age of the affluent worker, flower power and the Beatles, did Labour do better than it did in the depressions of the 1930s and the 1980s? Had Hobsbawm pointed out to Edward Heath in the early 1970s that the forward march of Labour had halted more then two decades before, the Conservative Premier, faced with the battles over the Industrial Relations Act and the miners' strikes, would have been less than impressed.

If Hobsbawm is basically correct in his overall estimation of the limitations of the militancy of that period, it is difficult to see any significant increase in sectionalism compared with past strike movements such as that of 1918–22. Trade unionism still embraced a greater section of the working class in the 1980s than it did in the 1920s, including many of Hobsbawm's white collar groups, whilst the entry of women into the labour force provides the potential for greater unity and power.

The situation is more complex than Hobsbawm allows. He tends to see the past through rose-coloured spectacles, and focuses on changes in prosperity and the social structure at the expense of *politics*. He places little weight on the policies of past Labour governments and Labour's recent failure to provide any coherent, convincing policies. Any account of Labour's problems surely needs to integrate more emphasis upon *party policy and party performance* upon the way, for example, the 1974–79 government attempted to control and discipline its working-class base without delivering any meaningful reforms. And upon the way the party has simply adapted to Thatcherism without providing any compelling alternative to it. Both Hobsbawm and Hall exaggerate the automatically debilitating impact for Labour of changes in class and society. Studies continue to demonstrate continuing awareness of class and residual identification with the Labour Party amongst trade unionists (Devine, 1992; Goldthorpe and Marshall, 1992). What is missing is the intervention of an active agency capable of providing ideological leadership, political strategy and organisational mobilisation.

Ironically for a historian, Hobsbawm appeared by the 1990s to be correct in his thesis but to have got his history wrong. The forward march of Labour has been halted but it was halted in the late 1970s not in 1950. Advance was progressively reversed in the 1980s. The political options available to stem retreat are limited. In the unlikely event that Labour were to turn towards radical left policies it is clear that there is no electoral majority ready in waiting. Such a project would require a well resourced, imaginative mobilisation far from the minds of the existing leadership. It would thus require a struggle against that leadership for which the forces are presently unavailable, not forgetting the electoral consequences of another bout of infighting. The alternatives are 'one more heave', more of the same, in the hope that further incremental gains in the next election will push the Conservatives out. Or some arrangement with the Liberal Democrats whose policies differ marginally from Labour's, but many of whose supporters lean towards the Conservatives rather than Labour. By 1994 the deep unpopularity of the Conservatives and the fillip Tony Blair's leadership gave Labour produced new optimism. A danger was that the party would rely on disillusion with the Conservatives rather than positive policies bringing it to power.

Certainly some social force – why not the unions? – needs to qualitatively develop the policies which failed in 1987 and 1992. If Britain is to regenerate its economy and society there is a need for stronger welfare services, more jobs, more democracy at work, a fairer distribution of income, an attack on poverty. There is also a crying need for the refurbishment of the political system, yet the unions hold back from vigorously proposing specific electoral and constitutional reform. There has also been suspicion of the new social movements, feminists, environmentalists and community politicians. These groups lack the potential power of organised labour and the political reach of the Labour Party. They often speak for oppression the Labour Movement has neglected. Closer links would appear mutually beneficial. An effective orchestration of demands for a fairer society, a more efficient economy and a more radical democracy could turn the tide for Labour decisively.

Conclusions

Unions carry out political activities outside the framework of the party, but for those organising the majority of members, affiliation to the party still provides a fundamental anchor for politics. Whilst the relationship has represented more than simply the imbrication of political and industrial bureaucracies, involving additionally a web of activists at regional and local level, it has never acted as a stimulus for the political mobilisation of trade unionists. On the whole, it has acted to subordinate union politics to parliamentary politics and union leaders to Labour Party leaders, curbing the constituency activists in the process. The unions in the post-war decades played a secondary, stabilising role; voting power and financial muscle were rarely cashed in for *de facto* control over decisions. In the 1970s this position was streamlined through the development of a second corporate circuit involving direct links between the TUC and party chiefs. The early 1980s saw an extension of the unions' constitutional role but new rights were applied with circumspection and respect for the primacy of the party leaders. The later 1980s saw significant decline in Labour Party membership to a new low, decline in participation and professionalisation of the political function in party and unions. There was adaptation to Thatcherism; spin doctors and pollsters held sway. In 1992 more than 60 Labour MPs had worked as full-time union or party officials.

Industrial debilitation, inability to carve alternative channels to political influence through a relationship with Conservative governments, loyalty to Labour and the difficulties of creating any viable replacement party, left unions more dependent than ever on Labour. The victory in the political fund ballots meant that the unions staved off a body blow to their political role. That role remains extensive. But its reach is far weaker than in the 1960s or 1970s.

Firstly, the unions have been very seriously weakened as clients of a party which by 1992 had lost four successive general elections, a situation unknown since Labour first formed a government in 1924 and one which fundamentally circumscribes the unions' power by denying them access to government. Secondly, their hold over the party has been seriously weakened. This is important, for political failures appear more influential in Labour's decline than changes in the class structure. Labour's leadership has lost faith in developing traditional values and demonstrated inability to develop a compelling left alternative to Thatcherism. Like other social democratic parties it seems to have too readily accepted the limits on the role of the state in the new market based world economy. In this it has been followed by the unions who since 1983 have progressively shed left-wing politics. Thirdly, Labour Party modernisers have moved to restructure union-party links to further diminish union influence. The objective is a European-style framework which would formalise greater autonomy for a professionalised, centrist party leadership, reduce union representation and minimise financial problems through state aid for parties. A key issue confronting the unions by the 1990s was the fact that Labour was no longer *a party* let alone *the* party of government. And there were growing doubts as to the extent it remained *their* party.

Despite Labour's revived prospects since 1992 caution about the unions' future political success remains in order. Their loss of political influence has been serious and the dynamic of modernisation means that what is at stake is a historical redefinition of relations rather than, as Marsh asserts, 'a re-establishment of the traditional relationship between the unions and the Labour leadership' (1992, 162). Labour's leadership is taking advantage of a weakened union movement to go beyond merely fine-tuning existing links. It aims to formally redefine the terms of symbiosis as one part of a wider political adaptation. It wishes to reform itself as a centre social democratic party on the continental model with a relationship with the unions far less *organic* than that which has historically prevailed. The political fund ballots of 1995–96 will provide another test for the unions. The nature of their political affiliations will continue as an issue beyond that. At the moment the political fortunes of the unions remain tied, in violation of Citrine's dictum, to the fate of one party, a party in which they no longer enjoy 'most favoured person' status.

Further reading

Lewis Minkin, *The Contentious Alliance: Trade Unions and the Labour Party*, Edinburgh University Press, 1991, is a monumental and diverse work indispensable for any real understanding of party–union relations. Ralph Miliband's *Parliamentary Socialism*, Merlin Press, 1973, is a classic socialist critique of the Labour Party. Keith Ewing, *Trade Unions, the Labour Party and the Law: A Study of the Trade Union Act 1913*, Edinburgh University Press, 1982, is useful on the legal background. Derek Fatchett, *Trade Unions and Politics in the 1980s: The 1984 Act and Political Fund Ballots*, Croom Helm, 1987, updates matters and has interesting information on CLPs in the 1980s.

A wealth of detail on Labour Party membership is contained in Patrick Seyd and Paul Whiteley, *Labour's Grassroots: The Politics of Party Membership*, Clarendon Press, 1992. Colin Hughes and Patrick Wintour, *Labour Rebuilt*, Fourth Estate, 1990, outlines Kinnock's restructuring of the Labour Party with admiration, whilst Richard Heffernan and Mike Marqusee, *Defeat From the Jaws of Victory: Inside Kinnock's Labour Party*, Verso, 1992, is far more critical. Andrew Taylor, *Trade Unions and Politics*, Macmillan, 1989, briefly compares the UK with a number of other countries such as the USA, Germany and Japan.

8

Journey into Europe

'The only card game in town is in a town called Brussels and it is a
game of poker where we have got to learn the rules and learn them
fast.' TGWU leader Ron Todd, speaking to the 1988 TUC,
voiced a remarkable change. Just seven years earlier Congress had
voted for withdrawal from the European Union. It might fairly be
said that Britain joined the EU in 1972 – the unions in 1988. After
decades of disinterest and hostility the standing ovation which
greeted Commission President Jacques Delors' address to the
Congress symbolised the unions' transformation from Euro-
phobes to Euroenthusiasts. Casting insularity to the winds the
TUC established an EU strategy committee. Positive reports
poured from Congress House. By 1991 GMB leader John
Edmonds was declaring the 'eccentric' British industrial relations
system would be replaced by a new model based on EU initiatives.
When in 1992 TUC General Secretary Norman Willis became
President of the ETUC, it seemed to set the seal on the sea change
in attitudes.

An obvious impulse in the unions' European revolution was
problems at home; most important were developments in the EU
itself. The dynamic towards integration had been restrained by
the crisis of the mid-1970s. After the 1980s recession and resolution of the argument over Britain's budgetary contributions, particularly from 1985 with Delors as President of the Commission,
the EU moved towards a Single European Market. The necessity
for fair competition and civilised liberalisation produced the

'social dimension' and the acceptance in December 1989 of the Social Charter by all member states except Britain. By 1993, despite the vicissitudes of the Exchange Rate Mechanism, the Treaty of Maastricht timetabling progress to economic and monetary union had been adopted. The unions thus face the challenge and the opportunity of the Single Market and new industrial relations initiatives. Above all there is the imperative, with the growth of globalisation and economic convergence of practical internationalism, of building unity between workers at every level from the shopfloor to industrial secretariats. This chapter examines the unions' European adventure.

The unions and the EU: the background

As debate on Britain's membership of the EU intensified from the 1960s three distinct tendencies could be discerned within the unions. The pro-European faction was small but united, organised with Labour Party supporters in the *Labour Committee for Europe*. The anti-community faction embraced a coalition of the left who viewed the EU as 'a capitalist club', moderates who supported national sovereignty and Atlanticists who identified with the US and Britain's role as a junior world power. The pragmatists, dominant until the 1970s, were based on the TUC and focused on the terms of entry (Teague, 1989, 29–31). Despite these divisions the TUC did attempt to overcome its isolation and played a positive role in the creation of the ETUC. Unions in the nine EU countries except Ireland, together with centres from the Nordic countries, Austria, Spain and Switzerland affiliated. By the 1980s 35 union centres from 21 countries were involved (Baranouin, 1986).

Britain formally joined the EU on 1 January 1973, 16 years after the Treaty of Rome. The TUC first opposed Edward Heath's initiative on the basis that Britain's economic prospects would be better outside on the terms negotiated. The 1972 Congress, blown by anti-Conservative militancy, declared 'opposition in principle' to membership and voted to campaign for withdrawal and boycott EU bodies. The anti-marketeers, strengthened by the collapse of the pragmatists into their camp, carried the day (TUC, 1972, 274, 446).

When Wilson's 1974 Labour administration put the revised terms to a referendum, the TUC remained opposed. Apart from dissatisfaction with the new terms they were concerned with 'issues of sovereignty as they related to the sovereign rights of the British Parliament and to the freedom of public and private industry and institutions' (TUC, 1975, 221–2). However, the unions were divided in practice, with 'Trade Unions Against the Common Market' and the 'Trade Union Alliance for Europe' both campaigning in the referendum.

The decisive 2:1 vote in favour of membership necessitated a re-appraisal of TUC policy. At the 1976 Congress the boycott of EU committees was ended. The TUC again became active in Europe, leading a push through the ETUC to motivate co-ordinated EU action on unemployment (Dorfman, 1977). An element of disillusion with the immobility of EU institutions, a lingering wish the referendum result had been different, the backlash against the Labour government and the revival of alternative strategies based on the national economy and import controls coalesced to produce votes for withdrawal at the 1980 and 1981 Congresses.

The terms of entry were a continual goad to opposition. Britain paid the price for its procrastination over the EU in the decade and a half after the war. The period from 1975 to 1984 was, moreover, one in which the EU was in the doldrums and British unions preoccupied with their own difficulties. Positive hopes were of creating an insulated island of socialist progress in contrast to the capitalist EU. Prompted by the Labour Party leadership's rejection of radicalism, new realism in the TUC and hostile messages from EU unions, things began to change. The TUC full-time staff had from 1981 attempted to convince the General Council of the need for a more constructive policy, and from 1983 re-alignment with the Labour Party's changing approach (Trower, 1990, 7–8).

Sometimes overlooked is the process of re-negotiating Britain's budgetary contributions. Changes in the Common Agricultural

Policy continued through the early 1980s culminating in Mrs
Thatcher's widely advertised triumph at the Fontainebleau
Summit in 1984. This reduced Britain's contributions and
weakened the props of the anti-EU platform. The drive since
1979 to integrate Britain into the world economy increasingly
eroded the potential of any national economic strategy. The political exclusion of the unions opened their eyes to wider horizons.
However, change was gradual. The EU remained a muted issue
on the British political agenda despite the moves towards the
Single European Act.

The international interests of British capital and the desire to
balance between the EU and the US combined with a sense of
national superiority to delay Britain's entry. The arrangements
and political culture which developed without Britain provided
pretexts for continued hostility. The unions were influenced by
these factors and by the chauvinism rooted in Britain's imperial
past and the benefits obtained from it (Nairn, 1972). Nonetheless,
as Teague points out, this does not explain the oscillations in the
TUC and the consistently pro-European line of some unions. He
argues that all factions in the continuing debate saw economic
policy in national terms. Critics viewed the EU as an instrument of
capitalism which could thwart left policies. Even supporters and
pragmatists did not see any significant role for supra-national
policies in economic decision-making. Assessing the position to
the mid-1980s he concluded:

The overriding impression is that no serious thought has been given to
the type of policies that could be implemented at the European level
which would advance the interests of the trade unions . . . All of the
factions appear to be meshed within the logic of national economic and
industrial planning . . . none of the factions had anything positive to say
about the EU's role in a strategy for renewed economic growth (Teague,
1989, 40, 42).

Change and transformation

The negative nature of union policies in the first decade of
Britain's membership is summed up by the failure to project any

serious strategic response. No special mechanisms were established by the TUC, still less affiliated unions, to deal with EU issues. They were consigned to one member of the International Department with substantive issues being dealt with by 'subject departments'. The EU figured marginally in TUC activities and in 1977 NALGO expressed concern at the failure to monitor developments. After 1983 the General Council related more to EU realities. Conversion was in train before 1988: in 1984 Congress accepted the Vredling Directive, while serious assessment of moves to a single market commenced in 1987. The 1987 General Election was a watershed. In its aftermath Labour ditched its already eroded critical stance. The Party developed a strong pro-EU orientation consistent with the move away from national economic policies. The General Council fell in line. At the heart of the change was not only the TUC's national disorientation, but its concern with the consequences of the impetus to EU economic integration.

A White Paper, approved by the Council of Ministers in 1985, contained 300 measures intended to remove physical, technical and fiscal barriers to free movement of capital and labour within the EU by the end of 1992 and create a Single European Market. There would also be harmonisation of the technical standards of goods and services to be traded in the new market. More problematic was the question of minimum standards covering the conditions of work of those producing goods and services – *the social dimension*. The 1992 project was a response to the problems EU capital faced in competition with the US and Japan. The Commission hoped these measures would stimulate centralisation of capital, more transnational enterprises, more internal competition and more efficiency in a bigger market of 320 million people. The year '1992' would represent a qualitative leap forward from customs union to common market. To stimulate progress the Single European Act replaced unanimity with 'qualified majority voting' for decisions taken by the Council of Ministers on proposals relevant to the SEM. Moreover, as former German Chancellor Helmut Schmidt put it 'Who ever heard of a single market with eleven different currencies?' (Wise and Gibb,

1993, 292). In early 1988 the Council of Ministers established a committee to discuss a timetable for moves to economic and monetary union.

Awareness of the importance of these developments brought home key points to the TUC. It was now clear that the EU would move in the direction of a common macroeconomic policy framework. EU policies would exercise increasing influence on what happened in Britain. Interest groups had to be inside or outside EU economic processes: those standing in the middle of the road would get knocked down. There was little chance of EU withdrawal for there was little chance of Britain achieving economic success outside the EU. More specifically, the SEM presented major problems for British workers. With increased competition the weak could go to the wall and many British enterprises were weak compared with their EU comparators.

The TUC staff were handed the high cards. In a series of papers culminating in the statement, *Maximising the Benefits, Minimising the Costs*, they argued that British industry, already weakened by the Thatcher experiment and on the periphery of the EU, was far from well placed in relation to the 'Golden Triangle' centred on Amsterdam, Bonn and Paris. In key areas it lacked size and economies of scale; its locus had moved towards low technology, low growth areas of the economy. Its record on training, investment and productivity was poor. With free movement of capital and increased competition a particular danger was relocation of companies in low cost EU states such as Greece and Portugal, and 'social dumping'. Acceleration in the growth of transnational companies would pose new challenges for collective bargaining (TUC, 1988b).

However, the TUC discerned potential benefits. Embattled in Britain, they grasped eagerly at a favourable prognosis such as the Commission report published in early 1988:

Costs will be down. Prices will follow as business under the pressure of new rivals previously protected is forced to develop fresh responses to a novel and permanently changing situation ... The SEM will propel Europe onto the blustery world stage in the 1990s in a position of competitive strength and on an upward trajectory of economic growth into the next century. Such additional growth following the progressive impact of EU market integration could in the space of a few years put between four and five percentage points on the Community's domestic product (Cecchini, 1988, xix, xvii).

Strong emphasis was placed on possible extension of collective and individual rights atrophied by Conservative employment legislation, renewed attention to workers' participation and the availability of EU funds for economic restructuring and job creation. The TUC stressed the utility of provisions in the Single European Act for 'Social Dialogue' and the EU conception of social partnership between management and unions. They concluded however: 'Britain is not well placed to gain.' The government was a 'fundamental stumbling block' (TUC, 1988b, 10–11). In these circumstances the TUC felt it could play a national leadership role. If the unions were able to slough off old orientations and embrace new opportunities they could utilise the changing situation to claw back recent losses.

A key figure in the transformation was Jacques Delors. A proselytiser for European unity, Delors wished to mobilise as many forces as possible behind its banner. His emphasis on workers' rights in the developing Social Charter acted as a lightening conductor. In his address to the September 1988 TUC Delors declared that social dialogue and collective bargaining were essential pillars of democratic society. There *would be* an effective social dimension to the Single Market and he was offering British unions a role in it as architects (TUC, 1988). His message to trade unionists was clear: 'you have totally failed to defeat the Prime Minister in this country but you have an opportunity through Brussels and Strasbourg to bring in social legislation helpful to your cause' (Letwin, 1992, 287).

The new line was affirmed by the response of Mrs Thatcher. Slow to catch the drift of EU developments she was supportive of the Single Market as an incarnation of economic liberalism. By mid-1988 she had taken stock of the impetus to integration. Her Bruges speech signalled opposition; by 1989 she was assuring the unions there would be no 'socialism by the back door' or 'by the back Delors'. By that time the TUC was seeking to strengthen EU legislative initiatives and EU wide collective bargaining. And there was a significant move away from the old faith in national economic strategy: 'It will be impossible in the long run to successfully conduct economic policy in isolation from the move towards economic and monetary union within Europe' (TUC, 1990a, 3).

Since 1988 the pro-European orientation has remained fixed, although suspicion is still reflected in some unions. The Maastricht Treaty promised difficulties. The proposals for a central bank, the tight criteria on convergence of national economies, the limits on budget deficits could all cause difficulties. The Treaty was opposed by a number of unions, notably NALGO and MSF. The TGWU was critical and at times echoes of the old rhetoric of the EU as a capitalist club re-emerged. Nonetheless, the majority of unions held the line, supporting further progress to integration through a common currency and a central European bank. The majority view was that despite unpalatable aspects of the Treaty the only alternative – a Britain outside the EU – was simply not a viable option.

EU politics and legislation

In their new enthusiasm the unions neglected some of the difficulties and exaggerated others. It was arguable that 'social dumping' would not be as prevalent as suggested. In the TUC scenario member states like Spain and Portugal would hold down the social wage limiting imports from Germany and France and increasing exports to those countries. Companies and jobs would move to low wage economies forcing Britain to follow a similar path. But price sensitive, labour intensive industries where the impact of the Single Market would be greatest are in decline in the EU. What is involved in many investment decisions is not just the attraction of lower wages in Portugal but of higher productivity in Germany. Moreover, by 1992 intensification of the Conservatives' low cost approach suggested Britain was, if anything, a 'beneficiary', not a victim, of social dumping. On the other hand, the determination and ability of the British government to oppose a level playing field could not be exaggerated. Whatever the economic realities the Conservatives fervently believed the social dimension would increase labour costs and unemployment. The less Britain had to accept EU legislation the better its economy would be able to compete. Mrs Thatcher had not wrought deregulation in industrial relations to see them re-regulated from Brussels. Given its distinctive worldwide pattern of economic activity Conservative Britain was determined to protect its interests inside and *outside* the EU, in the USA as well as Germany. It was determined to resist attempts to limit its manoeuvrability through more integration or more legislative controls.

The unions' positive view of the EU as a source and legitimation of protective legislation and a stimulus to stronger collective bargaining was firmly based. But there was a tendency to over-estimate the social dimension, glossing over the fact it was more about regulating competition than protecting workers, that there were real differences in the EU as to its legislative role with the emphasis on equality and health and safety rather than employment protection across the board – still less collective rights. This was related to the limited reach of the EU legislative process and the ability it gave member states to influence the content and form of legislation and its final realisation in national practice. From the second half of the 1980s, moreover, a significant change was the move of power from the Commission to the Council of Ministers and summits of Prime Ministers. A brief résumé of the development of the EU social framework illustrates some of these limitations.

Economic liberalism
Despite the political inspiration of the architects of the EU its early development was infused by support for the free market and free trade. Thus the Treaty of Rome 1957 sought to ensure free movement of labour and outlaw discrimination. Article 119 provided for equal pay for equal work and Article 123 established a Social Fund to provide for retraining and resettlement. Article 117 looked good but was declaratory, stating that member states

'agree upon the need to promote improved working conditions and an improved standard of living for workers so as to make possible their harmonisation while the improvement is being maintained'. Thus in terms of substance the social and industrial relations aspects of the Treaty were minimal.

From market to community

From the early 1970s the success of the Common Market led to greater emphasis on social issues. 'The Community had to be seen to be more than a device to enable capitalists to exploit the common market; otherwise it might not be possible to persuade the peoples of the community to continue to accept the discipline of the market' (Shanks, 1977, 12). Moves to extend good practice across the EU coincided with its enlargement and policies of intervention in many member states. The Social Action Programme of the 1970s produced directives on equal pay and equal treatment at work, collective dismissals, transfer of employment and insolvency. But the base for legislation remained limited. These directives stemmed from the Treaty of Rome, Articles 100 and 235, which provided for the harmonisation of laws and regulations in member states which *directly affected the functioning of the common market* or were deemed necessary to attain community objectives.

Slowdown

The measures of the 1970s demonstrated the difficulties in creating an EU framework for industrial relations. Action under Articles 100 and 235 required *unanimity* – with the consequent prospects of delay, compromise and veto. This describes the position between 1979 and 1984. To some extent this was due to the British government using its veto, for example, over the proposed directive on temporary work and fixed term contracts, but also to negative attitudes from employers and other member states. The Vredeling Directive on worker participation, first introduced in 1980, failed to progress. The ruling ethos was one of deregulation and flexibility in contrast with the corporatist mood of the previous decade.

Renewed progress

Renewal of the social dimension took account of the blocking potential of the requirements for unanimity in Articles 100 and 235 of the Treaty of Rome. Under Article 118 of the Single European Act the Council could adopt by *qualified majority* voting directives which lay down minimum requirements to encourage improvements in the working environment or health and safety of workers (a qualified majority consisted of 54 votes out of the possible 76 in the Council). And Article 118B gave the Commission powers to promote 'the dialogue between management and labour at European level which could if the two sides consider it desirable, lead to relations based on agreements'.

The Community's general powers to legislate were also changed. Qualified majority voting now applied under Article 100A to measures which had as their object the establishment and operation of the internal market. However, under Article 100A (ii), unanimity was still necessary for measures 'relating to the rights and interests of employed persons'. Therefore qualified majority voting was only extended to the area of working environment and health and safety: other employment issues still required unanimity in the Council. Although there was a possibility of taking a broad view of 'working environment' and 'health and safety', the legislative powers of the EU remained circumscribed.

The Social Charter

The Social Charter adopted in 1989 was a declaration of principle, not a form of legislation. Its range was wide: it covered conditions of employment, minimum pay, freedom of association, the right to bargain and strike, training, and health and safety (see p. 324). Its language was affirmative but amorphous, with vague references to 'fair remuneration' and 'a decent standard of living'. It saw implementation of its broad principles occurring through EU or national initiative or through collective bargaining.

However, the Charter was accompanied by an Action Programme to facilitate implementation. But this eliminated all reference to collective bargaining and freedom of association as objects of EU community action. This was justified by the developing principle of *subsidiarity*. This means that legislation should be initiated *at the lowest level where it can be effectively introduced*. Many of the Charter's principles were not to be implemented at community level but left to member states to implement themselves. Of the principles which *were* seen as suitable for EU action many were to be introduced by 'recommendations' or 'opinions' not binding on member states. Of the 17 draft directives, 10 dealt with health and safety issues. The Action Programme thus reflected both the limitations of the Charter and the commissioners' limited powers of legislation under the Single European Act.

The Social Charter: a Summary

The preamble emphasises the importance of the social dimension in the light of the 'impending completion of the internal market' and extends the notion of social rights to all citizens of the EU whether working or not. The implementation of these rights should not prejudice those which are more advanced already existing in individual member states.

Title I: fundamental social rights

- **Rights of freedom of movement** (paras 1–8) covers rights to freedom of movement, freedom to pursue an occupation, equal treatment, recognition of qualifications, frontier regions, subcontracted labour, social protection and public works contracts.
- **Employment and remuneration** (paras 9–10) covers freedom to pursue an occupation and access to placement services free of charge.
- **Living and working conditions** (paras 12–13) covers improvements in these areas, including working time, employment contracts, employment regulations (governing areas like redundancies and bankruptcies), annual paid leave and weekly rest periods.
- **Social protection** (paras 14–15) covers access to social security cover and minimum income for the unemployed.
- **Freedom of association and collective bargaining** (paras

16–18) covers freedom of association, union recognition and right to strike, settlement of disputes and contractual agreements between employers and workers. Para. 18 urges the development of the 'social dialogue'.

- **Vocational training** (paras 19–20) covers training opportunities, training and retraining systems and the freedom for every EU citizen to enrol for occupational training on the same terms as any national of the member state where the course is to take place.
- **Equal treatment** (para. 21) covers identification of implementation of equal treatment between men and women.
- **Information, consultation and participation** (paras 22–3) covers 'appropriate lines' for such rights, especially for workers in multinationals and in cases of technological change and restructuring. Particular attention to transfrontier workers.
- **Health and safety** (para. 24) covers further harmonisation in this area, with particular regard to public works.
- **Children and adolescents** (paras 25–7) covers minimum employment age (16), equitable remuneration, training and labour regulations.
- **Elderly** (paras 28–30) covers living standards, minimum income and social protection.
- **Disabled** (para. 31) covers integration into working life, including training, accessibility, transport and housing.

Title II: Implementation   (Paras 32–5) Member states to take appropriate steps to guarantee these rights. Commissioner to draw up plan and related instruments and to report back regularly thereafter on implementation of these rights to the Council of Ministers, European Parliament and Economic and Social Committee.

The Social Chapter

The Treaty of European Union agreed at Maastricht in December 1991 took matters further. The Treaty included a Protocol on Social Policy and an Agreement made between the 11 member states *excluding Britain*. The Protocol declared the intention of the 11 'to continue along the path laid down in the 1989 Social Charter'. The Agreement included changes in some of the Treaty of Rome's provisions on social policy and raises questions as to whether the 11 are entitled to develop legislation not binding on all members. The practical consequence is likely to be the majority going it alone with the eventual results affecting Britain.

The first important change at Maastricht involved Article 1 of the Treaty which redrafted and strengthened Article 117 of the Treaty of Rome. The objectives of the EU now included the promotion of employment, improved working conditions, social protection and dialogue between management and workers.

Under Article 2 qualified majority voting was to cover not only health and safety, but working conditions, information and consultation of workers, equality between men and women, and the integration of those excluded from the labour market. This was then *immediately limited* by Article 2, 3 which demands unanimity for legislation on social security and social protection of workers, protection on termination of employment, collective defence of the interests of workers and employers (including co-determination), conditions of employment for third country nationals residing in the EU and financial contributions for job creation. Finally, Article 2, 6 excludes from the EU legislative process 'pay, the right to association, the right to strike or the right to impose lock outs'.

The Agreement announced other important changes. Article 2,4 gave signatory states the opportunity to entrust management and unions with the implementation of directives at their joint request. The Social Dialogue was strengthened by giving the Commission the task of 'promoting the consultation of management and labour at community level' and taking relevant measures to support it. Before submitting proposals on social policy the Commission now has to consult management and unions. If both social partners come to an agreement the Commission can propose its implementation through the EU process. However, the principle of subsidiarity is explicitly stated in Article 3B. The community shall act 'only if and insofar as the objectives of the proposed action cannot be sufficiently achieved by the member states and can, therefore, by reason of the scale or effects of the proposed action, be better achieved by the Community'.

Social Europe after Maastricht

Maastricht undoubtedly represented a significant move forward. The extension of qualified majority voting was important. So was the new role in policy creation for employers and unions. There were increased prospects that many of the Chapter's proposals would become law. The move to monetary union had spurred on the social dimension. Yet the process remains contradictory and rooted in the subordination of social policy to neo-Liberal market economics. Neither the EU unions, on the retreat in the early 1980s, nor the isolationist British unions, were influential in the Single Market project. It was orchestrated by the Commission but influenced in the mould of market deregulation by the lobby of EU big capital, the Roundtable of European Industrialists, and companies becoming affected by transnational factors (Sharp, 1989, 217–19).

The Social Chapter is not a recipe for neo-corporatism or EU-wide harmonisation. It constitutes a minimum, broadly defined, set of principles which would provide the basis for limited legislation embodying minimum standards and a stimulus to collective bargaining. The objective was not to replace or restrict the market or increase union power but to provide some co-ordination to curb the inefficiencies of market competition and stimulate progressive, innovative management. The collectivists including the EU unions always had limited aims and did not get all they wanted by any means. Key concessions were made to Mrs Thatcher over the Charter and John Major over the Chapter. The resulting legal framework, far from constituting an embryonic collective labour code, reflects 'the ambiguities and spirit of compromise made inevitable by a two way conceptual clash between collectivism and liberalism in labour market regulation and between solidarity and subsidiarity in the framing of Community policies' (Rhodes, 1991, 254). Maastricht was a step forward but elements of opposition to the development of a strong social dimension remain not only from Britain but from Ireland, Spain and Portugal, and from UNICE, the EU employers' federation. For the unions the social dimension is not something already realised to be cashed in. It has to be fought for. The unions' bargaining power is important and for the British unions a major limitation. Moreover, the deteriorating economic situation in the EU, the costs of German reunification and problems with the ERM may well arrest further progress towards monetary union. This in turn will affect progress on social legislation.

The Social Chapter: the arguments

At Maastricht the British government went straight for an opt-out refusing negotiations which might have further diluted the Social Chapter – a position which will be difficult to sustain in the coming years. *But it is still bound by the social clauses of the Treaty of Rome and the Single European Act.* Its opt-out gave the other EU members the opportunity to begin to develop a significant EU legal framework. Its growth, which Britain would not be able to influence, would produce more tensions and surely lead other member states to press for Britain's inclusion. Nonetheless, the government continued to vigorously press the case against the Social Chapter.

The government case
1 Since 1979 Conservative governments have removed obstacles to the efficient operation of the labour market. Encouragement of flexibility and removal of rigidities produced a trans-formation of industrial relations inconceivable in the two pre-vious decades. 'Lifting the burden' on business through employment legislation produced an economic miracle in the 1980s. The Social Chapter will take us back to the bad old days.
2 By reimposing burdens on business the Social Chapter aims to improve standards to the level of the most profitable employers

and harmonise labour market rules on the model of the most regulated countries. The result will be higher costs for employers, higher prices for consumers, fewer jobs for workers and erosion of Britain's economic efficiency and competitive edge. If employers cannot reduce wages to bear the costs of improvements they will sack workers. Particular groups of protected workers, women for example, will suffer most, as companies will not hire them.

3   The Social Chapter cannot be justified on grounds of efficiency or equity. Legal rights as an employee are not much use – indeed they are a barrier to being hired – when you do not have a job. Not only is it a charter for the destruction of jobs but the chapter interferes with the freedom of the individual restored by the Conservative revolution in employment law. As the Institute of Directors put it, backing the government case: 'the individual and the rights of the individual which include the right to make a contract with another individual to provide employment services should be the foundation of social policy'. The social dumping argument is overdone. We have not seen a flight of German capital to Portugal or Scotland. The Social Chapter is an attempt to placate the unions and the better off EU countries. Free competition should involve competition over the price of labour. The Social Chapter will not protect EU workers from competition from the Third World.

4   The problems the Social Chapter can cause are exacerbated by the Treaty of Maastricht. The extension of majority voting could unleash an avalanche of measures from Brussels. In all the circumstances Britain had no option but to opt out.

The unions' response

1   The beneficial impact of Conservative legislation is questionable and who dares talk of an economic miracle after the recession of the 1990s? Nonetheless, the Social Chapter would leave much of that legislation intact: it does not apply to the right to associate or to strikes, picketing or pay. The Chapter is limited. Mrs Thatcher's characterisation of it as 'Marxist' shows how ridiculous such criticisms are. It does not involve

levelling up to the *best* standards. The objective is to establish *minimum* standards: witness the maternity directive which gets nowhere near Denmark's provisions, or the restrictions on working time which get nowhere near Germany's tight limits. Even the TUC's description of the social dimension 'a shorthand description of a decent society' exaggerates the nature of what is a very basic floor of rights.

2 Britain is simply in no position to compete with Taiwan and South Korea and welfare rights need not be a burden on business. Sweated labour – by 1990 a third of all full-time workers in Britain received pay below the Council of Europe's decency threshold – is an incentive to inefficient production eschewing innovation. When many British employers face better technologically tooled up EU competitors they will seek to survive by reducing costs. Welfare legislation can play a role in forcing employers to become more efficient and innovative. Reducing standards and allowing high unemployment favours wage-cutting and survival of the *least fit*. The government's approach is a barrier to innovation, forward investment and the search for new markets. An employment environment which emphasises welfare and participation rather than fear and insecurity can generate greater adaptability, higher morale and *higher productivity*. Equity in itself cannot be ignored; to some degree equity is related to efficiency.

3 Most employees are not in a position to negotiate with employers who can pick from scores of others with the same skills. Britain had a minimum floor of employee rights for most of this century. Its erosion has not kept unemployment at bay. Countries like Germany have continuously wiped the floor with Britain economically whilst maintaining superior welfare standards. Employers themselves do not see employee rights as a significant burden. In Germany strong unions and employment protection has closed cheap labour routes to employers, forced them to invest, develop training, work *with* employees to create 'a virtuous circle of upmarket industrial restructuring' (Streeck, 1991).

4 Britain needs the Social Chapter because its workers need

basic protections. With one sixth of the EU's population, Britain has far higher proportions of unemployed and impoverished workers. Its legislation on employment protection is way down the EU league table and only restrained from collapse by the requirement of EU membership. The Conservatives are the only important European party to oppose the Social Chapter. It is doubtful just how long Britain's EU partners will allow this pariah in their midst, a Taiwan loosely attached to the EU. In the end Britain will have to make up its mind whether it is a member of the EU – or not.

The unions and the social dimension

The real lesson of the government's reaction to Maastricht may be that they have given up hope of competing with France and Germany. John Major's track is not so much a slow one as a cheap one. He hopes to attract inward investment seeking a low cost, low quality workforce. Yet labour costs and product price are only one aspect of competition, together with research and development, quality and service. Indeed 'in a growing number of key sectors, the basis of competition is shifting to emphasising product quality not just costs. Attractive sites for new investment are increasingly those supplying skilled workers and efficient infrastructures' (Stopford and Strange, 1991, 1). Deregulation and fear of unemployment does not encourage the motivated, participative, satisfied workforce able to compete on quality as well as cost (Grahl and Teague, 1990, 219–20). Put crudely, for investors who want high skills, high tech and high quality it will be Germany calling. Britain's low pay, low benefits and low quality will attract investors who want low skill work and a cost advantage. This makes the position of the unions difficult. There is justification for the twin-track approach, developed by the TUC since 1988, of trying to strengthen the EU legislative framework and attempting to build on it through developing transnational bargaining and extending the scope of national bargaining. But there are tremendous problems. Let us look in more detail at the various ingredients in the unions' approach and their potential.

Exploiting EU legislation

The views of some unions have been simplistic and overly optimistic, witness: 'The Social Charter gives unions a new bargaining weapon. It will soon be converted into law' (GMB, 1990, 1). Maastricht gives unions cause for encouragement but the exclusion of key issues from the Agreement is important. So is subsidiarity. And so are the qualifications. For example, Article 1 strengthens the objectives of the EU but in the context of 'the need to maintain the competitiveness of the Community economy'. Article 2,2 extending qualified majority voting also requires that directives stimulate only minimum requirements for gradual implementation. It stresses the need to 'avoid imposing administrative financial and legal constraints in a way which would hold back the creation and development of small and medium sized undertakings'. Fundamentally for the unions both their government and their employers' organisations have rejected the Social Charter and Maastricht Social Chapter *in principle*. If Britain's isolation and pursuit of deregulation cannot last forever there are presently real limits to the EU, an engine of harmonisation.

Even if Britain was to participate in Maastricht's social process its legal fruits are likely to be more delayed and diluted than the unions would like. It is unfair to cite the Transfer of Undertakings (Protection of Employment) Regulations, 1981, the Equal Pay (Amendments) Regulations, 1983, the Sex Discrimination Act, 1986, and provisions on retirement, maternity and health and safety in the 1989 and 1993 legislation as evidence of all that can be achieved in a decade and a half. The process is likely to be more extensive and speedier in the future. But we should not expect an avalanche of protective legislation. The government will do the minimum to comply with EU initiatives.

Recent gains have centred on health and safety. Between 1988 and 1993, 18 directives were adopted, signalling the impact of qualified majority voting. These directives have produced important changes in British law in employers' obligations, fire safety and the protection of employees, such as the rights in the 1993 Trade Union Reform Act protecting employees stopping work in hazardous situations from dismissal. How far paper rights will be recognised in practice, given the weakening of enforcement mechanisms is questionable. With other initiatives the British government took diversionary action. Employment Minister David Hunt indulged in a spoiling process, which he stated, had 'drawn the teeth' of the directive on working time. The basic provision is for a 48-hour a week ceiling but member states can make exemptions for particular categories of worker. There are also provisions for obligatory breaks, minimum rest periods, limits on night shifts and minimum paid holidays. Having weakened the directive, Britain in 1993 refused to join the other member states in accepting it. Instead the government appealed to the European Court on the grounds it did not fall under the health and safety provisions of the EU legislation and required unanimity, not majority voting.

Similar attrition was mounted against the directive on pregnancy. This completed the EU legal process in 1993 again being treated under Article 118A as a health and safety issue. As a result of British attitudes the original proposals for 14 weeks' maternity leave on full pay were changed to entitlement to not less than statutory sick pay. When the British government legislated on the basis of the directive in the 1993 Trade Union Reform Act the relevant clauses were criticised by the Equal Opportunities Commission as inadequate and failing to fully comply with EU requirements. With the draft on European Works Councils (see Chapter 4) the strategy was different. The government declared all out opposition. They were backed by the CBI, arguing that Works Councils would provide a base for union assertion, higher costs and transnational collective bargaining. The issue was a matter for voluntary action and employer prerogative not legislation.

No less than seven EU directives motivated provisions of the 1993 Trade Union Reform Act covering maternity rights, sex discrimination, health and safety, redundancy consultation, written particulars of employment and transfer of undertakings. Their significance, however, was qualitatively diminished by other measures hostile to the unions which dominated the statute. Judgments such as those extending the Transfer of Employment regulations to public employment and the 1994 House of Lords' decision that British law on part-time workers' redundancy and unfair dismissal rights breached EU legislation again demonstrated the potential. In the areas on which the EU has most legal purchase, equal opportunities and health and safety, it is influencing British legislation; its impact on the shape of employment legislation as a whole has, as yet, been minor. Further change is likely to be part of a protracted process because of the limits on the EU's jurisdiction and a non-sympathetic national government restricting initiatives even where there is jurisdiction.

The TUC has done its best to overcome these difficulties. A *File on Europe* was published from 1988 explaining how EU institutions worked and how unions could influence them. National and regional briefings for union officers and a programme of educational courses were developed. A '1992 contact point' was established at Congress House. The social dimension was made the subject of serious lobbying through the ETUC and strengthened links with the EU Economic and Social Committee. Together with ETUC members, general council representatives met with Vasso Papandreou, the Social Affairs Commissioner, and sought further implementation of the Social Charter by representations in the Parliament and Council of Ministers. The TUC opened an office in Brussels and established a European section at Congress House. By 1991 it was realising that all its problems did not begin and end with a hostile Conservative government. It reported that 'the major obstacles to progress have been the limits to the Community's competence as set out in the Treaties, and the recalcitrance of the Council of Ministers' (TUC, 1991, 164).

Building the social dialogue
Article 118B of the Single European Act gave the Commission legal authority to promote *dialogue* (not consultation or bargaining) between management and unions at EU level. This

task had already commenced when the Commission initiated conferences between the ETUC and UNICE at Val Duchesse, Brussels, in 1985. In their first phase the Val Duchesse meetings produced a series of joint opinions rather than agreements on economic problems and brought in CEEP, the public sector employers. The ETUC went along with the view that the joint opinions should be voluntary instruments, the basis for collective bargaining not legislation, as they wished to establish in the employers' eyes the legitimacy of the social dialogue. In 1989 the creation of a steering group from the ETUC, CEEP and UNICE, which would be regularly consulted by the Commission on industrial issues and legislation, was seen as a further step in legitimising the role of the social partners. Their involvement in Maastricht was viewed as a major breakthrough, not least because of the strong support to joint agreement offered by UNICE. In 1991 the social partners established a working group which negotiated what became the content of the Agreement on Social Policy. An accord between ETUC and CEEP/UNICE in October 1991 contained the substance of the changes later agreed at Maastricht which strengthened the role of the social dialogue and collective bargaining in developing EU directives.

Described by its General Secretary as 'a milestone' the influence of the joint negotiations on the Treaty represents some change of line by UNICE, given earlier opposition to the Social Charter. UNICE agreed, however, to a broad framework, not a detailed EU-wide industrial relations system or the detailed content of future directives. Emilio Gabaglio, General Secretary of the ETUC argued, 'The agreement of 31 October paves the way for a new stage in the social dialogue based on a veritable bargaining dimension' (*Social Europe*, 1991, 16).

Whether a real bargaining dimension can develop, putting flesh on the skeleton of the few EU sectoral agreements arrived at by transnationals and union groupings, is a major question. British unions excluded from the fruits of the dialogue will still be involved in its development through the ETUC. They can exploit this by supporting EU level and sectoral agreements which, at least if they involve health and safety, equality, working conditions and consultative arrangements, can become legally enforceable for the 11 Social Chapter signatories. If their direct impact on Britain is denied by the government opt-out they can still act as standards and as political pressure points. The ability of the social dialogue to go forward in the deteriorating economic situation would demonstrate the strength of what still appears a fragile growth. Nonetheless, development strengthens a social framework which unlike that in Britain involves the unions. But the existence of labour exclusion in major competitors like Japan and the US means the Commission must keep an eye to the development of 'arrangements which respect not only socially desirable norms on European industrial relations but also accommodate the necessity for economically competitive European enterprises' (Roberts, 1992, 10).

Developing transnational bargaining

The Social Dialogue has had some echo in European level arrangements for information and consultation established in largely French owned multinationals in the 1980s. Gold and Hall found such bodies in 11 major companies. In BSN, Bull, Péchinery, Elf Aquitaine, Nestlé and Thomson Consumer Electronics there were joint agreements. In 5 further companies, Allianz, Mercedes Benz, Rhône-Poulenc, Saint Gobain and Volkswagen, there were informal arrangements. In 2 cases, BSN and Volkswagen, consultation involved important aspects of industrial relations. But these kind of arrangements covered a tiny number of multinationals. And they specifically excluded bargaining rights (Gold and Hall, 1992).

Current evidence for European level collective bargaining is negligible: it is viewed in the literature as 'rather a distant possibility' and 'not a foreseeable prospect' (Marginson, 1992, 543; Roberts, 1992, 7). Given the power multinationals wield compared with weakened unions, this is scarcely surprising. In the past, international secretariats or rank and file groupings have established sustained information exchange links between workers, if on a small scale. Perhaps the most famous example of rank and file links during the 1960s and 1970s was the joint committee of workplace representatives in Dunlop-Pirelli involving British and Italian trade unionists. Amongst the international trade secretariats the International Metalworkers' Federation was particularly active. Sometimes, as at Philips Electronics, they gained access to management which was terminated once the unions sought to make talks meaningful by discussing company investment. But examples of unions moving from international dialogue to international assistance and international bargaining have been rare. In the 1980s some local authorities, notably the GLC through its Popular Planning Unit, lent support to the development of transnational union committees in Philips, Ford and Kodak. But once again the hopes held out for international collective bargaining (Levinson, 1972) proved over-optimistic.

A number of surveys in the 1970s and 1980s found little evidence of international collective bargaining. It existed only in industries such as entertainment and shipping where service delivery crossed national boundaries. Studies stressed a degree of management support was necessary and it has been argued that the position of large employers, particularly those who play an important role in employers' organisations, will be central to future EU developments. UNICE has in the past opposed European level collective bargaining on the grounds that it would reduce employers' room to manoeuvre in different labour markets and provide unions with an entry into key decisions such as investment (Sisson, 1991). For the unions there were major problems: language; expense; the difficulties of organising meetings; different industrial relations systems; different legislation; different unions on different sites; the unions' desire to preserve their sovereignty; their fear of usurpation by direct links between lay representatives; and employee insularity (Northrup and Rowan, 1979; Haworth and Ramsay, 1984).

Reviews in the 1990s have emphasised employer opposition as a continuing obstacle (Rhodes, 1991, 272). Groups of workers such as those in Ford of Europe have established European Co-ordinating Committees which exchange information on key issues such as pay, working time and training. The repeated refusals of Ford to agree to European level talks has meant they have had to bargain separately, not together. Some writers suggest that on the union side difficulties in the 1970s and 1980s were exacerbated by recession, political differences amongst unions and poor infrastructure at ETUC level and, more contentiously, that circumstances are moving in the unions' favour (Henley and Tsakalotos, 1992).

One analysis argues that where companies are organised on a European basis, with a unified ownership and management structure and integrated production arrangements with workers in different countries producing similar goods and services, there may be a stimulus towards joint bargaining arrangements. This will be influenced by the ability of unions to see the potential, organise links and pressure management, as well as the political climate and the industrial relations and legislative framework. Initiatives at EU level, from the extension of the scope of product markets through the 1992 measures to favourable legislation, can affect the situation. Nonetheless, future exploitation of favourable opportunities suggests the development of transnational *consultation*, not transnational *bargaining* (Marginson, 1992).

European employers are taking social dialogue to mean just that. They see a role for unions in transnational issues; it is a consultative not a bargaining role. Despite this, unions are making positive efforts to build closer links. The ETUC has been attempting to build on the social dialogue accord embodied in Maastricht and the draft directive on European Works Councils. They argue that European wage negotiations are premature but framework agreements dealing with other issues could be reached at EU level and then implemented by national and sectoral negotiations. They have taken a particular interest through their industry committees in the works councils already established in companies like Bull and BSN and pressurised the Commission directly and via the Economic and Social Committee to introduce the draft directive on European Works Councils. If EU bargaining is distant, co-ordination of effort proceeds. In October 1992 EU unions organised a one hour rail strike in seven different countries to protest privatisation initiatives. In April 1993 the ETUC called a day of action and international rally at Maastricht to protest rising unemployment, and the strike against pit closures in Britain was timed to coincide with it.

There is no doubt that the ETUC, now representing 47 million workers across Europe, has gained in efficiency and reach over the last decade. It remains a lobbying body, not a bargaining agent. How far its affiliates would be willing to hand over power to the ETUC and accept united policies in a move to an EU bargaining system is an interesting question given the difficulties the TUC faces with *its* affiliates. At the moment the ETUC employs a secretariat of less than a dozen to cover an ever widening agenda. Its resources are dwarfed by those of the employers and the thousands of lobbyists bombarding EU bodies on their behalf, and this situation is even worse in relation to the resources available to the industry federations. If the unions are to have a greater impact on EU legislation and the co-ordination of bargaining efforts they will need more resources at EU level and a transfer of sovereignty from the national centres.

National bargaining: an EU dimension?

As the move towards a single market gathered momentum the TUC urged unions to appoint a full-time officer with responsibility for EU issues, strengthen links with unions on the mainland, take advantage of education on EU developments, develop language training and raise the implications of EU integration with employers. Affiliates were advised to ask employers to provide details of EU links and the impact of the single market on the enterprise and establish joint machinery for dealing with problems at local, national and EU levels. Unions should use EU standards and comparisons in bargaining and attempt to gain greater purchase on investment plans, product development and training (TUC, 1989a). As the convergence process gathered momentum with Britain's entry into the ERM in 1990 the TUC unsuccessfully offered the government talks on pay, productivity and training to ensure the ability of British industry to meet the challenge (see p. 220).

Some unions shared the TUC's new urgency. The GMB, for example, welcomed the social dimension and sought to strengthen it by increased contact with ETUC bodies and the six ETUC industry committees on which it was represented. There were similar responses from the AEU, EETPU, UCW and USDAW. Other unions such as NALGO and TGWU were more critical. A handful of unions such as the NUM and ISTC remained hostile to the single market and had little to say on the social dimension. Despite a majority for the TUC's position, divisions remained (Trower, 1990, 23–36).

It was also clear that employers, reflecting the attitude of the CBI, demonstrated little interest in new consultative or bargaining initiatives and demonstrated minimal reaction to the Social Charter (Wood and Peccei, 1991). Some declared their opposition to legislation on the Charter and prevaricated over action (Towers, 1992, 88). There were breakthroughs such as the much publicised agreement between the GMB and Keiper Recaro, a German vehicle components company which agreed to incorporate the Charter in collective agreements. Such innovations remained few and far between. The extent to which the standards in the Social Chapter and consequent legislation could be realised and diffused depended on bargaining and bargaining power. Yet the development of a European dimension to British collective bargaining in the early 1990s was stunted by the already diminishing reach and power of that bargaining. In Britain collective bargaining embraced a declining proportion of the workforce and so of course did the unions. This was hardly a healthy basis for introducing bargaining over the Social Chapter issues and developing negotiations of transnational rather than national scope. Even at the zenith of union density and bargaining coverage, links in the UK between different sites of the same enterprise had been limited (Terry, 1985). By the 1990s British collective bargaining was moving not upwards but downwards and the move to decentralisation contrasted with sectoral negotiations in much of the EU and the TUC's aspiration for transnational bargaining. The erosion of legal support for bargaining in Britain and the political exclusion of the unions raised the question of whether British unions would be left out of such transnational initiatives as did emerge.

Links between British unions and their EU counterparts have been well advertised. John Edmonds of the GMB claimed that at the end of the 1990s his union would be linked with at least six European unions through cross-frontier deals and amalgamations. The AEU worked hard at establishing links with European metalworkers and emulation of the German unions influenced its '35-hour week' campaign in 1990. There have been discussions about a European air pilots' union. The state of play and co-ordination on the ground however was demonstrated by Hoover in 1993. In return for production being switched from Dijon to Cambuslang the AEEU accepted an 11-month pay freeze, flexibility, fixed term contracts and a no strike clause. In the face of protests by the French unions the Scottish TUC condemned the move but the AEEU declared it had nothing to be ashamed of. In the same month Rockwell Graphic Systems announced they were relocating their plant from Nantes to Preston, Lancashire. Had the Scottish and French workers been members of the same union the problem could well have been minimised. But links remain only at the level of contacts and meetings. Transnational mergers appear far off and when British unions competed for negotiation rights at new plants of the West German company Bosch, as they did in 1992, few suggested that the relevant union was IG Metall, membership of which could institutionalise links with German workers and boost bargaining power in Britain.

The dilemma facing British unions is a frustrating one. They are seeking to overcome problems in this country by spreading their wings in Europe. But the possibility of successful international flight is undermined by their weakness on their own ground. The ability to develop transnational bargaining and exploit EU legislation is constrained by the deficiencies of the unions in Britain. Naturally, they turn to the state but legislation on basic issues such as organisation, bargaining rights and industrial action remain the preserve of Westminster, not Brussels. So does discretion over political and economic decisions which affect the strength of unions. Yet if full advantage is to be taken of EU developments strong unions are needed to ensure favourable variants of EU directives are translated into national law and enforced. Transnational bargaining requires unions with the capacity to bring powerful multinationals to the table. The unions' loss of national power was instrumental in their turning to Europe. It continues to limit what they can achieve there.

A European industrial relations system?

Writers who have emphasised the influence on industrial relations of external factors such as market conditions and technological development have suggested that an increase in integration would produce convergence (Kerr *et al.*, 1960). Yet it is correctly remarked that:

Most of today's member states have been members of the Community for 20–30 years, sharing in many fields the same market and technological base without producing any general homogenisation of industrial relations (Due *et al.*, 1991, 91).

This is not to say that with increasing market integration and a growing legislative framework convergence is ruled out in future. Moreover, some would argue that whilst the period since the 1960s has not seen homogenisation it has certainly witnessed the emergence of common trends. There has undoubtedly been across western European in the 1980s and 1990s a weakening of corporatist arrangements; a new emphasis on deregulation and curbs on public expenditure; a decline in union density and changes in the labour force composition unfavourable to trade unionism; higher sustained levels of unemployment; growth in flexibility and part-time and temporary employment; and a move away from national bargaining. Nonetheless what is striking about industrial relations in the EU in the 1990s is its continuing diversity.

Union membership and density vary widely, from Denmark where more than 80% of the workforce are in unions to Portugal and France with around 10% density. Most EU countries faced declines in density in the 1980s with France, Italy and the UK encountering real difficulties. Since then countries like Italy and the Netherlands with density around 35% have made a comeback. In Germany density, at around 40%, has overtaken that in Britain. If we add East German members to the DGB's 7.9 million workers the German unions are now the biggest in Europe. Differences in ideology, politics and culture remain important. The German unions with their consensual, participative approach are very different from their counterparts in France and Italy, still marked by a now waning tradition of political differentiation; or indeed the adversarial approaches which have characterised British unions. It is difficult to compare the position in Spain, and to some degree France, where employees often identify with unions without joining them, with Britain with its historic belief that all employees should be members.

Differences between unions are related to wider social arrangements. If 'the majority of EU countries remain committed to forms of labour relations that are at least weakly corporatist in character' (Henley and Tsakalotos, 1992, 578) this judgement hides a wide range of varying approaches. In most member states bargaining arrangements are based at industry level – only Portugal and Spain emulate Britain's decentralisation. Whilst only Denmark and the Netherlands have central framework agreements, in countries like Germany there is a high degree of bargaining co-ordination motivated by strong employers' organisations. As we have seen, all member states except Britain accept the need for legal underpinning to the labour market and an EU dimension whilst national legislation, though varying, usually provides more rights for *regulated* trade unions than exist in the UK.

There are clear differences in the operation of the labour market. Most members regulate working hours – Denmark is with Britain an exception – but the maximum varies widely. British workers work longer. More than 46 hours a week is worked by 38% of men and 13% of women compared with EU averages of 15% and 6%. And they work more irregular hours than their counterparts in other member states. The incidence of part-time working also varies with around 44% of women working part-time in Britain compared with 8% in Greece. In countries like Greece and Portugal there are still strong proportions of the labour force concentrated in agriculture. The league table of wages also demonstrates a north–south split, with Britain increasingly going south to join Greece, Spain and Portugal as a low wage economy.

Despite economic pressures – similar changes in industrial structure and employment patterns and the extension of markets – and political pressures from the EU towards convergence what stands out is the stubborn resilience of national systems of industrial relations. This is related in turn to enduring economic and political differences. One detailed study found 'common trends but continuing and, in some aspects, increasing variety and heterogeneity of national models . . . persistent national diversity in the face of cross national pressures towards convergence' (Ferner and Hyman, 1992, xvii).

Some writers have sought to categorise the differences between member states as representing three different traditions and systems of industrial relations. **The Roman-German system** is found in Belgium, France, Germany, Greece, Italy, Luxembourg and the Netherlands. The state is here a central actor in industrial relations. The constitutions of these states guarantee fundamental rights to associate and bargain whilst there is also strong employment protection legislation. **The Anglo-Irish system** emphasises voluntarism with the state playing a minimal role. **The Nordic system** centres on national framework agreements between unions and employers' associations with the state acting very much as a backstop when required (Due *et al.*, 1991).

This categorisation is useful but too broad in blending the quite important differences between, say, Belgium, Italy and Greece or Finland and Denmark. It is also rather static. The system in Britain was different in quite significant ways in the 1990s from the 1960s. In the 1970s the British system moved slightly in the direction of the Roman-German system. In the 1980s it moved significantly in the direction of the USA and Japan. Nonetheless the schema demonstrates the limits to convergence after four decades of the EU but also the possibilities of limited future convergence. There is not a one-to-one relationship between legislative change and changes in practice but the development of the Social Chapter and successful progress to economic and monetary union are likely to encourage both. Encourage but not determine. Common legislation operates within limits and is circumscribed by susidiarity. UNICE is opposed to any European industrial relations system and national union centres remain jealous of their prerogatives (Roberts, 1992, 8). There are, moreover, different paths to economic convergence. The belief that decentralised bargaining is a barrier to downward convergence of inflation rates under the ERM prompted the TUC initiatives on co-ordinated bargaining of 1990. They were rebuffed by a government which depended on rising unemployment and *ad hoc* public sector wage restraint to achieve that aim. In the end greater convergence in industrial relations will depend on greater convergence between economies – easier planned then achieved.

Beyond the European Union

A neglected aspect of TUC attempts to cultivate links with the state was its relations with the Colonial Office and Foreign Office established by the 1940s. The TUC was also a major player in the creation and operation of the ICFTU, influenced from its inception by the CIA through AFL officials. When the US autoworkers explicitly raised the question of CIA funding in the 1960s the TUC took no action. The problem was temporarily resolved by the AFL's secession until 1981. Relations between the TUC and the Americans had never been easy. Whilst the TUC helpfully turned a blind eye to AFL support for US interests and puppet unions across the globe, it was increasingly willing to develop links with *ersatz* unions in the USSR and Eastern Europe.

By the 1970s the TUC was in direct receipt of state funding for its Third World programme. The secretary of its International Department was appointed from the Foreign Office, his deputy was seconded to the Foreign Office, and government officials debriefed TUC staff after overseas visits. Whilst the International Department was responsible for almost a third of TUC expenditure it was alleged that it did little to monitor the operations of multinationals, arm British workers and encourage practical international links at industry and company level, or help Third World workers in struggle. Its stance was a mixture of inertia and silent support for US politicisation programmes in the Third World (Thomson and Larson, 1978). By the late 1970s the TUC's compromising junketing with Stalinist police chiefs masquerading as union leaders, which culminated in lukewarm support for the emergence of Solidarnosc in Poland, was also coming under criticism.

The turn to Europe represented a much needed opportunity to open a new chapter in internationalism. Its coincidence with the disintegration of Stalinism and the renewal of trade unionism in Russia and Eastern Europe was timely. The world trade union movement was changing fast. Progress in many countries from South Africa to Brazil, the disintegration of the WFTU and the intensification of globalisation and integration, incarnated not only in the EU but in the Free Trade Agreement between the US, Canada and Mexico, demonstrated the challenge to trade unionists to forge a new internationalism located in solidarity and self-interest which transcends empty rhetoric. The new commitment to Europe is a necessary beginning. Unions also need to look further afield.

Conclusions

The conversion to Europe is a dramatic episode in union history. It lay not simply in opportunism but awareness of changing reality: a desire to take advantage of a perceived pro-union wind in Europe to turn the anti-union tide in Britain was located in an understanding that purely national economic strategies provided no alternative. It demonstrated again the nature of British unions as defensive reactors rather than positive initiators. The unions have since demonstrated the zeal of the convert. They have understood that there is no future for Britain outside the EU, or as a reluctant passenger, and entered into the spirit of membership to create a democratic social Europe. Their resistance to the lure of old arguments of national economics and national sovereignty in the Maastricht debate and their determination to grasp the opportunities coalescence of capital gives for coalescence of labour demonstrated that realism mixed with opportunism had hardened into relatively principled, if self-interested, policy. Nonetheless their ability to achieve goals set has been limited. Prospects have been exaggerated, difficulties minimised. *Tendencies* to global economic integration are just that and are only slowly reflected in political developments. Nation states still play an important role in linking local economies to the global system. The British state is determined to block greater integration and social legislation, which it sees as inimical to British capital's worldwide role, and maintain a 'two-tier EU'.

The problem is that British unions are attempting to develop a weak neo-corporatism at European level when the nation state is still a powerful reality, and supra-national institutions minimally developed, when most important political levers remain located at national level in the hands of a hostile government and when unions across Europe are weak. The national polity and industrial relations system remain key determinants circumscribing supra-national regulation. The EU legislation still consigns decisions on collective rights and the processes of wage determination to national regulation. Even in the supra-national sphere outcomes are constrained by subsidiarity. Within the EU the picture is a diverse one – but trade unionism and corporatist arrangements have waned since 1980. The establishment of an EU industrial relations system is distant. Prospects for transnational bargaining are limited. The ETUC is not in a position to mount major campaigns. Translation into practice of EU standards depends on collective bargaining – at the very time unions' bargaining power is declining. For British unions there are no easy options *anywhere*. The irony is that growing union weakness prompted the turn to Europe; continuing weakness limits their ability to fully exploit the possibilities of the EU.

On the positive side a valuable bridgehead was established at Maastricht. The unions have begun to grapple with the intricacies of international economic strategy. We are seeing support for the democratisation of EU institutions, increasing the powers of the Parliament, liberalising the Commission and emphasising the importance of EU elections. How long a 'two-tier EU' and the contradiction between the *laissez-faire* policies of the British government and the more regulatory approach of the Commission and other member states can continue is debatable, but it is an explosive contradiction.

Conversion to Europe is healthy and overdue. Born out of national problems it provides the basis for practical inter-nationalism. Internationalism cannot stop at Brussels; it has to embrace Eastern Europe and the Third World; but the emphasis on the EU as an arena for progressive struggle is the right one. While EU developments can help the unions to outflank the British government, they can in the end act only as salve and not antidote. Playing a part in constructing the international state is severely limited by a hostile nation state. There is no alternative to confronting the deep-seated industrial and political problems unions face at home.

Further reading

A good book to introduce you to the development of the EU and the background to present issues is Juliet Lodge, ed., *The European Community and the Challenge of the Future*, Pinter, 1989. Paul Teague and John Grahl's *Industrial Relations and European Integration*, Lawrence & Wishart, 1992, looks at the background to current controversies and the possibility of an EU-wide system of industrial relations. Michael Gold, ed., *The Social Dimension: Employment Policy in the European Community*, Macmillan, 1993, is also good reading. Anthony Ferner and Richard Hyman's *Industrial Relations in the New Europe*, Blackwell, 1992, is an excellent survey of the current position in 17 European countries. Mark Wise and Richard Gibb, *Single Market to Social Europe*, Longman, 1993, is up to date on developments from the Single European Act to Maastricht.

9

Worker participation and industrial democracy

Industrial democracy and worker participation in management were important issues in the 1960s and 1970s. Work-ins and occupations, experiments in participation at British Steel and British Leyland, worker co-operatives at Triumph-Meriden and Fisher Bendix were all part of a resurgence which produced new policies from the TUC. This culminated with the 1977 Bullock Report. Since 1979 interest has diminished but worker participation remains a significant issue for the unions for at least four reasons. In employee involvement and profit sharing they face modern variations on old themes. The Labour Party has maintained a commitment to extending rights and representation in the enterprise. EU initiatives continue to attract attention. Finally it is suggested that, as collective bargaining wanes and workers are further excluded from important decisions, participation could become an alternative means of representing workers' interests. Are participation schemes a means of giving the workforce real control over the enterprise and a stake in the economy? Or are they a means of legitimising management control and the *status quo*? Should unions support or oppose them? In this chapter we examine some of the issues.

Democracy at work: the arguments

Opinion in the unions has been and remains divided over these issues.

The case for

Extension of democracy Political democracy makes the government of the nation accountable to its citizens. Yet many important decisions taken directly by employers elude political control. Measured by the canons of political democracy the government of the enterprise is autocratic. Those who take fundamental decisions are not answerable to employees. Collective bargaining does provide workers with a voice in some of the decisions which affect their working lives. The differences between the formal rights of political democracy and the uncertainties of collective bargaining make direct comparisons unsustainable. Collective bargaining is an unsatisfactory mechanism for democratic control: its effectiveness depends on employees' ability to organise and employers' willingness to bargain. The results of collective bargaining are dependent, not on reason or democracy, but on the degree of power employees can bring to bear against employers. This, in turn, is dependent upon economic and political factors over which employees have little control. Employees spend a large proportion of their lives at work. Work is crucial to the way we live. Our investment is at least as significant as that of shareholders. We should have a guaranteed voice in decisions. Democracy at work is justified in its own right and its absence means that democracy in society is diminished.

Extension of participation Participation is essential to democracy and an important means of political education. Democracy should involve more than voting in parliamentary elections. To function optimally, democracy needs activists, and that does not just mean MPs. The power structures governing work give employees limited opportunities to participate in significant decisions. Even collective bargaining is carried on *for* rather than *by* most workers. Greater participation in industry will strengthen parliamentary democracy by creating more aware, creative citizens. Participation schemes are limited. They spur further moves to democracy.

Alienation from work Work should be a rich, satisfying

experience with ability to develop our potential. For all too many of us, life at work involves toleration rather than gratification. We experience stress and boredom. We do not like our jobs. We work largely for the money. Alienation is related to the authoritarian nature of decision-making in the enterprise. If we possess more autonomy and responsibility and are able to participate in important decisions, we will achieve greater self-realisation: almost every study carried out shows increased work satisfaction and improved motivation is derived from genuine extensions of workers' powers over decisions (Brannen, 1983).

Greater efficiency and productivity   If workers are satisfied, they are better motivated and more productive. They possess knowledge management fails to draw on and abilities management fails to develop. Participation improves the quality of decision-making. A whole range of studies of experiments in participation demonstrate remarkable increases in productivity. As the 1982 TUC–Labour Party statement commented, 'accountability in economic decision-making is not an inefficient luxury but is essential to improving economic performance'.

Better industrial relations   Employees are better educated and critical, less prepared to accept old-style authoritarianism. Attempts to go on in the old way have played their part in low morale and industrial conflict. As the Bullock Committee observed: 'employees have become less prepared to accept unquestioningly unilateral decisions by management and have shown a readiness to challenge a decision if it seems to have ignored their point of view or to affect them adversely' (Bullock, 1977, 23). Mechanisms for worker participation will facilitate a move from conflict to co-operation.

The case against

The right to manage   The enterprise is a team; every team needs a captain. Each member does not have to face up to the full consequences of his or her actions. There is an opportunity for shirking, at little cost to the individual even though overall output suffers. We need a group to monitor performance. This 'control' will require an incentive, a right to the profits. In the interests of maximising efficiency, the controller is vested with property rights in the enterprise from which all management ultimately derive their authority. Separation of decision-making from ownership has led to economic decline. The 'British disease' would become terminal if decision-making powers were to be further dispersed amongst employees who have no ownership rights, no real stake in the enterprise and no incentive to commit themselves fully to its goals.

Work and politics are different things   Our goal at work is to produce goods and services, to answer demand in the most efficient fashion. What is involved is *different* from what is involved in the political process. Management requires technical and economic skills, a grasp of a bewildering variety of functions, research and development, accountancy, sales and supervision. It requires complex decisions to be taken by experts. At times, it requires secrecy. Everybody can participate fully in the political process; they cannot participate to the same degree in industrial decision-making. If we try to apply political democracy to industry through electing managers, taking decisions through votes of the workforce, or bargaining between management and unions in the boardroom, we shall fall flat on our faces. The most important decisions in industry are dictated by economic calculation. Taking them is the province of professional management. 'The trouble with socialism,' Oscar Wilde said, 'is that it will take up too many evenings.' Workers would find increased participation too demanding – look at its absence in the political system.

The productivity myth   It is doubtful whether participation is the answer to the problem of productivity. Poor productivity is the product not so much of poor motivation as of inadequate investment, training and outmoded technology. Experiments in participation which show productivity shooting through the roof are small scale. Carried out under special circumstances, for short periods, their implications have been exaggerated. Even if productivity does increase and there is *some* evidence to back this view, this could lead to a variety of results: increased efficiency could lead to workers losing jobs and working harder. The assertion that participation produces 'improved industrial relations' – a problematic term in itself – also lacks firm evidence to back it.

Workers' participation is a con-trick Workers are only interested in decisions which directly affect their own jobs (Wall and Lischeron, 1977). The initiative for participation schemes has generally come from management. Their aim has been to weaken workers' power, undermine the unions and commit the employees to management goals. Advocates of industrial democracy portray its development in terms of gradual, organic evolution. In reality, schemes of participation and democracy have come and gone in cycles. It has been popular with the bosses when unions have been powerful and popularised as a means of defusing threats to management control. Most participation schemes are limited. There is no evidence they lead to real democracy. If unions fall for such schemes they will compromise their independence and ability to represent their members.

The historical record

We can shed more light on these arguments if we address the evolution of these ideas. Those who embraced industrial democracy earlier in the century were clear about two things. Industrial democracy meant workers controlling and owning the enterprise; it meant replacing the capitalist system with a socialist society. Syndicalist ideas which influenced the unions in the period from 1900 emphasised the role of workers rather than the state in winning control of their industries and then directly governing them. Leaders such as James Connolly and Tom Mann saw the role of the rank and file and militancy as central in constructing industrial unions which through the general strike could take control of their industries and provide the apparatus for their government. Real democracy, industrial democracy, would replace the parliamentary surrogate. As an intrinsic part of 'the Great Unrest' of this period and the impact of the Russian Revolution these ideas challenged Labourism, which responded in the 1918 Labour Party constitution by promising public ownership of industry with 'the best obtainable system of popular control'. Syndicalism exercised strong influence in the railways, the mines, the post office and in engineering. A gradualist variant was Guild Socialism developed by thinkers such as Arthur Penty and A. P. Orage and popularised by G. D. H. Cole. Unions developing on an industrial basis would move beyond collective bargaining and become **guilds** through which the workers would run industry.

Many unions adopted proposals for workers' control of industry in their rule books. But the influence of these ideas was undermined by the response of capital and the state, the inter-war recession, the defeat of the General Strike and consequent developments in the TUC and the Labour Party. The establishment of the Whitley Committees was part of an attempt to replace aspirations to workers' control with co-operation and participation of workers in making companies more productive. Human relations ideas and the influence of Elton Mayo's *The Human Problems of an Industrial Civilisation* gained ground. The enterprise was a unity. Management had to develop participative techniques to reintegrate alienated workers into existing goals and systems of control: Mayo's 'teachings became accepted doctrine amongst British personnel managers for many years' (Clegg, 1970, 189). As the TUC and Labour Party developed clearer strategies for regulating rather than replacing capitalism, the idea that nationalised industries would combine state ownership with subordination to capitalist economy and the authority relations of the private enterprise – urged by Herbert Morrison against initial opposition from union leaders like Ernest Bevin – won the day.

The limits of the post-war settlement were seen in the new nationalised corporations. The TUC supported the idea that members of the board should be appointed by and responsible to the state, not the workforce. The new bosses were technocrats and former owners. Trade unionists who did serve had to surrender 'any position held in or any formal responsibility, to the Trade Union'. The only formal change was the extension of joint consultation. Carrying on from the wartime Joint Production Committees, Joint Consultation Committees, a dilute form of participation, were supported by many union leaders themselves influenced by human relations ideas (Child, 1969). Opposition, even from unions such as the NUM and NUR, was limited. Rather than being utilised, as R. H. Tawney suggested, as a laboratory to experiment with new methods of democracy, the nationalised industries affirmed 'normality'. With the return of the Conservatives in 1951 and the onset of boom, industry remained undemocratised.

Renewed militancy produced new interest. The new left which developed from 1956 emphasised the continuing subordination wage labour imposed on workers and continuing alienation in the 'age of affluence'. The Institute of Workers' Control with Ken Coates and Tony Topham as its driving force exercised a real influence amongst a minority of union activists. It argued that workers should extend control, eroding management prerogative at the workplace, educating themselves through demands for a social audit which would open the books of companies and demonstrate the social costs of capitalist economy. Growing political consciousness would lead workers to confront the decisive historic questions of ownership and self-management of industry.

The introduction of worker directors at British Steel in 1968 heralded a new round of management-sponsored participation schemes influenced by European developments. Even productivity bargaining was proclaimed as strengthening participation, although the Donovan Commission rejected workers on the board in favour of the reform of collective bargaining. The TUC, from 1968, particularly after Britain's entry into the EU in 1972, embraced board level representation. This possessed the potential to redistribute power towards unions. Essentially it took corporatist emphases a stage further by consolidating union influence on the enterprise and bringing power sharing and bargaining into the boardroom. It could mellow sectional militancy and replicate the TUC's national political role in industry. This period culminated in the acrimonious debate that followed the Bullock Report.

The years since constitute the age of employee involvement, the response capital and the new conservative state offered first to Bullock and the threat of EU initiatives and then to the changing conditions neo-*laissez-faire* engendered. Employee involvement is part of human resource management, intended to commit workers to the management-set goals of the enterprise. Successive Conservative governments, fundamentally opposed to any extension of genuine participation and regarding management prerogative as sacrosanct, have supported this approach.

Democracy and its opponents

It is clear from what we have said that terms such as 'industrial democracy' and 'worker participation' are often used interchangeably to cover very different concepts and mechanisms. Is it helpful to lump together representation on company boards, consultation schemes, information disclosure and worker co-operatives in one composite category? Some writers file suggestion schemes and newsletters under 'employee involvement' which is then subsumed under 'worker participation', in turn assimilated to 'industrial democracy'. Some define democracy in the broadest terms as 'any theory or scheme as long as it is based on a genuine concern for the rights of workers particularly their right to share in the control of industrial decisions' (Clegg, 1960, 3). This kind of approach which then goes on to identify collective bargaining and joint consultation with industrial democracy confuses matters. The essence of joint consultation, for example, is that management provides workers with information about decisions they have made or intend to make and then listens to the workers' views. But management retains the prerogative to make the decision. In making it, they may or may not take into account the workers' views. It is not meaningful to describe such schemes as 'worker participation in management decision-making', still less 'industrial democracy'.

Our brief historical survey discloses a number of broad

categories. **Industrial democracy** transforms the ownership and authority relations of the enterprise as part of a wider strategy of transforming economy and society. Industrial democracy is justified in relation to democratic theory. To truly parallel even the present political system, industry would require self-management in which decisions would be taken directly or by means of representative institutions, by all employees. **Self-management** would require that the workers should not only have *control* of decisions but also *own* the assets of the enterprise. Control without ownership is as inadequate as ownership without control, represented at its most indirect and infirm by traditional policies of nationalisation. The democratisation of ownership, **economic democracy**, is just as essential. Any real and enduring system of industrial democracy would require planning between enterprises and major changes unattainable within a capitalist framework. This has always been the perspective of a minority of trade unionists.

Participation is often defined as 'any process whereby workers have a share in the making of managerial decisions'. But we need to exclude triviality. **Worker participation in management** gives workers a *share in power through a significant voice in significant decision-making mechanisms*. It is not industrial democracy but its *purpose* is to erode management prerogative and cede part of their decision-making rights to the workforce. The Bullock proposals involved worker participation. **Employee involvement** does not: it cedes no significant participation in decision-making to workers in terms of the *scope* of the issues covered and the *levels* at which it occurs. Worker participation may involve a step towards industrial democracy in intention and/or practice or be regarded as a final step in itself and perhaps a roadblock to further progress. The aim may be power sharing within the existing framework, or participation may be part of a strategy for its replacement. It has been used, as in Germany, to substitute for collective bargaining. A strong impetus from management's side has been the view that the *status quo* requires refurbishing, that things must change to remain the same, that in Allan Flanders's phrase 'to regain control management should share it'. For management, worker participation has been sometimes, not always, a response to challenges to its power.

From the union side it may be part of a strategy to strengthen capital and the fruits it delivers to the workforce, a means of extending bargaining, a link in the chain to self-management, or a threatening attempt to bypass unions by establishing an alternative channel for worker aspirations. Participation may be far from transformative and become part of the conventional landscape, as in Germany, or carry potential for further change. Schemes may be ambiguous and unstable, their final outcome indeterminate. There may, therefore, be an element of risk to capital, fear that for the workers an inch may become a yard, limited participation may stimulate an appetite for more. Management may therefore sponsor or oppose participation. Unions may support even management-sponsored schemes to inject them with their own goals or oppose them as a trap presaging disempowerment. The form participation takes and its outcome depend on the existing consciousness and competence and the wider balance of forces between labour and capital. Whilst many trade unionists have always rejected participation in favour of collective bargaining, since the 1960s it has received increased support.

Employee involvement and joint consultation are, in contrast, most usefully termed **management communication and involvement techniques**. They are worker participation only *in the minimal sense achieved by deletion of management decision-making.* Their *purpose* is not to erode management rights but unambiguously to strengthen them. The voice given workers is at *levels* and over a *range* of issues which are *insignificant in terms of overall corporate decision-making.* Employee involvement is embedded in pre-set production imperatives and involves mechanisms which, even if turned to workers' purposes, as when consultation involves bargaining, carry little democratic significance and remain 'soft on power'. Genuine participation modifies management prerogative. Real democracy transforms society. Quality circles and team briefings touch the fringes of management decision-making. They are, at best, **pseudo participation**, used to appropriate workers' knowledge and legitimise decisions already made by management (Pateman, 1970).

We need to examine specifically and in detail the provenance, sponsorship, objectives and unfolding of particular schemes in the context of overall power and authority relations. However unsatisfactory, these broad definitions provide a framework to judge initiatives advertised as worker participation and industrial democracy, for all too many of the pretenders aim at reinforcement of the *status quo*. Such strategies can have unintended consequences and provide potential openings for those who seriously desire to create industrial democracy.

Even broad distinctions offer some antidote to discourse which appropriates emancipation and empowerment to legitimise the interests of those opposed to industrial democracy. Some writers criticise conflation of quite different phenomena under the 'democracy and participation' rubric but themselves maintain the practice. Ackers *et al.* urge the replacement of Ramsay's image of 'cycles' of employer interest by 'waves', for waves come in different shapes and sizes. But waves of different shapes and sizes remain waves: industrial democracy is a different *genus* from employee involvement which is again different from the worker participation of the 1970s. This analysis still runs the three together (1992, 1993). Another common example is the much used continuum model: employee participation runs along a line from nil or dilute forms to workers' control and self-management. This elides the abrupt dislocations between concepts such as joint consultation, bred by human relations, and workers' self-management, a transformative socialist ideal, and the *antagonism* between them. The continuum is in reality chasmatically punctuated by conflict-driven discontinuity. The model in contrast is suggestive of seamless progression: it implies employee involvement and self-management are essentially cut from the same cloth.

Coates emphasises the enduring nature of employer opposition to any erosion of prerogative (1994, 105) and Ramsay the conjuring up of ersatz participation to arrest democratic aspirations, which falls into triviality or decay once the threat to the existing system subsides (1977). Ackers *et al.* point out the growth of employee involvement in the 1980s lacks a militant threat to property and authority relations to respond to. It is true as they argue that state and employers have taken initiatives in periods of union weakness as well as strength. These have typically involved dilute forms of participation. For example, the essential nature of employee involvement as an HRM technique characterises it as a response to harder market competition. Its dressing up as kitsch participation denotes its relation in a cheap labour, low skill economy, to EU initiatives. The initial impulse of the Conservatives was to parry EU pressures: 'we already have participation, we call it employee involvement'. Perhaps even more fundamentally, management is still faced as in the 1960s and 1970s with 'the threat' of a more educated workforce.

Management initiatives are informed by a number of purposes. As with Whitleyism they may be intended to canalise and neutralise militancy. Joint consultation appears more a cosmetic concession to distract attention from the fact that nationalisation changed little and firm up the distinction between collective bargaining and management prerogative. The schemes of the 1960s and 1970s represented corporatism in the enterprise. Employee involvement has been a response to engaging the educated workforce, to union weakness, the EU climate and market pressures. Some schemes have been motivated by paternalism and philanthropy.

In general, 'managerial prerogatives have been vigorously defended' (Poole, 1986, 17). In the process management has strengthened opposition in the unions. Trade unionists have over the long haul supported collective bargaining against participation, which has been suspected of compromising independence and establishing an alternative channel for activity, a potentially conflicting focus for loyalty (Ursell, 1983). Labourist horizons were affirmed in acceptance of the Morrisonian public corporation. Although by the 1970s the position of the TUC had changed, the unions have never attempted to build support for participation and democracy in any sustained way amongst members. Whilst workers demonstrate a desire for more control over their immediate work environment their aspirations for participation in key management decision-making processes are limited (Wall and Lischeron, 1977).

Workers on the board

The worker-director schemes of the 1960s and 1970s and the Bullock Report thus still merit scrutiny as the major example of a union-driven attempt to introduce participation on a general, collectivist, statutory basis. As late as 1967 a TUC working party chaired by TGWU leader Jack Jones saw the major means for widening union influence as extension of collective bargaining. Change in policy was related to increased conflict, EU membership, the growth of multinationals, industrial restructuring and closures. The TUC's 1974 statement, *Industrial Democracy*, argued there were limits to the ability of even extended bargaining to deal with fundamental decisions over investment, location and closure. New forms of joint regulation were necessary to put the unions on the inside track and take bargaining into the boardroom. The TUC had no desire to socialise the enterprise. Rather, unions' corporatist responsibilities needed new articulation at company level to operate successfully at state level. Joint regulation and political exchange now required unions to be inside the boardroom, although once there they would maintain their distinct identity. Company structure should be revised to create a two-tier board framework with a supervisory board on European lines overseeing a smaller executive board. To give workers 'a degree of joint control over all the major decisions of the company – closures, redundancy, major technological changes, mergers, etc. – their representatives, appointed through union machinery, should have half the seats on the supervisory board.

The Bullock Report

The 1974 Wilson government regarded the issue as a hot potato. A Committee of Inquiry, chaired by Lord Bullock, was not established until August 1975 and did not report until January 1977. The terms of reference demonstrated unequivocal commitment to the idea of worker-directors. But by the time the report was published, the Social Contract, whose most radical edge it represented, was well past its zenith.

The committee was split. The majority recommended single-tier boards be retained. In private companies with more than 2,000 employees, they should consist of equal numbers of shareholders and employee representatives. The third element in Bullock's '2x + y' formula was a smaller number of directors to be drawn from the ranks of relevant experts, academics, lawyers, accountants and scientists. Employee representatives would be appointed through 'single channel' union machinery. Unions would establish Joint Representative Committees to regulate the new system, but the employee directors could not be mandated by the shopfloor. Finally, company law would be amended so that all directors would be charged with acting in the interests of shareholders *and* employees. The employer representatives produced a minority report. Change should develop through voluntary means from the bottom up. It should culminate in employee representation on a supervisory board where one-third of the directors would be employee representatives.

The report came under assault from the CBI. The unions themselves were split down the middle. The NUM, the EETPU, the AEU and the GMB all registered strong reservations or outright opposition from a variety of different standpoints. The 1977 TUC Congress produced a woolly compromise resolution. More than a year after the report the government produced a watered down White Paper. Action on this was, in its turn, delayed by splits in the cabinet and finally the 1979 General Election intervened.

The public sector

Bullock's brief was limited to the private sector. The worker directors introduced in BSC in 1968 sat only on divisional boards, which were purely advisory. They were selected by management from a union list and they were not accountable to the unions. The British Leyland scheme established in 1975 was also limited. In the car division, factory committees elected divisional committees which then elected union representatives to the Cars Council, where they sat with management representatives. The committees possessed no decision-making powers. They were quite separate from collective bargaining structures. In the event of disagreements on the participation committees, executive responsibility lay with management. The experiment in the Post Office, in contrast, was based on the '2x + y' model. However, employee representatives were appointed by the government from union recommendations and some were full-time union officials rather than employees as envisaged in the Bullock blueprint.

Employer opposition and Thatcherism arrested further developments. Yet the Bullock Report and the consequent controversy remain of enduring relevance in their statement of many of the key problems and arguments involved. Bullock is still an essential departure point for any re-examination of the problem of participation.

Workers on the board: the critique

Employer opposition   The CBI's stance represented orchestration of the positions of finance and industrial capital, the big multinationals and smaller capital. However, as Labour's commitment wilted and as capital, relating to developing Thatcherism, moved rightwards, the CBI conference took an ever firmer line and jettisoned its commitment to back-up legislation (Strinati, 1982, 171–8). The intensity of opposition might appear surprising when Donovan took the view that 'to regain control management had to share it' and Bullock could be perceived as simply a further step in this direction. But those sections of capital most affected saw the proposals as too dangerous, particularly the multinationals, who wished to maintain flexibility in their UK operations. Whilst boardroom representation *might* have advantages in terms of increased efficiency, it *definitely* constitutes a threat to the status and prerogatives of managers (Coates, 1980; Hodgson, 1984). Certainly, the specific nature of trade unionism in the mid-1970s, particularly its strength in the workplace, made Bullock a different proposition for most employers from the introduction of co-determination in Germany, in the face of weak or non-existent trade unionism. The nub of the CBI's criticism was summed up in the minority report:

We are completely opposed to the introduction into existing Boards of representatives of special interests of any kind which might provoke confrontation or extend the scope of collective bargaining into top level management. The dilution of management expertise, the confusion of objectives and the risk of a blocking vote seems to us to be a sure recipe for decline in management leadership and initiative; this is basic to our views and is not simply a question of proportions (Bullock, 1977, 176).

The CBI case was the traditional case: management must be left to manage. There was room for consultation and involvement, but workers should not be entitled to any real initiatory or determinant voice in strategic decisions. Having staved off legislation, the CBI contented itself with support for employee involvement. Managers of all types remained strongly opposed to board level representation (Cressey *et al.*, 1981, 42).

Opposition from the unions Criticism from the union side was sometimes based on opposition to class collaboration. Alternatively, it stemmed from the view that unions' objectives were best attained through collective bargaining. Many of the criticism centred on details. It was claimed, for example, that under the '2x + y' formula the TUC's demand for joint regulation and 50–50 representation was diluted. Union representatives would usually be outvoted. One of the 'independent' experts on the Bullock Committee had subsequently resigned to become director of the CBI. It was also pointed out that employee representatives could not be mandated by the unions and that, in certain cases, they would have to maintain confidentiality. In practice, shareholder representatives would connive to ensure that real decision-making moved away from formal meetings of the board. The unions should hold out for the TUC proposals – *half the seats* on the board.

A second line of attack indicted the intention of the exercise: Bullock specifically saw participation providing new legitimacy for management. Evidence of the realisation of Bullock's theorising could be cited, for worker-director schemes *have* been implemented, albeit with minority employee representation in private industry. Such schemes have been initiated by management, incorporated managerial perspectives and achieved little for union goals (Chell, 1983). Introduced on a wider scale, they would lead to incorporation of the unions. Worker-directors would become isolated and ultimately urge acceptance of job loss and more effort. For once management objectives were endorsed, profit maximisation would be the only imperative. The BL scheme was often cited as an example of this. Supporters of participation cannot escape the central problem: in the end, employers are in business to make a profit and there is a conflict between wages and profits. In short, attempts to democratise the enterprise without changing the economic system are doomed in the face of the necessities of capitalist production: 'reform of the authority relations of the factory is impotent in the absence of structural reform of the production relations of society' (Clarke, 1977, 364). Unions should avoid contamination, extending collective bargaining and direct action against the day when transformation of capitalism would be on the agenda.

Workers on the board: the justification
One counter-argument stresses the inconsistency of a position which emphasises the centrality of union democracy and ignores the equally important issue of democratising the enterprise. The CBI's defence, 'it is unwise to impose democracy' could be equally applicable to the unions. If a healthy industrial democracy is only attainable by voluntary means, why should the implementation of democracy in the unions, where it is already more developed than in the enterprise, require the force of law? Many supporters of participation concede the Bullock proposals were far from perfect. Certainly, any system will provide the unions with problems. Vigilance is required. But results are not determined in advance. What happens will depend on various factors, but at least partly upon the will of the unions to make arrangements work in a fashion which advances the interests of their members. The purpose *may* be incorporation. Intentions do not determine outcomes. It remains open whether employee representatives will be co-opted by management, or alternatively, will succeed, if they receive adequate backing from the unions, in

extending the reach of union interests.

Moreover, such assertions tend to over-emphasise the confidence and unity of employers and the weakness of labour. It would be wrong to understate the power of capital; there is no assurance that a changed economic and political situation would not reopen disagreements between the employers. Or, that the unions would not be able to take advantage of such divisions by strategies of which participation could constitute one component.

Pursuit of profit does not dictate *specific* behaviour by employee-directors. British Steel is different from ICI which is, in its turn, different from EMI or Komatsu. Firms operate in different product and labour markets. They have different profit levels, different policies and react to problems in different ways. Capital is not a monolith and directors will have a range of discretion in decision-making. It is, moreover, quite possible that in the event of conflict between stewards and employee-directors, the position taken by the directors might well be just as justifiable as that taken by the stewards. Worker-directors may represent a *step forward* in strategies to transform patterns of ownership and economic regulation (Tomlinson, 1982).

Finally, the evidence that participation experiments have led to incorporation is mixed. The studies carried out for Bullock on board representation in the EU showed its overall impact was minimal. In British Steel, worker-directors did adopt a managerial approach and did not challenge the financial logic of the corporation. There was little to show that they had played a role in weakening the unions (Brannen, 1983). In BL where there were redundancies and undermining of shopfloor organisation, the role played by participation remains undemonstrated. The company was already in dire straits and the workplace leadership had already committed themselves to support managerial strategies. Certainly the scheme acted as a useful propaganda vehicle for management to make their case and the unions did not find it an effective instrument for the modification of company policy (Willman and Winch, 1985).

A study of the Post Office found that the employee representatives did challenge management positions but had only marginal impact, although greater than in the case of BSC, reflecting perhaps stronger representational arrangements. The researchers concluded: 'there was no evidence that the experiment was leading to any greater incorporation of the union into the philosophy and practices of management than might already have occurred through collective bargaining: board representation was not weakening the unions' bargaining strength, or autonomy, or their ability to oppose management in the interest of their members' (Batstone *et al.*, 1983, 11, 120).

The argument for supporting worker-directors, therefore, is based on a rejection of fatalism: their role is not predetermined. Evidence which demonstrates that they have little impact could be related to the limited nature and scale of the systems which have been implemented. A national system backed by law and strong unions could provide very different results.

The extension of collective bargaining

British trade unionism reached its limits in tentative approaches to participation. The only significant attempt broke on the rocks of employer opposition, state hesitancy and internal divisions. Against those who argue for an 'insider' role, critics still urge extension of collective bargaining as a more assured path to progress.

The arguments for

1 Collective bargaining is tried and tested, the central method of trade unionism responsible for the advances unions have made. Its results are impressive and it enables unions to maintain independence. Worker-directors, in contrast, will be explicitly and intimately involved in management policy and thus constrained in opposing its consequences. Board representation legitimises the view, antagonistic to trade unionism, that industry is a team in which we all have the same interests.

2 Industrial democracy is already embodied in collective bargaining. The basic characteristic of democracy is the existence of an opposition, and the opposition in the workplace to

the government of management is the union. If the union were to dissolve itself into management through boardroom representation we would end up with industrial despotism (Clegg, 1960).

3 Collective bargaining has made inroads into issues such as hiring and firing, staffing levels, technology and the speed of work. Management prerogative has been challenged over promotion, pricing, location, mergers and closure. As the TUC–Labour Party Liaison committee put it, 'collective bargaining has evolved and is evolving to meet new needs and circumstances. New areas continuously arise where collective bargaining can be used to extend joint control'.

4 The potential of collective bargaining remains unrealised. For example, the idea of planning agreements was developed in the 1970s as a means of creating tripartite agreements between government, employers and unions which would provide the latter with closer involvement in enterprise decision-making. Little came of these initiatives under Labour, owing to a lack of will, but they have been taken up by radical local authorities. The establishment in the early 1980s of the Greater London Enterprise Board was closely followed by the creation of similar bodies in West Yorkshire, Merseyside and Lancashire. The West Midlands Enterprise Board invested over £10 million in more than 30 companies spanning the industrial spectrum. GLEB adapted the idea of the planning agreement into the 'enterprise plan'. Whenever it intervened to regenerate local industry it made its assistance conditional upon joint planning by the board, management and unions.

5 The potential inherent in collective bargaining is also illustrated by the Lucas Aerospace Shop Stewards' Alternative Corporate Plan. The Lucas Combine Committee initiated a research programme which mobilised the knowledge and experience of the workforce. The plan sought to draw the sting of the management argument that redundancies were inevitable, by demonstrating that an alternative range of products, technically and commercially viable but also socially useful could be manufactured. It pressed for the replacement of

arms production by rail/road vehicles, kidney machines and domestic space heaters. The Lucas plan had three main strengths: it raised the question of the *nature* of production; it moved the unions off the defensive terrain of simply saying 'no' to management decisions by projecting detailed alternatives, which raised the question 'who manages Lucas?'; and it pre-figured the socially beneficial purposes for which production could be organised were the creativity of the workforce to be given free rein. The popularity of the plan and the degree to which it gripped the imagination of other groups of workers is incontestable; many other groups of workers took up the idea.

The arguments against

1 Collective bargaining has been primarily defensive, failed to raise the share of wages and played a role in bureaucratising unions. Nearly all the objections made to participation can be levelled at collective bargaining: it can legitimise the role of management, secure compliance in their decisions and under-mine the unions' independent role. Taken a stage further, these criticisms have been levelled at trade unionism itself.

2 Collective bargaining does not constitute industrial democracy. An organised opposition is not the essential hallmark of demo-cracy; many democracies have got along fine without it. More-over, the fact that unions are in this model 'an opposition which can never become the government', shows how strained the analogy between collective bargaining and democracy is. The determinant feature of democracy is the accountability of the leadership to those they lead. Collective bargaining provides no formal mechanisms for such accountability. In Britain today there is not even minimum legislation requiring employers to recognise unions and the efficacy of collective bargaining varies tremendously.

3 Whilst it would be wrong to ignore its achievements, collective bargaining has typically embraced a limited range of issues and has restricted management prerogative through a negative veto, rather than acting as a channel for the positive assertion of workers' interests. It has operated at the margins. It has done

little to influence strategic decisions on investment, mergers and closures. Its success has declined with the distance travelled from immediate job-related issues. Bargaining over strategic issues is very different and much more difficult than bargaining about wages or hours of work and requires the adoption of formal participation machinery. Unions would be mad to pass up an opportunity to move closer to the sites of primary decision-making through participation. Worker representatives can bargain in the boardroom at least as well as on bargaining committees, which are also remote from their members.

4 The planning agreements of the 1970s achieved nothing. The only full planning agreement developed by the Labour government was with Chrysler. There was no union involvement in its negotiation. Its success in extending the ability of the unions to determine strategic decisions was starkly exemplified in 1978, when Chrysler's US management sold off the UK subsidiary to Peugeot-Citroen, without even informing government or unions. The spate of local authority initiatives remain small scale and suffer from the subordination of local to central government and the extensive strengthening of Whitehall dominance since 1980. Witness the fate of the GLC. They do not provide a compelling precursor for a national strategy of economic regeneration and increased worker participation.

5 The Lucas Alternative Plan was inspiring. Nonetheless, management refused to negotiate on it and it was never implemented. Instead, management successfully carried through redundancies. It is difficult to see how alternative products suggested in the plan could be produced and marketed successfully by the individual enterprise in the absence of a national system of planning or, at least, extensive state support. The Lucas plan, rather than reaffirming the possibilities of collective bargaining, embodied in its genesis a recognition of the limitations of collective bargaining in dealing with capital and, in its progress, the failure of trade unionists to create an adequate substitute for an outmoded form. It is difficult to see its results as 'a new trade unionism in the making'. Workers'

plans fared no better elsewhere. United Biscuits' employees in Liverpool developed what was described as 'the most detailed alternative plan ever prepared by unions in Britain to deal with a closure'. The company stated:

The alternative plan presented by the unions and the constructive spirit and content of the discussions demonstrates that very difficult decisions can be examined responsibly on the basis of full access to available information. For a small group of shop stewards to achieve in so short a time this level of knowledge and competence in handling that knowledge is most impressive. Sadly their efforts and the efforts of all those who have supported them have not enabled the company to reverse the decision.

The closure went ahead.

Participation and bargaining

It is true that the 1970s saw some increase in the scope of bargaining, and the extent of informal job controls was greater than in other European countries (Storey, 1980; Leijnse, 1980). Controls over staffing, output and demarcations remained limited, largely defensive, fragmented and vulnerable, protecting workers 'without substantially circumscribing employers' room for manoeuvre' (Hyman and Elger, 1981, 144). Unions' ability to influence strategic decisions was limited because of the 'at a distance', reactive nature of collective bargaining. One study found only 19 out of 150 strategic decisions involved the unions who were responding to agendas already determined by management (Wilson *et al.*, 1982).

The limits of collective bargaining in a favourable environment suggest it possesses *inherent* weaknesses and requires supplementing with 'insider' strategies. Since the 1970s unions have been urged to bargain over issues such as training and new technology (TGWU, 1992). However 'union policy towards training can be characterised as defensive rather than offensive and few bargaining initiatives have occurred' (Rainbird, 1990, 172). Both technology and training would appear issues where participation would facilitate union influence. It has proved difficult for unions to influence the initial set of choices on the nature of technological innovation through conventional means. Yet the nature of new technology and the way initiatory decisions go, often dictate subsequent impact on work organisation and seriously circumscribe later bargaining. The potential of boardroom representation to pre-empt, initiate and get in at the start of corporate decision-making would suggest, given what appear to be structural limitations to the reach of collective bargaining when the going is good, and significant weakening when it is heavy, that participation remains important. The incorporation–legitimation of capital argument, partly based on an exaggerated profile of pre-existing union independence is, in the light of possible alternatives, unconvincing. There are dangers. Given the existing limits of collective bargaining and 'direct action', what would remain a leap in the dark merits favourable consideration. Certainly in conditions of stronger trade unionism and a more favourable economic position.

In the 1970s extension of collective bargaining may have appeared an alternative. Declining access for workers to key decisions as collective bargaining has waned has re-emphasised the important of alternative forms of representation. However, the problem remains: employer opposition is tenacious and the factors militating against collective bargaining militate against participation. The lessons of the Bullock experience are that progress necessitates a general, strategic, well resourced initiative based on sustained education of the membership. It would require a united movement with the will and the power to overcome strong opposition. In today's conditions this is unlikely.

The European dimension

The EU initiative likely to immediately affect Britain is the 1991 draft directive on European Works Councils. This would apply to all companies or groups with at least 1,000 workers in the EU and at least 100 in two or more member states. It would require the establishment of European Works Councils, group wide trans-national forums, in every such enterprise on the request of the workforce. The role and composition of the Council would depend on agreement between the employer and a special negotiating body of workers' representatives. In the event of failure to agree on the nature and functioning of the Council it would have minimum rights to meet annually with top management to receive information on the company's activities and plans and the right to be consulted on any proposals 'likely to have serious consequences for the interests of the employees'. This would cover closures, relocation, mergers, organisational change and new production methods. The Works Council would have up to 30 members – existing employee representatives or specially elected for the purpose.

European Works Councils were high on the agenda of the 11 member states accepting the Maastricht Social Protocol. Around 90 major British based firms would be affected, including 59 of the top 100 companies and a further 260 with plants in Britain (Marginson *et al.*, 1993). The proposals provide no explicit role for unions – this would be left to individual states. The council's role would be limited to *information* and *consultation*. The Draft Directive states final decisions remain 'exclusively the responsibility of management'. Despite this, the initiative has been opposed by UNICE, the European Employers' Federation, and stridently by the CBI and the British government. Nonetheless, in 1993 Ford joined the ranks of the largely French owned companies which have European Works Councils, agreeing to establish a forum covering its 100,000 workers in Belgium, Britain, Germany, Spain and Portugal, embracing full-time officers and shop stewards.

Whilst legislation would benefit the unions the proposals are limited in terms of participation. Progress has been slower on the proposed directive which would require 'European Companies' to establish either board level representation, works councils or alternative transnational arrangements. The TUC has therefore looked with increasing approval at the German system of co-determination. A resolution at the 1991 Congress suggested aspects of the German system might be adopted in Britain and the TUC organised a fact finding visit in 1992. The strongest system of co-determination, in the coal and steel industry, which provides for equal numbers of worker and shareholder representatives on supervisory boards, a workers' veto on the appointment of the labour director and Works Councils certainly merits scrutiny (Hall, 1993). The problem is again obvious: employers are more hostile to significant developments than they were at the time of Bullock, and the state even more opposed.

Employee involvement

Since 1979 communication and involvement techniques have held the stage. Management inspired, voluntary, individualist in ethos, they give unions a minor role. They carry little ambiguity and little risk for management: their potential for evolution into significant participation is small. Managers 'support most employee involvement practices so long as these do not radically affect their control function within the firm' (Poole and Mansfield, 1992, 207). The provisions of the 1982 Employment Act require undertakings with more than 250 workers to report annually on arrangements for providing information to employees, consulting regularly with employees or their representatives, encouraging involvement through profit sharing and share ownership and achieving a common awareness on the part of employees of financial and economic factors affecting enterprise. This slender state underpinning demarcates the boundaries of employee involvement.

Joint consultation

Some observers argued there was a decline in joint consultative committees as strong workplace organisation developed in the 1950s and 1960s. Recent research emphasises their continuity through the post-war period (McInnes, 1985). By 1980 consultative committees covered more than a third of establishments and there had been an increase in the 1970s. Joint consultation went hand in hand with collective bargaining. Of itself it represented little threat to union functions (Brown, 1981; Daniel and Millward, 1983).

There was little change in the early 1980s, decline in private industry balancing growth in the public sector. Consultative committees were more common in larger, unionised enterprises and in a third of cases higher level committees were used for negotiations. Between 1984 and 1990 the proportion of workplaces with committees dropped from 34% to 29%. This was the product of change in the private sector, compositional changes and the decline of larger establishments in manufacturing. The most important matters discussed were production and employment issues and government legislation. Two-thirds of managers and workplace representatives believed committees had some influence on management decisions. Separate committees dealing with health and safety were recorded in a quarter of establishments, although there was an increase in managers taking decisions on those matters without consultation (Millward *et al.*, 1992, 151ff.).

Joint consultation has been seen by management as a means of encouraging a joint interest view of the enterprise, improving communications and drawing on employee resources. It has been seen by unions as a means of bypassing shop stewards, a useful means of gaining information on management intentions or a talking shop. At times it has been used to replace or compete with collective bargaining, more commonly it has co-existed as a complement. It is a dilute form of participation which has constituted a minimal threat to the unions and in some cases has been useful to them. What is unclear is the extent to which, with collective bargaining on the wane, it is becoming a channel for bargaining on the retreat.

Communication and involvement techniques
It is asserted that streamlined communication systems can change employee attitudes, make them more aware of market restraints, and improve motivation through newsletters and videos. This involves transmission and minimal participation. The second strand involves employees more, with the emphasis on active appropriation of employee skills and knowledge to solve problems of production and organisation and facilitate change in efficiency through quality circles, job redesign and total quality manage-

ment. The use of these techniques has burgeoned with new initiatives recorded in 45% of establishments in 1990 compared with 35% in 1984. Innovation seems to have been stronger on the communications front with more initiatives reported on 'more information to employees' and 'more two-way communication' than on autonomous work groups or quality circles. Growth was concentrated in the service sector and in unionised workplaces (Millward *et al.*, 1992, 175–6).

Some have seen TQM, which seeks to embed quality concerns in the production process through employee involvement, as promising increased participation (Hill, 1991). However, its goals of consumer satisfaction, continuous improvement and increased profit, as well as the production system and authority relations in which it occurs, are given, set by management. Any worker autonomy is at the margins, limited to decisions over work organisation. This is the involvement of the puppet show. Such approaches have been, as yet, limited in their impact on unions and responses have been mixed (see p. 134). Their value to unions which have embraced them, such as the AEEU, remains unclear. A wide range of unions have formed links with the Industrial Involvement and Participation Association and unions such as the TGWU which have been suspicious have had to come to terms with these techniques. The TGWU has sought to make all aspects of employee involvement the subject of negotiation, ensure representation is always through union channels, and that team working is under shop steward surveillance. Yet at Rover, between 1987 and 1992, it was forced by fear of job loss into almost complete co-operation in lean production with TQM, continuous improvement and team working.

Financial involvement

Profit sharing schemes as a means of eroding worker resistance are as old as capitalism. Since 1978 the state has encouraged a number of such initiatives. Kenneth Clarke has urged:

We need to do away once and for all with old fashioned 'them' and 'us' attitudes in industry. Successful companies in a modern economy need to involve their employees – share ownership, profit related pay, employee share ownership plans co-operatives – they can all help us to achieve the essential goals of competition and co-operation; competition in our economy and co-operation within our companies (Clarke, 1987).

Conservatives argue a financial stake will turn the worker into 'economic man and woman'. Attitudes will change, they will come to embrace the goal of profit, they will identify with management, they will work harder. Financial participation is another individualistic anti-collective technique to further management goals. Again the participation element is shallow. It does not touch authority relations or, generally, ownership. Mrs Thatcher's vision 'an employee should not only be working in the shop floor or in the office. He should be present at the AGM as a shareholder' has remained largely unrealised. There is little employee participation in the design or operation of these initiatives (Baddon *et al.*, 1989).

State support has come through tax relief. The 1978 Finance Act provided support for deferred profit sharing schemes where profits are used to purchase shares. The 1980 Act facilitated Save As You Earn share schemes. In 1987 help was given to profit related payments and in 1989 to Employee Share Ownership Plans. Later budgets increased tax concessions. This has produced substantial growth in financial involvement. Direct profit related payment schemes have proved the most popular, spreading to around 40% of establishments by 1990, whilst around a third had some form of profit sharing arrangement. The 1990 WIRS survey found the proportion of the workforce covered by share ownership schemes increased from 22% in 1984 to 34% in 1990. Nonetheless, share distribution remains restricted. Under 30% of share schemes authorised by the Inland Revenue to 1990 were open to all employees: 'all workforce' schemes offered workers nearly £3,000 on average whereas the average value of shares under options issued to executives was six times that amount. Even in the highly favourable conditions of privatisation, employees in British Gas owned 855 shares each worth around £2,000 in 1991, whilst seven executives owned 1.5 million shares worth £3.5 million (Nichols and O'Connell Davidson, 1992; Millward *et al.*, 1992, 264–5).

Whilst employees approve of these schemes there is little evidence they have changed attitudes or had more than marginal impact on industrial relations, although one survey found industrial relations worse and financial performance better in companies with financial involvement than in those without it. Some schemes, such as British Telecom, involve penalties for industrial action but this is unusual. The unions' historic antipathy – until the mid-1980s the TUC described such initiatives as 'not so much an encouragement of individual shareholding as an attack on collective institutions' – has flaked. The TUC was concerned that these schemes discriminated between private and public sectors, dynamic and declining industries, employed and wageless. They gave workers little enhanced say in decision-making. Tied financially to inefficient management or a declining industry workers could end up losers. By the 1990s USDAW's 'We are not against them nor are we very enthusiastic' was more representative, although some unions are more positive and interest was demonstrated in other forms of financial involvement such as the management of pension schemes and, wider, the Swedish Wage-Earner Funds (Poole and Jenkins, 1990; Millward *et al.*, 1992, 266).

Worker co-operatives

Worker co-operatives, businesses owned and controlled by their workers, consist of older organisations such as the Scott Bader Commonwealth, 'new start' co-operatives which blossomed from the 1960s in publishing, bookselling, printing and wholefoods, often with a radical or alternative lifestyle orientation, and 'rescue' co-operatives, established to stave off closure. Worker co-operatives seem to combine the benefits of economic democracy and workers' self-management. In the 1970s, older co-operatives were joined by 'rescue' ventures at Meriden, Kirkby Manufacturing and Engineering and the *Scottish Daily News*. They originated in struggles against closure and were financially aided by the 1974

Labour government and championed by Tony Benn, Secretary of State for Industry. Labour's Industrial Common Ownership Act, 1976, was intended to stimulate co-operatives. The recession of the 1980s provided further impetus.

The GMB and the Welsh TUC established support services for members interested in establishing co-operatives. This was reinforced by support from Labour local authorities. By 1984, the Greater London Enterprise Board had invested over £1 million in 36 co-operatives. More than 70 Co-operative Development Agencies sponsored by councils were established and the number of worker co-operatives was estimated to have increased by 1990 to more than 1,600, with a workforce of over 10,000 concentrated in retail distribution, catering, food-processing, printing and publishing, and building and allied services. In the 1990s co-operatives have been given a further fillip by CCT and Employer Share Ownership Plans. It is claimed co-operatives have similar average performance and life expectancy to the orthodox enterprise and that their record is good, given that many are established for job protection rather than to seize growth opportunities.

The renaissance of interest is illustrated by the publicity accorded the Mondragon experiment in Spain. Established in 1956, in the Basque country, on the ruins of a small bankrupt firm, the network now covers 150 co-operatives in a range of industries and provides more than 18,000 jobs. It has its own bank, with 84 branches, and its own training and research and development agencies. Mondragon has benefited from intimate links with a homogeneous community. Despite a concentration in hi-tech industries, Mondragon embraces co-operatives in agriculture, education and housing. A general assembly of workers elects a governing non-executive board which, in turn, appoints management. A social council represents workers through a cell based system, linked to the governing board. There is no union representation; indeed, striking is punishable by expulsion or fines.

Co-operatives have had support from the Labour Party. Unions have given strong support and back-up expertise, more to save jobs than develop democracy. Apart from a handful of cases, they have been reluctant to commit funds. The scheme launched by

Kenneth Clarke in 1987 was seen as ending Tory ideological opposition to co-operatives. However, different political philosophies give different emphases to co-operatives as the vehicle for defence of jobs, small business-led growth, alternative forms of economic organisation or guarantors of alternative lifestyles. The Conservatives, for example, are supporters of 'employee buyouts', particularly in the public sector.

Why should workers succeed in a venture in which entrepreneurs failed? A partial answer is that, whereas the ownership structure and authority relations in the conventional enterprise alienate employees and limit commitment, the co-operative is liberating because it gives all employees a direct responsibility in the enterprise. Co-operators have a real stake. Supporters of co-operatives can point to increases in productivity and lower unit costs. At KME there was an increase in output from 7,000 to 13,000 radiators per week and a significant increase in the company's market share.

The injection of public money can be justified on grounds of job creation and alternative costs of unemployment. Unions should support co-operatives because of rule-book objectives such as the TGWU's 'the extension of co-operative production and distribution'; because co-operatives redistribute resources away from monopoly ownership; and because successful co-operatives can raise the self-confidence of workers, question the immutability of established methods of organisation, and generate demands for more democratic experiments.

It can be argued that this view fails to face unpalatable realities. Workers will normally be dependent on external finance. Financial institutions are likely to impose tight constraints. Their caution, particularly if the co-operative arises from an economic failure, will be boosted by ideological mistrust. Often survival can only be guaranteed through excessive self-exploitation: 'you will have to work like you never worked before' Jack Spriggs, chair of the KME co-operative, told its new owners. This can mean, as at Meriden, co-operators work below union rates. This entails a minimal role for unions and can be seen as an invitation to other employers to undermine collective bargaining. It can mean, as at

Meriden, that professional management is brought in at professional rates and that orthodox principles of work organisation, differentials and discipline re-emerge. A detailed study of KME found authority became centralised and leadership was exercised by a small elite, with little part played by the unions or by the majority of workers in decision-making (Eccles, 1981). In the end, financial pressures led to the collapse of all the 'Benn co-operatives'.

One lesson is that co-operatives need well thought out structures to involve the members in decision-making. But even well-developed democratic mechanisms will not work in the absence of a will to democracy and participative values. The origin of some co-operatives in job protection may cause problems, particularly if the strongest motivation comes not from the workforce, but from union officials or politicians. The need to counteract the antagonistic non-participative environment draws attention to the enduring importance of education.

The position of some on the left is more straightforward: 'you cannot build islands of socialism in a sea of capitalism'. Most co-operatives, it is asserted, either fold, or become conventional enterprises. The first GLC-supported co-operative is often taken as an example. When GEC declared its intention of closing Associated Automation, a telephone subsidiary, the GLC purchased the plant and equipment for around £100,000 and turned it over to a co-operative in which the workers invested part of their redundancy payments. Within a year, the new co-operative folded, amidst recriminations. The lesson drawn is that co-operatives can distract workers from a fight to force their employer to maintain jobs. On the right, co-operative failures are sometimes seen as an affirmation of the benefits of the orthodox capitalist enterprise.

But there are still those who believe co-operatives can play a role in a future strategy for industrial democracy. The failure of co-operatives has been seen as evidence that the road to democratisation is long and hard and that it is simplistic to see new ventures producing transformation in attitudes and a sudden upsurge in the desire to participate. Even with a change of structures, you still need to work at involvement and stimulate participation. On the other hand, it has been argued that there is no iron law stemming from the need for maximisation of profits which inevitably dooms co-operatives to collapse or degeneration back to capitalist principles. The framework for profit determination is looser than this view allows, as is demonstrated by the diversity of approaches utilised by conventional firms. Similarly, whilst it is clear that management is necessary as a function, the scope that *does* exist for its reform should not be minimised on the basis of one or two ill resourced experiments.

Conclusions

By the 1970s participation had become an important part of the Labour Movement's agenda. Reversal of its advance demonstrated the limitations of corporatism in Britain and the tenacious opposition of employers to any genuine significant restructuring of the hierarchical enterprise in favour of the workforce. It was facilitated by the inability of the unions to convincingly develop, let alone conclude, an educating debate amongst their members and put all their power behind an agreed strategy. Even in the 1970s industrial democracy in the sense of the restructuring of economic and authority relations and the planning of production by the workforce was not on the agenda, and it is arguable whether successful participation would have opened a path to it. Since then, only employee involvement techniques for maintaining employee disempowerment remain on offer, demonstrating again that capitalism can absorb almost anything and regurgitate it as its opposite. Initiatives from Europe continue to loom; it would be unwise for unions to place too much reliance on them.

The unions have never been hotbeds of demands for democracy or participation. There has always been a minority tradition which has sought socialist change or an insider role in capitalism. Nationalisation and Bullock highlighted the constraints of Labourism and the limits of opposition tendencies. Participation remains an important if divisive issue given the limitations of collective bargaining in dealing with key issues and its erosion in the 1980s. The TUC looks to the EU but has not produced any integrated strategy to replace Bullock and deliver on EU proposals. Reformers wish to modify the authority structure of the enterprise but accept its existing economic objectives. Radicals wish to change both its government and economic ends. They divide into those who see participation as a path towards industrial democracy and those who see it as a trap to co-opt unions. The first group are therefore willing to examine participation schemes. The second group argue workers should preserve their independence, extending bargaining and unilateral controls in combination with wider strategies for socialist transformation.

Opponents of participation are faced with growing management power, the erosion of shopfloor control and collective bargaining. For it is clear that 'growth in inequality in wages and earnings . . . is being matched by a widening in the inequalities of influence and access to key decisions about work and employment' (Millward, 1994, 133). Supporters of participation also face intractable problems – the assertive opposition of capital and the state but also the defensive caste of British trade unionism inadequately geared to operate within the sophisticated apparatuses of multinational capital. And, in this context, organisation, skills and knowledge are an essential part of power. Whilst there may be real choices between different policies, different means of implementation and different timescales and, whilst enterprises may be judged on a range of complex accounting indices and may be long-term profit 'satisfiers', rather than short-term profit maximisers, in the end, there are structural systemic constraints. The enterprise is part of the capitalist system and is required to perform according to the imperatives of that system.

None of this is a decisive argument against participation. It underscores the difficulties a weakened movement with questionable commitment will encounter. The failure to implement Bullock illustrated the limitations of union power in the 1970s. There is little evidence to sustain the view that unions possess sufficient unity and muscle to implement a similar strategy in the 1990s. The irony for the unions is that when participation was on offer they did not want it enough. When they need it, it is not on the menu. This sums up the short termism and lack of strategic forward thinking which in this, as in other areas, has limited success. Increasing recognition that so many of the problems of industrial relations arise from the way work is organised, and the increasing disenfranchisement of workers from decision-making does not make solutions any easier. Nonetheless, if progress is to be made on these central questions it remains essential that participation and industrial democracy continue to figure on the political agenda.

Further reading

Two good books which discuss the ideas of democracy and participation are Alan Fox, *Man Mismanagement*, Hutchinson, 1985, and Caroline Pateman, *Participation and Democratic Theory*, Cambridge University Press, 1970. A good account of the socialist tradition can be found in Ken Coates and Tony Topham, eds., *Workers Control: A Book of Readings*, Panther, 1970. Paul Blumberg, *Industrial Democracy: The Sociology of Participation*, Constable, 1968, provides an excellent account of the history of participation experiments. Laurie Baddon *et al.*, *People's Capitalism?*, Routledge, 1989, is helpful on recent developments. Mary Mellor, Janet Hannah and John Stirling, *Worker Co-operatives in Theory and Practice*, Open University Press, 1988, is a stimulating read.

The state of the unions

As the twentieth century closes, unions face fundamental challenges over issues they thought laid to rest in its early years: they
are not as powerful as they were. The question arises whether the
period 1945–75, the high tide of union influence, was itself
exceptional. Nonetheless, unions still constitute a significant and
powerful interest and there is intensive debate about the nature
and extent of change. This chapter draws together the strands of
change, examines its importance and scrutinises the degree to
which union power has diminished since the 1970s. It examines
some of the alternatives facing the Labour Movement if it is to
regroup after the reverses of recent decades.

The contours of change

Since the late 1970s the motor of development has been a
complex, explosive interaction of economic and political factors,
with the politics of neo-Conservatism responding to and
amplifying economic and industrial tendencies hostile to the
Labour Movement. Thatcherism has been inflated and distorted
particularly by its opponents: it remains a reality. Dating historical
changes is an arbitrary process. We need to attend to continuity,
the gradual unfolding of developments key to today's situation
through the post-war period and the new emphasis reflected by
Labour governments after the economic jolts of the 1970s. But it
is *change* that is most striking and on deeper examination it is

change that characterises this period. Despite precursive developments in the 1970s, 1979 remains an important turning point for British trade unions. The years 1979 to 1987 saw the rise and political dominance of Thatcherism. From 1988, driven by economic failure and divisions over Europe, it was in retreat, but Labour and the unions were unable to reap the benefits. The new conservatism failed to reverse economic decline. It did facilitate a changed political economy. Fragile and limited as it was besides the coherence some theorists lent it, it contributed to weakening the unions without solving the problems they allegedly caused.

The transformation in density, the longest, most significant haemorrhage of members in union history has been fundamental. Membership of all unions dropped by 4 million between 1979 and 1992, membership of TUC unions by almost 5 million. By 1992 the gains of the 1960s and 1970s had melted away: unions had the same number of members as in 1951. The view that unions were returning to a pre-1968 post-war normality was outmoded by continuing membership loss. Overall density of employees and the unemployed declined to a post-war low of 37%, compared with 55% in 1979; density of employees to 42%. For TUC unions the figures were 34%, compared with 52% in 1979, and 30% in comparison with 49% in 1979 (see Chapter 1).

TUC unions suffered most. The TGWU saw membership halved despite mergers. MSF and the GMB, more active in mergers, were around a third and a quarter smaller by 1992, whilst UCATT had shed 192,000 members. The NUM had more than 250,000 members in 1979, 8,000 by 1993. The face of trade unionism has been changed: Actors' Equity dwarfs the NUM. Decline has however been uneven. NALGO had 753,000 members in 1979 and 759,000 in 1992, NUPE 692,000 in 1979 and 550,000 in 1992. Many non-TUC bodies increased membership, the most obvious being the Royal College of Nursing. Individual unions increased their membership in different years. Even in a bad year, like 1991, 28 TUC unions made overall gains. These were typically small, insufficient to offset past losses. In the late 1980s the TGWU recruited 250,000 new members annually but still lost members overall.

Significant decline has occurred in the past. Between 1920 and 1933 overall membership dropped from 8.4 million to 4.4 million, and overall density from 45% to 22%. Recovery thereafter demonstrates that restoration of fortunes is possible. The difference with today is that by the early 1990s, after 12 years of sustained decline, membership loss was *speeding up* not slowing down. The pattern of employment growth that developed in the late 1930s, the full employment fashioned in the war years, the long post-war boom, the conditions that stimulated the recovery in union membership, appear extremely unlikely to be reproduced. The new mass production factories of the 1930s and 1940s were more conducive to trade unionism than the growth of private services of the 1990s. Utility of comparison with the very different economy and society of half a century ago is limited.

The drop in membership has borne most heavily on 'unionate' unions and rendered trade unionism very much a public sector phenomenon. Decline is clearly related to unfavourable economic circumstances, specifically unemployment. But it continued as the economy came out of recession and then as jobs grew and unemployment fell. The business cycle changed, the downward trend in membership did not. In the boom years of 1988 and 1989 membership of TUC unions fell by 5% and 2.7% before declining sharply as recession re-emerged, by 5% and 6% in 1991 and 1992. Membership loss has thus been sustained through recession and economic upswing. Even in the two recessions of the early 1980s and early 1990s fall in membership was greater than the fall in employment: in 1981–82 employment fell by 5.6%, membership by 11.6%.

The seriousness of this situation is compounded by decline in collective bargaining. The most authoritative survey found substantial decline in recognition between 1984 and 1990: the proportion of establishments recognising unions fell from 66% to 53%, with negotiating rights 'withering away through lack of support from employees'. The coverage of collective bargaining has diminished: 'The fall was stark, substantial and incontrovertible' (Millward *et al.*, 1992, 352). Collective bargaining was becoming a minority phenomenon, increasingly decentralised and more restricted in scope, 'fewer issues were subject to joint regulation in 1990 than in 1980' (Millward *et al.*, 1992, 353). The incidence of derecognition increased. The coverage of workplace organisation declined. It remained intact where collective bargaining continued to flourish. It proved unable to resist intensification of labour and reorganisation of work. Workplace trade unionism was more marginal than in previous decades. Nevertheless, for most of this period real wages were increasing, coming under pressure only in the early 1980s and early 1990s, and the trade unionist's premium over non-members was maintained. However unions were unable to avoid greater *dispersion* of wages and regressive redistribution of income and wealth from 1979 (Chapter 2, Chapter 3).

By 1993 the strike rate, often taken as an indicator of combativity and union strength, had declined significantly. The number of strikes was the smallest since records began. There appeared a clear distinction between the aggressive successful militancy of the 1960s and 1970s and the defensive, less successful industrial conflict of recent years. The unions stabilised their financial position after the body blows of the early 1980s but remained insecure and employer dependent institutions. Collective *laissez-faire* was finally laid to rest, replaced by loss of autonomy, circumscription of legal protection and detailed regulation of union activity. The new Conservative state has saddled the unions with an irksome and all enveloping framework of law (see Chapter 6). The kind and quality of union democracy is under challenge from business union and plebiscitary formulations. Internal relations are defined in terms of full-time professional managers diagnosing consumer desires mediated less by activists, more by consultants and market research (Chapter 4). These tendencies are paralleled in the Labour Party so that we are confronted with moves not only to business unionism but to a weakened, more fragmented *Business Labour Movement*, articulated more sensitively to capitalist logic (Chapter 7). There has been a reversal of the impetus to workers' participation in industry, strengthening of management prerogative and renewed confidence in capitalist authority relations (Chapter 9).

Whilst it would be wrong to minimise the extent to which there has always been division and disunity, recent tendencies have produced greater disaggregation and loss of cohesion in the Labour Movement. Management-controlled decentralisation of bargaining strengthened tendencies to sectionalism and enterprise identification. Fragmentation has been encouraged by failure of co-ordinated projects and lack of political success and has weakened the role of the TUC.

In the political sphere, too, change has been far reaching and significant. The unions suffered political exclusion and their influence on the state was less than at any time since the 1930s. Their social and industrial legitimacy was called into question (Chapter 5). Labour lost an unprecedented four consecutive general elections and failed to mobilise its historic constituency. As the failures of capitalism were made manifest it was the party of capitalism which benefited from a new *dominant minority party* system. As the Conservatives rode recession and the removal of Mrs Thatcher Labour proved unable to benefit, even as the Major government plumbed new depths of unpopularity and economic difficulty. The period from 1979 was one in which the dominance of policies antagonistic to trade unionism spread across the spectrum and Labour was drawn into a broad market consensus.

The left in the Labour Party associated with the unions was decisively weakened, the Communist Party disintegrated and no significant left organisation developed outside Labour's ranks. The successful resolutions at the 1980 conference demanding restrictions on movement of capital, increased spending on public utilities, a wealth tax, 'a substantial cut in arms spending', a 35-hour week and acceptance that 'Britain's social and economic problems can only be resolved by socialist planning', appeared in the 1990s from another world. Tony Benn's removal from the executive in 1993 symbolised the sea change. After the miners' strike there was no half way significant base for left opposition in the unions. The TGWU–MSF–UNISON axis was increasingly the voice of protest calming into grudging acquiescence in Labour Party policy. The union broad lefts, where significant, have, by and large, settled down as internal electoral and resolutionary machines. They have exercised little influence in reversing the direction of politics. Union leaders saw the reduction of their influence in the Labour Party formalised at the 1993 conference. Many accepted that even the election of a Labour government would not dissolve their difficulties (see Chapter 7).

Such a government would have to interact with the economic change which has contributed to the union-hostile environment and in its turn stimulated developments such as EU integration. Structural change in economy and industry is not epochal or transformative – at least as yet – in the way those who inflate limited, sometimes contradictory tendencies into new systems claim. It is real, growing and unfavourable to trade unionism. Capitalism is more volatile, less regulated. Markets are harder and there is increasing competition between states to attract capital. Conservative policies have abolished exchange controls and opened Britain up to a world market pressing down on potential pro-union options, such as corporatism, on a cheap labour basis. The system seems set in a recession–sluggish recovery–shallow boom cycle. This is exacerbating Britain's relative decline and limiting the margin for concessions. Whilst far from endangering capitalist stability it places constraints on the full employment based recovery favourable to union resurgence.

Full employment has increasingly crumbled in the developed economies and its importance as a goal has been downplayed by politicians. In Britain we have done without it for almost two decades. Strict deflationary regimes adopted internationally to squeeze out inflation have produced sustained high levels of unemployment. In Europe the commitment to the ERM and Maastricht circumscribe future state intervention to use interest rates, exchange rates, increased public spending and borrowing to achieve full employment. The Labour Party's commitment to full employment and its priority for a future Labour Government has been questionable. The ravages inflicted on manufacturing since 1979 and the apparent inability of services to deliver full-time jobs constitute further impediments. Internationalisation sets limits on reflation by individual states and the political will for a co-ordi-nated international offensive to realise full employment is far from evident. Whilst current attempts to turn Britain into a low wage, low job economy are unlikely to overcome competition from the Pacific rim and achieve economic regeneration, any return to the conditions of the post-war boom, in which unions waxed, appears unlikely. Britain's economic future appears to lie along the hard road to greater international collaboration. These developments do not determine union decline. They make its reversal difficult.

The debate on decline

This snapshot suggests, as did many commentators from the mid-1980s, unions in the throes of serious decline, facing a 'crisis', although whether they had been *permanently transformed* remained an open question (Towers, 1989, 164; Marsh, 1992). Others had no doubt change was transformative and enduring. Decline was linked to deep-seated changes in industrial relations and workers' attitudes, from collectivism to individualism, conflict to co-operation (Bassett, 1986). Analysts impressed by loss of membership and political influence and the successful imposition of new legislation saw change as politically induced, fundamental and lasting. The unions had been tamed; erosion of their power was an undoubted achievement of Thatcherism (Kavanagh, 1987, 243; Gamble, 1988, 126). Some saw union decline as the result of systemic changes which were structural and inexorable (Lash and Urry, 1987). By 1987 Norman Willis, General Secretary of the TUC, felt unions faced 'a serious crisis, challenges more profound than at any time in the movement's long history'. As these challenges worked their way through, some academics asserted we had seen the 'dissolution of the labour movement . . . the counter-revolution of our time' (Phelps Brown, 1990, 11).

An opposing view emphasised the resilience of the unions, asserting density of 43% and membership of 9 million after a dozen years of attrition represented a reasonable response. For most of the period workplace organisation stood up well. Collective bargaining, if diminished, remained central whilst the trend of wages was attributed to continuing strength. Much of the legislation had had minimal impact. Important continuities in industrial relations meant reversal was possible. It was argued by the mid-1980s that Thatcherism often meant 'business as usual', with 'surprisingly little evidence of a dramatic shift of bargaining power away from the unions' (McInnes, 1987, 136ff.). Examining membership, density, wages, workplace organisation, union finances and political developments it was argued that by 1988 unions had responded to difficulties 'remarkably well':

Those who believe in a crisis of the labour movement have made a series of analytical errors. They have mistaken short-term cyclical trends such as the decline in union membership, strike frequency and bargaining power for long-term secular trends. All previous evidence suggests that these three indicators will rise again as the economy moves out of recession . . . (Kelly, 1988, 289).

Survey evidence demonstrated important continuities in workplace organisation (Batstone, 1984; Millward and Stevens, 1986). It was urged that the evidence for change in workers attitudes and the composition of the working class was slight; success in the political fund ballots demonstrated political resilience. Alternatively whilst unions were 'generally less influential' at both national level and the workplace this could be reversed when economic conditions returned to 'normality' (Kelly and Richardson, 1989, 143).

By the 1990s, proponents of resilience were arguing that the view that compositional change had weakened union membership was lacking in substance. Whilst union bargaining power declined to 1986, it recovered in the late 1980s, evidenced by industrial action in 1989 and rising wages as productivity slowed (Kelly, 1990, 49).

Clarification of these issues has been bedevilled by problems of terminology, differing values and theoretical frameworks. There are inevitably different estimations of what constitutes a 'crisis' or a 'counter-revolution'; of which measure of density we should take; whether we should emphasise the position of TUC unions or all unions; of what the contemporary position should be measured against; of whether today's density is healthy – compared with France or the USA – or unhealthy – compared with 1979; of whether the pint pot is half empty or half full. Different views on the strength of the challenge the unions have faced may affect views of how well they have responded. We may reach different conclusions if we see the stuff of trade unionism as workplace organisation or if we emphasise the political dimension. Assessments which emphasise collective bargaining and which address largely the industrial fate of *the unions* may differ from those which see unions as economic and political agents of social change, *part of a movement*.

Since 1979 the situation has changed rapidly. Judgements aimed at an evolving situation are necessarily fallible. It was easier to discern change at the workplace in the early 1990s than in the mid-1980s and more evidence was available by then. There are real limits to the evidence. Small scale case studies may not be generalisable. Anybody who has seen union officers or managers filling in survey forms or even being interviewed may question the results. Power is an elusive concept and changes difficult to measure. Generalisations have to be made but the multitude of different situations and levels they encompass inevitably limits their utility.

The supporters of decline theory have been correct in insisting on the dynamic of change and its seriousness for unions. Proponents of union resilience usefully emphasise the unevenness and complexity of change and differential impact on different levels of the movement. The supporters of decline are sometimes too emphatic: the movement has been weakened not dissolved. We cannot say decline is terminal. The advocates of resilience have been too optimistic in their suggestions that change has been limited and temporary. We cannot say it will be reversed. Some proponents of qualitative change have been in danger of encouraging fatalism by over-emphasising its progress – the stern inevitability of loss of power brooks no interference. The resilience theorists have at times been unduly optimistic, downplaying real changes in the political and economic framework and in danger of breeding complacency: if 'nothing much has really changed' not a great deal needs to be done to set things right.

Debate on factors propelling decline in membership can be

dealt with first. The macroeconomic environment, particularly unemployment and growth in real wages, clearly played a role as rising wages depressed incentives to membership and rising unemployment increased the force of employer sanctions. But if the business cycle constitutes an almost complete explanation (Carruth and Disney, 1988) it is difficult to understand why membership failed to increase as unemployment declined and wage growth slowed in the late 1980s. Similarly, the argument that changes in workforce composition largely explain decline leaves the difficulty that these developments were in train in the 1970s, when membership was increasing. Whilst there may be no automatic link between these changes and membership loss some relationship seems likely given the problems unions face in organising part-time workers in new or small, scattered workplaces with high turnover (Hyman, 1991b, 623). The best view seems that of WIRS:

There can be little doubt that some of the decline in trade union membership and representation arose from compositional change. The decline of heavy manufacturing industries with their concentrations of male manual workers, the tendencies towards smaller workplaces, the steady rise of the service sector, the contraction of the public sector, the rising proportion of overseas owned workplaces, the increase in part-time employment, all these changes worked against union membership (Millward *et al.*, 1992, 356).

Again, whilst the contribution of changing state policy and legislation cannot be ignored, to attribute the entire drop in density to legislation (Freeman and Pelletier, 1990) is simply not consistent with what we know about the impact of the legislation (see Chapter 6) which took effect after, not before, serious decline in density, and ignores completely the well researched links between density and the macroeconomic framework. All of these factors as well as changes in employers' attitudes and the halting union response played *some* role (Metcalf, 1991). But we need to know something about their relative significance. The break with full employment, the continuing high level of unemployment, the brevity of the late 1980s fall in the number of jobless, the reassertion of high unemployment in the early 1990s, *this, inter-acting with continuing industrial and compositional change based on the collapse of manufacturing*, must be accorded prime importance. Changes in the labour force had been occurring in the 1960s and 1970s; but not in the context of such high unemployment. That mass unemployment was the initiator and driving force of decline is suggested by the higher rate of membership loss in the two recessions. That changes in the labour force and industry played a role, reinforced by legislation, wider state policy and by the late 1980s employer resilience, is clear from the continuing dynamic of decline between the recessions, as documented in detail in the 1984–90 WIRS.

The question of measuring change in power relations is even less tractable. Recent discussion has attempted to move beyond 'commonsense' estimations of the balance of forces between unions and employers ,based on membership figures, wage movements and strike statistics, to more rigorous frameworks. Attempts to develop Weberian definitions of power, 'the success of one group in obtaining compliance with its will regardless of the opposition of others' – the most ambitious is Martin, 1992, – have met with limited success (see also Batstone, 1988). They have produced long lists of factors to be addressed without providing the equipment to measure their interaction and assess the changing outcomes of union–employers–state transactions. We can assess broadly, and to a degree subjectively, whether employers or unions are successful in industrial struggle or controlling change in industrial relations. Achieving greater precision is elusive: it is difficult to determine with exactitude what the changing objectives are of both sides in wage negotiations or a strike, what power factors influence outcomes and how we assess them in win-lose terms.

In assessing the changing position of unions we are dealing with imperfect instruments and subjective judgements. It helps if we define our framework. In this book *we have examined unions not simply in terms of collective bargaining or workplace organisation but as the expression of social class conflict, core components of a Labour Movement operating at the workplace and nationally, in the industrial the industrial and political spheres, and possessed of an economic and social mission.* Thus estimations of political and economic change as well as industrial change weigh heavily in the scales. Who is in government, the distribution of income, the pattern of wealth ownership, the level of employment, are important, as well as average earnings. The industrial is constrained by the economic and political. Unions must be examined in their overall context not as the subjects of a limited institutional analysis of job regulation, but as the subjects of a political economy of industrial relations (Hyman, 1975, 31).

It helps, secondly, if we disentangle three related but to some extent distinct issues: union decline, change in industrial relations and change in workers' attitudes. Taking each issue in turn it appears incontrovertible that there has been a crisis of **representativeness**: with two-thirds of workers outside the bedrock organisations of the working class it is difficult to establish a claim to speak for that class, to aggregate its interests, to assert its values. In intimate relation to this, it appears incontestable that in comparison with preceding decades **union power** declined substantially and secularly from 1979 and that by the mid-1980s this decline was significant. **Labour market changes**, centrally higher unemployment and the new distribution of jobs, weakened union power, reducing membership, making recruitment harder and increasing worker dependence and insecurity. Developments in training, limiting union control over labour supply and new technology and curbing job controls had only a restricted impact. **Product market changes**, the abolition of exchange controls and EU developments, led employers to respond to stronger competitive pressures with strategies for work reorganisation and intensification of labour. **The state** was insulated from labour and more dependent on capital. Its policies supported capital's reinvigoration through deregulation and a new **legal environment** which strengthened employer sanctions against unions and the workforce and constrained their response. With the balance of power between management and unions shifting gradually and cumulatively, management opted for a strategy of compliance through wage concessions, influenced by higher profits and ability to pay. This was reinforced by firm reassertion of management prerogative which initially stopped short of derecognition but has increasingly turned to it. Higher real wages and then, in the 1990s, a second recession further strengthened both acquiescence and decline.

This represents a general assessment. Trends from 1979 increased diversity. In some enterprises and workplaces there was an increase in union power. Assessing the movement as a whole there was an erosion of power. TUC unions are the core of British trade unionism. The fact they now organise only 34% of the employed and 30% of the total workforce demonstrates the reduced legitimacy, credibility and bargaining power of a movement which seeks effectively to represent and protect the majority of the working class.

All levels of the movement are affected. The evidence suggests that whilst workplace organisation was relatively protected from the changes in political economy and power to the mid-1980s it has cumulatively felt their impact. To argue that national loss of power goes hand in hand with continuing strength at the workplace is now highly questionable. The view that 'the situation is not fundamentally different from the late 1960s when the Donovan Commission analysed shop steward power' (Martin, 1992, 178) is very wide of the mark. The workplace organisation Donovan examined was, whatever its weaknesses, assertive, confident, underpinned by full employment and *growing*. Today as we saw in Chapter 3 it is under pressure and declining.

The key union mechanisms, collective bargaining, industrial action and political involvement have suffered. Union power in previous decades was essentially negative. But the unions were able to exercise a veto over key industrial and political issues and on occasions take the initiative. From 1979 the veto was far less effective. In 1972 and 1974 the miners were able to defeat governments. In 1984–85 they were themselves crushed. Between 1969 and 1974 the unions were able to immobilise legislation from both Labour and Conservative governments. In the 1980s such resistance was brushed aside and a far more restrictive legal edifice successfully erected. In the 1960s and 1970s unions had some progressive impact on the distribution of national income. By the 1990s capital's share was greater than in 1979 and an inegalitarian and diverse dispersal of wages had occurred. In the 1960s and 1970s Harold Wilson won four elections. Since 1979 his successors have lost four, cutting the unions off from political power. The ambitions of 1979 to extend collective bargaining and refashion the structure of the enterprise appear distant memories.

The decline in power has been sustained over a decade and a half; the current is still running strongly. Evidence that union power revived in the late 1980s, limited largely to strike outcomes in 1989, ignores cumulative debilitation – as well as the weakening of collective bargaining and workplace organisation, then proceeding along with membership loss – and, if granted, represents a small, temporary resurgence in a sustained downward trajectory.

This is to argue that the unions' bargaining power has diminished not evaporated. In the 1990s the unions are still able to win battles. The very length of the retreat; the extensive remoulding that has taken place; the potent mix of political, economic and structural factors which have driven change; the failure to take advantage of the upturn that did come in the late 1980s; the fact that future upturns seem likely to be union friendly in only a limited way; all this makes reversal of present trends very difficult. Even if the political situation changes, 'normality' is very different from 1979. Across the century it is the post-war years that appear abnormal and the argument that unions will naturally revive in an upturn is dubious.

The Labour Movement has been confirmed as the bearer of a secondary, derivative, negative, limited power, severely circumscribed by economic change and state initiatives. In terms of the real, if exaggerated, gains it made in representativeness and strength in the period to 1979 it has, since the mid-1980s, been faced with *a crisis*, a turning point, a time of danger. That certain sections have maintained their bargaining power should not detract from this general judgement. However, the crisis is somewhat less acute if we turn to change in industrial relations and workers' attitudes. As we saw in Chapter 3, 'the evidence for a major shift in manual worker values is very thin' (Gallie, 1988,

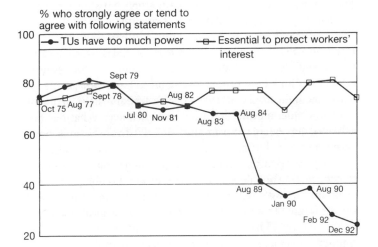

Figure 10.1 *Opinion poll attitudes to unions*
Source: MORI.

478). Workers generally have not rejected 'them and us' attitudes or reversed their views on collective organisation. There has been no crisis of worker loyalty. We must not confuse *change in the balance of forces between employers and unions with shifts in attitudes to unions or a move towards unitary conceptions on the part of workers* (Whitston and Waddington, 1992). The reach of Thatcherite values has been limited and the increase in public support for unions significant (Edwards and Bain, 1987; Rentoul, 1989). Despite the decline in industrial action, continuing strikes and the results of ballots demonstrate unions' continued ability to mobilise members (Kelly, 1990). And their popularity and position in public esteem has grown with their difficulties (see Figure 10.1). Eight out of ten people still view unions as essential to defend workers interests.

Moreover, as we saw in Chapter 3, there has been no transformation in the institutions and practices of industrial relations. There is ominous evidence of management reappraising union recognition. Management prerogative and individual bargaining have blossomed. Traditional structures have come under pressure; but no alternative union free, human resource based unitary system has come to replace them. Indeed 'HRM issues are rarely pursued to the point where the industrial relations system is threatened' (Guest, 1989, 43). In the public sector industrial relations culture has become more conflict based and adversarial. Fundamentally, Conservative administrations have weakened labour without solving the problems of capital. What has been achieved has been a power shift in industrial relations not an enduring trend shift in the British economy (Nolan, 1989).

Thus we reach the limits of change, limits somewhat short of transformation and terminal decline. Power has ebbed, driven by economic change and political coercion. Whatever its volition, retreat is real. As yet it is not propelled by ideological disaffection and desertion. The working class has not turned against the Labour Movement. This goes to the question of the permanency and stability of change. It demonstrates the limits to Conservative success. For as Lukes observes 'is it not the supreme exercise of power to get another or others to have the desires (or in this case attitudes) you want them to have?' (1974, 23).

Future strategies

The conditions for union organisation rooted in class conflict and exploitation still exist. Contemporary trends suggest workers need unions more than at any time since 1945. Arbitrariness and injustice at work are on the increase and when workers most need the protection of the law it is denied them. In 1993, a third of the workforce lacked protection against unfair dismissal as British employers refused to accept the basic standards of their EU counterparts. Insecurity, intensification of work, coercive casualisation, growing inequalities in rewards and exclusion from any voice in the destiny of the enterprise stand out as important trends eating into overall quality of life. Deregulation and the reassertion of the view of workers as 'factors of production' demands a resurgence of trade unionism. The National Association of Citizens Advice Bureaux has published widely publicised

reports on the low pay and poor working condition that charac-
terise union free workplaces. At the 1993 Conference of the
Institute of Personnel Management its director general claimed
'The creation of a permanently casualised industrial peasantry
with little protection and no stake in the future cannot be in the
interests of organisations or society'. Positively the Labour Movement can still point to the union mark-up – union members still do
better than their non-union counterparts – and the failures of
Conservative governments. No serious alternative to trade
unionism as a vehicle for representation and protection has yet
emerged. The ball is in the unions' court. Can they harness the
resentment and bitterness that has developed and ensure it produces a collective oppositionary response rather than cynicism
and demoralisation?

Non-members are not fundamentally opposed to membership;
they cite lack of availability or inability to help with their specific
problems as reasons for non-membership (see Chapter 2). There
is nothing in the nature of working part-time that disposes such
workers against membership. There is nothing intrinsic in being
female, working in an office, carrying out supervisory functions,
paying a mortgage, which is antagonistic to paying a union subscription. Small, scattered work units, part-time workers and high
turnover do make for problems. Where unions have a base matters
are facilitated: the density of part-time workers is lower than
full-time, but where part-timers are concentrated and work with
full-time staff who are union members the difference is
diminished (Bain and Price, 1983, 24; Batstone and Gourlay,
1986). If Sainsbury's now employs more staff than Ford the
average size of its supermarkets is growing and many resemble
small factories. Low pay, speed-up, lack of job security and legal
protection may in many situations provide a spur to membership:
'The staff in most stores will tell you that they are greatly over-
worked, under severe strain and feel physically and mentally
drained at the end of the working day' (Smith, 1987, 26).

Unions have to enable workers to set these problems in a
framework which demonstrates their susceptibility to collective
solutions based on union membership. These workers are not

dockers, miners or car workers. Unions have to respond to *their* work culture and *their* problems to extend awareness of mutual dependency and construct a new collective, solidaristic consciousness, which will differ in some aspects from that of past generations of trade unionists. This will require new approaches to the specific exploitation women workers, black workers, part-time and temporary staff endure, weaving this into a new fabric of mutual concern and co-operation. Recruiting members and establishing organisation requires more conscious, planned effort than in earlier decades, more resources, more strategy, more finesse. In the absence of a supportive political, legal and economic context, restoration of union fortunes to pre-1979 levels seems utopian; some retrenchment and advance appears possible. It will depend on imaginative action by the unions themselves.

Growth and renewal?
In the new environment unions have pursued new policies on recruitment and mergers. Whilst the latter may provide economies of scale they involve concentration of existing members rather than the overall growth vital to a change in union fortunes (see Chapter 1). Some writers have emphasised the key role in such growth of economic and political factors. Favourable state policy, low unemployment and rising inflation provide essential conditions for *aggregate* growth. In their absence unions will simply be competing for shares of a declining market (Bain, 1970). Others have argued that union activity can make some impact in increasing the overall number of members. In the 1960s and 1970s unions such as the TGWU and GMB grew differentially in ways which suggested a significant role for leadership and organisational factors (Undy *et al.*, 1981). Even if we accept that structural factors act as a powerful constraint on growth, effective policies are important to structure perceptions of unions, to project unions as the answer to workers' problems and enrol them in membership. Whilst the specific relationship between environment and union action remains a matter of debate, unions can have some impact on structural factors and where those are given

interact with them effectively or fruitlessly. Even agnosticism should suggest activity.

In the post-war period unions were geared up to servicing existing members not recruiting new ones. Growth from the late 1960s saw extension of membership where unions already had a base, through shop steward activity, the closed shop and check-off. Full-time officers were not significantly involved in recruitment (Bain, 1970; Robertson and Sams, 1978). This continued into the early 1980s with only around 15% of establishments with unorganised workers experiencing recruitment activity (Millward and Stevens, 1986, 70). Significant groups of workers were arguably unorganised because no attempt had been made to organise them (Beaumont and Harris, 1990). By 1986 only 23 TUC unions had recruitment officers and officers generally ranked recruitment as a low priority activity. From the mid-1980s investment in recruitment was greater. Even in unions where officers were expected to allot time to recruitment, accountability to existing members acted as a check on change (Kelly and Heery, 1989).

However in 1986 the TGWU initiated its *Link-Up* campaign aimed at low paid, temporary and part-time workers complemented by television advertising. ASTMS and TASS tried mailshot recruitment in Bracknell and Milton Keynes. The GMB in conjunction with a design consultancy produced a video magazine and launched *Flare*, the Campaign for Fair Laws and Rights in Employment, aimed at the casual workforce, as well as initiatives in the white collar sector. In 1987, USDAW joined in with a campaign aimed at similar workers. It has been estimated that 79% of unions organised a specific recruitment campaign 1985–89 compared with 39% in the early 1980s. These were often not specifically targeted and lacked dedicated officers and budgetary support. By the early 1990s there was 'little evidence to show unions have developed systematic and coherent strategies' (Mason and Bain, 1992, 44). Recruitment was given high verbal priority, less support when it came to resources. Attention to non-union establishments remained limited (TUC, 1989b). The TUC and nearly all the big unions have employed consultants to diagnose the needs of members, run surveys and market research and examine the efficiency of existing organisation.

With a union like USDAW losing 25% of its membership every year retention of members also assumed a new urgency. The TUC has emphasised the importance of new services in both recruitment and retention particularly in 'attracting members in newer industries. . .and particular groups of workers with no tradition of trade union organisation'. This approach has been strongly supported by the GMB. In 1989 the TUC introduced its *Union Law* scheme providing legal advice from 2,500 solicitors on non-employment as well as work related issues. In 1990 the Unity First Credit Card supported by 30 unions was unveiled. A wide range of unions has offered financial packages, life assurance, car insurance and discount schemes. Some claim what members want *primarily* from unions is expert advice and advocacy, increasingly in the negotiation of individual contracts. Some unions such as the IPMS have established individual contracts hot-lines. It was argued that where unions faced barriers but where workers held favourable attitudes towards them, such as hotels and catering, adequate recruitment resources were not being deployed (McCauley and Wood, 1992). Yet unions such as NUCPS which actually increased its membership in 1993 emphasised the importance of an active campaigning approach.

It has been urged that unions should give up the strike weapon and as an alternative build broad alliances to mobilise public opinion to deliver union objectives (Bolton, 1993). Others have felt that more aggressive policies may prove more attractive than the modern 'friendly society' approach, citing correlations between strike rates and growth in the past (Kelly, 1990, 59). Unions have certainly employed and extended traditional methods. Derecognised at Shell, the TGWU organised a public boycott of the company's products, leafletted garages and petitioned the European Parliament for an inquiry into the company. MSF has employed similar methods to recruit in insurance companies. The NCU produced videos for Mercury employees and respondents to their pay survey of the company consisted of a majority of non-members. As part of targeting particular groups unions have cut subscriptions for certain categories, notably the unemployed, encouraged members to seed recruitment by establishing links with schools and attempted to recruit students and those on government training schemes. The TUC in 1988 established a Youth Forum and affiliates have strengthened their structures to represent young people.

Another emphasis has been on 'organising the employer' by offering partnership and a range of benefits from single union agreements to management consultancy and industrial training. Despite criticism of the sweetheart deals and market based unionism of the AEEU many other unions have followed in their wake. The left led MSF organised seminars for employers claiming:

the growth and prosperity of the region cannot be separated from the needs of local employers to secure a long-term higher growth rate . . . investment by itself will not provide success; it will require the effective management of change. There is an urgent need to establish good in-company communications and industrial relations . . . MSF believes it has a lot to offer both sides of industry in this respect.

Recognising the crucial impact of employer attitudes on growth this strategy asserts:

if labour unions are to reverse the decline in membership they must facilitate achievement of beneficial workplace outcomes that cannot be realised in non-union work environments whilst simultaneously lessening the disparities in economic performance between union and non-union companies (Hirsch, 1989, quoted in Metcalf, 1991).

Problems and prospects
Success has been limited. Unions have singularly failed to retain unemployed members, the biggest ingredient in the haemorrhage of membership. By 1992 all but two of the top 20 TUC unions allowed unemployed workers to retain membership free or on reduced subscriptions. Whilst MSF stood out with 29,000 unemployed members – perhaps because it paid unemployment benefit – most were like BIFU, with 320 unemployed members and COHSE with 100 such members. TUC figures showed part-time

workers accounting for only 16% of the membership of the top 20 unions in 1993 – a decline in percentage terms since 1989. Individual unions have succeeded in stemming or reversing membership decline. Others have won the battle in particular years. A wide range of unions attests to the importance for them of an active campaigning approach. But in terms of overall membership figures the new emphasis on recruitment and retention has not succeeded – although we do not know how matters would stand without it.

Two things seem clear: unions are not the puppets of structural change, but environmental factors are placing firm limits on what union activity can do to repair their ravages. There are also fundamental problems with union responses to membership loss. For unions, recruitment drives aimed at organising sizeable employers will be more cost effective than individual recruitment. Employer hostility and competition between unions for groups who appear likely members can still make this kind of recruitment expensive for financially tight organisations, whilst leaving low density areas untouched. Moreover it is sometimes the financially weaker unions such as USDAW or BIFU who are well placed to recruit in low density areas but lack resources compared with 'closed' unions such as ISTC or the GPMU. Competition may involve duplication of effort, keeping subscriptions low and offering concessions to employers. Thus mergers may appear an easier, more cost effective route to growth, economies of scale and elimination of competitors. It is argued that in today's situation where growth is costly, recruitment policy is based on unions competing over easy pickings in high density areas and looking for mergers. What is lacking is expansionary attempts to recruit in low density areas rather than competition for shares of a declining market. The present approach is likely to produce continuing overall decline, at best stagnation. Greater control of harmful competition and co-ordination of recruitment is necessary (Willman, 1989).

Whether the conditions for greater regulation and closer co-operation exist is another matter. TUC moves to strengthen Bridlington and the work of the Special Review Body from 1987 were extremely useful in raising the issue of recruitment and providing detailed labour market analysis. The two pilot schemes involving TUC co-ordination mounted at Trafford Park, Manchester and London Docklands met with mixed success and have not been emulated. Union autonomy and competitive attitudes are ingrained. Cutbacks in TUC activities raise questions about future initiatives. Recruitment does not figure in the slimmed down list of TUC core functions. The 1993 legislation undermines its regulatory functions.

There are also problems with the financial services strategy. Many of the workers unions need to recruit do not inhabit the world of consumerism. Members with money to spare may prefer specialist bodies. If they want these services from their unions there is no evidence that they want them at the expense of what they regard as the unions' pivotal function: bargaining to improve their wages and conditions of employment. Unless the unions can effectively assert their role as successful bargainers, credit cards, videos and Filofax are unlikely to reverse their decline. Non-employment benefits exercise only marginal influence on members' reasons for joining unions. New members are not attracted by non-work services and demonstrate little interest in them (Chapter 4). Emphasis on services should be an addition to existing union functions not a substitute for them. Unions have to be essentially fighters not friendly societies. To voluntarily transform themselves into servicing organisations like BUPA or the AA, as advocated by some, (Bassett and Cave, 1993) would not be to solve the problem but to give up on its solution.

Past periods of union growth 1916–20, 1968–74 were fuelled by militant action (Cronin, 1979). But today's constraints are very different from those applying then. The favourable economic and political conditions of the late 1960s and 1970s have evaporated, the very factors fuelling decline constrain aggressive action. An increase in successful militancy and effective publicising of it would undoubtedly provide the unions with a fillip. Those who urge the replacement of industrial action with alliances with the churches and Conservatives to mobilise public opinion have only to look at what finally transpired in the 1993 dispute over pit closures. Certainly the generation of militancy and its relationship to workers' perceptions of trade unionism, and wider, to the development of radical or conservative politics, requires more detailed investigation.

Attempting to increase membership by offering management increasingly committed collaboration also raises problems. Its implementation has not provided an antidote to membership loss. Most single union deals have involved no guarantee of membership and in companies like Nissan density has remained low. Of itself the beauty contest suggests union weakness. Employer sponsorship of a union has a price. If unions accept a junior partnership on management's terms, alienation of membership and decline in its own resources, ability to act and utility to management can occur. In the end, the union has little to sell; for its ability to secure membership compliance is strained. Many attempts to seed the enterprise culture and develop HRM bypass unions. Many employers do not see the need for a weak, semi-independent subaltern and reject partnership with the unions. The stance of employers will undoubtedly remain crucial to membership trends. There are still more effective ways of securing employer compliance than the compromise of essential adversarial functions. If unions become part of management they may secure greater legitimacy with the employer at the cost of support from the employee.

The facts of decline have proved stubborn in the face of initiatives informed by many of these approaches. By the 1990s the limited success of direct efforts led unions to turn once more to support for legal procedures to be introduced by a future Labour government in line with the EU Social Charter. The intractability of economic and political factors highlighted again the importance of a friendly government.

Alternatives

The strength of Labourism has been its emphasis on an all embracing movement, mobilising the values of collectivism, equality, solidarity and unity as an integrating force for class action. It is under pressure from the factors discussed in this book, economic change, the growing heterogeneity of the labour force and fragmentary impulses induced by political and industrial weakness. Recent decades have thus placed tremendous strains on Labourism. But it has always been characterised by eclecticism, contradiction and confusion in philosophy and practice. It has asserted the independence and autonomy of unions and the need to transform capitalism, but has sought close collaboration with employers and state. The unions have demanded greater involvement in the running of the enterprise but have backed away from formal mechanisms for participation. They have accepted the political–industrial division and the sanctity of the constitution and worked closely with capital but have employed anti-capitalist rhetoric and at times mobilised against the state. The political impulse of their leaders has been towards corporatism but they have been historically hamstrung by the tension between demands for free collective bargaining and demands for more economic planning which would limit collective bargaining. Labourism has always uneasily combined the practice of competing philosophies of trade unionism which have surfaced in recent years and inform the approaches discussed in the previous section. Discussion of these may help unions to address and reformulate their role.

Much advice offered to unions would see them move towards **business unionism**, best exemplified by the AEEU. We can recognise strands of business unionism in recent TUC statements which deny inherent conflict between capital and labour, stress partnership and advertise collective bargaining as a vehicle for increased productivity and work restructuring (TUC, 1993). In this view many of the components of the union-hostile environment are irreversible. They bring Britain into line with other countries and have to be accepted and exploited if unions are to survive. Trade unionism is not so much a movement as a business which has to sell its services to management and its members in a professional competitive fashion. Unions have to explicitly recognise their dependence on the enterprise, the centrality of profit and market performance and the harmful nature of conflict. If unions co-operate in flexibility and training initiatives and educate their members in the imperatives of the market more jobs will be secured; greater efficiency will trickle-down in higher wages and better conditions. Unions must compete for members. They are service organisations not activist based democracies. Replacing class conflict with the market they should eschew extensive involvement in politics. They may incline to one party but should not be too closely identified with it.

Business unionism cuts with the grain. It is linked to tendencies to fragmentation and heterogeneity in the Labour Movement and increased competitive pressures on enterprises. The problems are fundamental and perennial: it is a strategy for more sectionalism and greater dissolution of the Labour Movement, whilst there are serious doubts as to whether employers want the partnership they are offered. With workers' fortunes tied to markets, the strong survive, the weak go to the wall. The reality of conflict at the workplace and the consequent necessity for independent organisation has stubbornly reasserted itself. Business unionism by progressively alienating union from members, through its actions as an arm of management, progressively atrophies the sinews of mobilisation. Others will come to take up the independent oppositionary role which has proved necessary and resilient through history.

Since 1979 **corporatist trade unionism** has continued to assert itself. The election of a Labour government more responsive to the unions could, it is argued, qualitatively improve their situation. In the early 1980s hopes were high for a new improved Social Contract. Chastened by Thatcherism trade unionists would realise that the last Labour government failed not because of the inadequacies of corporatism but because it was not corporatist enough. If the government were to offer reflation, full employment, economic planning and the unions firmer control over sectional militancy the electorate would respond. By the 1990s hopes of a 1970s style return to the corridors of power had dimmed, but many trade unionists still believed that a progressive future involved a further experiment in corporatism.

The strength of this view lies in the understanding that for the unions Labour still represents an improvement over the Conservatives and the complexion of government is still important to their future. Corporatist approaches assert the unity of the Labour Movement and carry the promise of counteracting tendencies to fragmentation. Much would hang on the content of political exchange and there is no past tradition of success to draw upon. Labour's policy-making and constitutional change has been informed precisely by the desire to avoid any significant role for the unions in government should it be returned to power. Changes in economics, industrial structure and in collective bargaining make any formal, developed incomes policy unlikely. The return of Labour would help the unions. The recreation of any fully fledged corporatism or even the 1974–79 model seems unlikely. Milder forms influenced by the EU remain on the agenda.

The influence of Marxist and socialist conceptions of trade unionism waned with militancy in the 1980s. Within this tradition Lenin has lasted better than the 'optimists'. Recent Marxist analysis veers towards syndicalism. It is too focused on industrial action. Placing its faith in mass strikes as the engine of insurgency it neglects the broader political plane and the *construction* of political consciousness before and during strikes. For example, if Marxists entered the mass strike situation from a position of powerful political purchase with revolutionaries organised in a strong party, entrenched in Parliament, in key positions in the unions, the education system and the mass media, the position would be dramatically different than if they entered such a situation as a negligible force – the position which has prevailed throughout recent history. In other words there is always the need for a strategy which combines support for industrial militancy with broader encroaching control. If socialists are not able to win converts in significant fashion outside the situation of mass industrial action, their ability to act within it through a powerful party capable of mobilising in all sectors of society will be qualitatively diminished.

We have seen since the 1970s a weakening of the limited purchase Marxists had in the unions. In the 1980s in the absence of any strong Marxist political current the cudgels were taken up by Arthur Scargill and the NUM. **Semi-syndicalist trade unionism** embodied the view that major industrial action could, almost of itself, transform the economic and political situation leftwards and produce a change of government. It emphasised the educational power of leadership and industrial action. It was based upon a belief in the willingness of workers to respond to strong leadership despite unfavourable economic and political circumstances, a favourable view of the potential power of labour in action in relation to capital and the state and a rejection of the distinction between the industrial and political. It urged that trade unionists should exploit all opportunities to develop and generalise industrial action which could remove the Conservative government and replace it with a left led Labour alternative.

The hold of semi-syndicalist unionism was based upon the balance of forces prevailing in the 1960s and 1970s. Its influence in the 1980s was based on an attempt to veto the ending of the post-war compromise. With full employment, a 'weak' state and the availability of minimal solidarity it was able to score successes, although its viability as a weapon of social change was limited by the lack of complementary socialist encroachment in the political arena. The impact of the new political economy of Thatcherism eroded the base for mobilisation and the assertiveness of workplace organisation, diminished solidarity and provided the basis for a 'strong' state response. The destruction of the NUM, the conduct of the pit closures dispute of 1993 and the general ebbing of industrial action demonstrate the weakness of militant trade unionism in the 1990s.

In any prescription for revival the questions of workplace organisation, union democracy, workers' participation and legal reform demand attention. Strong workplace organisation has been a healthy feature of the union landscape important to demo- cracy, participation and power. It seems to this writer that any sustained regeneration of labour will required renewal at the workplace and a new strategic bargain with the Labour Party as part of the programme of a future government. It will require reconstruction of more politically conscious, participative, solidaristic shop steward organisation with wider horizons than in the past and workplace organisation which nurtures in its members a sharp sense of involvement in a wider movement. This has several dimensions. Workplace organisation would be more extensive horizontally, with effective links, compared with the past, across the employing enterprise and the industry; and vertically, with greater articulation between the workplace and union. This could only be based on a new reconciliation of the interplay of sectional and general, of independence and unity in the construction and assertion of the general and strategic interest of labour against the immediate and particular. This would require a new programme for economic renovation centred on workers' participation, redistribution of income and wealth and fundamental reform of the institutions of British society. It would require a bargain agreed in advance of government with the Labour Party embracing employment, wages, taxation and the welfare state. Such a project would necessitate reform and recasting of current labour law in the form of a charter of workers' rights as part of wider constitutional change. It would involve a recharging of activism and mobilisation and a rejection of current conceptions of intra-union relations increasingly based on the polarity of professional experts and passive members. If we define trade unionism as a commodity to be sold rather than a responsibility of class, community and citizenship we will debilitate collectivism and democracy.

The Labour Movement urgently needs to rework past definitions of the general interest to confront not only economic exploitation but oppression in all its forms in and beyond the workplace. Unions cannot – nor should they try to – transform themselves into community groups or political parties. Their central economic functions defending workers in the production process are necessary and honourable. Accepting that class remains the dominant antagonism in society they possess a potential power which the new social movements, community, environmental and consumer groups, lack. Unions have often lacked in turn the keen appreciation of oppression these groups possess. Alliances could be mutually fruitful and play a role in union resurgence.

The prospects for these kind of changes are, it has to be said, far from good. They would involve not the dashing cavalry charge, the sudden major explosion of discontent that dissolves difficulties but the slow, patient reconstruction of the labour movement that exists now, taking advantage of such small explosions as are likely to occur. As we have seen there is little evidence of resurgence at the workplace; particularism, decentralisation, and enterprise confinement are important tendencies whilst many union leaders, enthusiastically embracing business union conceptions of internal democracy, see little role for strong workplace organisation and activism.

The USA

Many seeking answers to the dilemmas of the unions have looked abroad. The emphasis on financial services and TUC co-ordinated recruitment have come from the USA. Can we see the future of British trade unions in America today? If so it looks like a future of declining influence. Membership dropped from 22 million in 1975 to 16 million by 1990 with density today at around 15%. More than 60% of members work in 5 industries: state employment, construction, transport, private services and distribution. There is a trend to deunionisation, with trade unionism confined to the traditional industrial states in the north east and mid-west. The USA encountered much of the structural and compositional changes Britain has recently faced earlier and more intensively. Unlike the British unions the Americans are not facing a sudden trauma. Real union growth only developed in the 1930s when the 'New Deal' produced the National Recovery Act 1933 and the Wagner Act providing bargaining rights. Membership at 4 million in 1935 had grown to 14 million by 1945. But like their Japanese counterparts American workers suffered a frontal assault from employers in the post-war years. The Taft-Hartley legislation restricted industrial action. Decline continued during the long boom. Density fell in the 1950s, 1960s and 1970s. A weakened trade unionism failed to break out of the areas in which it possessed a historic hold. Today less than 10% of private sector workers carry union cards.

America has always been the heartland of business unionism. George Meany, long-time President of the AFL-CIO, regularly declared his love of the profit system and abhorrence of strikes. He solved long ago the problems of British unions: 'Frankly I used to worry about the membership, about the size of the membership. But quite a few years ago I just stopped worrying about it because to me it doesn't make any difference' (Moody, 1988, 125). Business unionism depends for success on high profits. When these decline, collective agreements embody concessions and 'givebacks' from the workforce. In 1988 three-quarters of all agreements covering more than 1,000 workers contained concessions. US Labour has never built its own party although it possesses links with the Democrats. Dominated by business unionism it has never seen itself as a social movement. It has enthusiastically embraced the *status quo* and the consequences of limited internal democracy can be seen from the fact that three of the last five Presidents of the Teamsters have served prison sentences. As an example of the limits of business unionism the USA would seem to provide lessons of what to avoid rather than emulate.

Sweden

If supporters of the market have looked to the USA, supporters of corporatism have traditionally looked to the Nordic countries. Sweden was long characterised as the most successful country in the world with a per capita income second only to Switzerland. At the centre of its industrial relations were centralised negotiations between employers and unions. Framework agreements related wages to full employment, price stability, economic growth and income distribution. Solidaristic wage policy related increases to the position of employers in the export industries. The agreed rates were then paid across industry keeping wages higher than they might have been and penalising employers in the less efficient enterprises, whilst restraining wage growth in the more competitive, dynamic, export sectors.

With more than 80% of all employees union members this

system worked. The government outlined broad economic goals staying on the sidelines whilst LO, the TUC, bargained with the SAF, the major employers' association, applying pressure as required. Lower level agreements were negotiated within the national framework and whilst there was wage drift it was not experienced as a major problem. Stability based on a small labour force, neutrality in two world wars and the presence of the union supported Social Democrats in government uninterruptedly until the 1970s was enhanced by the insider role given Swedish trade unions in administering unemployment benefit, and later profit sharing arrangements. The Swedish example demonstrated that it was possible for unions, even with a relatively small public sector and an economy organised on market lines, to achieve agreement with capital and the state which exchanged co-operation for substantial economic concessions, full employment and a high social wage.

From the 1970s the problems of the world economy increasingly affected Sweden. The public sector, employing an increasing proportion of the labour force, exerted more pressure on wages. Export oriented employers were more sensitive to the trade cycle and exporting capital abroad, wage drift and inflation all increased and there were tensions between LO and the Social Democrats who were out of office 1976–82. In the 1980s internationalisation of the Swedish economy proceeded apace. With important markets in Germany and Britain key employers turned to the EU, whilst multinational mergers and deals increased. From 1983 centralised negotiations came under pressure; by 1988 they had broken down with wage drift at record levels. In 1990 the government introduced regressive tax reforms and an LO backed wage freeze. Discontent and world recession contributed to the return of a Conservative government.

Nonetheless, the successes of the Swedish approach in maintaining full employment, economic growth, high rewards and high union membership are undeniable. Since 1985 growth has fallen behind and inflation exceeded the OECD average. But through the recessions of the 1970s and 1980s full employment was maintained. It stayed at under 2% until 1990 when far higher levels took hold. The Swedish experience holds lessons as an example of the possibilities of combining a strong working class movement, curtailing the power of capital, with economic growth. Its success in reconciling full employment, economic efficiency, high wages and rising union membership merits attention as an alternative to the deregulated market model of Japan and the USA. Nevertheless we are talking about a working population of 3 million in a country with an untypical history. With tendencies to globalisation, the impact of recession and membership of the EU limiting future choices, the relevance of the Swedish case to other, different countries remains questionable.

Conclusions

Decline in union power has produced important changes, but has not yet achieved the qualitative transformation of industrial relations or the attitudes of the labour force which figures in government rhetoric. As idea and reality the Labour Movement has been weakened. It remains a strong social force – a force for good in society. But events have confirmed the limits of its power, the reactive nature of that power and its powerful tendency to adapt to change within capitalism. Economic, political and industrial trends continue to militate against trade unionism. New approaches are important if a descent to US levels of unionisation and consequent remoulding of industrial relations are to be avoided.

Tendencies to business unionism gain strength from increasingly competitive markets and internal differentiation in unions and industry, centrally from the importance of employer support if loss of membership is to be arrested. It is doubtful if business unionism is an answer for more than a minority. In a situation of continuing economic decline the margin for general concessions to trade unionists is slender. It has an obvious attraction in certain market situations, particularly for groups of skilled and secure workers and could provide protected enclaves on the model of the craft trade unionists of the last century or the American unions today. However, as the American practice of concessions and layoffs demonstrate, those who live by the market die by the market. Business unionism is as unlikely to benefit the majority of workers in the twenty-first century as craft trade unionism did in the nineteenth century. A generalisation of business unionism would appear a prescription for numerical decline, continued disaggregation of the Labour Movement, as employees identify with employers and markets not their fellow workers, and a reduction in the political influence and social weight of the unions.

In this light, corporatism appears to many a more attractive proposition. The problem is that whilst business unionism flows with the tide towards employer and market, corporatism, with the state and regulation at its heart, runs against it. Possessing less power and less cohesion, unions are less attractive partners for co-option. There is far less zest for state regulation of industry, greater need to compete to attract capital and less need for the state to institutionalise union strength, now sapped. The decline in union coverage, controlled decentralised bargaining, the weakening of shop stewards, the heterogeneity of the labour force and its adjustment to market imperatives argue against resurrection of concertation. In many countries the period to the early 1980s saw successful corporatist-style arrangements produce lower levels of unemployment and industrial conflict, and real increases in the social wage compared with countries with free market arrangements. Since the 1980s, corporatism has waned: the difficulties can be seen from the Swedish experience. In Britain free collective bargaining has benefited many workers. It is questionable whether the unions and the TUC would be able to deliver on any bargain over wages which required control of workers who feel they do better in an unregulated system. Even in the 1960s and 1970s corporatist arrangements possessed instability and a limited lifespan, whilst governments operating incomes policies were swiftly put to the electoral sword.

Nonetheless if return to the 1970s is unlikely, any future Labour government will involve the unions in formal consultative processes such as the National Economic Assessment promised in the 1992 election. The Conservatives' resort to public sector wage restraint shows the limits of market regulation. It is possible political change could produce a modified form of corporatism which could involve unions in discussion of wages, employment legislation, labour market policy, training, income distribution and the development of EU directives. For the unions optimism must be centred on their restored popularity and the possibility of Labour in government.

The maintenance, indeed reassertion, of a strong political dimension seems essential and the return of a Labour government indispensable to any significant improvement in the position of the unions. Many on the left see this as a catalyst to a revival of militancy. It would undoubtedly provide a shot in the arm for socialists but in all probability as the prelude to a renewal of socialist reconstruction rather than a recipe for speedy resurgence.

Some argue militancy could push a Labour government left-wards. Maybe. But if the left have failed to elect a Labour government determined to carry out a radical programme, why should they then be able to infuse money militancy with socialist consciousness? Why should a right-wing Labour government be pushed leftwards by a strike wave? More likely is a re-run of 1978–79. An alternative constructive scenario would see a successful period of party–union co-operation. The developments of recent decades cannot be easily undone. The problem for socialists is that they are faced with an overwhelming majority in the unions whose horizons are sturdily bound by the economic and social *status quo*, and a majority of the conscious political minority whose perspective remains one of mild reform. To change this is the work not of years, but of decades. Moreover, a Britain moving in the direction of socialism would face massive economic and political difficulties from a hostile world.

These constraints may not be insuperable. They must be confronted, not ignored or minimised. The problem for socialists remains how to successfully transform the consciousness of trade unionists who want more out of capitalism and are far from convinced, particularly after the history of the regimes in the USSR and Eastern Europe, of the need for an alternative. Even disillusion with the *status quo* is constrained by a realistic understanding of the sheer difficulty of creating a more democratic economy and society. None of this is decisive in terms of politics. We may feel the capitalist system is so inefficient and unjust as to make its replacement an imperative whatever the odds. It does raise fundamental questions about the role of unions in socialist politics.

There are no easy answers to the problems afflicting British unions. A diversity of response is likely. Particular groups of workers will maintain strong organisation and bargaining power but the struggle between unity and sectionalism, solidaristic movement and fragmented bargaining in British trade unionism is tilting towards the latter. Whether decline and disaggregation can be arrested remain conjectural. What is clear is that the present predicament of the Labour Movement is not susceptible to glib solutions. Alternatives to the *status quo* appear to possess limited resonance and face powerful constraints. Although there is deep disillusion with neo-Conservatism the tendencies it has unleashed still hold the stage. The future of trade unionism remains uncertain and insecure. What is clear is that the future will not be simply determined by economic and social forces. The activity of working people, their struggle to control capital and the market and create a new collective solidarity, will remain central.

Further reading

Phillip Bassett, *Strike Free: New Industrial Relations in Britain*, Macmillan, 1986, and Phillip Bassett and Alan Cave, *All for One: The Future of the Unions*, Fabian Society, 1993, assert the case for the new individualism and a business union approach. John Kelly's *Trade Unions and Socialist Politics*, Verso, 1988, argues a very different view and provides stimulating analysis of many of the difficulties unions face. Roderick Martin's *Bargaining Power*, Clarendon Press, 1992, attempts to pin down the elusive concept and assess the current balance between unions and employers. Michael Goldfield, *The Decline of Organised Labour in the United States*, University of Chicago Press, 1988, Kim Moody, *An Injury to All: The Decline of American Unionism*, Verso, 1988, and Thomas Geoghegan *Which Side Are You On?*, Farrar Straus, 1991, provide useful analyses of the situation in the USA. Walter Korpi, *The Working Class in*

Welfare Capitalism, Routledge & Kegan Paul, 1978, and Anders Kjellberg, 'Sweden: can the model survive?' in Anthony Ferner and Richard Hyman, eds., *Industrial Relations in the New Europe*, Blackwell, 1992, detail the background and position in Sweden. Marino Regini, ed., *The Future of Labour Movements*, Sage, 1992, provides stimulating analyses of the issues facing unions in Western Europe and North America.

References

B. Abel-Smith and R. Stevens, 1967, *Lawyers and the Courts*, Heinemann

ACAS, 1980, *Industrial Relations Handbook*, HMSO

ACAS, *Annual Reports*, 1986–1991

P. Ackers, M. Marchington, A. Wilkinson and J. Goodman, 1992, 'The use of cycles? Explaining employee involvement in the 1990s', *Industrial Relations Journal*, 23, 4

V. Allen, 1954, *Power in Trade Unions*, Longman

V. Allen, 1957, *Trade Union Leadership*, Longman

V. Allen, 1971, *The Sociology of Industrial Relations*, Longman

P. Anderson, 1965, 'Origins of the present crisis', in R. Blackburn and A. Cockburn, eds, 1967

P. Anderson, 1967, 'The limits and possibilities of trade union action', in R. Blackburn and A. Cockburn, eds, 1967

P. Anderson, 1987, 'Figures of descent', *New Left Review*, 161

P. Armstrong, A. Glynn and J. Harrison, 1984, *Capitalism Since World War II*, Fontana

M. Artis and D. Cobham, 1991, *Labour's Economic Policies 1974–79*, Manchester University Press

K. Ascher, 1987, *The Politics of Privatisation*, Macmillan

J. Atkinson, 1985, 'The changing corporation', in D. Clutterbuck, ed., 1985

S. Auerbach, 1990, *Legislating for Conflict*, Clarendon Press

S. Auerbach, 1993, 'Mrs Thatcher's Labour Laws: slouching towards Utopia?', *Political Quarterly*, 64, 1

B. Avis, 1990, 'British Steel: a case for the decentralization of collective bargaining', *Human Resource Management Journal*, 1, 1

R. Bacon and W. Eltis, 1976, *Britain's Economic Problem*, Macmillan

L. Baddon, L. Hunter, J. Hyman, J. Leopold and H. Ramsay, 1989, *People's Capitalism?*, Routledge

G. Bain, 1970, *The Growth of White Collar Unionism*, Oxford University Press

G. Bain, ed., 1983, *Industrial Relations in Britain*, Blackwell

G. Bain and F. Elsheikh, 1976, *Union Growth and the Business Cycle*, Blackwell

G. Bain and R. Price, 1983, 'Union growth: dimensions, determinants and destiny', in G. Bain, ed., 1983

J. Banks, 1974, *Trade Unionism*, Collier, McMillan

B. Baranouin, 1986, The *European Labour Movement and European Integration*, Pinter

D. Barnes and E. Reid, 1980, *Government and Trade Unions, the British Experience 1964–79*, Heinemann

P. Bassett, 1986, *Strike Free: New Industrial Relations in Britain*, Macmillan

P. Bassett, 1991, 'Unions and Labour in the 1980s and 1990s', in B. Pimlott and C. Cook, eds, 1991

P. Bassett and A. Cave, 1993, *All for One: The Future of the Unions*, Fabian Society

E. Batstone, 1984, *Working Order*, Blackwell

E. Batstone, 1988, 'The frontier of control', in D. Gallie, ed., 1988

E. Batstone, I. Boraston and S. Frenkel, 1977, *Shop Stewards in Action*, Blackwell

E. Batstone, A. Ferner and M. Terry, 1983, *Unions on the Board*, Blackwell

E. Batstone and S. Gourlay, 1986, *Unions, Unemployment and Innovation*, Blackwell

J. Beale, 1982, *Getting it Together: Women as Trade Unionists*, Pluto Press

P. Beaumont, 1992, 'Annual review article: 1991', *British Journal of Industrial Relations*, 30, 1

P. Beaumont and R. Harris, 1990, 'Union recruitment and organising attempts in Britain in the 1980s', *Industrial Relations Journal*, 21, 4

A. Bennett and S. Smith-Gavine, 1988, 'The percentage utilisation of labour index', in D. Bosworth, ed., 1988

H. Beynon, 1973, 1984, *Working for Ford*, Penguin

H. Beynon, 1983, 'The politics of the British factory', *Critique*, 16

H. Beynon, ed. 1985, *Digging Deeper: Issues in the Miners' Strike*, Verso

T. Bilton, K. Bonnet, P. Jones, M. Stanworth, K. Sheard and A. Webster, 1986, *Introductory Sociology*, Macmillan

D. Bird, 1993, 'International comparisons of labour disputes in 1993', *Employment Gazette*, December

R. M. Blackburn, 1967, *Union Character and Social Class*, Batsford

R. Blackburn and A. Cockburn, eds, 1967, *The Incompatibles*, Penguin

R. Blackwell and P. Lloyd, 1989, 'New managerialism in the civil service', in R. Mailly *et al.*, eds, 1989

D. Blanchflower and A. Oswald, 1988, 'The economic effects of trade unions', *Employment Institute*, 3, 10

P. Blyton, 1992, 'Steel: a classic case of industrial relations change in Britain', *Journal of Management Studies*, 29, 5

P. Blyton and P. Turnbull, eds, 1992, *Reassessing Human Resource Management*, Sage

G. Bolton, 1993, *Unions: A New Direction*, Democratic Left

A. Booth, 1985, 'The free rider problem and a social custom model of trade union membership', *Quarterly Journal of Economics*, 100, 1

D. Bosworth, ed., 1988, *Working Below Capacity*, Macmillan

P. Brannen, 1983, *Authority and Participation in Industry*, Batsford

H. Braverman, 1974, *Labor and Monopoly Capital*, Monthly Review Press

British North American Committee, 1988, *New Departures in Industrial Relations*

C. Brown, 1984, *Black and White Britain*, Heinemann

W. Brown, ed. 1981, *The Changing Contours of British Industrial Relations*, Blackwell

W. Brown, 1986, 'The changing role of trade unions in the management of labour', *British Journal of Industrial Relations*, 24, 2

W. Brown, 1993, 'The contraction of collective bargaining in Britain', *British Journal of Industrial Relations*, 31, 2

W. Brown and S. Wadhwani, 1990, 'The economic effects of industrial relations legislation', *National Institute Economic Review*, 31, February

W. Brown and J. Walsh, 1991, 'Pay determination in Britain in the 1980s: the anatomy of decentralisation', *Oxford Review of Economic Policy*, 7, 1

H. Phelps Brown, 1966, 'The influence of trade unions and collective bargaining on pay levels and real wages', in W. McCarthy, ed., 1985

H. Phelps Brown, 1990, 'The counter-revolution of our time', *Industrial Relations*, 21, 1

Lord Bullock, 1977, *Report of a Committee of Inquiry on Industrial Democracy*, HMSO

B. Burkitt and D. Bowers, 1979, *Trade Unions and the Economy*, Macmillan

D. Butler and D. Kavanagh, 1992, *The British General Election of 1992*, Macmillan

A. Campbell and J. McIlroy, 1981, *Getting Organised*, Pan Books

A. Carruth and R. Disney, 1988, 'Where have two million trade union members gone?', *Economica*, 55

A. Carruth and A. Oswald, 1989, *Pay Determination and Industrial Prosperity*, Oxford University Press

CBI, 1987, *Change at Work*

P. Cecchini, 1988, *The European Challenge: The Benefits of a Single Market*, Wildwood House

M. Chadwick, 1983, 'The recession and industrial relations: a factory approach', *Employee Relations*, 5, 5

E. Chell, 1983, 'Political perspectives on worker participation', in C. Crouch and F. Heller, eds, 1983

J. Child, 1969, *British Management Thought*, Allen & Unwin

J. Child, ed., 1973, *Man and Organisation*, Allen & Unwin

J. Clark and Lord Wedderburn, 1983, 'Modern labour law: problems, functions and policies', in Lord Wedderburn *et al.*, eds, 1983

K. Clarke, 1987, 'Speech to the Industrial Society', *Employment Gazette*, May

T. Clarke, 1977, 'Industrial democracy: the institutionalised suppression of industrial conflict', in T. Clarke and L. Clements, eds, 1977

T. Clarke and L. Clements, eds, 1977, *Trade Unions under Capitalism*, Fontana

T. Claydon, 1989, 'Union derecognition in Britain in the 1980s', *British Journal of Industrial Relations*, 27, 2

H. Clegg, 1960, *A New Approach to Industrial Democracy*, Blackwell

H. Clegg, 1970, *The System of Industrial Relations in Great Britain*, Blackwell

H. Clegg, 1976, *Trade Unionism under Collective Bargaining*, Blackwell

H. Clegg, 1979, *The Changing System of Industrial Relations in Great Britain*, Blackwell

T. Cliff and C. Barker, 1966, *Incomes Policy, Legislation and Shop Stewards*, London Industrial Shop Stewards' Defence Committee

R. Clifton and C. Tatton-Brown, 1979, *Impact of Employment on Small Firms*, Department of Employment Research Paper 6

D. Clutterbuck (ed.), 1985, *New Patterns of Work*, Gower

D. Coates, 1980, *Labour in Power*, Longman

D. Coates, 1983, 'The question of trade union power', in D. Coates and G. Johnston, ed., 1983

D. Coates, 1989, *The Crisis of Labour: Industrial Relations and the State in Contemporary Britain*, Philip Allan

D. Coates, 1994, *The Question of UK Decline, the Economy, State and Society*, Harvester

D. Coates and G. Johnston, eds 1983, *Socialist Arguments*, Martin Robertson

D. Coates, G. Johnston and R. Bush, 1985, *A Socialist Anatomy of Britain*, Polity Press

D. Coates and J. Hillard, eds, 1986, *The Economic Decline of Modern Britain: The Debate Between Right and Left*, Wheatsheaf

S. Cohen and P. Fosh, 1988, *You are the Union*, WEA

T. Colling, 1991, 'Privatisation and the management of industrial relations in the electricity industry', *Industrial Relations Journal*, 22, 2

T. Colling, 1993, 'Contracting public services', *Human Resource Management Journal*, 3, 4

H. Collins, 1982, 'Capitalist discipline and corporatist law, II', *Industrial Law Journal*, 11, 3

Commission for Racial Equality, 1992, *Part of the Union?*, CRE

P. Cosgrave, 1985, *Thatcher: The First Term*, Bodley Head

D. Cox, ed., 1992, *Facing the Future*, University of Nottingham

P. Cressey, J. Eldridge, J. MacInnes and G. Norris, 1981, *Industrial Democracy and Participation: A Scottish Study*, Department of Employment

I. Crewe and M. Harrop, eds, 1989, *Political Communications: The General Election Campaign of 1987*, Cambridge University Press

R. Crompton and G. Jones, 1984, *White Collar Proletariat*, Macmillan

J. Cronin, 1979, *Industrial Conflict in Modern Britain*, Croom Helm

M. Cross, 1988, 'Changes in working practices in UK manufacturing 1981–88', *Industrial Relations Review and Report*, 415

C. Crouch, 1982, *Trade Unions: The Logic of Collective Action*, Fontana

C. Crouch and F. Heller, eds, 1983, *Organisational Democracy and Political Processes*, Wiley

J. Curran, 1989, *Employment and Employment Relations in the Small Firm*, Kingston Polytechnic

P. Curwen, 1986, *Public Enterprise: A Modern Approach*, Wheatsheaf

W. Daniel, 1987, *Workplace Industrial Relations and Technical Change*, Pinter

W. Daniel and E. Stilgoe, 1978, *The Impact of Employment Protection Laws*, Policy Studies Institute

W. Daniel and N. Millward 1983, *Workplace Industrial Relations in Britain*,

Heinemann

J. O'Connell Davidson, 1990, 'The commercialisaton of employment relations: the case of the water industry', *Work, Employment and Society*, 4, 4

P. Davies and M. Freedland, 1993, *Labour Legislation and Public Policy*, Clarendon Press

Department of Employment, 1983, *Democracy in Trade Unions*, HMSO

Department of Employment, 1992, *People, Jobs and Opportunity*, HMSO

F. Devine, 1992, *Affluent Workers Revisited: Privatism and the Working Class*, Edinburgh University Press

L. Dickens, M. Jones, B. Weekes and M. Hart, 1985, *Dismissed: A Study of Unfair Dismissal and the Industrial Tribunal System*, Blackwell

L. Dickens and G. Bain, 1986, 'A duty to bargain? Union recognition and information disclosure', in R. Lewis, ed., 1986

R. Disney, 1990, 'Explanations of the decline in trade union density in Britain: an appraisal', *British Journal of Industrial Relations*, 28, 2

M. Dodgson and R. Martin, 1987, 'Trade union policies on new technology', *New Technology, Work and Employment*, 2, 1

G. Dorfman, 1977, 'From the inside looking out – the TUC in the EEC', *Journal of Common Market Studies*, 15, 4

G. Dorfman, 1983, *British Trade Unionism against the Trades Union Congress*, Macmillan

J. Due, J. Madsen and C. Stroby-Jensen, 1991, 'The social dimension: convergence or diversification in the single European market?', *Industrial Relations Journal*, 22, 2

P. Dunleavy and C. Husbands, 1985, *British Democracy at the Crossroads*, Allen & Unwin

S. Dunn and J. Gennard, 1984, *The Closed Shop in British Industry*, Macmillan

J. Eaton and C. Gill, 1983, *The Trade Union Directory*, Pluto Press

T. Eccles, 1981, *Under New Management*, Pan Books

M. Edwardes, 1984, *Back From the Brink*, Pan Books

P. Edwards, 1985, 'Myth of the macho manager', *Personnel Management*, April

P. Edwards, 1987, *Managing the Factory*, Blackwell

P. Edwards and G. Bain, 1988, 'Why are trade unions becoming more popular?', *British Journal of Industrial Relations*, 26, 3

P. Edwards and P. Marginson, 1988, 'Trade unions, pay bargaining and industrial action', in P. Marginson *et al.*, 1988

P. Edwards and C. Whitston, 1991, 'Workers are working harder: effort and shopfloor relations in the 1980s', *British Journal of Industrial Relations*, 29, 4

R. Edwards, 1979, *Contested Terrain*, Heinemann

J. Elgar and R. Simpson, 1993, *The Impact of the Law on Industrial Disputes in the 1980s*, Centre for Economic Performance, LSE

T. Elger, 1990, 'Technological innovation and work reorganisation in British manufacturing in the 1980s: continuity, intensification or transformation?', *Work Employment and Society*, special issue

T. Elger, 1991, 'Task flexibility and the intensification of labour in UK manufacturing in the 1980s', in A. Pollert, ed., 1991

P. Elias and K. Ewing, 1982, 'Economic torts and labour law', *Cambridge Law Journal*, 41, 2

J. England, 1981, 'Shop stewards in Transport House: a comment upon the incorporation of the rank and file', *Industrial Relations Journal*, 12, 5

G. Evans, 1993, 'The decline of class divisions in Britain?', *British Journal of Sociology*, 44, 3

S. Evans, 1985, 'The use of injunctions in industrial disputes', *British Journal of Industrial Relations*, 23, 1

S. Evans, 1987, 'The use of injunctions in industrial disputes, May, 1984-April 1987', *British Journal of Industrial Relations*, 25, 3

S. Evans, J. Goodman and L. Hargreaves, 1985, 'Unfair dismissal, law and changes in the role of trade unions and employers' associations', *Industrial Law Journal*, 14, 2

P. Fairbrother, 1984, *All Those in Favour: The Politics of Union Democracy*, Pluto Press

P. Fairbrother, 1990, 'The contours of local trade unionism in a period of restructuring' in P. Fosh, E. Heery, eds, 1990

P. Fairbrother and J. Waddington, 1990, 'The politics of trade unionism: evidence, policy and theory', *Capital and Class*, 41

D. Fatchett, 1987, *Trade Unions and Politics in the 1980s: The 1984 Act and Political Fund Ballots*, Croom Helm

A. Ferner, 1989, *Ten Years of Thatcherism: Changing Industrial Relations in British Public Enterprises*, Warwick Papers in Industrial Relations, University of Warwick Industrial Relations Research Unit

A. Ferner and R. Hyman, eds, 1992, *Industrial Relations in the New Europe*, Blackwell

B. Fine and R. Millar, eds, 1985, *Policing the Miners' Strike*, Lawrence & Wishart

D. Finegold and D. Soskice, 1988, 'The failure of training in Britain',

Oxford Review of Economic Policy, 4, 3

A. Flanders, 1970, *Management and Unions*, Faber

T. Forester, ed., 1985, *The Information Technology Revolution*, Blackwell

P. Fosh, 1981, *The Active Trade Unionist*, Cambridge University Press

P. Fosh, 1993, 'Membership participation in workplace unionism: the possibility of union renewal', *British Journal of Industrial* Relations, 31, 4

P. Fosh and C. Littler, eds, 1985, *Industrial Relations and the Law in the 1980s: Issues and Future Trends*, Gower

P. Fosh and E. Heery, eds, 1990, *Trade Unions and their Members*, Macmillan

P. Fosh, H. Morris, R. Martin, P. Smith and R. Undy, 1993, 'Politics, pragmatism and ideology: the wellsprings of conservative union legislation, 1979–1992', *Industrial Law Journal*, 22, 1

D. Foster, 1993, 'Industrial relations in local government – the impact of privatisation', *Political Quarterly*, 64, 1

A. Fox, 1966, *Industrial Sociology and Industrial Relations*, Research Paper 3, Royal Commission on Industrial Relations, HMSO

A. Fox, 1973, 'Industrial relations: a critique of pluralist ideology', in J. Child, ed., 1973

A. Fox, 1985a, *History and Heritage: The Social Origins of the British Industrial Relations System*, Allen & Unwin

A. Fox, 1985b, *Man Mismanagement*, Hutchinson

R. Freeman and H. Medoff, 1984, *What Do Unions Do?*, Basic Books

R. Freeman and J. Pelletier, 1990, 'The impact of industrial relations legislation on British union density', *British Journal of Industrial Relations*, 28, 2

A. Friedman, 1977, *Industry and Labour: Class Struggle at Work and Monopoly Capitalism*, Macmillan

B. Fryer, A. Fairclough and T. Manson, 1974, *Organisation and Change in the National Union of Public Employees*, University of Warwick

G. Gall, 1993, 'What happened to single union deals?', *Industrial Relations Journal*, 24, 1

D. Gallie, 1988, 'Employment, unemployment and social stratification' in D. Gallie, ed., 1988

D. Gallie, ed., 1988, *Employment in Britain*, Blackwell

D. Gallie, 1989, *Trade Union Allegiance and Decline in British Urban Labour Markets*, ESRC

A. Gamble, 1988, *The Free Economy and the Strong State: The Politics of Thatcherism*, Macmillan

P. Garrahan and P. Stewart, 1992, *The Nissan Enigma*, Mansell

A. Giddens and J. McKenzie, eds, 1982, *Social Class and the Division of Labour*, Cambridge University Press

Sir I. Gilmour, 1983, *Britain Can Work*, Martin Robertson

A. Glyn, 1992, 'The productivity miracle, profits and investment', in J. Michie, ed., 1992

A. Glyn, 1992, 'The costs of stability', *New Left Review*, 195

A. Glyn and B. Sutcliffe, 1972, *British Capitalism, Workers and the Profits Squeeze*, Penguin

A. Glyn and J. Harrison, 1980, *The British Economic Disaster*, Pluto Press

GMB, 1990, *Getting Ready for the European Social Charter*

M. Gold and M. Hall, 1992, *European Level Information and Consultation in Multinational Companies: An Evaluation of Practice*, Office for Official Publications of the European Communities

J. Goldstein, 1952, *The Government of British Trade Unions*, Allen & Unwin

J. Goldthorpe, 1974, 'Industrial relations in Great Britain: a critique of reformism', in T. Clarke and L. Clements, eds, 1977

J. Goldthorpe, 1982, 'On the service class', in A. Giddens and G. McKenzie, 1982

J. Goldthorpe, D. Lockwood, F. Bechofer and J. Platt, 1968, *The Affluent Worker, Industrial Attitudes and Behaviour*, Cambridge University Press

J. Goldthorpe and G. Marshall, 1992, 'The promising future of class analysis', *Sociology*, 26, 3

G. Goodman, 1985, *The Miners' Strike*, Pluto Press

J. Grahl and P. Teague, 1990, *1992 – The Big Market – The Future of the European Community*, Lawrence & Wishart

F. Green, ed., 1989, *The Restructuring of the UK Economy*, Harvester

P. Gregg and S. Machin, 1992, 'Unions, the demise of the closed shop and wage growth in the 1980s', *Oxford Bulletin of Economics and Statistics*, 54, 1

M. Gregory, P. Lobhan and A. Thomson, 1985, 'Wage settlements in manufacturing 1979–84 – evidence from the CBI pay databank', *British Journal of Industrial Relations*, 23, 3

M. Gregory, P. Lobhan and A. Thomson, 1987, 'Pay settlements in manufacturing industry 1979–84', *Oxford Bulletin of Economics and Statistics*, 49, 1

M. Gregory and A. Thomson, 1990, *A Portrait of Pay 1970–82: An Analysis of the New Earnings Survey*, Blackwell

J. Griffith, 1991, *The Politics of the Judiciary*, Fontana

K. Grint, 1993, 'What's wrong with performance appraisal', *Human Resource Management Journal*, 3, 3

D. Guest, 1989, 'HRM: implications for industrial relations', in J. Storey, ed., 1989

M. Hall, 1993, *Works Councils for the UK? Lessons from the German System*, Warwick Papers in Industrial Relations, University of Warwick

S. Hall, 1988, *The Hard Road to Renewal: Thatcherism and the Crisis of the Left*, Verso

S. Hall and M. Jacques, eds, 1983, *The Politics of Thatcherism*, Lawrence & Wishart

S. Hall and M Jacques, 1990, *New Times*, Lawrence & Wishart

L. Harris, 1985, 'British capital, manufacturing, finance and multinational companies', in D. Coates and J. Hillard, eds, 1986

M. Harrison, 1960, *Trade Unions and the Labour Party*, Macmillan

J. Hatfield, 1978, *The House the Left Built*, Gollancz

N. Haworth and H. Ramsay, 1984, 'Grasping the nettle: problems with the theory of trade union internationalism', in P. Waterman, ed., 1984

F. Hayek, 1980, *1980s Unemployment and the Unions*, Institute of Economic Affairs

A. Heath, R. Jowell and J. Curtice, 1985, *How Britain Votes*, Pergamon Press

A. Heath, R. Jowell and J. Curtice, 1994, *Labour's Last Chance: The 1992 Election and Beyond*, Dartmouth Publishing

N. Heaton and J. Linn, 1989, *Fighting Back: A Report on Shop Steward Responses to New Management Techniques*, Northern College/TGWU Region 10

E. Heery and J. Kelly, 1988, 'Do female representatives make a difference?: women full-time officials and trade union work', *Work, Employment and Society*, 2, 4

E. Heery and J. Kelly, 1994, 'Professional, participative and managerial unionism: an interpretation of change in trade unions', *Work Employment and Society*, 8, 1

R. Heffernan and M. Marqusee, 1992, *Defeat from the Jaws of Victory: Inside Kinnock's Labour Party*, Verso

A. Henley and E. Tsakalotos, 1992, 'Corporatism and the European labour market after 1992', *British Journal of Industrial Relations*, 30, 4

B. Hepple, 1983, 'Individual labour law', in G. Bain, ed., 1983

P. Hewitt, 1993, *About Time, the Revolution in Work and Family Life*, Rivers Oram

S. Hill, 1991, 'Why quality circles failed but total quality management might succeed', *British Journal of Industrial Relations*, 29, 4

B. Hirsch, 1989, 'Firm investment behaviour and collective bargaining strategy', mimeo, University of North Carolina

E. Hobsbawm, 1989, *Politics For a Rational Left*, Verso

E. Hobsbawm *et al.*, 1981, *The Forward March of Labour Halted*, Verso

G. Hodgson, 1984, *The Democratic Alternative*, Penguin

R. Hoxie, 1917, 1977, *Trade Unionism in the United States*, Appleton-Century-Crofts

J. Hunt, 1982, 'A woman's place is in her union', in J. West, ed., 1982

L. Hunter and J. McInnes, 1992, 'Employer and labour flexibility', *Employment Gazette*, June

U. Huws, J. Hurstfield and R. Holtmaan, 1989, *What Price Flexibility? The Casualisation of Women's Employment*, Low Pay Unit

R. Hyman, 1971, *Marxism and the Sociology of Trade Unionism*, Pluto Press

R. Hyman, 1975, *Industrial Relations: A Marxist Introduction*, Macmillan

R. Hyman, 1979, 'The politics of workplace trade unionism', *Capital and Class*, 8

R. Hyman, 1991a, 'Plus ça change? The theory of production and the production of theory', in A. Pollert, ed., 1991

R. Hyman, 1991b 'European unions: towards 2000', *Work, Employment and Society*, 5, 4

R. Hyman, 1994, 'Industrial relations in western Europe: an era of ambiguity?', *Industrial Relations*, 33, 1

R. Hyman and R. Fryer, 1975, 'Trade unions: sociology and political economy' in J. McKinlay, ed., 1975

R. Hyman and T. Elger, 1981, 'Job controls, the employers' offensive and alternative strategies', *Capital and Class*, 15

R. Hyman and W. Streeck, eds, 1988, *New Technology and Industrial Relations*, Blackwell

Industrial Relations Review and Report 1991, 'Annualised hours: the concept of the flexible year', 448

P. Ingram, 1991, 'Changes in working practices in British manufacturing industry in the 1980s', *British Journal of Industrial Relations*, 29, 1

O. Jacobi, B. Jessop, H. Kastendiek and M. Regini, eds, 1986, *Technological Change, Rationalisation and Industrial Relations*, Croom Helm

C. Johnson, 1991, *The Economy under Mrs Thatcher 1979–1990*, Penguin

Sir K. Joseph, 1975, 'Is Beckerman among the sociologists?', *New Statesman*, 18 April

Sir K. Joseph, 1979a, 'Solving the union problem is the key to Britain's recovery', in D. Coates and J. Hillard, eds, 1986

Sir K. Joseph, 1979b, *Conditions for Fuller Employment*, Centre for Policy Studies

R. Jowell and C. Airey, eds, 1990, *British Social Attitudes*, Gower

O. Kahn-Freund, 1977, *Labour and the Law*, Stevens

O. Kahn-Freund, 1979, *Labour Relations: Heritage and Adjustment*, Oxford University Press

D. Kavanagh, 1987, *Thatcherism and British Politics*, Oxford University Press

J. Kelly, 1988, *Trade Unions and Socialist Politics*, Verso

J. Kelly, 1990, 'British trade unionism: change, continuity and contradictions, *Work, Employment and Society*, special issue

J. Kelly and E. Heery, 1989, 'Full-time officers and trade union recruitment', *British Journal of Industrial Relations*, 27, 2

J. Kelly and R. Richardson, 1989, 'Annual review article, 1988', *British Journal of Industrial Relations*, 27, 1

C. Kelly and J. Kelly, 1991, '"Them, and us" social psychology and the new industrial relations', *British Journal of Industrial Relations*, 29, 1

A. Kerr, 1992, 'Why public sector workers join unions', *Employee Relations*, 14, 2

C. Kerr, J. Dunlop, F. Harbison and C. Myers, 1960, *Industrialism and Industrial Man*, Cambridge University Press

I. Kessler, 1991, 'Workplace industrial relations in local government', *Employee Relations*, 13, 2

I. Kessler and J. Purcell, 1992, 'Performance related pay, objectives and application', *Human Resource Management Journal*, 2, 3

A. Kilpatrick and T. Lawson, 1980, 'On the nature of industrial decline in the UK', in D. Coates and J. Hillard, eds, 1986

J. Kingdom, 1991, *Government and Politics in Britain*, Polity Press

N. Kinnie and D. Lowe, 1990, 'Performance related pay on the shop floor', *Personnel Management*, November

I. Knight, 1979, *Company Organisation and Worker Participation*, HMSO

T. Kochan, H. Katz and R. McKersie, 1986, *The Transformation of American Industrial Relations*, Basic Books

LRD 1983, *Labour Research*, November

LRD 1988, *Labour Research*, March

LRD 1989, *Labour Research*, May

LRD 1990, *Labour Research*, September

LRD 1991, *Women in Unions: Action for Equality*

LRD 1993a, *Black Workers and Trade Unions*

LRD 1993b, *Labour Research*, September

LRD 1993c, *Labour Research*, June

M. Laffin, 1989, *Managing Under Pressure: Industrial Relations in Local Government*, Macmillan

S. Lash and J. Urry, 1987, *The End of Organised Capitalism*, Polity Press

N. Lawson, 1992, *The View From No. 11*, Bantam Press

R. Layard, P. Metcalf and S. Nickell, 1978, 'The effects of collective bargaining on relative and absolute wages', *British Journal of Industrial Relations*, 16, 3

R. Layard and S. Nickell, 1985, 'The causes of British unemployment', *National Institute Economic Review*, April

F. Leijnse, 1980, 'Workplace bargaining and trade union power', *Industrial Relations Journal*, 11, 2

S. Leman and J. Winterton, 1991, 'The restructuring of pit-level industrial relations in the UK coal industry', *New Technology, Work and Employment*, 6, 1

S. Letwin, 1992, *The Anatomy of Thatcherism*, Fontana

C. Levinson, 1972, *International Trade Unionism*, Allen & Unwin

R. Lewis, ed., 1986, *Labour Law in Britain*, Blackwell

R. Lewis and B. Simpson, 1981, *Striking a Balance: Employment Law After the 1980 Act*, Martin Robertson

S. Lipset, M. Trow and J. Coleman, 1956, *Union Democracy*, Free Press

J. Lodge, ed., 1989, *The European Community and the Challenge of the Future*, Pinter

F. Longstreth, 1988, 'From corporatism to dualism: Thatcherism and the climacteric of British trade unions in the 1980s', *Political Studies*, 36, 3

M. Martinez Lucio and S. Weston, 1992, 'The politics and complexity of trade union responses to new management practice,' *Human Resource Management Journal*, 2, 4

S. Lukes, 1974, *Power: A Radical View*, Macmillan

L. Mackay, 1986, 'The macho manager: it's no myth', *Personnel Management*, January

R. Mailly, S. Dimmock and A. Sethi, eds, 1989, *Industrial Relations in the Public Services*, Routledge

P. Marginson, 1991, 'Change and continuity in the employment structure of large companies', in A. Pollert, ed., 1991

P. Marginson, 1992, 'European integration and transnational management, relations in the enterprise', *British Journal of Industrial Relations*, 30, 4

P. Marginson, P. Edwards, R. Martin, J. Purcell and K. Sisson, eds, 1988, *Beyond the Workplace: Managing Industrial Relations in Multi-Plant Enterprises*, Blackwell

P. Marginson, M. Hall and K. Sisson, 1993, *European-Level Employee Information and Consultative Structures*, IPM

D. Marsden and M. Thompson, 1990, 'Flexibility agreements and their significance in the increase in productivity in British manufacturing since 1980', *Work, Employment and Society*, 4, 1

D. Marsh, 1992, *The New Politics of British Trade Unionism*, Macmillan

G. Marshall, D. Rose, C. Vogler and H. Newby, 1985, 'Class, citizenship and distributional conflict in modern Britain', *British Journal of Sociology*, 36, 2

R. Martin, 1968, 'Union democracy: an explanatory framework', *Sociology*, 2, 2

R. Martin, 1980, *TUC: The Growth of A Pressure Group 1868–1976*, Clarendon Press

R. Martin, 1992, *Bargaining Power*, Clarendon Press

R. Martin, P. Fosh, H. Morris, P. Smith and R. Undy, 1991, 'Decollectivization of trade unions? Ballots and collective bargaining in the 1980s', *Industrial Relations Journal*, 22, 3

B. Mason and P. Bain, 1992, 'Trade union recruitment strategies', *Industrial Relations Journal*, 22, 1

E. Matzner and W. Streeck, eds, 1991, *Beyond Keynesianism: the Socio-economics of Production and Full Employment*, Edward Elgar

W. McCarthy, ed., 1985, *Trade Unions*, Penguin

W. McCarthy, ed., 1992, *Legal Intervention in Industrial Relations, Gains and Losses*, Blackwell

W. McCarthy and S. Parker, 1968, *Shop Stewards and Workplace Relations*, Royal Commission on Trade Unions Research, Paper 10, HMSO

I. McCauley and R. Wood, 1992, 'Hotel and catering industry employees – attitudes towards trade unions', *Employee Relations*, 14, 3

J. McIlroy, 1983, *Industrial Tribunals*, Pluto Press

J. McIlroy, 1985, 'Police and pickets', in H. Beynon, ed., 1985

J. McIlroy, 1991, *The Permanent Revolution? Conservative Law and the Trade Unions*, Spokesman

J. McIlroy, 1992, 'Ten years for the locust: the TUC in the 1980s', in D. Cox, ed., 1992

J. McIlroy, 1993, 'Tales from smoke-filled rooms', *Studies in the Education of Adults*, 25, 1

J. McInnes, 1985, 'Conjuring up consultation', *British Journal of*

Industrial Relations, 23, 1

J. McInnes, 1987, *Thatcherism at Work*, Open University Press

J. McKinlay, ed., 1975, *Processing People*, Holt Rinehart & Winston

I. McLoughlin and S. Gourlay, 1992, 'Enterprise without unions', *Journal of Management Studies*, 29, 5

K. McNeil and C. Pond, 1988, *Britain Can't Afford Low Pay*, Low Pay Unit

D. Metcalf, 1989, 'Water notes dry up', *British Journal of Industrial Relations*, 27, 1

D. Metcalf, 1990, 'Union presence and labour productivity in British manufacturing industry: a reply to Nolan and Marginson', *British Journal of Industrial Relations*, 28, 2

D. Metcalf, 1991 'British unions: dissolution or resurgence?', *Oxford Review of Economic Policy*, 7, 1

J. Michie, ed., 1992, *The Economic Legacy 1979–1992*, Academic Press

K. Middlemas, 1979, *Politics in Industrial Society*, Deutsch

R. Miliband, 1969, *The State in Capitalist Society*, Weidenfeld & Nicolson

N. Millward, 1990, 'The state of the unions', in R. Jowell and C. Airey, eds, 1990

N. Millward, 1994, *The New Industrial Relations?*, Policy Studies Institute

N. Millward and M. Stevens, 1986, *British Workplace Industrial Relations 1980–84*, Gower

N. Millward, M. Stevens, D. Smart and W. Hawes, 1992, *Workplace Industrial Relations in Transition*, Dartmouth Publishing

P. Minford, 1985, 'Trade unions destroy a million jobs', in W. McCarthy, ed., 1985

L. Minkin, 1991, *The Contentious Alliance: Trade Unions and the Labour Party*, Edinburgh University Press

N. Mitchell, 1987, 'Changing pressure group politics: the case of the TUC 1976–84', *British Journal of Political Science*, 17, 4

K. Moody, 1988, *An Injury to All: The Decline of American Unionism*, Verso

R. Moore and H. Levie, 1985, 'New technology and the unions' in T. Forester, ed., 1985

M. Moran, 1974, *The Union of Post Office Workers: A Study in Political Sociology*, Macmillan

M. Moran, 1979, 'The Conservative Party and the trade unions since 1974', *Political Studies*, 27, 1

T. Morris and S. Wood, 1991, 'Testing the survey method: continuity and change in British industrial relations', *Work, Employment and Society*, 5, 2

T. Nairn, 1972, 'The left against Europe', *New Left Review*, 75

T. Nichols, 1969, *Ownership, Control and Ideology*, Allen & Unwin

T. Nichols and J. O'Connell Davidson, 1992, 'Employee shareholders in two privatised utilities', *Industrial Relations Journal*, 23, 2

N. Nicholson, G. Ursell and P. Blyton, 1981, *The Dynamics of White Collar Unionism*, Academic Press

P. Nolan, 1989, 'The productivity miracle?', in F. Green, ed., 1989

P. Nolan, 1992, 'Trade unions and productivity: issues, evidence and prospects', *Employee Relations*, 14, 6

P. Nolan and P. Marginson, 1990, 'Skating on thin ice? David Metcalf on trade unions and productivity', *British Journal of Industrial Relations*, 28, 2

J. Northcott and P. Rogers, 1984, *Microelectronics in British Industry: Patterns of Change*, PSI

N. Northrup and P. Rowan, 1979, *Multinational Collective Bargaining Attempts*, University of Pennsylvania Press

C. Offe, 1985, *Disorganised Capitalism*, Polity Press

C. Offe and H. Wiesenthal, 1985, 'The two logics of collective action', in C. Offe, 1985

S. Ogden, 1993, 'Water' in A. Pendleton and J. Winterton, eds, 1993

C. Pateman, 1970, *Participation and Democratic Theory*, Cambridge University Press

H. Pelling, 1988, *A History of British Trade Unionism*, Penguin

A. Pendleton and J. Winterton, eds, 1993, *Public Enterprise in Transition: Industrial Relations in State and Privatised Corporations*, Routledge

S. Perlman, 1928, 1970, *Theory of the Labour Movement*, Augustus Kelley

B. Pimlott and C. Cook, eds, 1991, *Trade Unions in British Politics*, Longman

M. Pinto-Duschinsky, 1989, 'Financing the General Election of 1987', in I. Crewe and M. Harrop, eds, 1989

M. Piore and C. Sabel, 1984, *The Second Industrial Divide: Prospects for Prosperity*, Basic Books

A. Pollert, 1988, 'The flexible firm: fixation or fact?', *Work, Employment and Society*, 2, 3

A. Pollert, ed., 1991, *Farewell to Flexibility*, Blackwell

M. Poole, 1986, *Towards a New Industrial Democracy: Workers' Participation in Industry*, Routledge

M. Poole and G. Jenkins, eds, 1990, *The Impact of Economic Democracy: Profit Sharing and Employee Shareholding Schemes*, Routledge

M. Poole and R. Mansfield, 1992, 'Managers' attitudes to Human

Resource Management: rhetoric and reality', in P. Blyton and P. Turnbull, eds, 1992

R. Price, 1986, *Labour in British Society*, Croom Helm

R. Price, 1988, 'Information, consultation and the control of new technology', in R. Hyman and W. Streeck, eds, 1988

J. Prior, 1986, *A Balance of Power*, Hamish Hamilton

F. von Prondzynski, 1985, 'The changing function of labour law', in P. Fosh and C. Littler, eds, 1985

J. Purcell, 1989, 'How to manage decentralised bargaining', *Personnel Management*, May

J. Purcell, 1991, 'The rediscovery of the management prerogative: the management of labour relations in the 1980s', *Oxford Review of Economic Policy*, 7, 1

J. Purcell and K. Sisson, 1983, 'Strategies and practice in the management of industrial relations', in G. Bain, ed., 1983

H. Rainbird, 1990, *Training Matters*, Blackwell

J. Ranelagh, 1992, *Thatcher's People*, Fontana

H. Ramsay, 1977, 'Cycles of control: worker participation in sociological and historical perspective', *Sociology*, 11, 3

T. Rees, 1992, *Women and the Labour Market*, Routledge

J. Rentoul, 1987, *The Rich Get Richer: The Growth of Inequality in Britain in the 1980s*, Unwin

J. Rentoul, 1989, *Me and Mine: The Triumph of the New Individualism*, Unwin Hyman

M. Rhodes, 1991, 'The social dimension of the Single European Market', *European Journal of Political Research*, 19, 3

B. Roberts, 1988, 'A new era in British industrial relations', in British–North American Committee, 1988

I. Roberts, 1992, 'Industrial relations and the European Community', *Industrial Relations Journal*, 23, 1

N. Robertson and K. Sams, 1978, 'The work pattern of union officers', *Industrial Relations Journal*, 9, 1

R. Rose and I. McAllister, 1986, *Voters Begin to Choose*, Sage

W. Runciman, 1966, *Relative Deprivation and Social Justice*, Routledge

Royal Commission on Trade Unions and Employers' Associations, 1968, *Report*, HMSO (The Donovan Report)

B. Sarlvik and I. Crewe, 1983, *Decade of Dealignment*, Cambridge University Press

H. Scarborough, 1986, 'The politics of technological change at British Leyland' in O. Jacobi, *et al.*, eds, 1986

J. Scott, 1982, *The Upper Classes*, Macmillan

J. Scott, 1985, *Corporations, Classes and Capitalism*, Hutchinson

J. Scott, 1991, *Who Rules Britain?*, Polity Press

P. Seyd, 1987, *The Rise and Fall of The Labour Left*, Macmillan

P. Seyd and P. Whiteley, 1992, *Labour's Grassroots: The Politics of Party Membership*, Clarendon Press

M. Shanks, 1977, *European Social Policy Today and Tomorrow*, Pergamon Press

M. Sharp, 1989, 'The community and new technologies', in J. Lodge, ed., 1989

K. Sisson, 1991, *Employers' Organisations and Industrial Relations: The Significance of the Strategies of Large Companies*, University of Warwick

K. Sisson, 1993, 'In search of HRM', *British Journal of Industrial Relations*, 31, 2

C. Smith, 1987, *Recruiting Women to the Trade Union Movement*, TGWU

P. Smith and G. Morton, 1993, 'Union exclusion and the decollectivisation of industrial relations in contemporary Britain', *British Journal of Industrial Relations*, 31, 1

Social Europe, 1991, 2

B. Spencer, 1989, *Remaking the Working Class? An Examination of Shop Stewards' Experience*, Spokesman

G. Standing, 1986, *Unemployment and Labour Market Flexibility: The United Kingdom*, ILO

T. Stark, 1990, *Income and Wealth in the 1980s*, Fabian Society

H. Stephenson, 1982, *Claret and Chips: The Rise of the SDP*, Michael Joseph

M. Stewart, 1991, 'Union wage differentials in the face of changes in the economic and legal environment', *Economica*, 58

J. Stopford and S. Strange, 1991, *Rival States, Rival Firms*, Cambridge University Press

J. Storey, 1980, *The Challenge to Management Control*, Routledge

J. Storey, ed., 1989, *New Perspectives on Human Resource Management*, Routledge

J. Storey, 1992, *Developments in the Management of Human Resources*, Blackwell

J. Storey and K. Sisson, 1990, 'Limits to transformation: human resource management in the British context', *Industrial Relations Journal*, 21, 1

W. Streeck, 1991, 'On the institutional conditions of diversified quality production' in E. Matzner and W. Streeck, eds, 1991

D. Strinati, 1982, *Capitalism, The State and Industrial Relations*, Croom

440   *References*

Helm

S. Tailby and C. Whitston, eds, 1989, *Manufacturing Change*, Blackwell

F. Tannenbaum, 1921, 1966, *The Labour Movement: Its Conservative Functions and Social Consequences*, Putnams

R. Taylor, 1993, *The Trade Union Question in British Politics: Government and Unions Since 1945*, Blackwell

P. Teague, 1989, 'The British TUC and the European Community', *Millennium*, 18, 1

N. Tebbit, 1988, *Upwardly Mobile: An Autobiography*, Weidenfeld & Nicolson

M. Terry, 1982, 'Organising a fragmented workforce – shop stewards in local government', *British Journal of Industrial Relations*, 20, 1

M. Terry, 1983, 'Shop steward development and managerial strategies' in G. Bain, ed., 1983

M. Terry, 1985, 'Combine committees – developments of the 1970s', *British Journal of Industrial Relations*, 23, 3

M. Terry, 1986, 'How do we know if shop stewards are getting weaker?', *British Journal of Industrial Relations*, 4, 2

M. Terry, 1989, 'Recontextualising shopfloor industrial relations', in S. Tailby and C. Whitston, eds, 1989

TGWU, 1992, *Negotiating for Training*

M. Thompson, 1993, *Performance Related Pay: The Employee Experience*, Institute of Manpower Studies

P. Thompson, 1989, *The Nature of Work*, Macmillan

D. Thomson and R. Larson, 1978, *Where Were You Brother?*, War on Want

A. Thornett, 1987, *From Militancy to Marxism*, Left View Books

S. Tolliday, 1985, 'Government, employers and shop floor organisation' in S. Tolliday and J. Zeitlin, eds, 1985

S. Tolliday and J. Zeitlin, eds, 1985, *Shop Floor Bargaining and the State*, Cambridge University Press

J. Tomlinson, 1982, *The Unequal Struggle: British Socialism and the Capitalist Enterprise*, Methuen

B. Towers, 1989, 'Running the gauntlet: British trade unions under Thatcher 1979–1988', *Industrial and Labour Relations Review*, 42, 2

B. Towers, 1992, 'Two speed ahead: Social Europe and the UK after Maastricht', *Industrial Relations Journal*, 23, 2

D. Trower, 1990, 'British trade unions and 1992: changing attitudes and policies', University of Manchester, MA thesis

P. Turnbull and S. Weston, 1993, 'Co-operation or control? Capital restructuring and labour relations on the docks', *British Journal of Industrial Relations*, 31, 1

H. A. Turner, 1962, *Trade Union Growth, Structure and Policy. A Comparative Study of the Cotton Unions*, Allen & Unwin

H. A. Turner, G. Clack and G. Roberts, 1967, *Labour Relations in the Motor Industry*, Allen & Unwin

TUC, 1952, 1961, 1970, 1972, 1974, 1975, 1980, 1982, 1984, 1985, 1988, 1990, 1991, *Report*

TUC, 1968, *Action on Donovan*

TUC, 1979, *Employment and Technology*

TUC, 1982, *Industrial Relations Legislation*

TUC, 1983, *Trade Union Strategy*

TUC, 1988a, *Maximising the Benefits, Minimising the Costs*

TUC, 1989a, *Europe 1992 – Progress Report*

TUC, 1989b, *Organising for the 1990s*

TUC, 1990a, *Managing the Economy Towards 2000*

TUC, 1991a, *Collective Bargaining Strategy for the 1990s*

TUC, 1991b, *The Involvement of Black Workers in Trade Unions*

TUC, 1993, *Evidence to House of Commons Committee on Employment*

R. Undy, V. Ellis, W. McCarthy and A. Halmos, 1981, *Change in Trade Unions*, Hutchinson

R. Undy and R. Martin, 1984, *Ballots and Trade Union Democracy*, Blackwell

G. Ursell, 1983, 'The views of British managers and shop stewards on industrial democracy', in C. Crouch and F. Heller, eds, 1983

USDAW, 1987, *Getting Involved: Members' Views and Priorities*

J. Vickers and G. Yarrow, 1988, *Privatisation: An Economic Analysis*, MIT

S. Wadhwani, 1990 'The effect of unions on productivity, growth investment and employment', *British Journal of Industrial Relations*, 28, 3

T. Wall and J. Lischeron, 1977, *Worker Participation: A Critique of the Literature and Some Fresh Evidence*, McGraw Hill

J. Walsh, 1993, 'Internalisation v. decentralisation: an analysis of recent developments in pay bargaining', *British Journal of Industrial Relations*, 31, 3

P. Waterman, ed., 1984, *For a New Labour Internationalism*, ILER

B. Webb and S. Webb, 1894, 1920, *The History of Trade Unionism, 1666–1920*, Longman

B. Webb and S. Webb, 1897, 1902, *Industrial Democracy*, Longman

K. W. Wedderburn, 1972, 'Labour law and labour relations in Britain', *British Journal of Industrial Relations*, 10, 2

Lord Wedderburn, 1983, 'The new politics of labour law', in W. McCarthy, ed., 1985

Lord Wedderburn, 1986, *The Worker and the Law*, Penguin

Lord Wedderburn, 1989, 'Freedom of association and philosophies of labour law', *Industrial Law Journal*, 18, 1

Lord Wedderburn, 1992, 'Laws about strikes', in W. McCarthy, 1992

Lord Wedderburn, R. Lewis and J. Clark, eds, 1983, *Labour Law and Industrial Relations: Building on Kahn-Freund*, Clarendon Press

B. Weekes, M. Mellish, L. Dickens and J. Lloyd, 1975, *Industrial Relations and the Limits of Law*, Blackwell

J. West, ed., 1982, *Work, Women and the Labour Market*, Routledge

J. Westergaard and H. Resler, 1976, *Class in a Capitalist Society*, Penguin

C. Whitston and J. Waddington, 1992, 'Why sign up? New trade union members' reasons for joining', *Industrial Relations Research Unit Research Review*, 6, University of Warwick

D. Widgery, 1976, *The Left in Britain, 1956–68*, Penguin

M. Wiener, 1985, *English Culture and the Decline of the Industrial Spirit 1850–1980*, Penguin

B. Wilkinson, 1983, *The Shop Floor Politics of New Technology*, Heinemann

R. Williams and R. Moseley, 1981, *Trade Unions and New Technology: An Overview of Technology Agreements*, University of Aston

R. Williams and F. Steward, 1985, 'Technology agreements in Britain: a survey 1977–83', *Industrial Relations Journal*, 16, 3

P. Willman, 1989, 'The logic of market-share trade unionism: is membership decline inevitable?', *Industrial Relations Journal*, 20, 4

P. Willman and G. Winch, 1985, *Innovation and Management Control*, Cambridge University Press

D. Wilson, R. Butler, D. Cray, D. Hickson and G. Mallory, 1982, 'The limits of trade union power in organisational decision-making', *British Journal of Industrial Relations*, 20, 3

M. Wise and R. Gibb, 1993, *Single Market to Social Europe*, Longman

D. Wood and P. Smith, 1989, *Employers' Labour Use Strategies*, Department of Employment Research Paper, 63

S. Wood and R. Peccei, 1991, 'Preparing for 1992?', *Human Resource Management Journal*, 1, 1

E. Wright, 1978, *Class, Crisis and the State*, New Left Books

E. Wright, 1985, *Classes*, Verso

S. Yeandle, 1984, *Women's Working Lives: Patterns and Strategies*, Tavistock

H. Young, 1989, 1991, *One of Us*, Macmillan

F. Zweig, 1948, *Labour, Life and Poverty*, Gollancz

Index